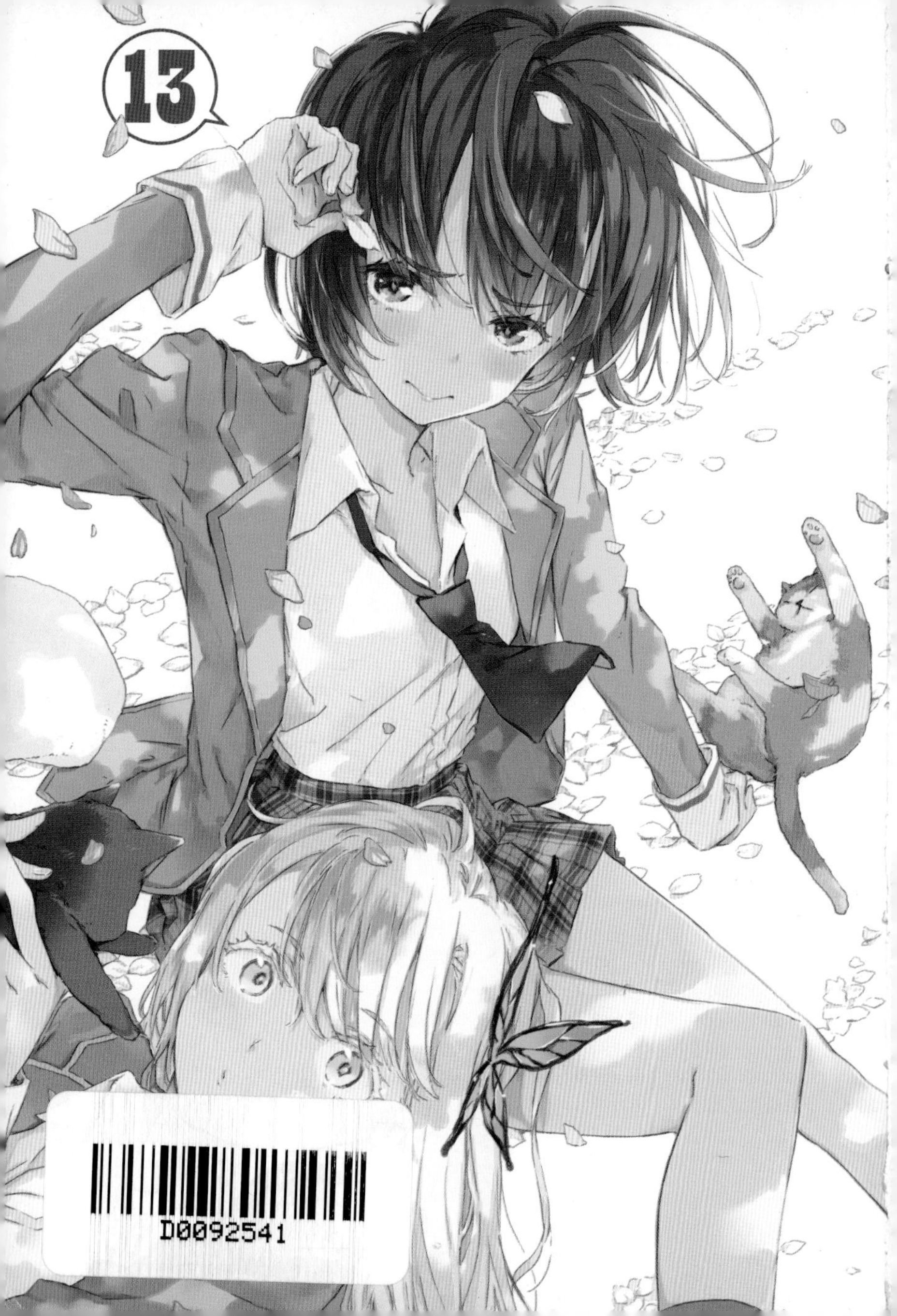
13

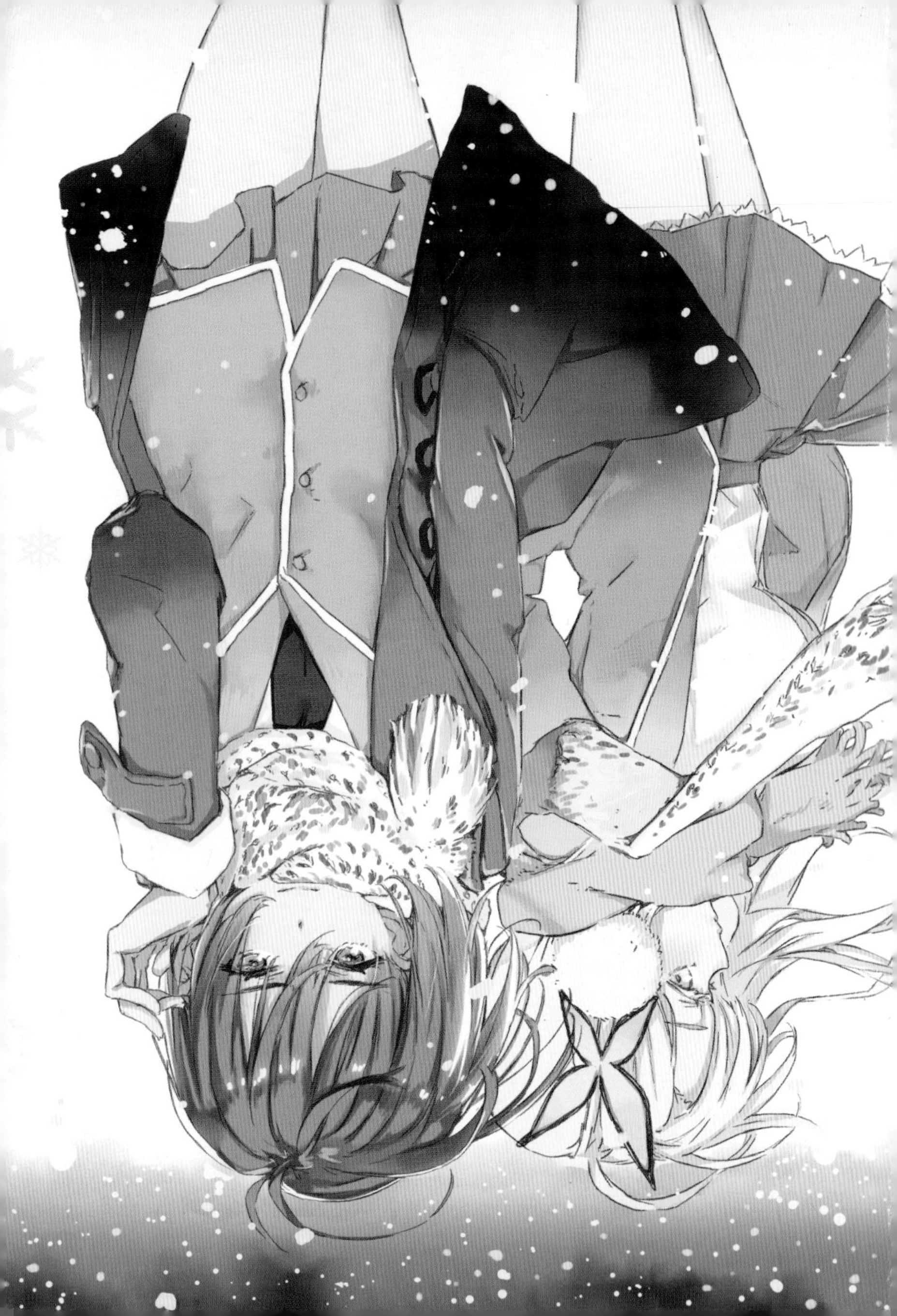

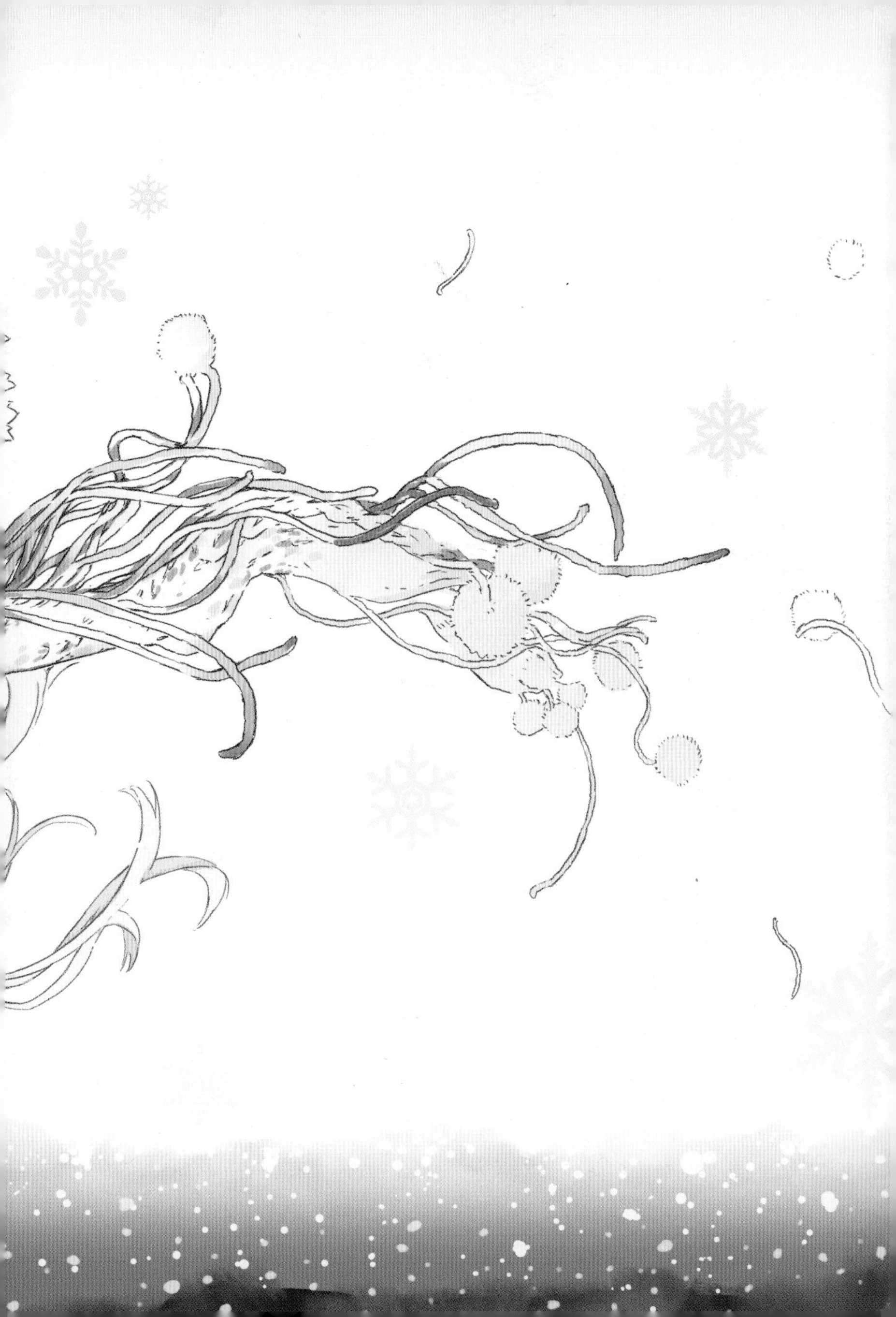

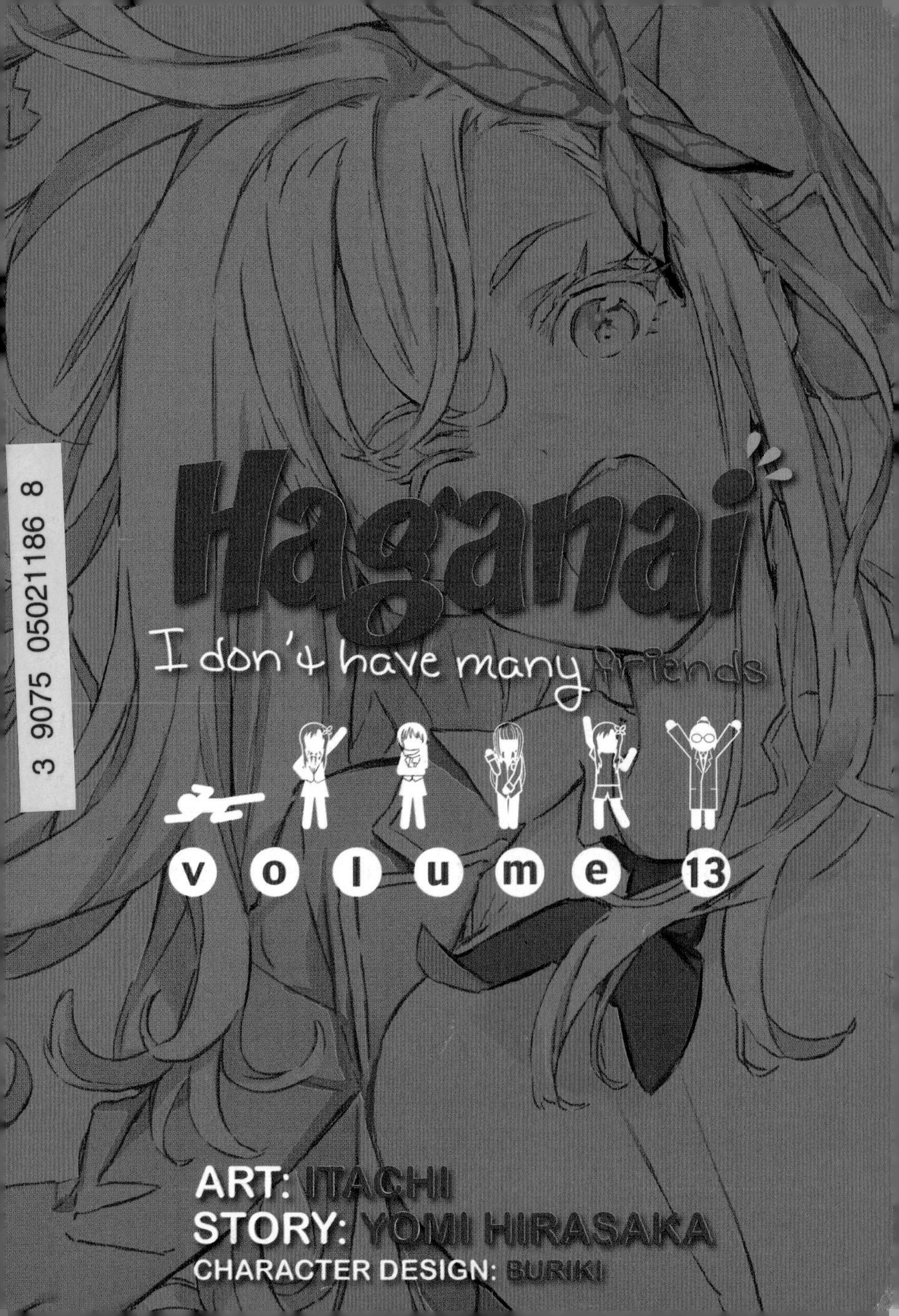

Haganai

I don't have many friends

volume 13

ART: ITACHI
STORY: YOMI HIRASAKA
CHARACTER DESIGN: BURIKI

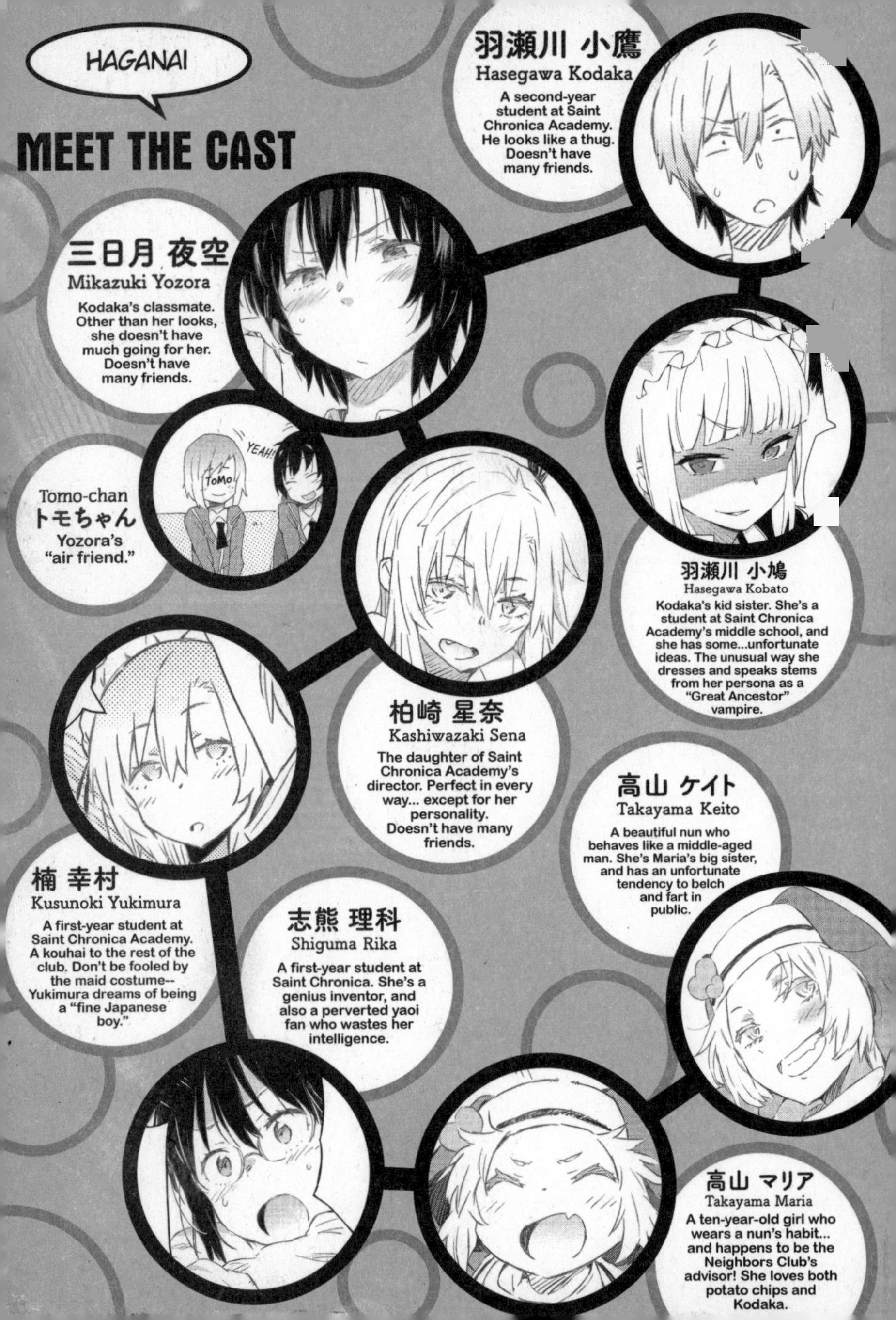
HAGANAI
MEET THE CAST
羽瀬川 小鷹
Hasegawa Kodaka
A second-year student at Saint Chronica Academy. He looks like a thug. Doesn't have many friends.
三日月 夜空
Mikazuki Yozora
Kodaka's classmate. Other than her looks, she doesn't have much going for her. Doesn't have many friends.
YEAH!
TOMO
Tomo-chan
トモちゃん
Yozora's "air friend."
羽瀬川 小鳩
Hasegawa Kobato
Kodaka's kid sister. She's a student at Saint Chronica Academy's middle school, and she has some...unfortunate ideas. The unusual way she dresses and speaks stems from her persona as a "Great Ancestor" vampire.
柏崎 星奈
Kashiwazaki Sena
The daughter of Saint Chronica Academy's director. Perfect in every way... except for her personality. Doesn't have many friends.
高山 ケイト
Takayama Keito
A beautiful nun who behaves like a middle-aged man. She's Maria's big sister, and has an unfortunate tendency to belch and fart in public.
楠 幸村
Kusunoki Yukimura
A first-year student at Saint Chronica Academy. A kouhai to the rest of the club. Don't be fooled by the maid costume-- Yukimura dreams of being a "fine Japanese boy."
志熊 理科
Shiguma Rika
A first-year student at Saint Chronica. She's a genius inventor, and also a perverted yaoi fan who wastes her intelligence.
高山 マリア
Takayama Maria
A ten-year-old girl who wears a nun's habit... and happens to be the Neighbors Club's advisor! She loves both potato chips and Kodaka.

The Neighbors Club

Previous club activity logs:

Hasegawa Kodaka, a lone wolf at a new school, and his gloomy classmate Mikazuki Yozora create a new club for unfortunate souls who desperately need to make friends. More and more students join, and with one exception(?), they're all beautiful--but unfortunate--girls. Next thing you know, the club is up to seven members! While trying to figure out ways to make friends, the club members play games and put on plays to entertain themselves, but they always end up veering wildly off course. The most recent fiasco? Discovering that the script Yozora "wrote" for the club's film for the school festival was plagiarized from a decade-old movie! The club has no choice but to start shooting a brand-new movie from scratch, using a script written by Sena...

Club Activity Log 51:

How She Responded

We finally began filming our movie.

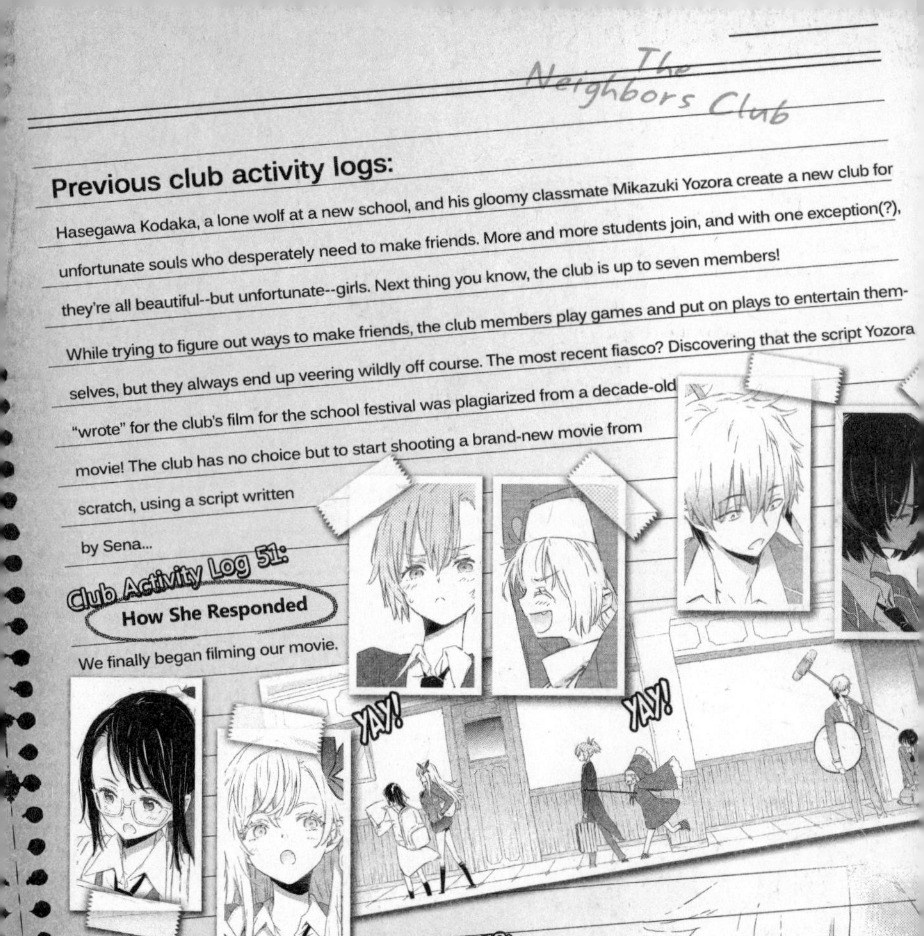
YAY!
YAY!

Club Activity Log 52:

Pegasus's Wild Fantasy

Sena and I learned we're betrothed!

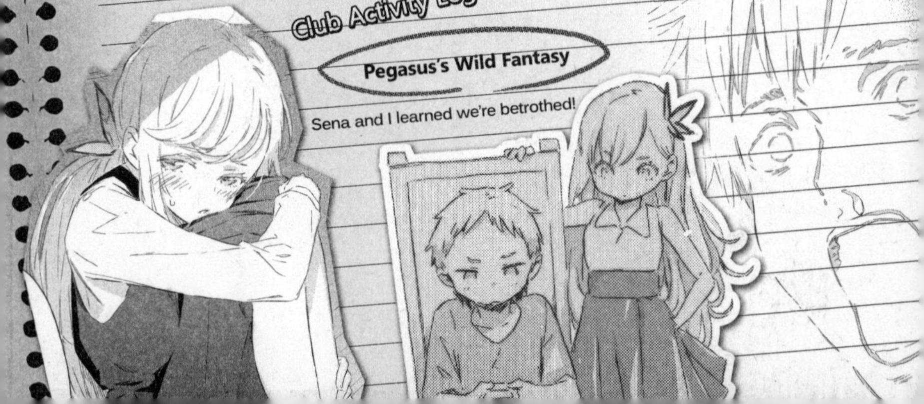

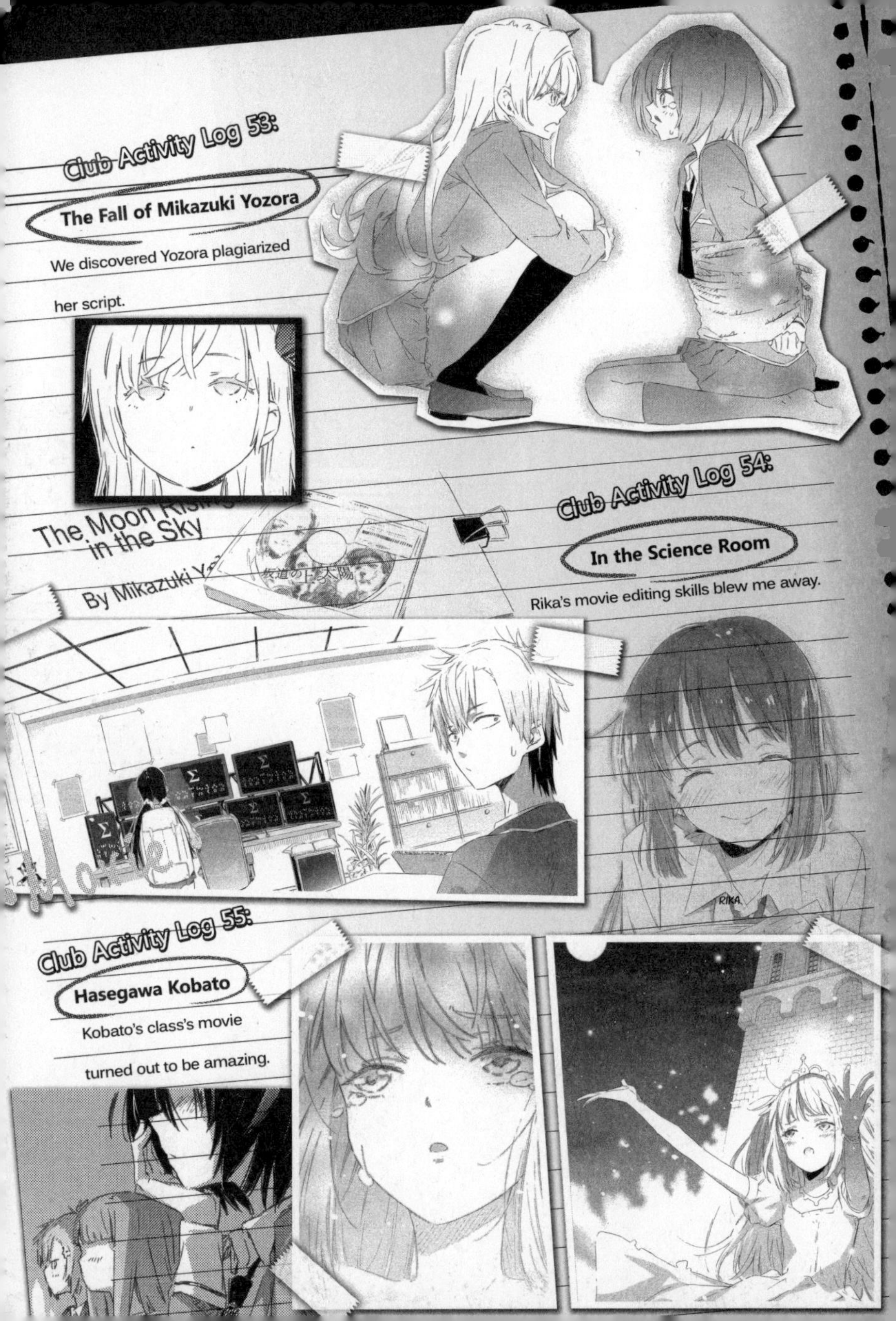
Club Activity Log 53:
The Fall of Mikazuki Yozora
We discovered Yozora plagiarized her script.
The Moon
in the Sky
By Mikazuki
Club Activity Log 54:
In the Science Room
Rika's movie editing skills blew me away.
RIKA
Club Activity Log 55:
Hasegawa Kobato
Kobato's class's movie turned out to be amazing.

Haganai

I don't have many friends

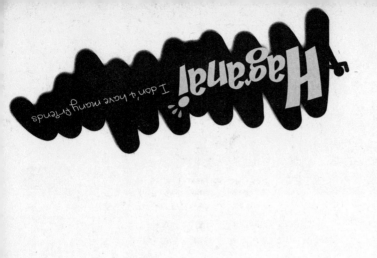

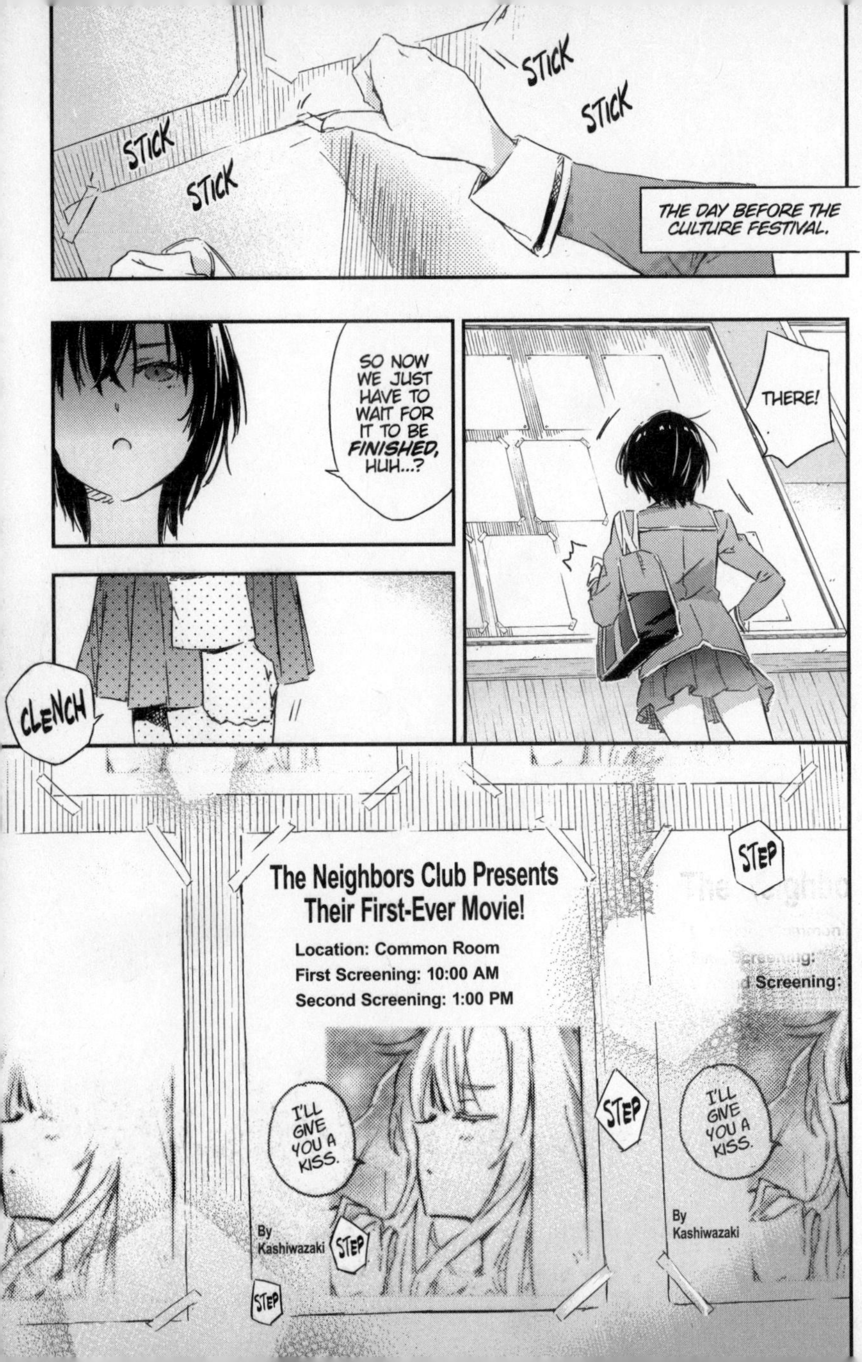
THE DAY BEFORE THE CULTURE FESTIVAL.
STICK
STICK
STICK
STICK
THERE!
SO NOW WE JUST HAVE TO WAIT FOR IT TO BE FINISHED, HUH...?
CLENCH
STEP
The Neighbors Club Presents Their First-Ever Movie!
Location: Common Room
First Screening: 10:00 AM
Second Screening: 1:00 PM
I'LL GIVE YOU A KISS.
By Kashiwazaki
STEP
I'LL GIVE YOU A KISS.
By Kashiwazaki
STEP
STEP

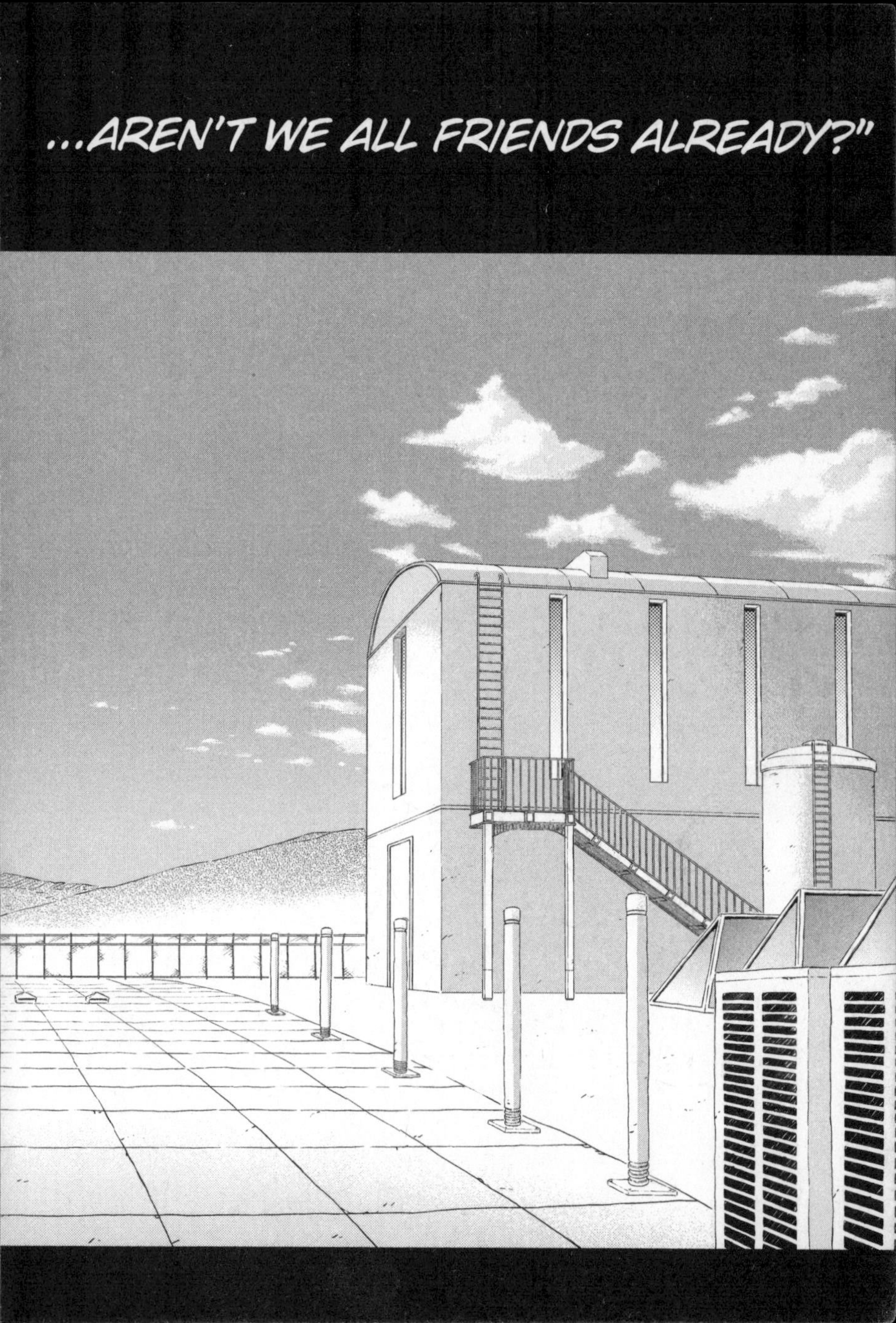
...AREN'T WE ALL FRIENDS ALREADY?"

"WHAT RIKA'S TRYING TO SAY IS...

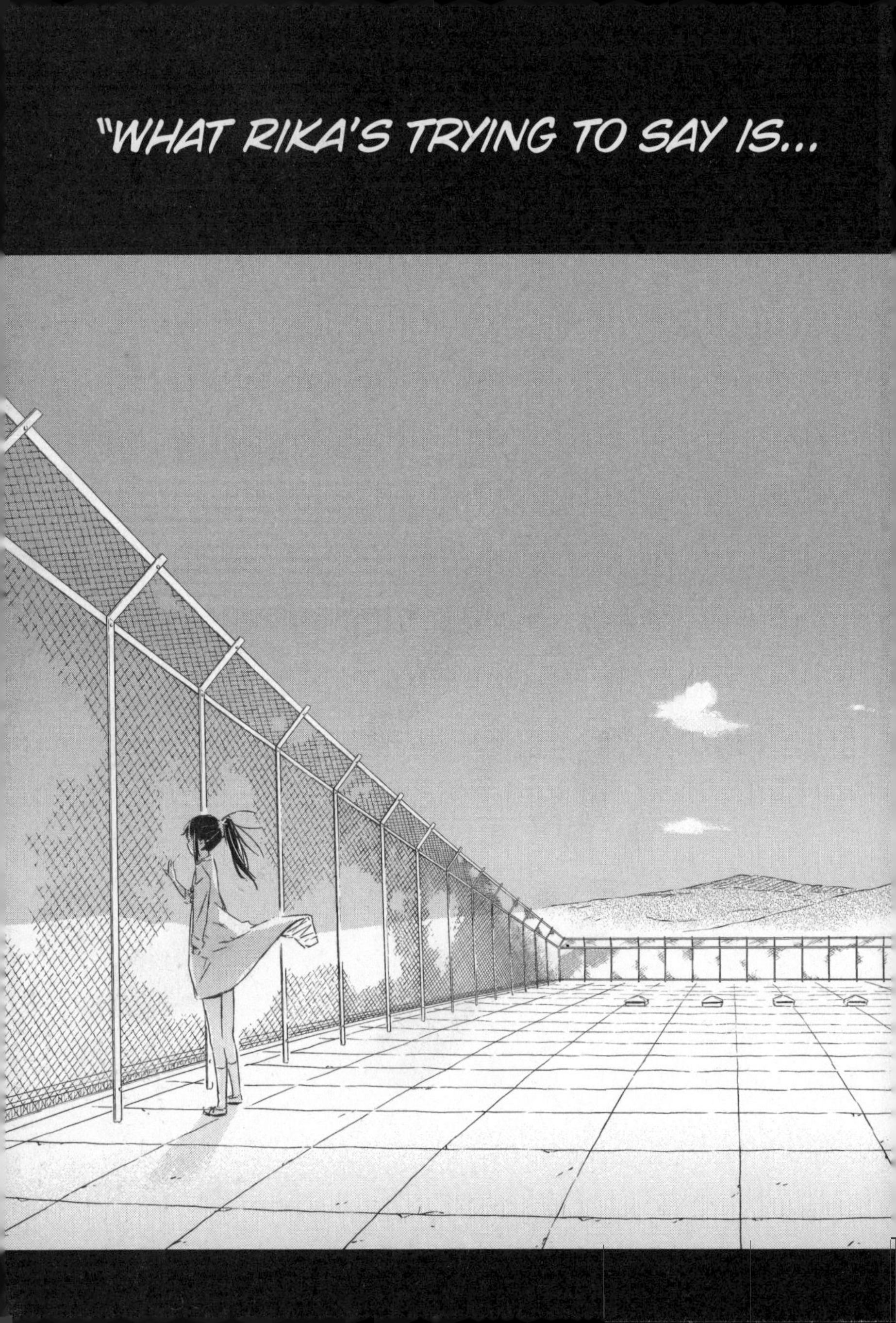

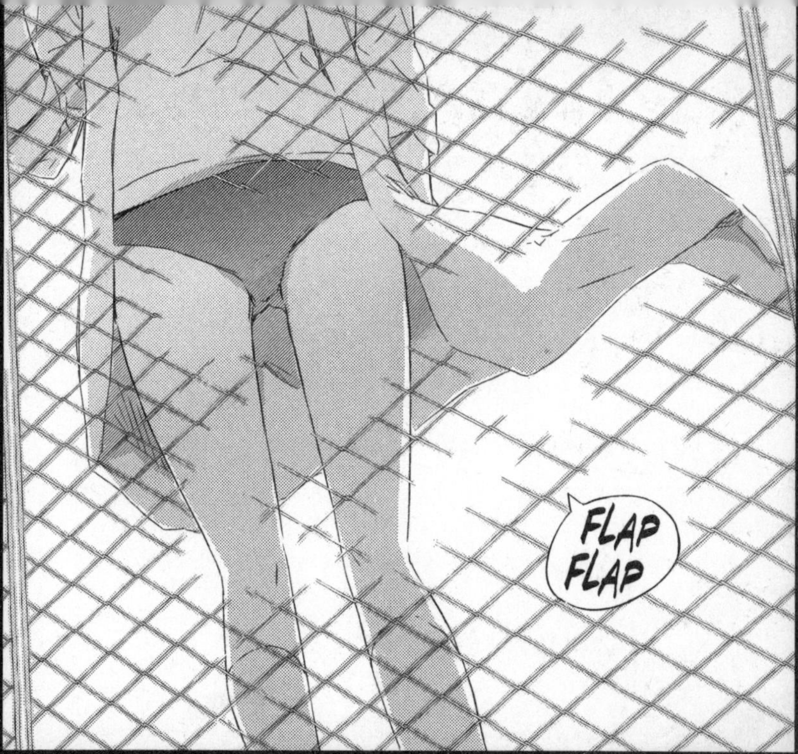
FLAP FLAP

Club Activity Log 56:
King Lear

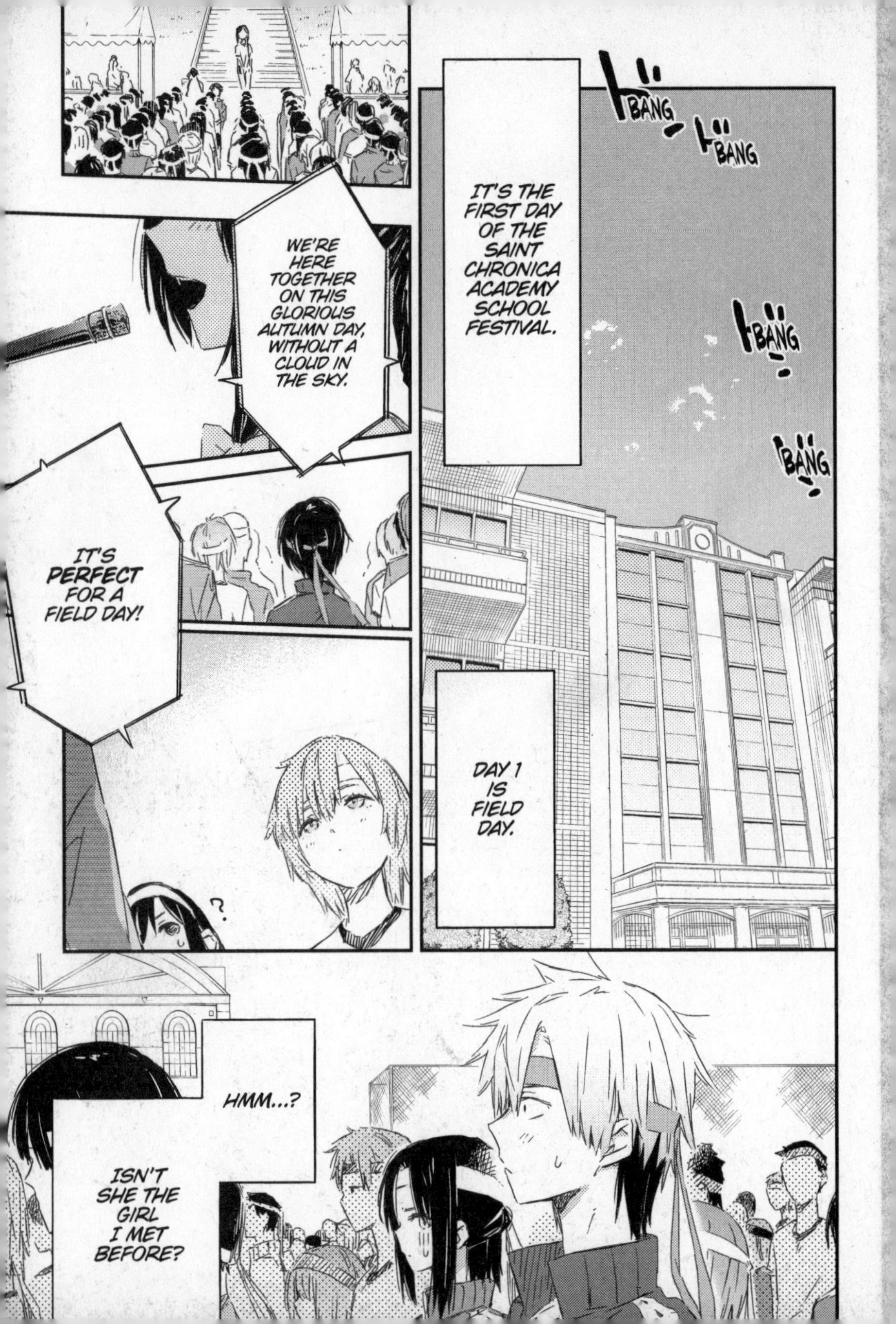
BANG
BANG
IT'S THE FIRST DAY OF THE SAINT CHRONICA ACADEMY SCHOOL FESTIVAL.
BANG
BANG
DAY 1 IS FIELD DAY.
WE'RE HERE TOGETHER ON THIS GLORIOUS AUTUMN DAY, WITHOUT A CLOUD IN THE SKY.
IT'S PERFECT FOR A FIELD DAY!
?
HMM...?
ISN'T SHE THE GIRL I MET BEFORE?

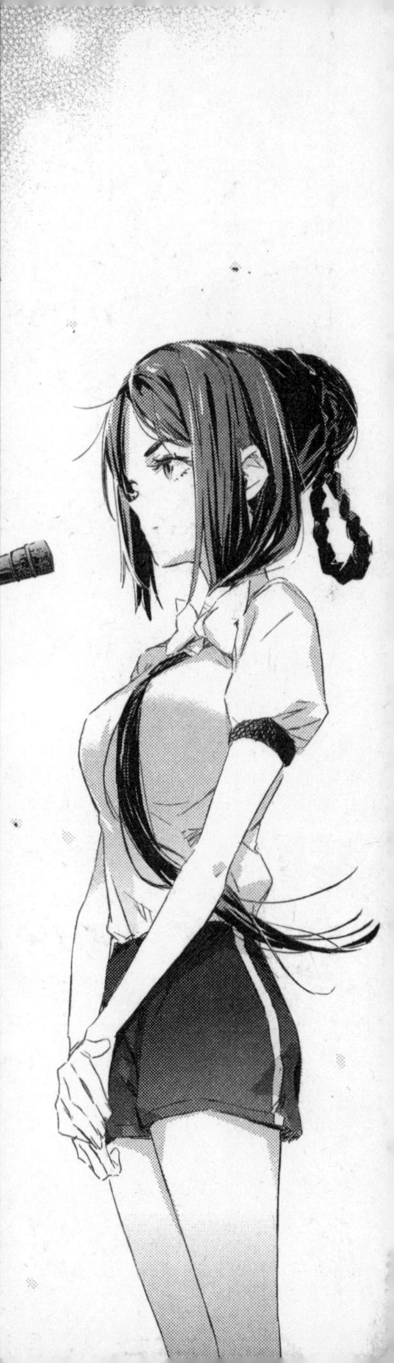
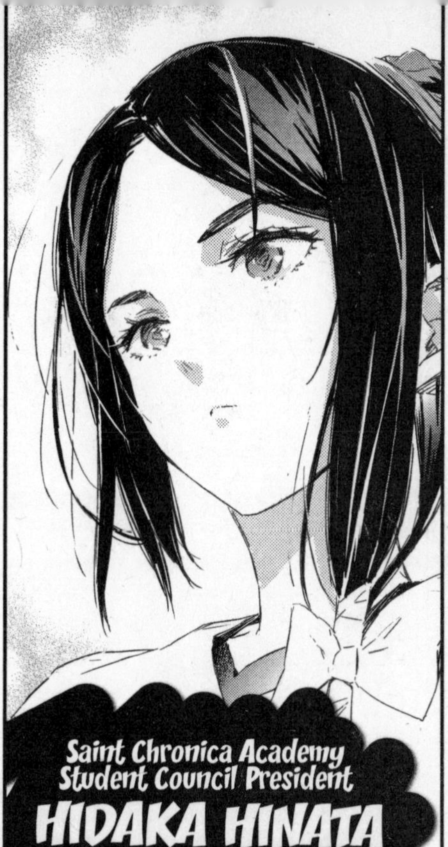
Saint Chronica Academy
Student Council President
HIDAKA HINATA
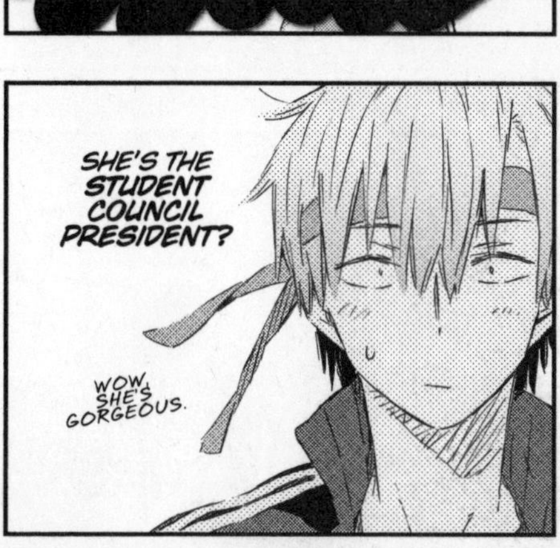
SHE'S THE STUDENT COUNCIL PRESIDENT?
WOW, SHE'S GORGEOUS.

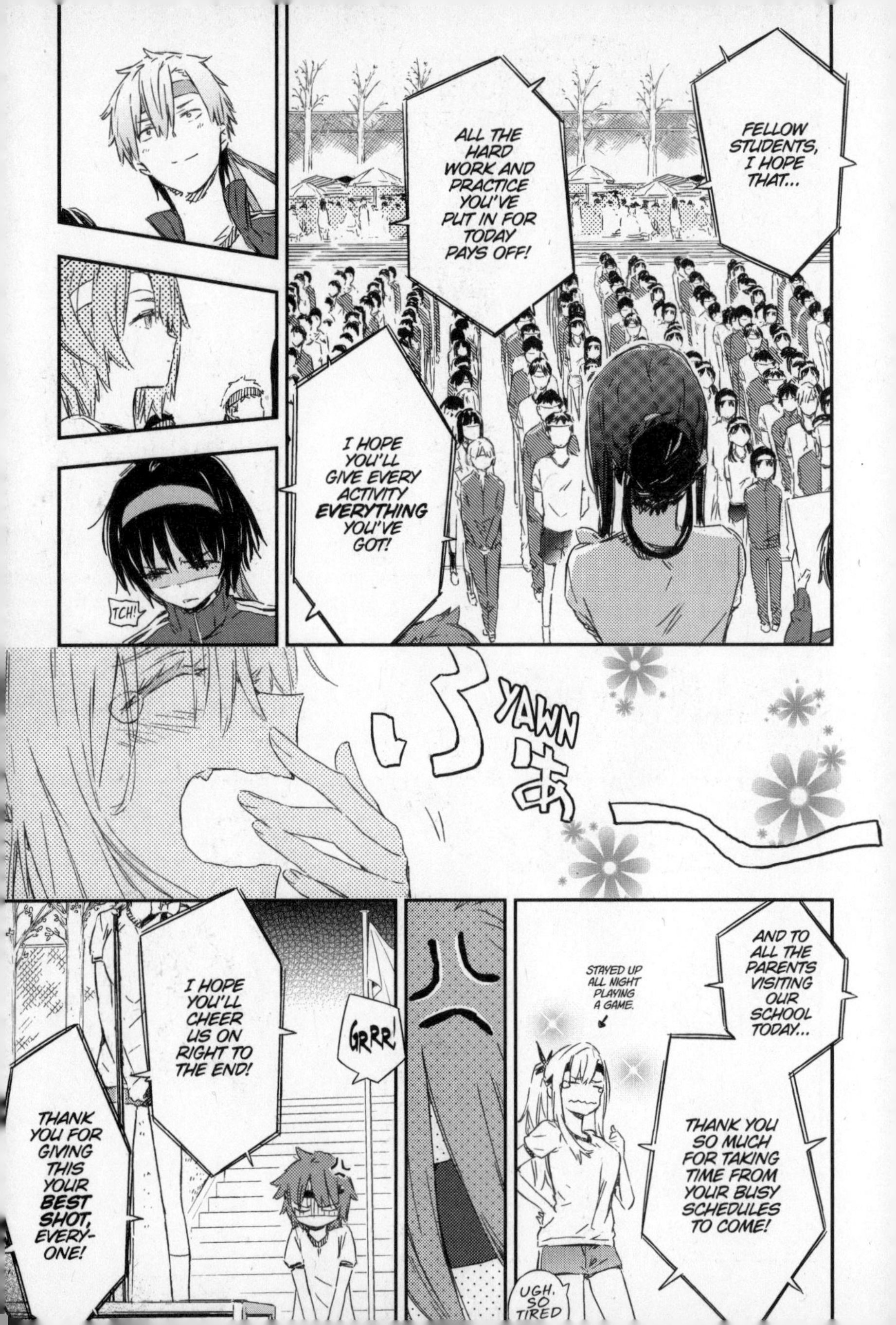
FELLOW STUDENTS, I HOPE THAT...
ALL THE HARD WORK AND PRACTICE YOU'VE PUT IN FOR TODAY PAYS OFF!
I HOPE YOU'LL GIVE EVERY ACTIVITY EVERYTHING YOU'VE GOT!
TCH!
YAWN
あ
AND TO ALL THE PARENTS VISITING OUR SCHOOL TODAY...
STAYED UP ALL NIGHT PLAYING A GAME.
THANK YOU SO MUCH FOR TAKING TIME FROM YOUR BUSY SCHEDULES TO COME!
UGH, SO TIRED
GRRR!
I HOPE YOU'LL CHEER US ON RIGHT TO THE END!
THANK YOU FOR GIVING THIS YOUR BEST SHOT, EVERY-ONE!

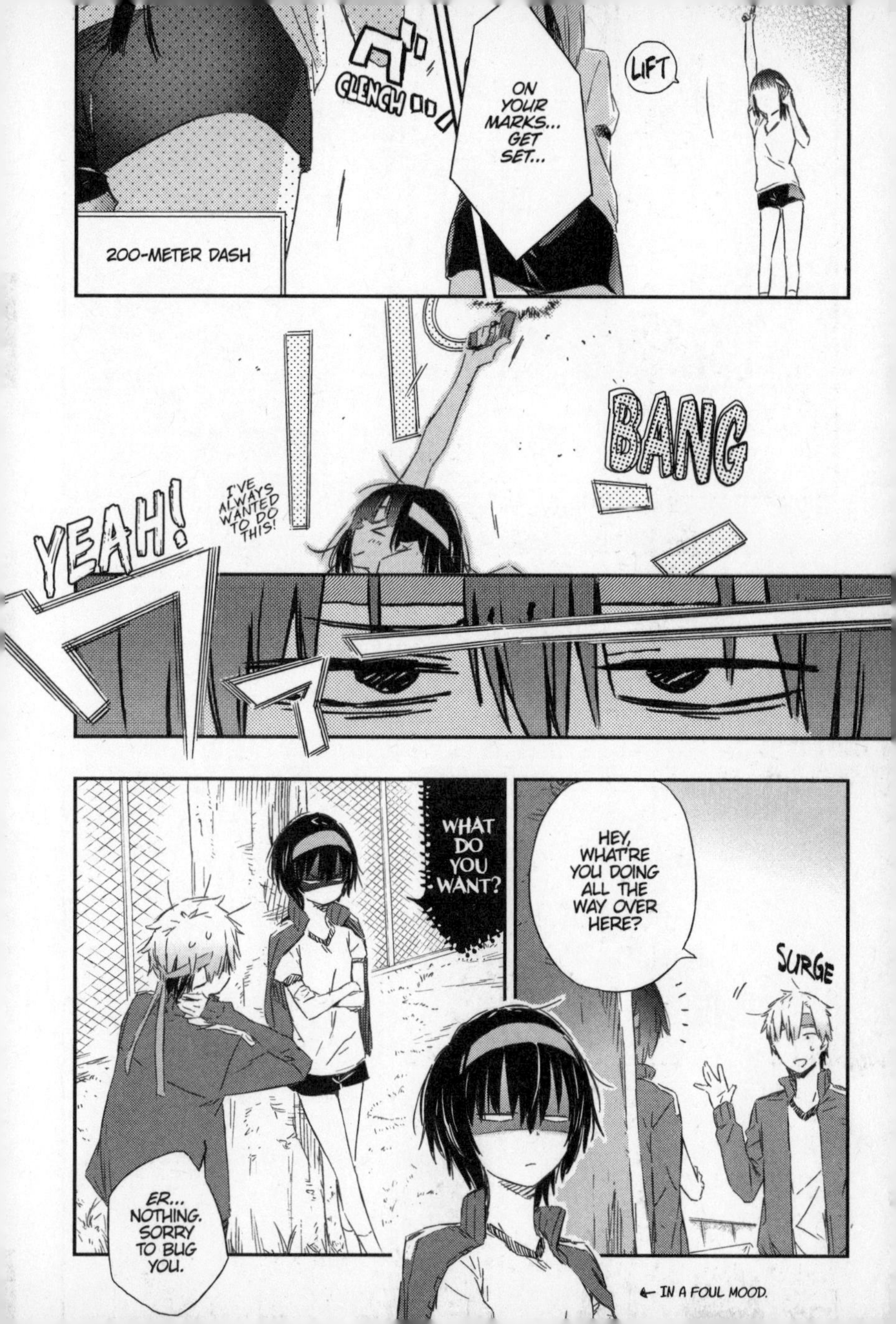
LIFT
ON YOUR MARKS... GET SET...
CLENCH
200-METER DASH
BANG
I'VE ALWAYS WANTED TO DO THIS!
YEAH!
HEY, WHAT'RE YOU DOING ALL THE WAY OVER HERE?
SURGE
WHAT DO YOU WANT?
ER... NOTHING. SORRY TO BUG YOU.
← IN A FOUL MOOD.

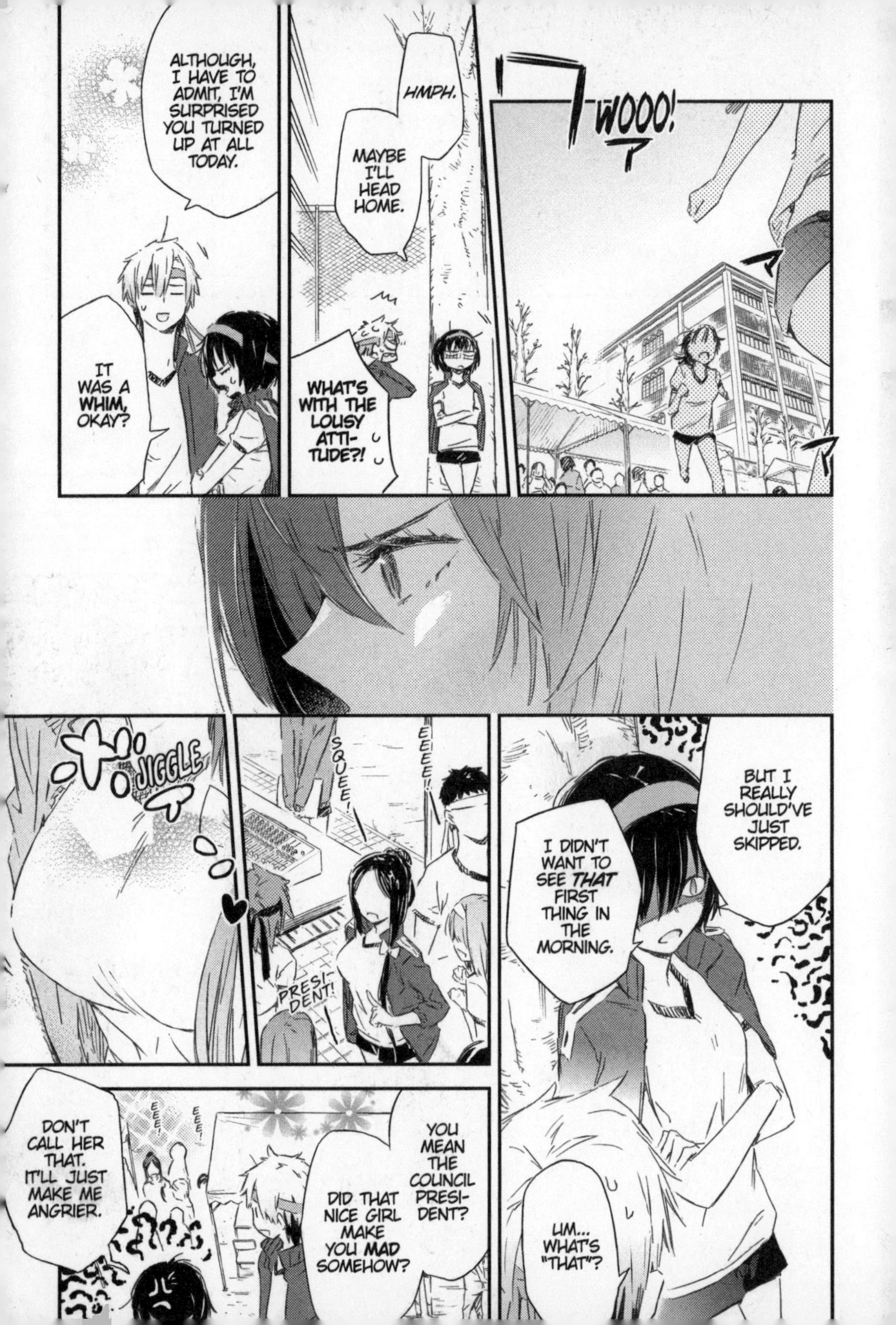
WOOO!
HMPH.
MAYBE I'LL HEAD HOME.
WHAT'S WITH THE LOUSY ATTI-TUDE?!
ALTHOUGH, I HAVE TO ADMIT, I'M SURPRISED YOU TURNED UP AT ALL TODAY.
IT WAS A WHIM, OKAY?
BUT I REALLY SHOULD'VE JUST SKIPPED.
I DIDN'T WANT TO SEE THAT FIRST THING IN THE MORNING.
EEEE!!
SQUEEE!
PRESI-DENT!
JIGGLE
UM... WHAT'S "THAT"?
YOU MEAN THE COUNCIL PRESI-DENT?
DID THAT NICE GIRL MAKE YOU MAD SOMEHOW?
EEE!
EEE!
DON'T CALL HER THAT. IT'LL JUST MAKE ME ANGRIER.

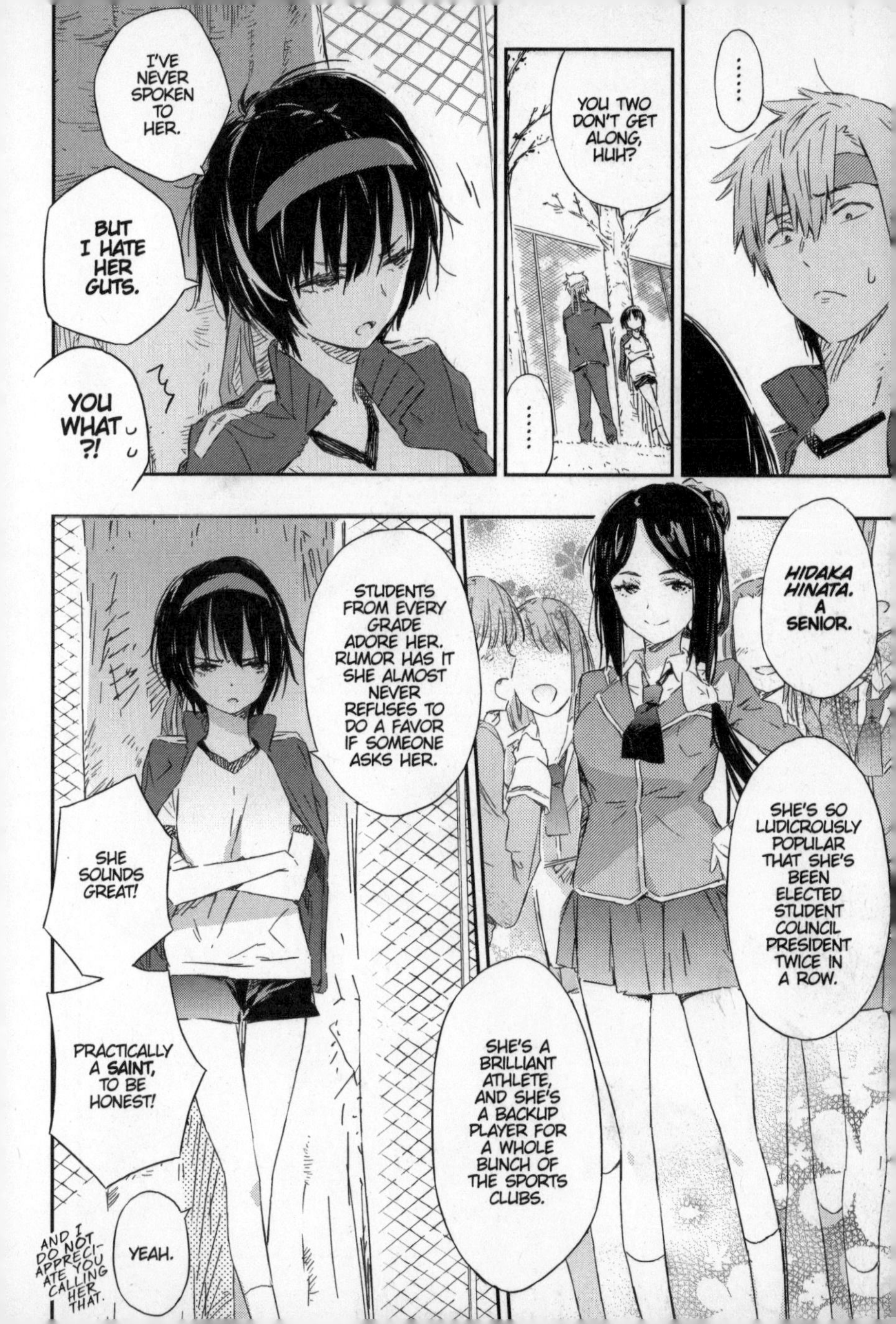
……
YOU TWO DON'T GET ALONG, HUH?
……
I'VE NEVER SPOKEN TO HER.
BUT I HATE HER GUTS.
YOU WHAT?!
HIDAKA HINATA. A SENIOR.
SHE'S SO LUDICROUSLY POPULAR THAT SHE'S BEEN ELECTED STUDENT COUNCIL PRESIDENT TWICE IN A ROW.
STUDENTS FROM EVERY GRADE ADORE HER. RUMOR HAS IT SHE ALMOST NEVER REFUSES TO DO A FAVOR IF SOMEONE ASKS HER.
SHE'S A BRILLIANT ATHLETE, AND SHE'S A BACKUP PLAYER FOR A WHOLE BUNCH OF THE SPORTS CLUBS.
SHE SOUNDS GREAT!
PRACTICALLY A SAINT, TO BE HONEST!
YEAH.
AND I DO NOT APPRECIATE YOU CALLING HER THAT.

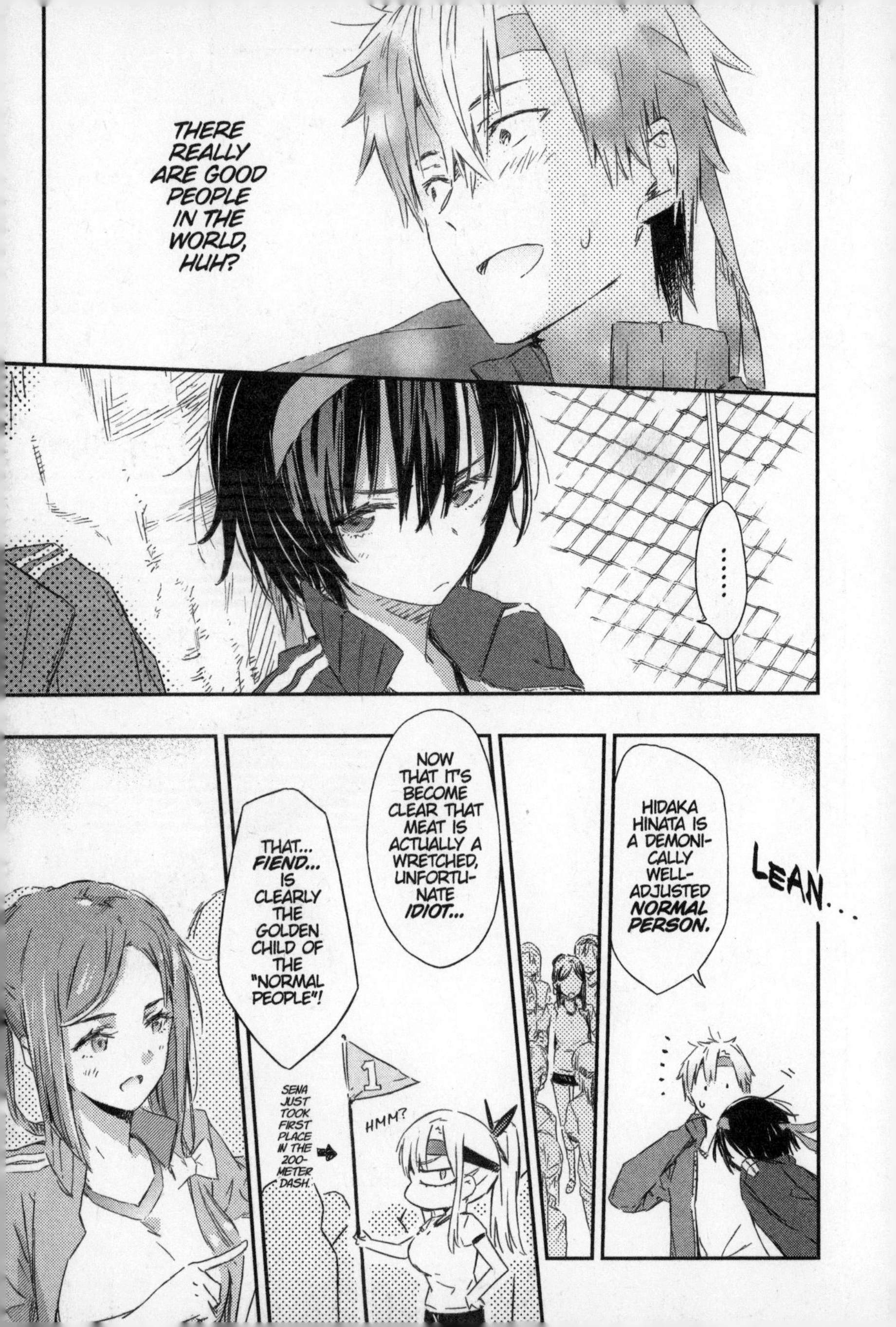
THERE REALLY ARE GOOD PEOPLE IN THE WORLD, HUH?
......
HIDAKA HINATA IS A DEMONICALLY WELL-ADJUSTED NORMAL PERSON.
LEAN...
NOW THAT IT'S BECOME CLEAR THAT MEAT IS ACTUALLY A WRETCHED, UNFORTUNATE IDIOT...
HMM?
SENA JUST TOOK FIRST PLACE IN THE 200-METER DASH.
THAT... FIEND... IS CLEARLY THE GOLDEN CHILD OF THE "NORMAL PEOPLE"!

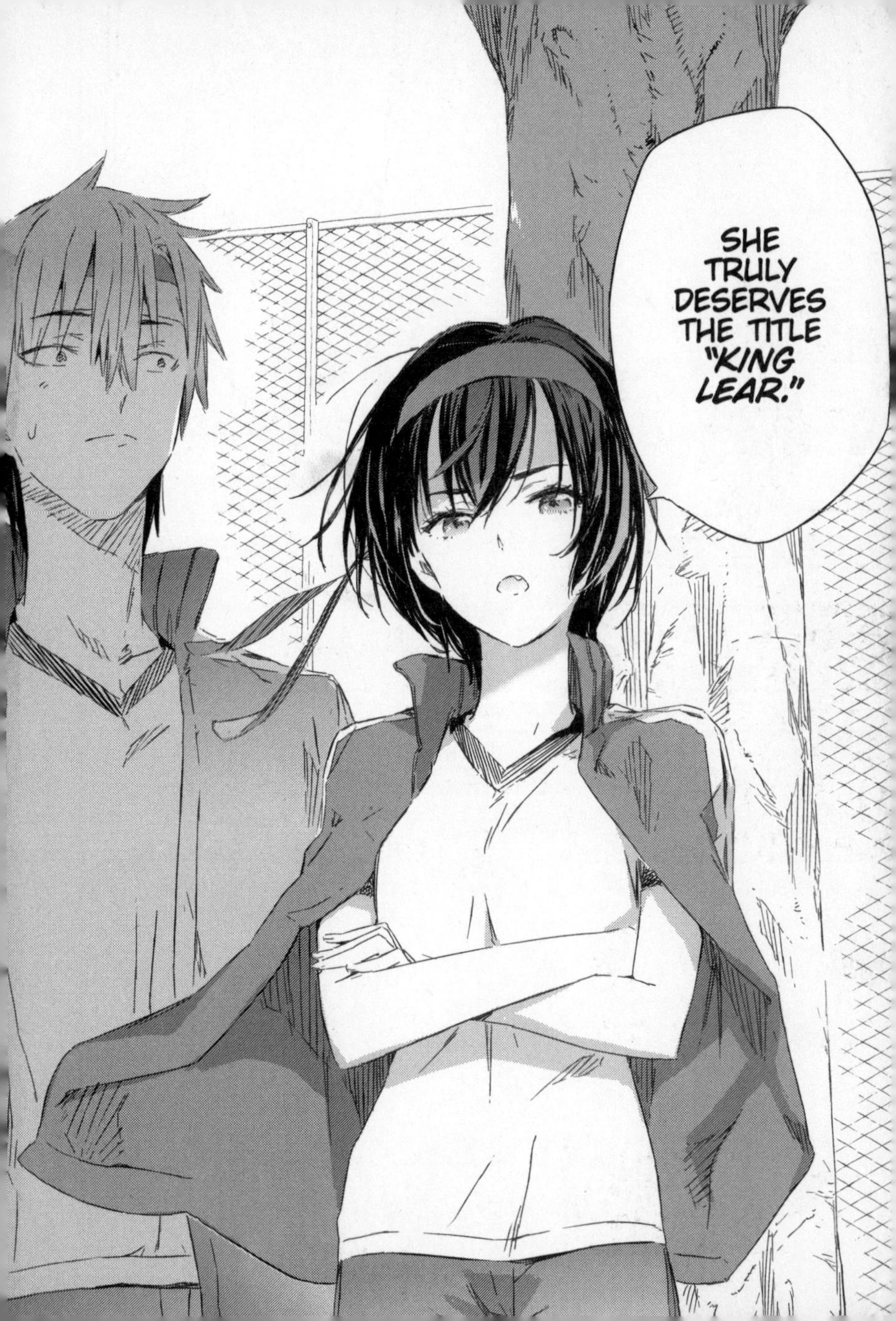
SHE TRULY DESERVES THE TITLE *"KING LEAR."*

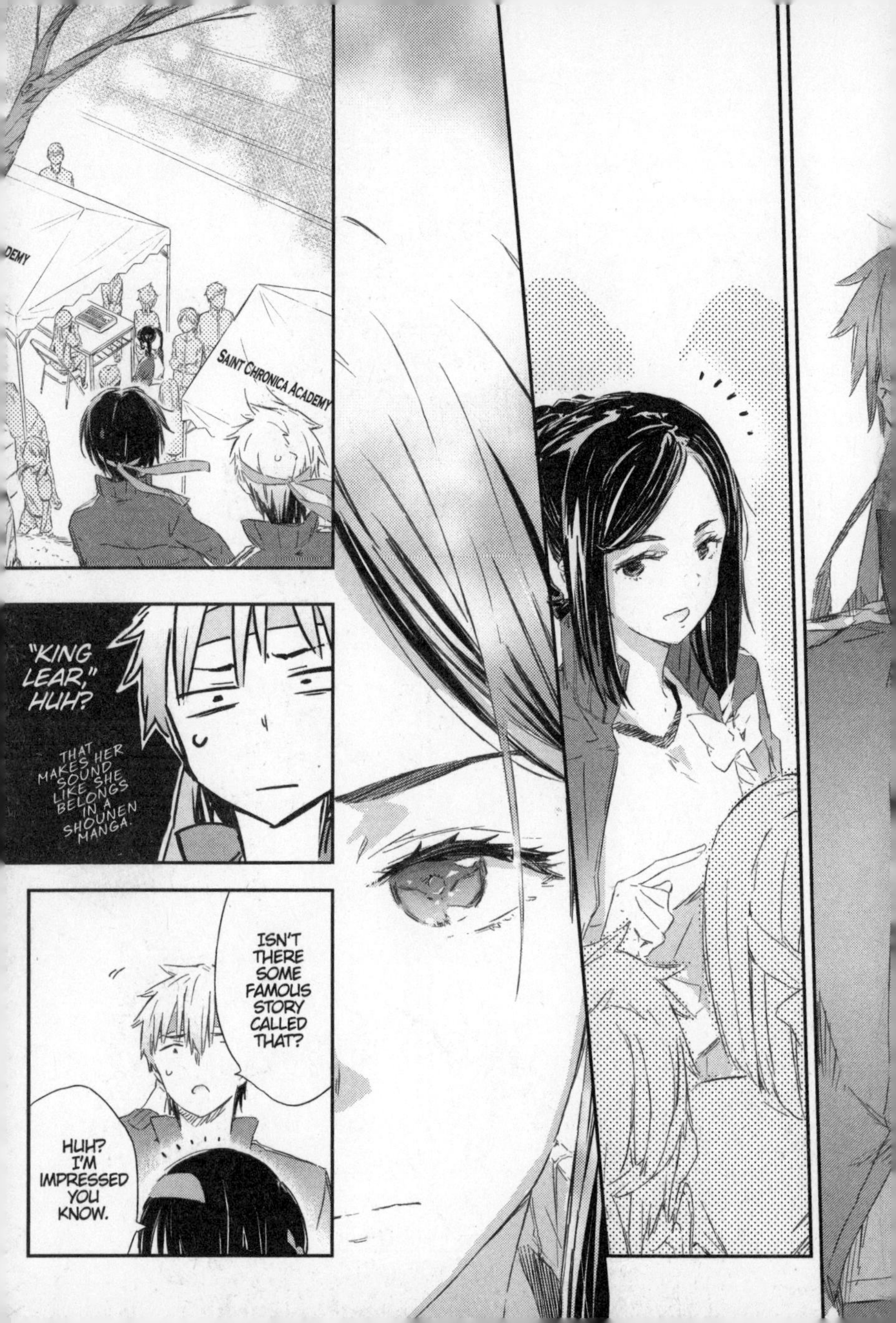
SAINT CHRONICA ACADEMY
"KING LEAR," HUH?
THAT MAKES HER SOUND LIKE SHE BELONGS IN A SHOUNEN MANGA.
ISN'T THERE SOME FAMOUS STORY CALLED THAT?
HUH? I'M IMPRESSED YOU KNOW.

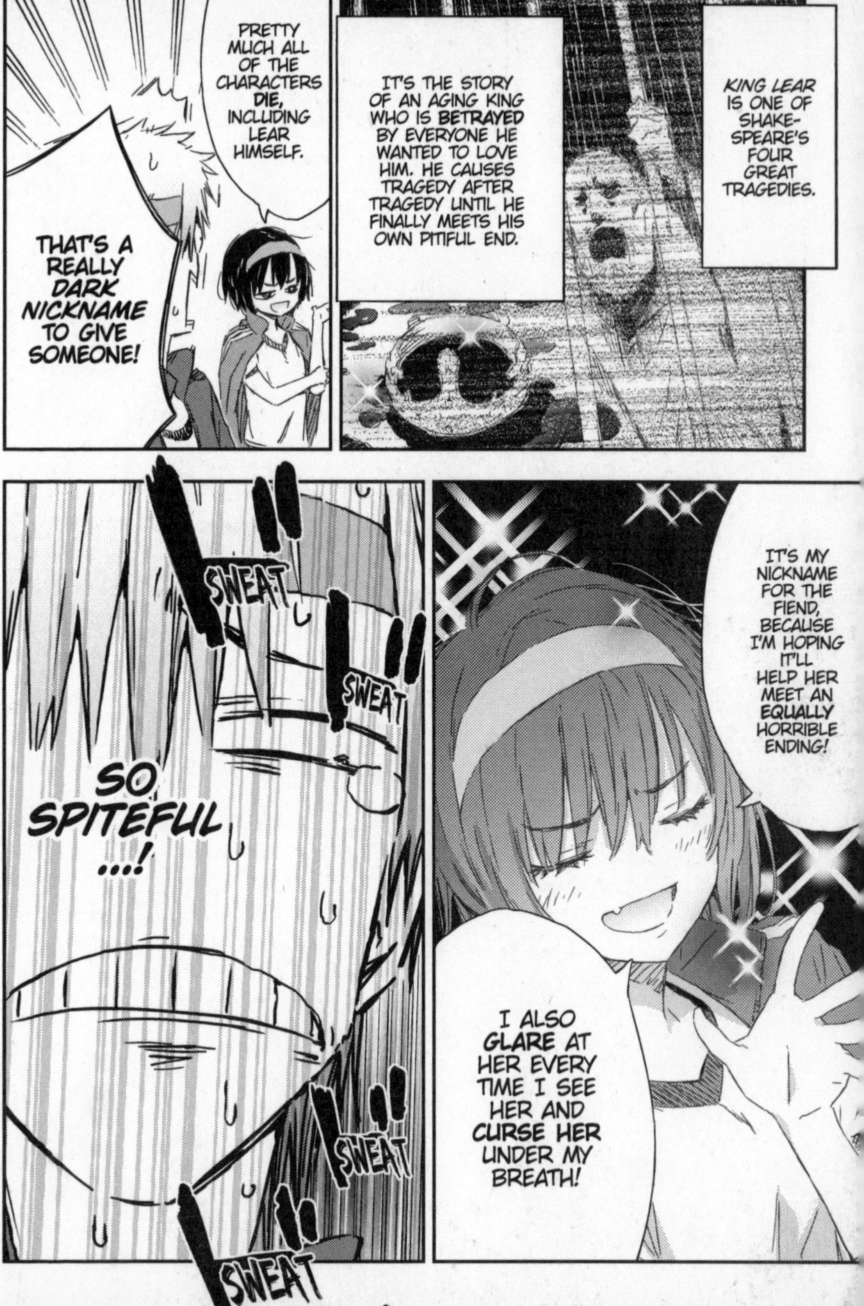
KING LEAR IS ONE OF SHAKE-SPEARE'S FOUR GREAT TRAGEDIES.
IT'S THE STORY OF AN AGING KING WHO IS BETRAYED BY EVERYONE HE WANTED TO LOVE HIM. HE CAUSES TRAGEDY AFTER TRAGEDY UNTIL HE FINALLY MEETS HIS OWN PITIFUL END.
PRETTY MUCH ALL OF THE CHARACTERS DIE, INCLUDING LEAR HIMSELF.
THAT'S A REALLY DARK NICKNAME TO GIVE SOMEONE!
IT'S MY NICKNAME FOR THE FIEND, BECAUSE I'M HOPING IT'LL HELP HER MEET AN EQUALLY HORRIBLE ENDING!
I ALSO GLARE AT HER EVERY TIME I SEE HER AND CURSE HER UNDER MY BREATH!
SWEAT
SWEAT
SO SPITEFUL ...!
SWEAT
SWEAT

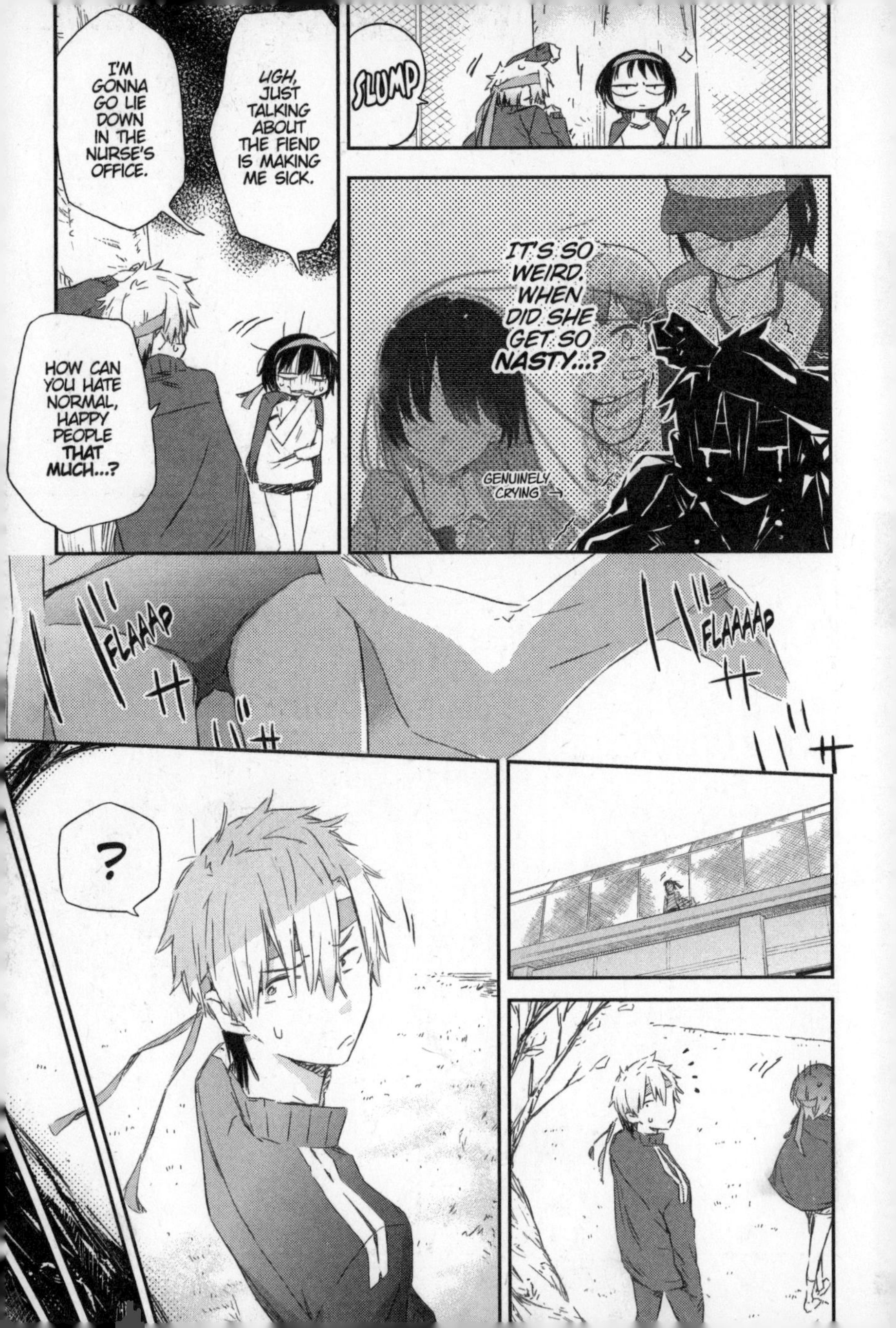
SLUMP
IT'S SO WEIRD. WHEN DID SHE GET SO NASTY...?
GENUINELY CRYING
UGH, JUST TALKING ABOUT THE FIEND IS MAKING ME SICK.
I'M GONNA GO LIE DOWN IN THE NURSE'S OFFICE.
HOW CAN YOU HATE NORMAL, HAPPY PEOPLE THAT MUCH...?
FLAAAAP
FLAAAP
?

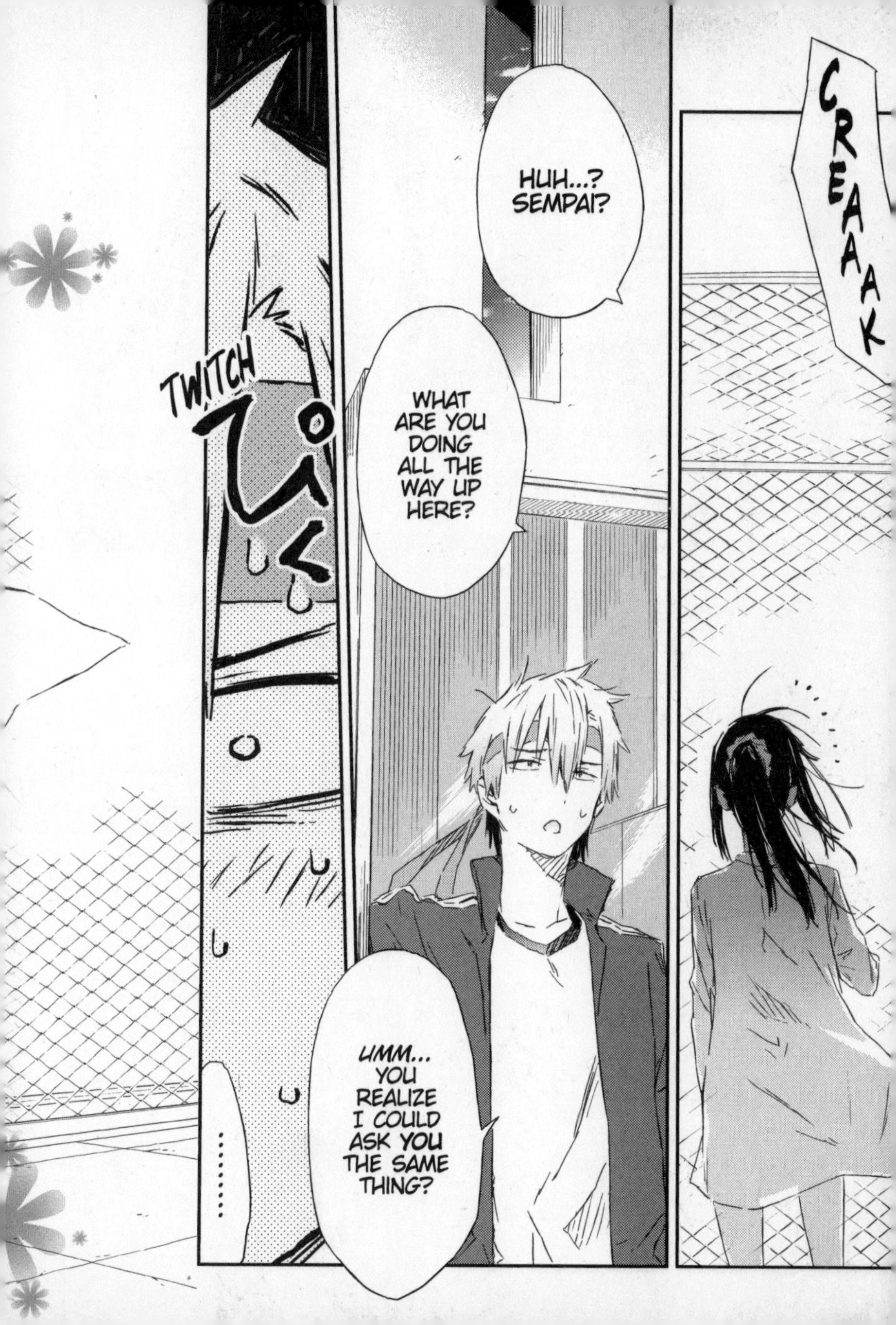
CREAAAK
HUH...? SEMPAI?
WHAT ARE YOU DOING ALL THE WAY UP HERE?
UMM... YOU REALIZE I COULD ASK YOU THE SAME THING?
TWITCH
ぴく
......

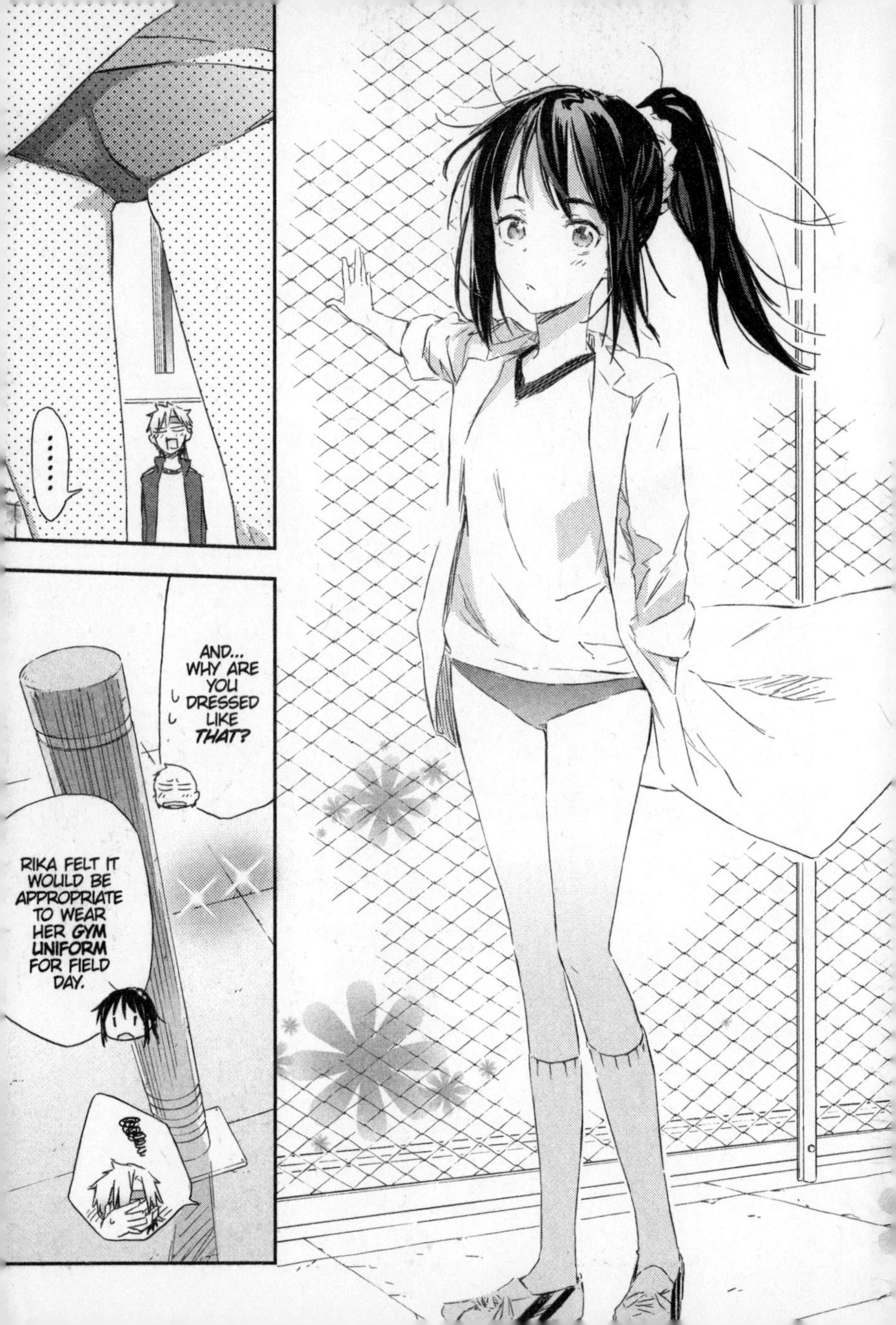
......
AND... WHY ARE YOU DRESSED LIKE *THAT?*
RIKA FELT IT WOULD BE APPROPRIATE TO WEAR HER **GYM UNIFORM** FOR FIELD DAY.

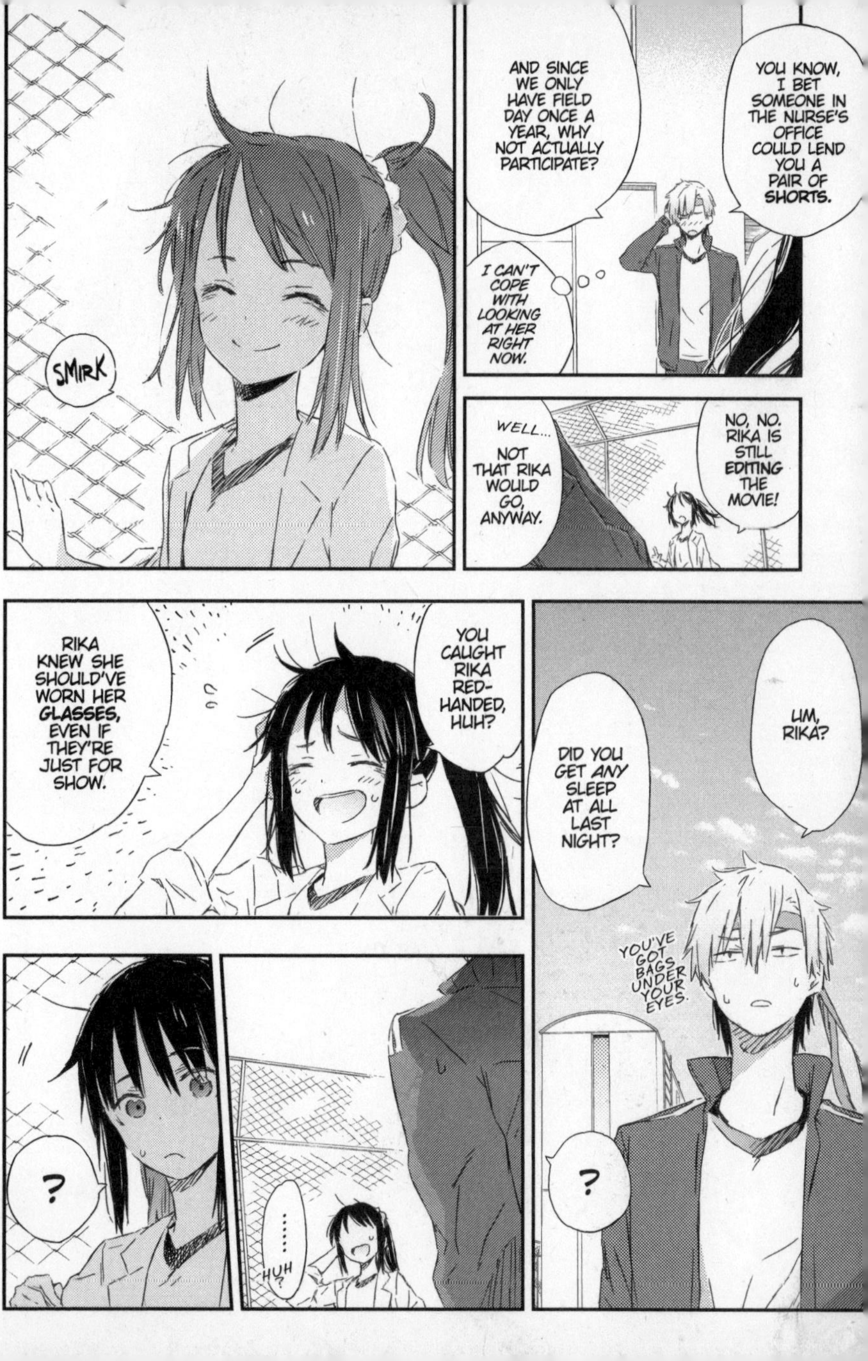
YOU KNOW, I BET SOMEONE IN THE NURSE'S OFFICE COULD LEND YOU A PAIR OF SHORTS.
AND SINCE WE ONLY HAVE FIELD DAY ONCE A YEAR, WHY NOT ACTUALLY PARTICIPATE?
I CAN'T COPE WITH LOOKING AT HER RIGHT NOW.
NO, NO. RIKA IS STILL EDITING THE MOVIE!
WELL...
NOT THAT RIKA WOULD GO, ANYWAY.
SMIRK
UM, RIKA?
DID YOU GET ANY SLEEP AT ALL LAST NIGHT?
YOU'VE GOT BAGS UNDER YOUR EYES.
YOU CAUGHT RIKA RED-HANDED, HUH?
RIKA KNEW SHE SHOULD'VE WORN HER GLASSES, EVEN IF THEY'RE JUST FOR SHOW.
?
......
HUH?
?

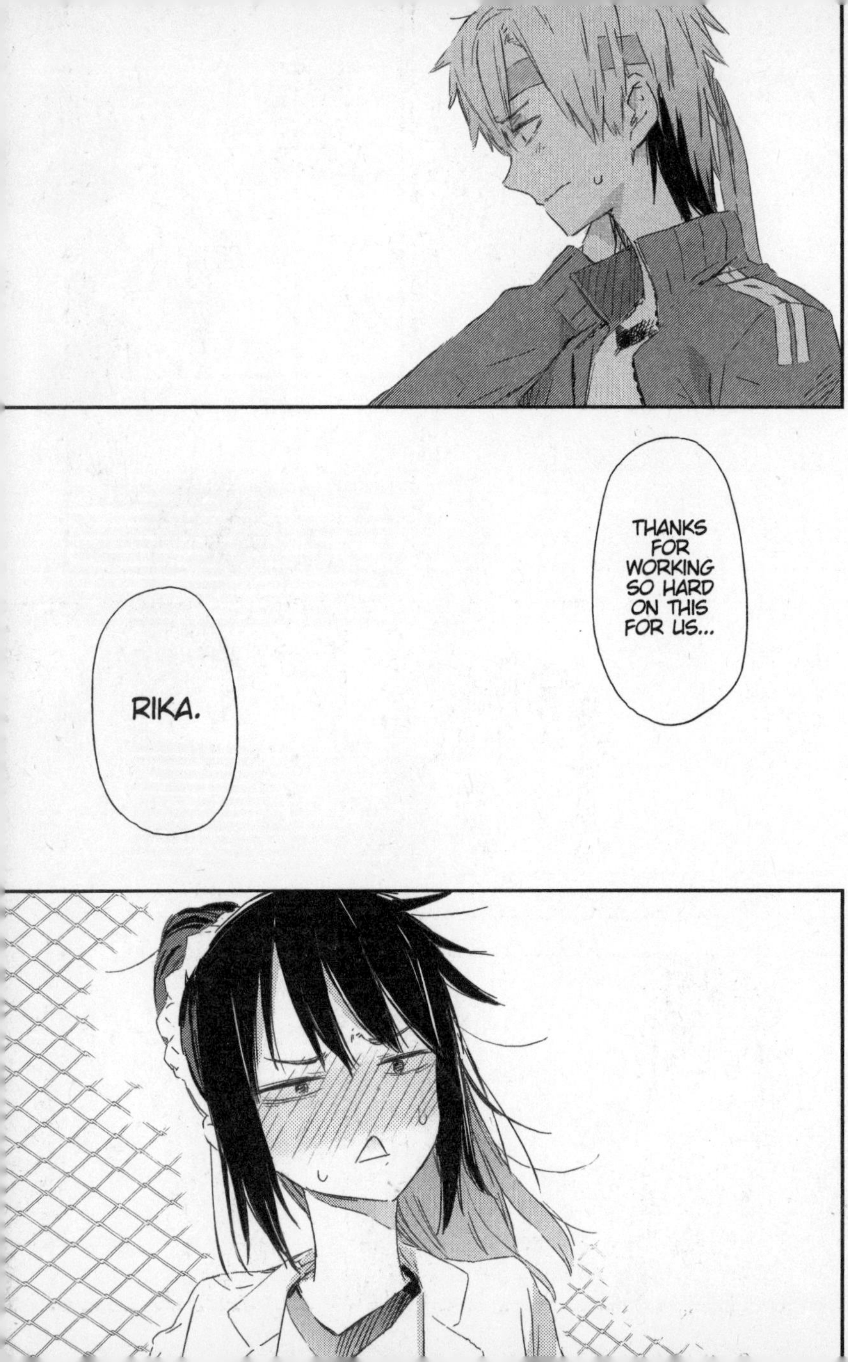
THANKS FOR WORKING SO HARD ON THIS FOR US...
RIKA.

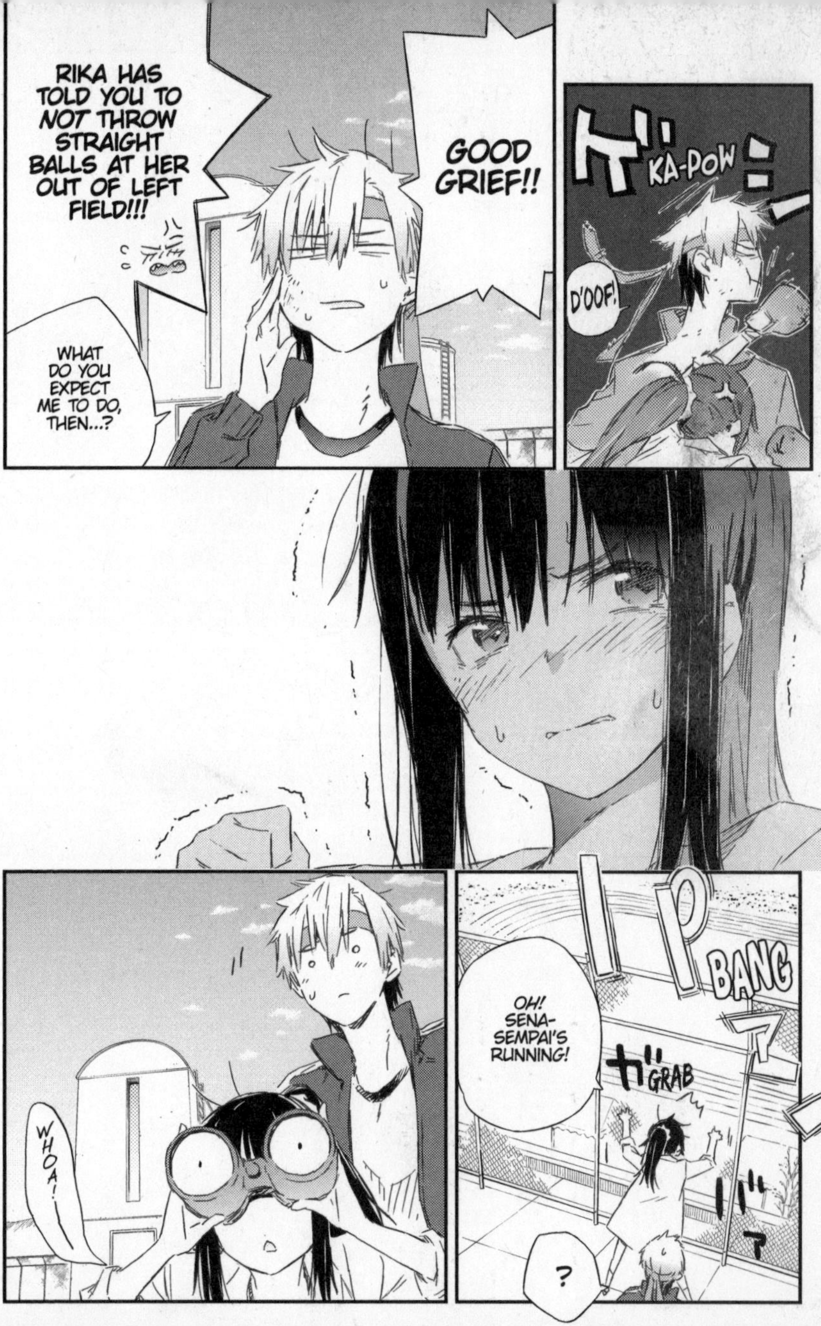
KA-POW!!
D'OOF!
GOOD GRIEF!!
RIKA HAS TOLD YOU TO NOT THROW STRAIGHT BALLS AT HER OUT OF LEFT FIELD!!!
WHAT DO YOU EXPECT ME TO DO, THEN...?
BANG
GRAB
OH! SENA-SEMPAI'S RUNNING!
?
WHOA!

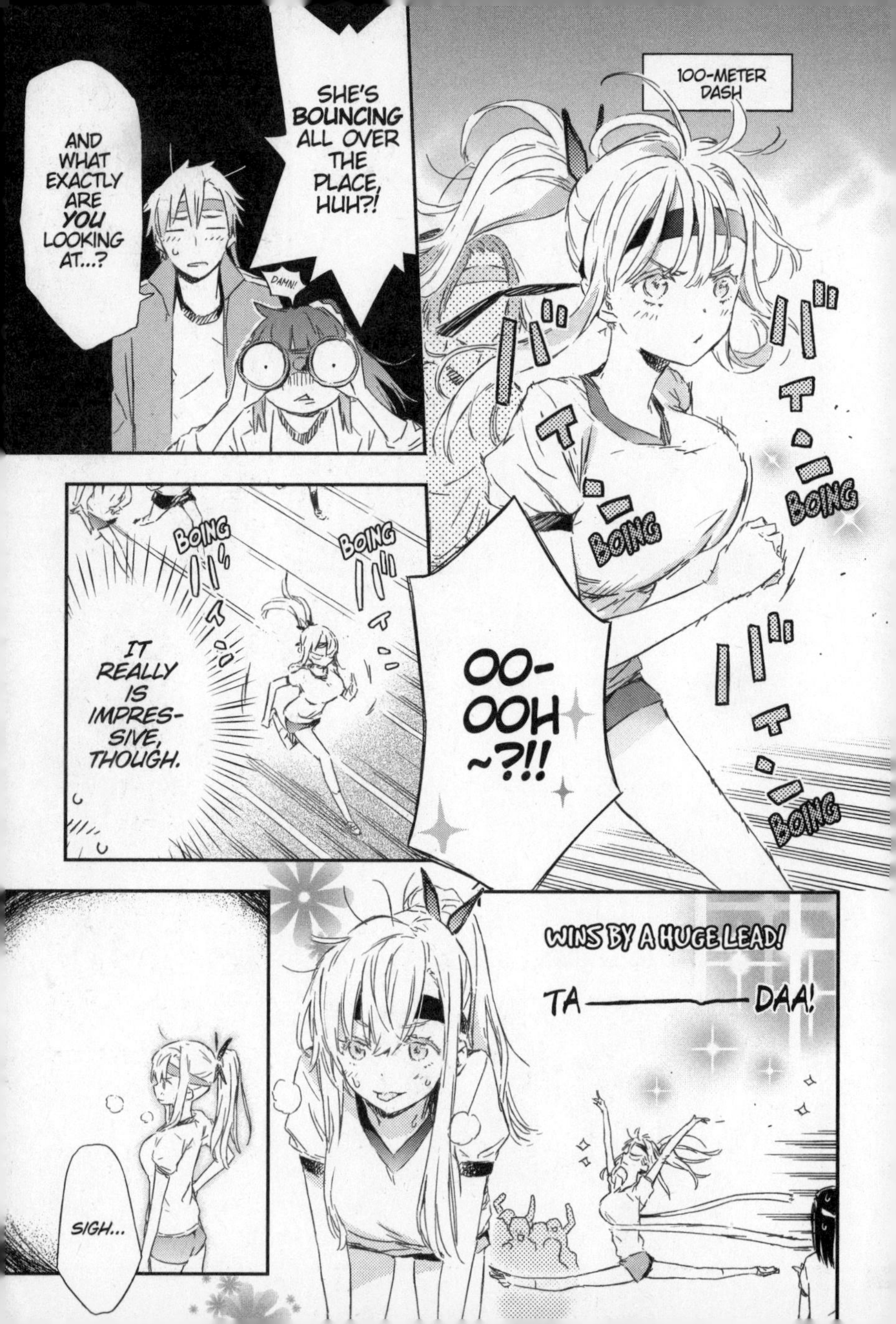
100-METER DASH
BOING
BOING
BOING
BOING
SHE'S BOUNCING ALL OVER THE PLACE, HUH?!
DAMN!
AND WHAT EXACTLY ARE YOU LOOKING AT...?
OO-OOH ~?!!
BOING
BOING
IT REALLY IS IMPRES-SIVE, THOUGH.
WINS BY A HUGE LEAD!
TA———DAA!
SIGH...

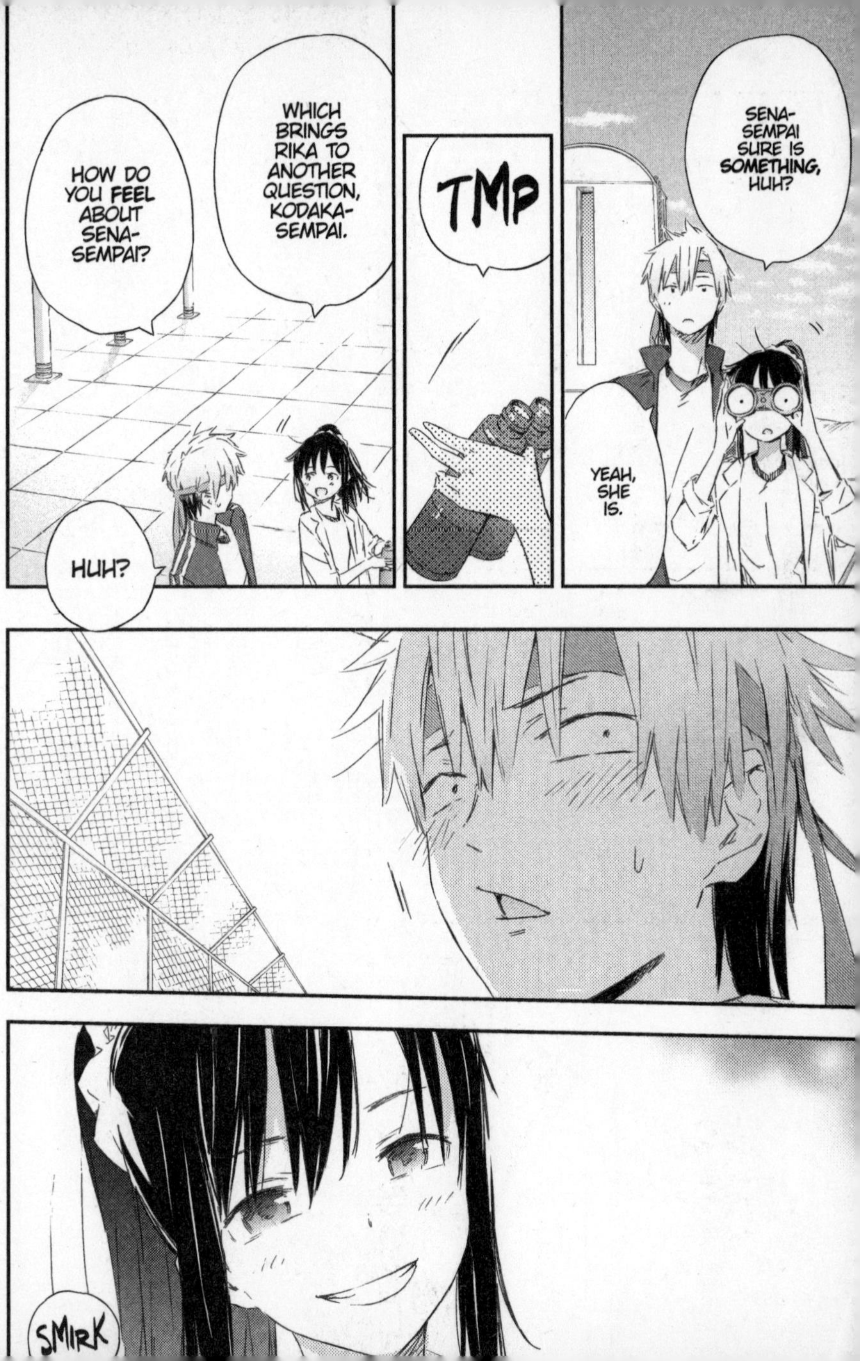
SENA-SEMPAI SURE IS SOMETHING, HUH?
YEAH, SHE IS.
TMP
WHICH BRINGS RIKA TO ANOTHER QUESTION, KODAKA-SEMPAI.
HOW DO YOU FEEL ABOUT SENA-SEMPAI?
HUH?
SMIRK

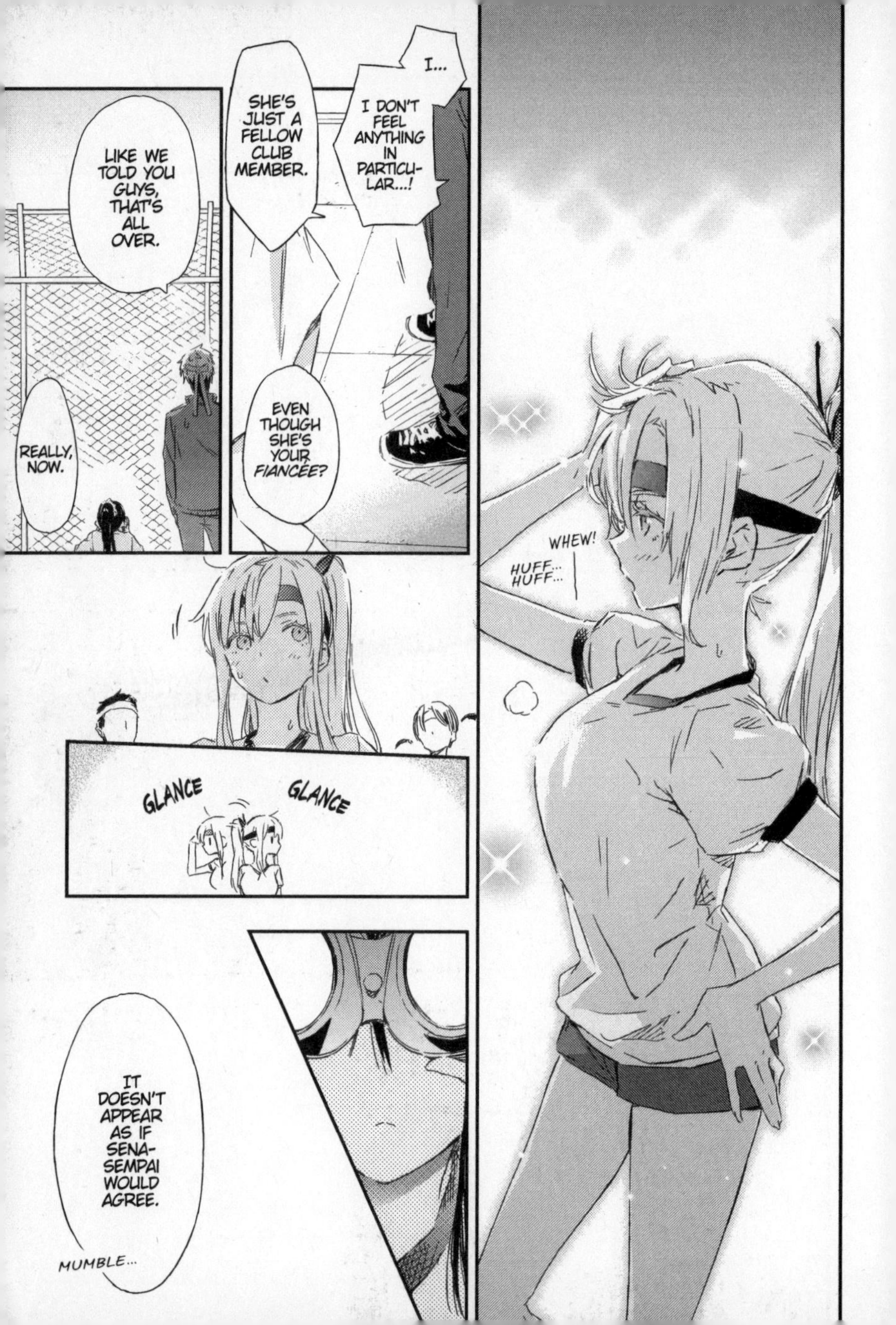
WHEW!
HUFF... HUFF...
I...
I DON'T FEEL ANYTHING IN PARTICU-LAR...!
SHE'S JUST A FELLOW CLUB MEMBER.
EVEN THOUGH SHE'S YOUR FIANCÉE?
LIKE WE TOLD YOU GUYS, THAT'S ALL OVER.
REALLY, NOW.
GLANCE
GLANCE
IT DOESN'T APPEAR AS IF SENA-SEMPAI WOULD AGREE.
MUMBLE...

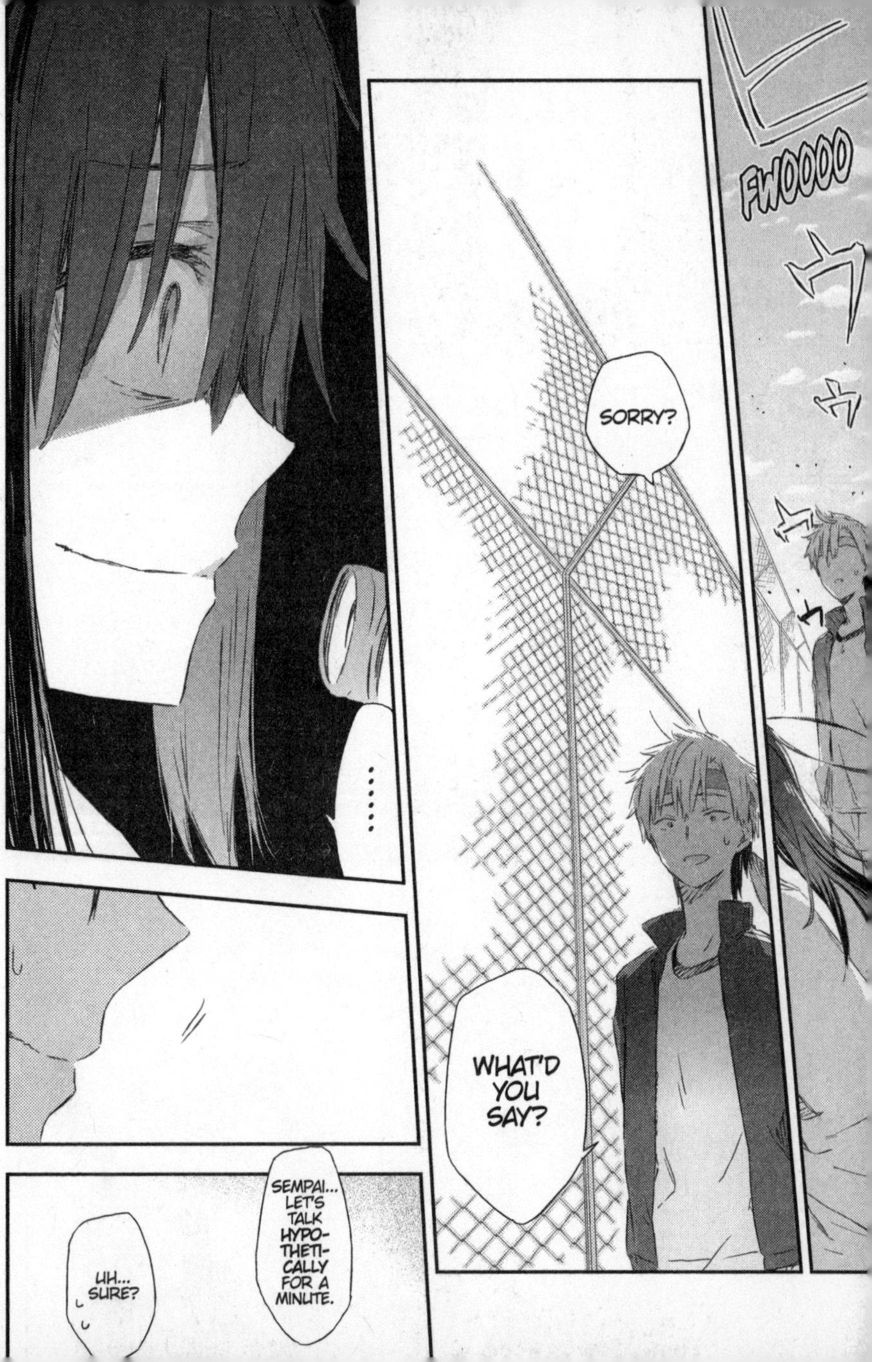
FWOOOO
SORRY?
WHAT'D YOU SAY?
......
SEMPAI... LET'S TALK HYPOTHETICALLY FOR A MINUTE.
UH... SURE?

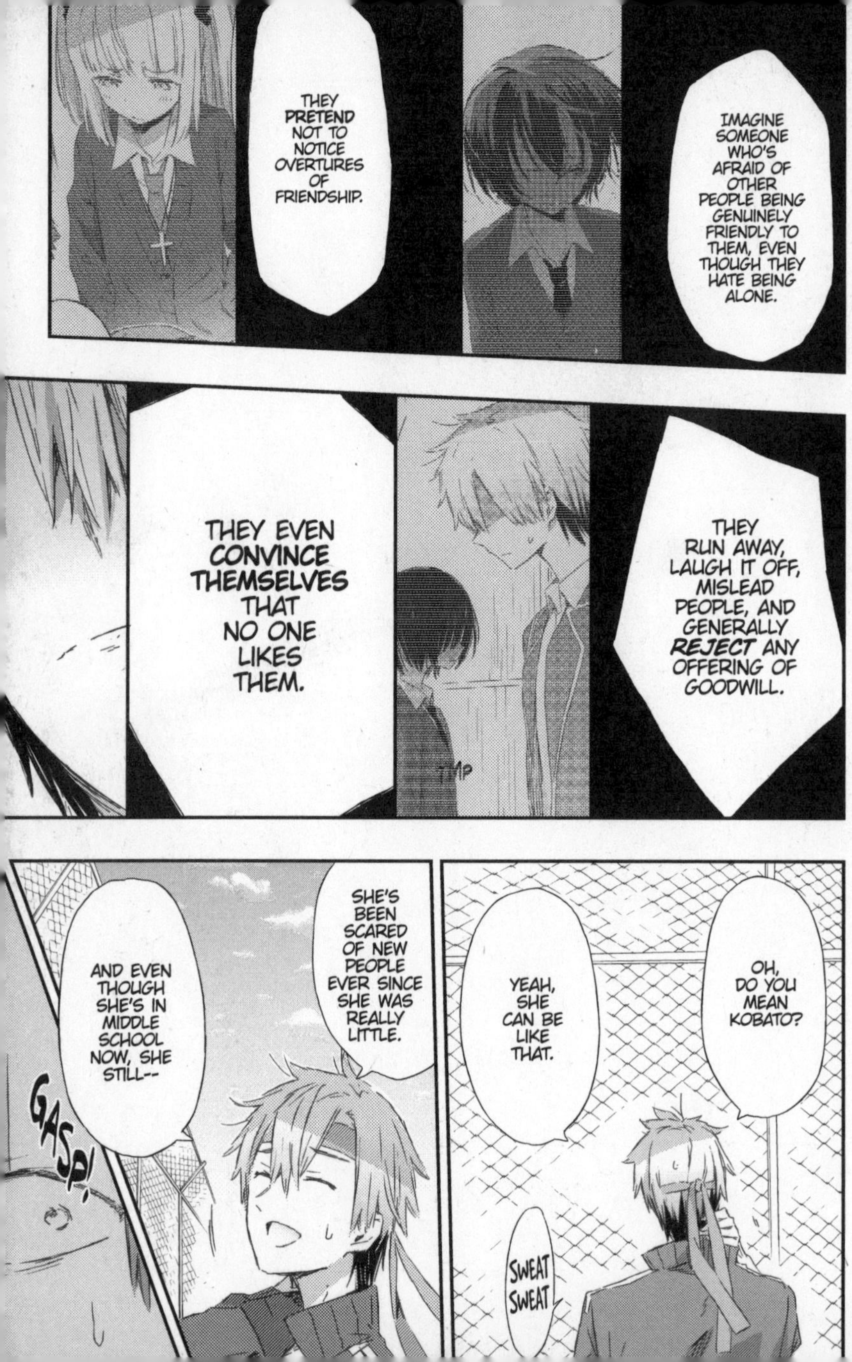
IMAGINE SOMEONE WHO'S AFRAID OF OTHER PEOPLE BEING GENUINELY FRIENDLY TO THEM, EVEN THOUGH THEY HATE BEING ALONE.
THEY PRETEND NOT TO NOTICE OVERTURES OF FRIENDSHIP.
THEY RUN AWAY, LAUGH IT OFF, MISLEAD PEOPLE, AND GENERALLY REJECT ANY OFFERING OF GOODWILL.
TMP
THEY EVEN CONVINCE THEMSELVES THAT NO ONE LIKES THEM.
OH, DO YOU MEAN KOBATO?
YEAH, SHE CAN BE LIKE THAT.
SWEAT SWEAT
SHE'S BEEN SCARED OF NEW PEOPLE EVER SINCE SHE WAS REALLY LITTLE.
AND EVEN THOUGH SHE'S IN MIDDLE SCHOOL NOW, SHE STILL--
GASP!

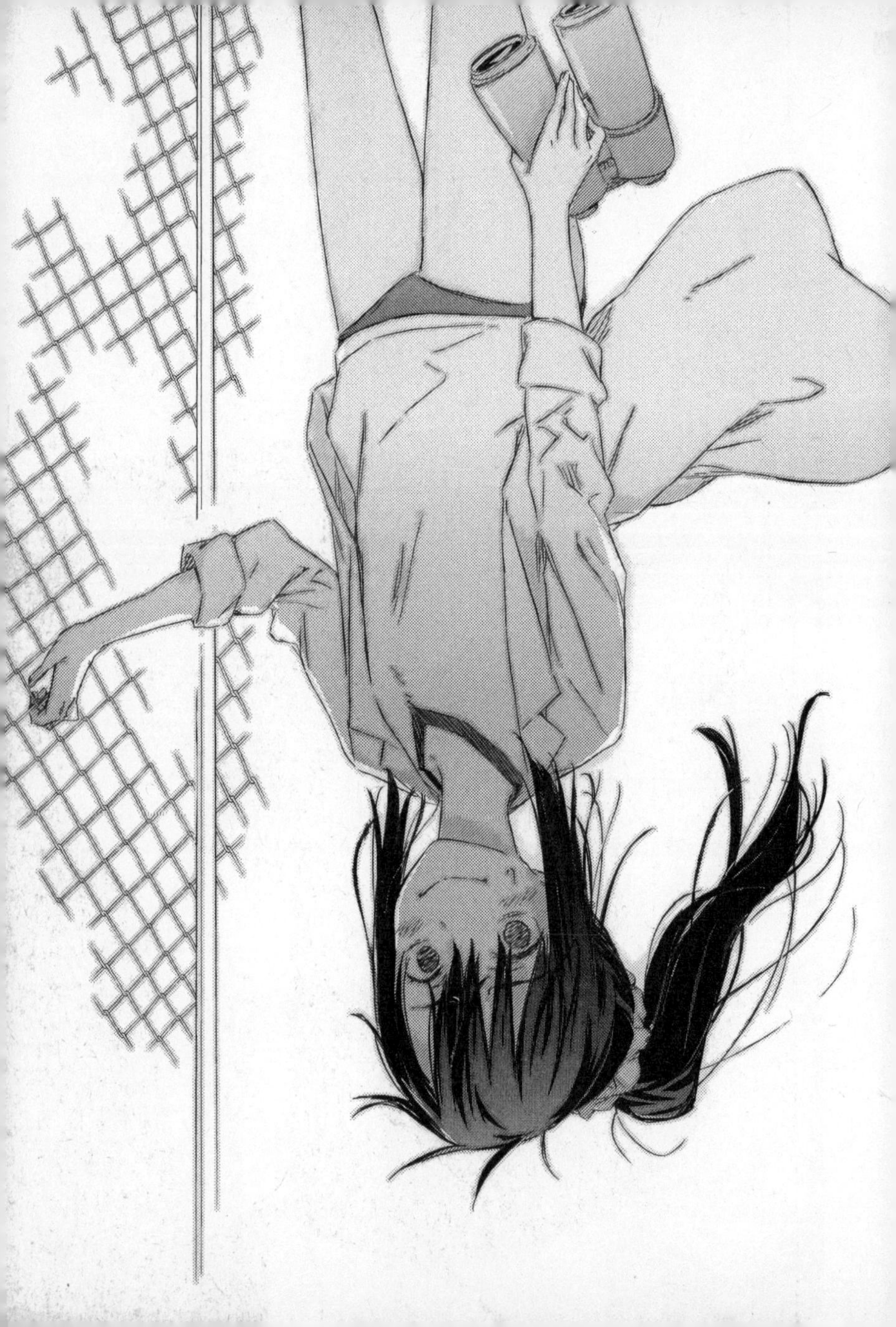

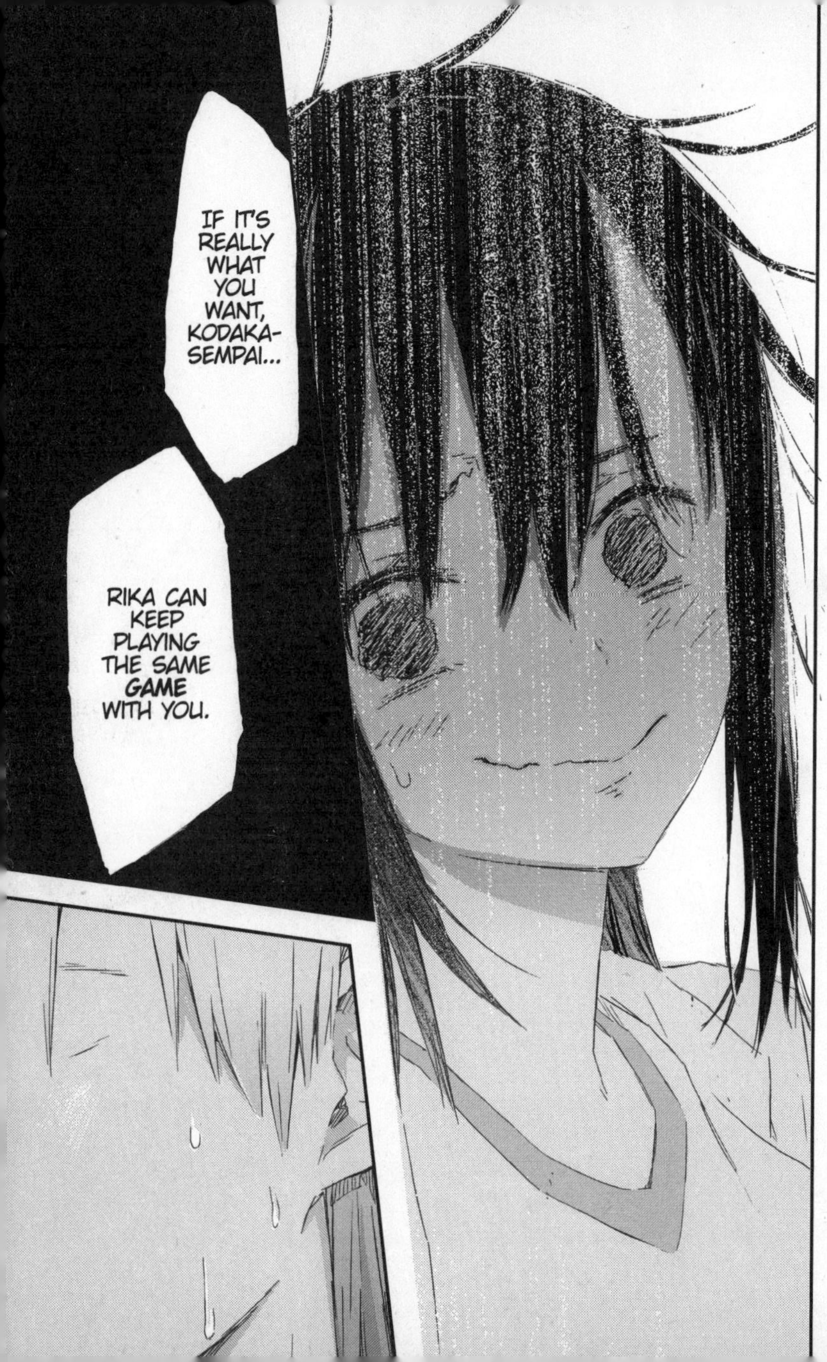
IF IT'S REALLY WHAT YOU WANT, KODAKA-SEMPAI...
RIKA CAN KEEP PLAYING THE SAME GAME WITH YOU.

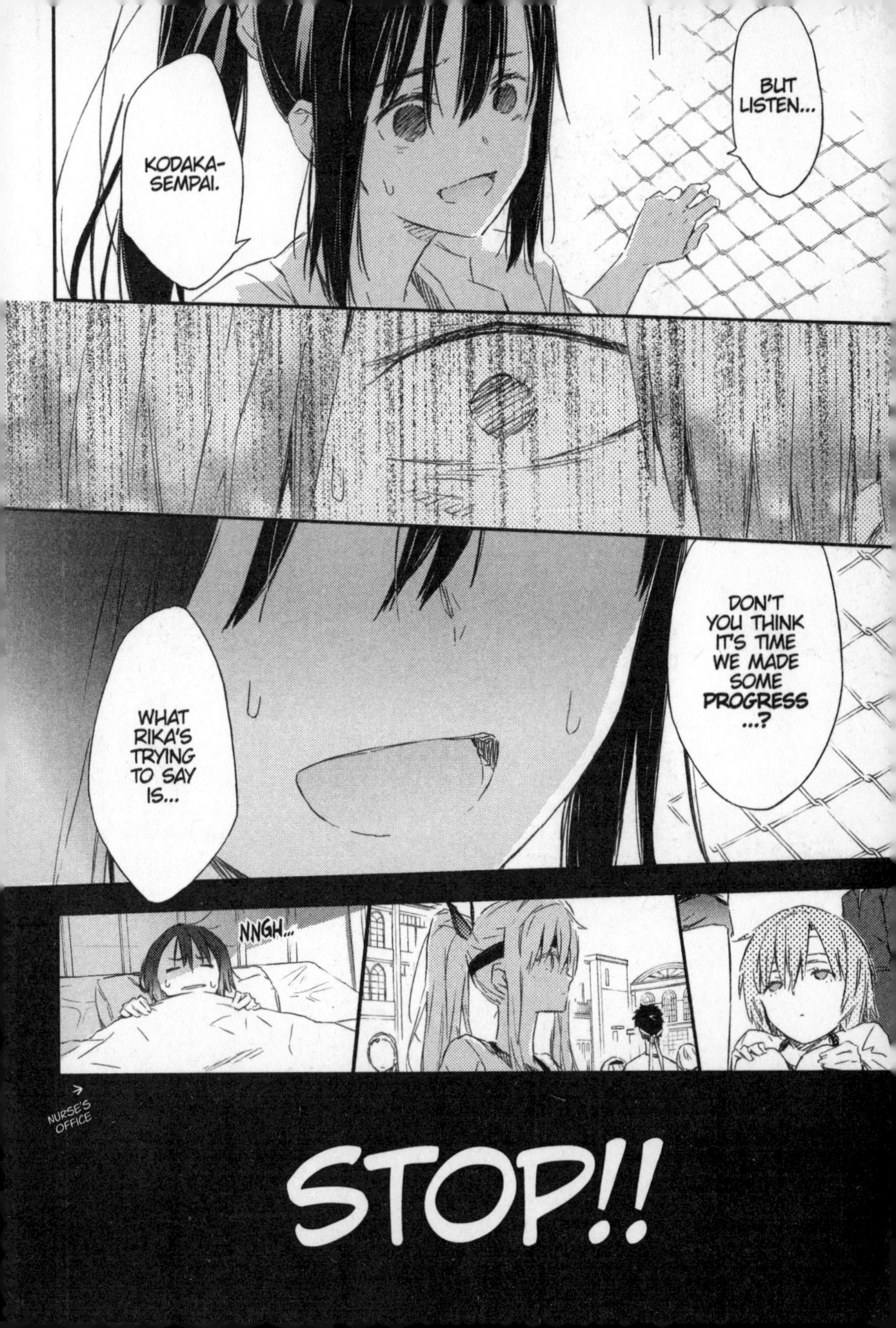
BUT LISTEN...
KODAKA-SEMPAI.
DON'T YOU THINK IT'S TIME WE MADE SOME PROGRESS ...?
WHAT RIKA'S TRYING TO SAY IS...
NNGH...
NURSE'S OFFICE
STOP!!

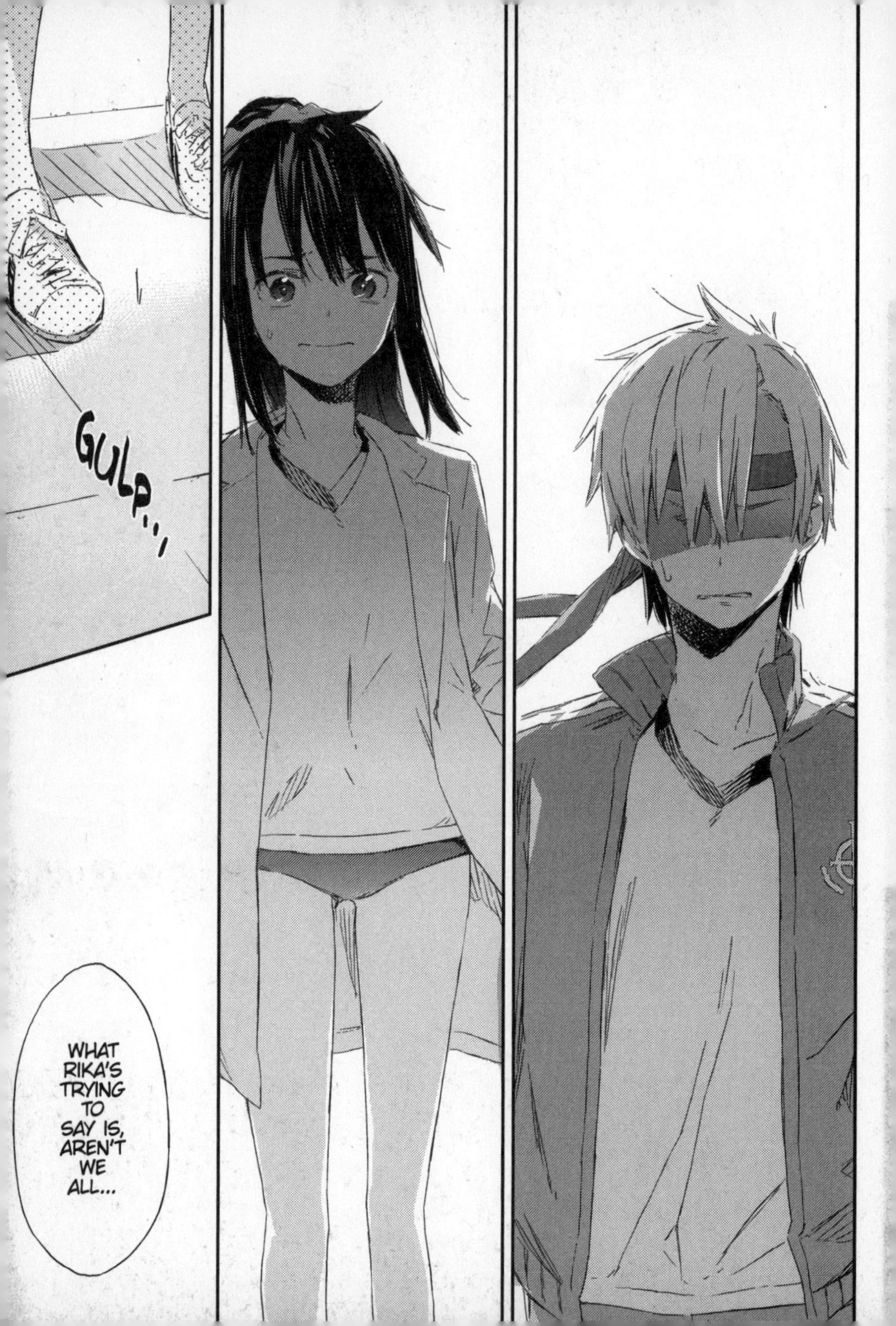
GULP...
WHAT RIKA'S TRYING TO SAY IS, AREN'T WE ALL...

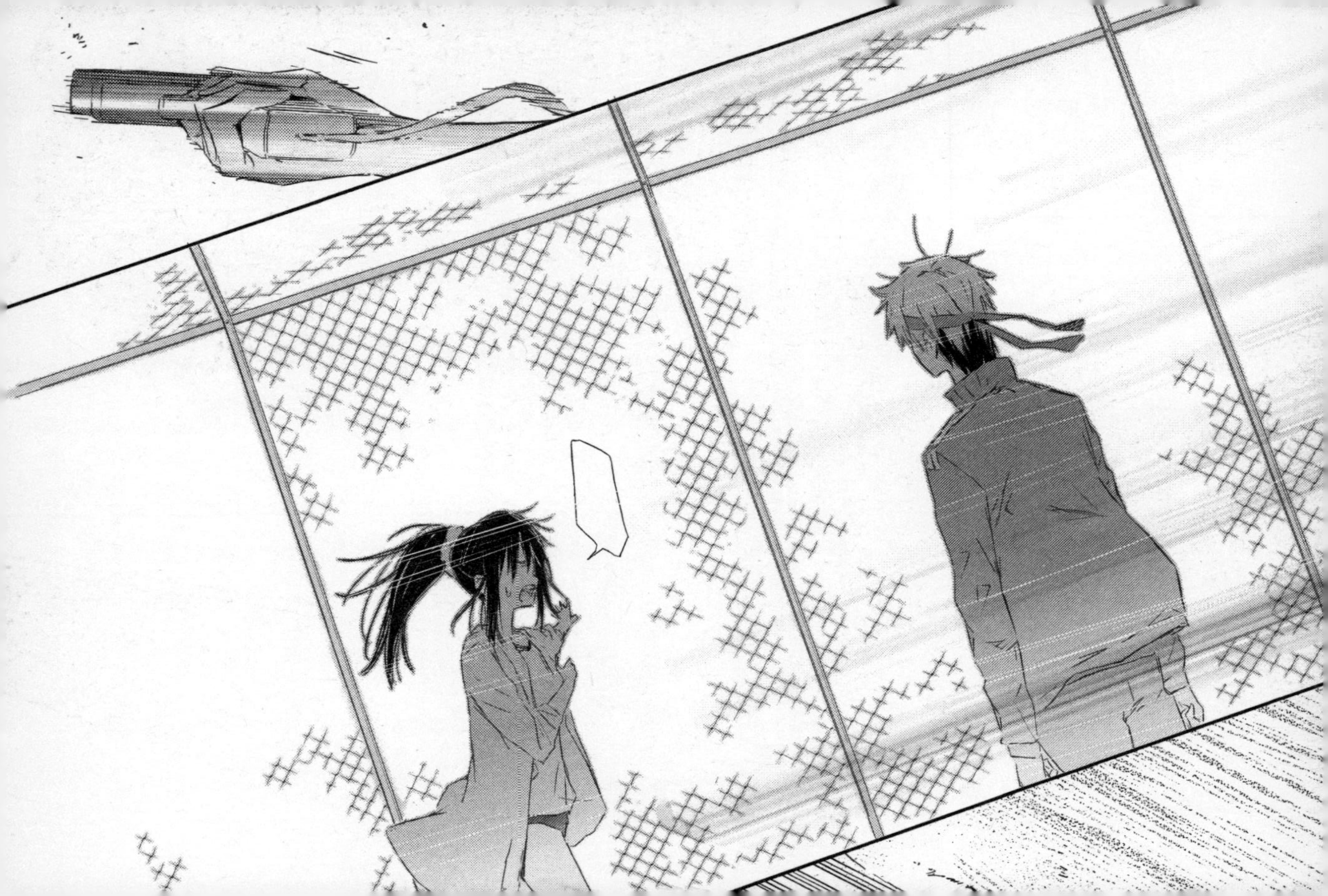

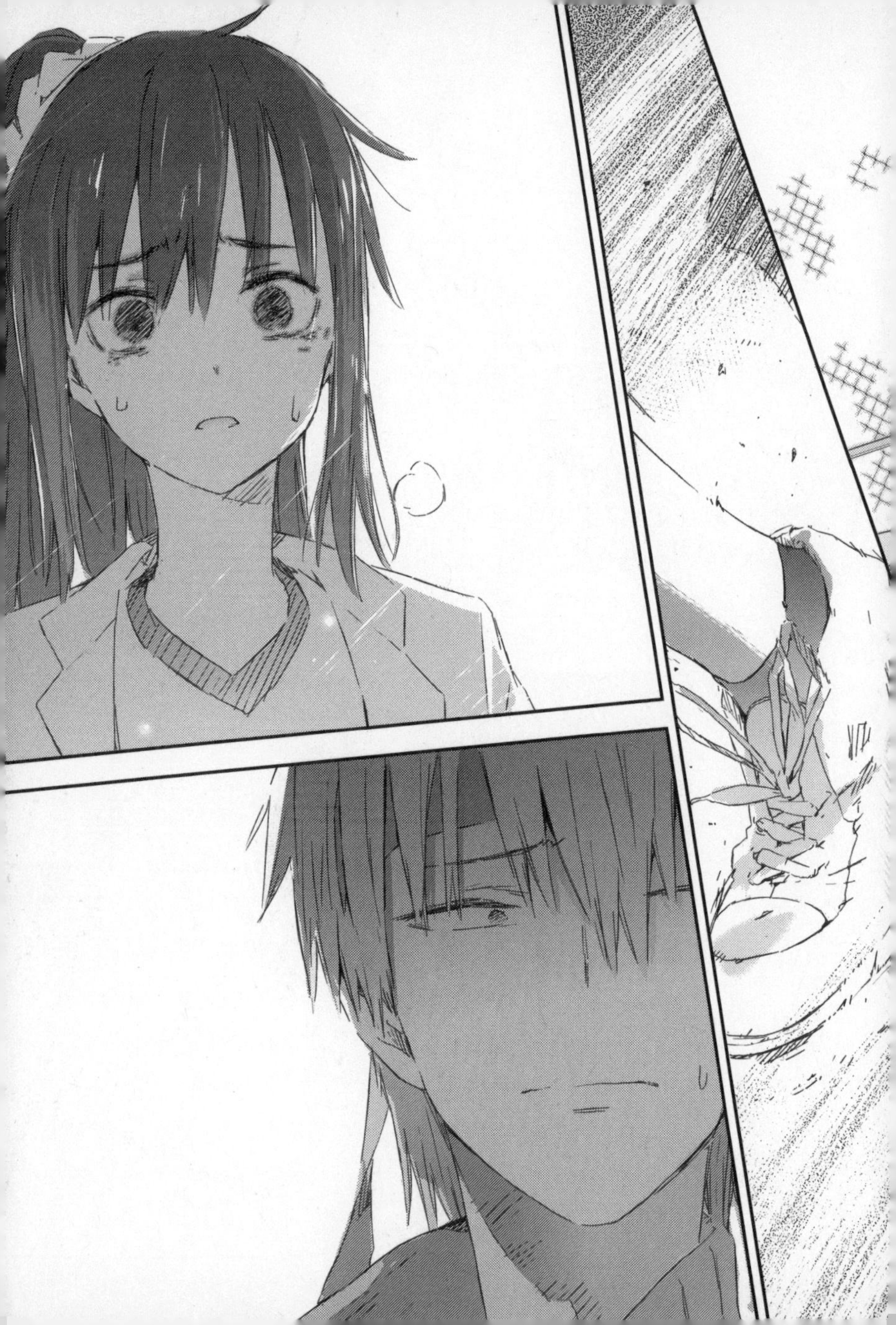

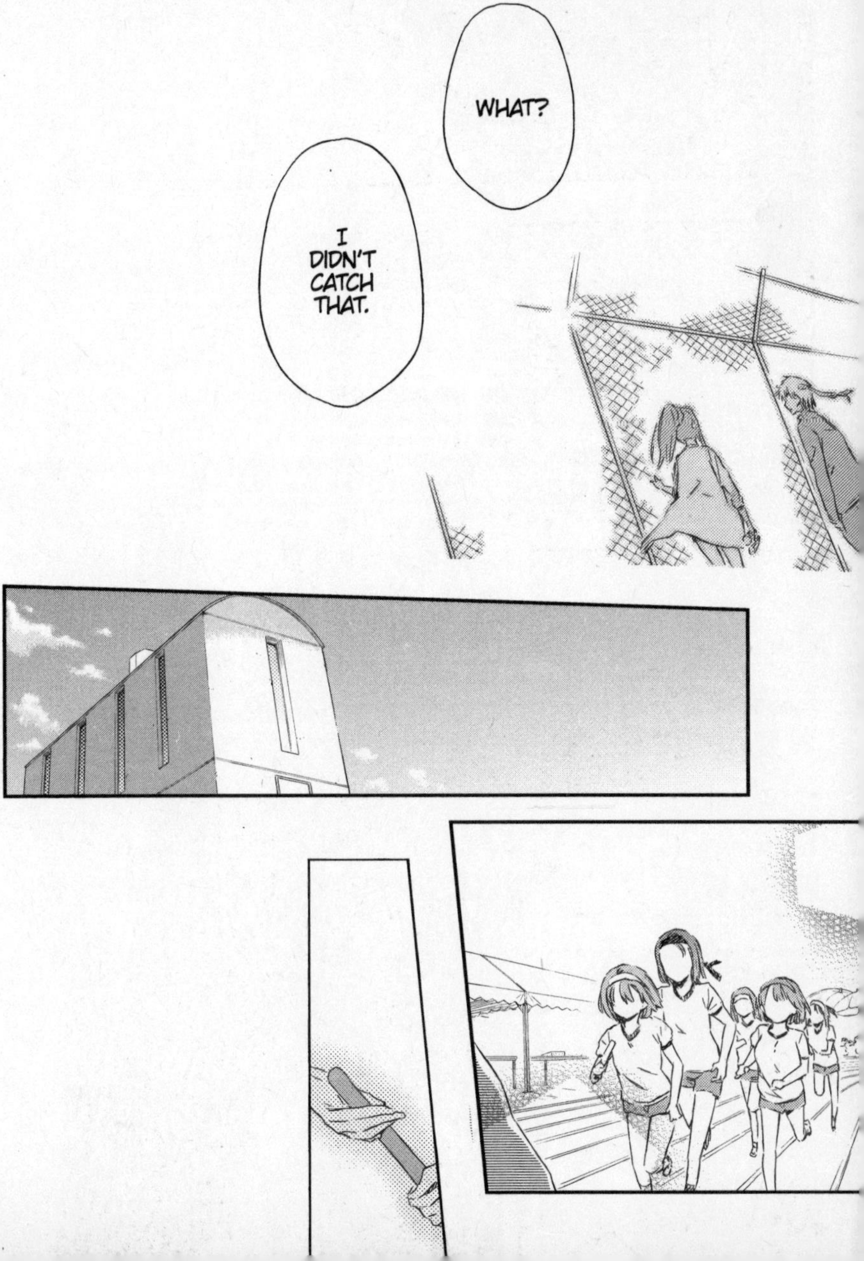
WHAT?
I DIDN'T CATCH THAT.

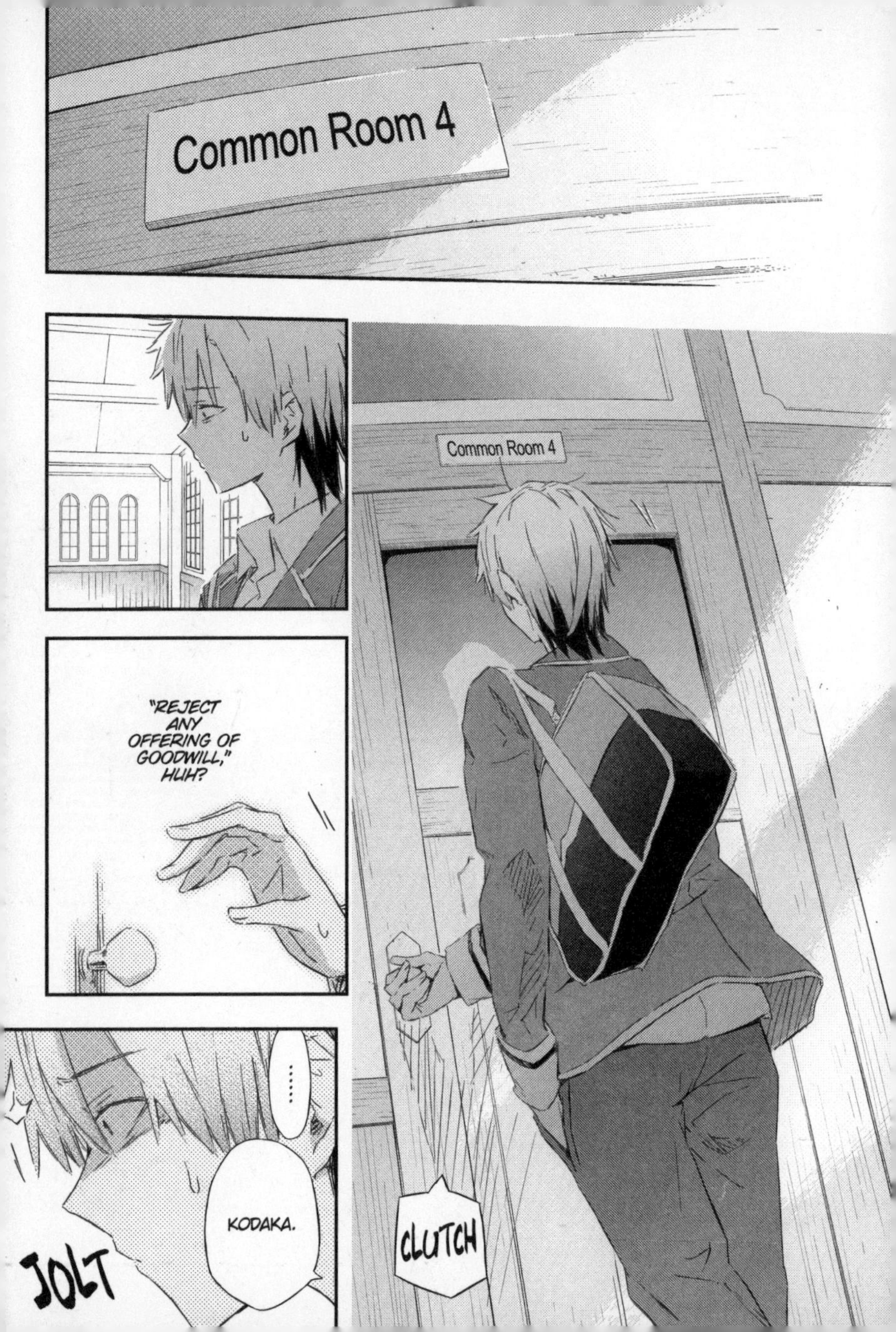
Common Room 4
Common Room 4
CLUTCH
"REJECT ANY OFFERING OF GOODWILL," HUH?
......
KODAKA.
JOLT

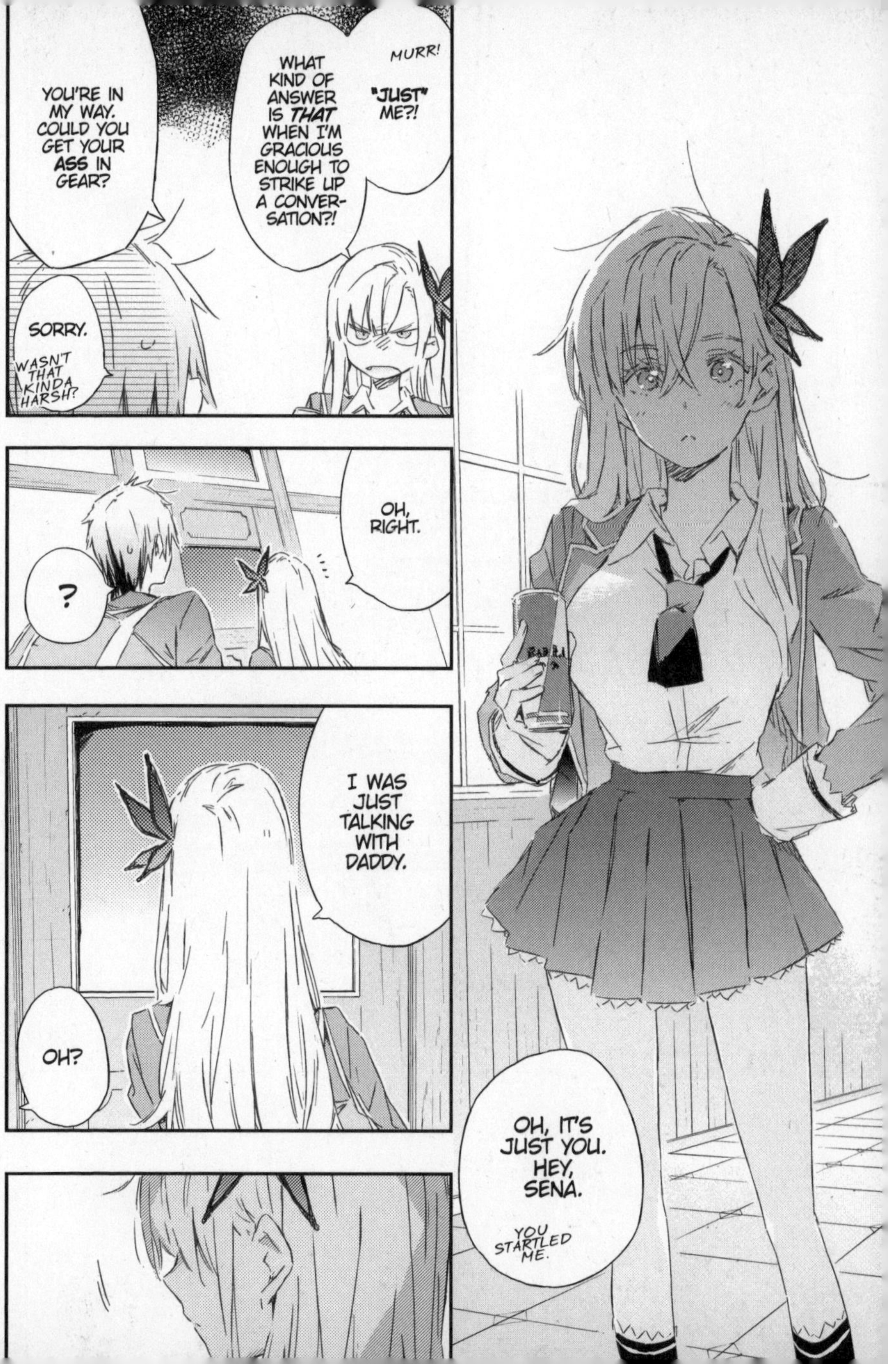
OH, IT'S JUST YOU. HEY, SENA.
YOU STARTLED ME.
MURR!
"JUST" ME?!
WHAT KIND OF ANSWER IS THAT WHEN I'M GRACIOUS ENOUGH TO STRIKE UP A CONVERSATION?!
YOU'RE IN MY WAY. COULD YOU GET YOUR ASS IN GEAR?
SORRY.
WASN'T THAT KINDA HARSH?
OH, RIGHT.
?
I WAS JUST TALKING WITH DADDY.
OH?

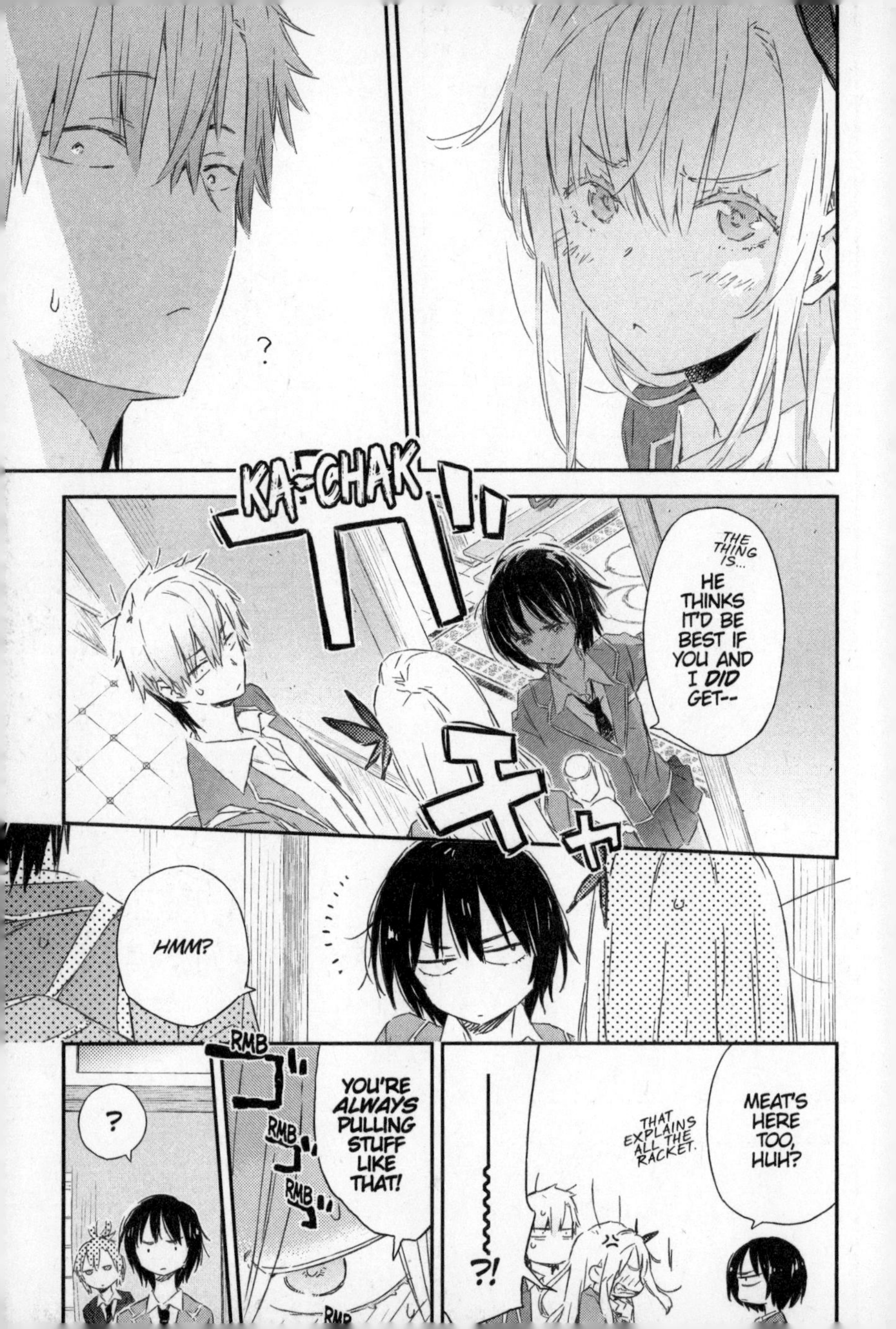
?
KA-CHAK
THE THING IS... HE THINKS IT'D BE BEST IF YOU AND I DID GET--
HMM?
MEAT'S HERE TOO, HUH?
THAT EXPLAINS ALL THE RACKET.
~~~~~?!
YOU'RE ALWAYS PULLING STUFF LIKE THAT!
RMB
RMB
RMB
RMB
?
~~~~~

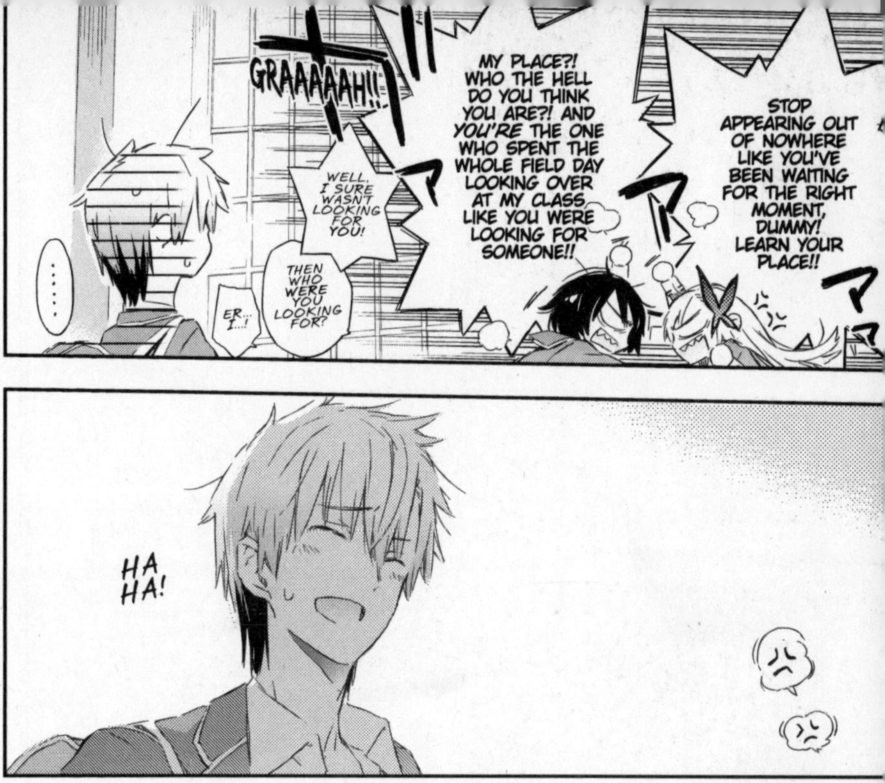
STOP APPEARING OUT OF NOWHERE LIKE YOU'VE BEEN WAITING FOR THE RIGHT MOMENT, DUMMY! LEARN YOUR PLACE!!
MY PLACE?! WHO THE HELL DO YOU THINK YOU ARE?! AND YOU'RE THE ONE WHO SPENT THE WHOLE FIELD DAY LOOKING OVER AT MY CLASS LIKE YOU WERE LOOKING FOR SOMEONE!!
GRAAAAAH!!
WELL, I SURE WASN'T LOOKING FOR YOU!
THEN WHO WERE YOU LOOKING FOR?
ER... I...!
......
HA HA!

"WHAT RIKA'S TRYING TO SAY IS, AREN'T WE ALL..."

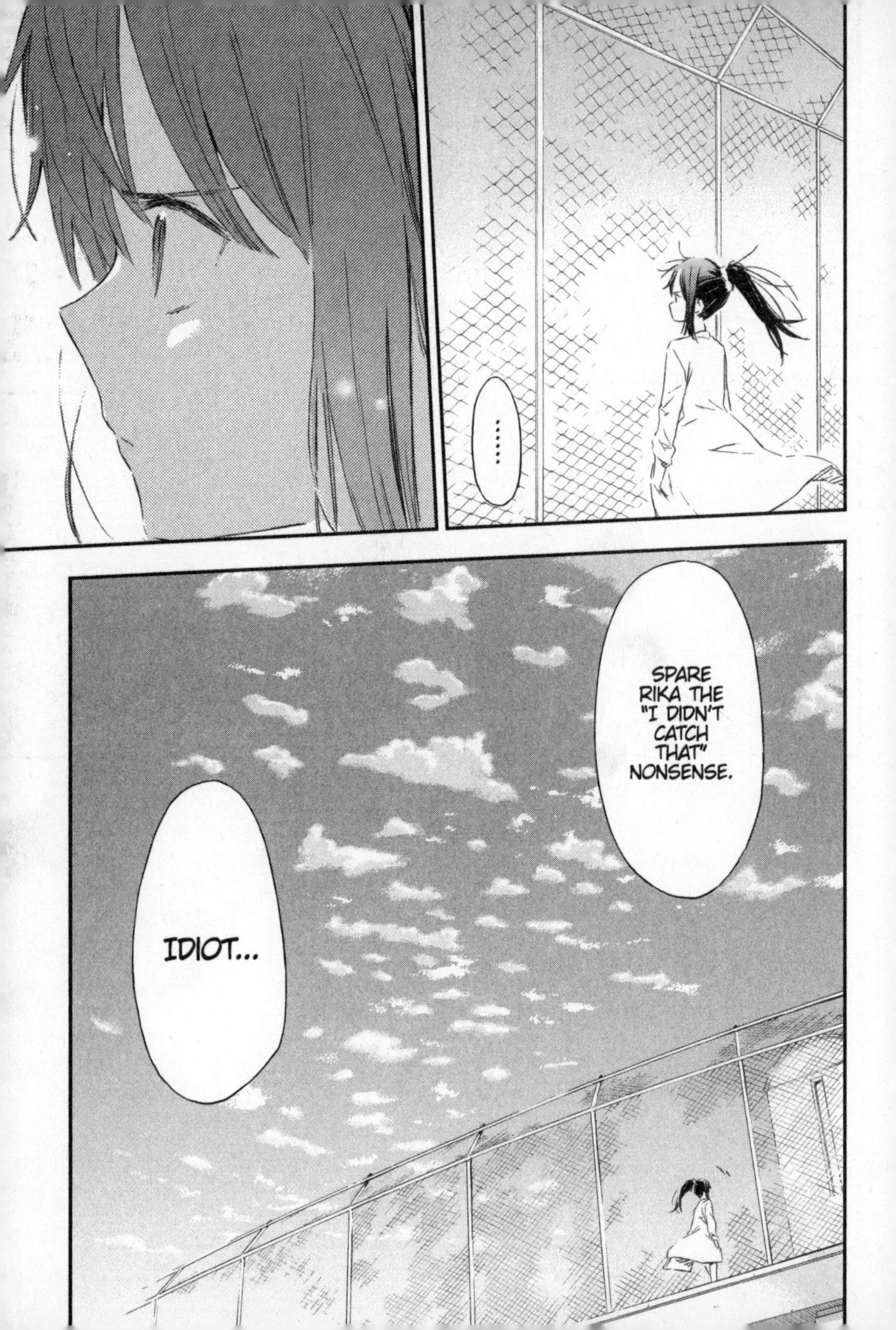
......
SPARE RIKA THE "I DIDN'T CATCH THAT" NONSENSE.
IDIOT...

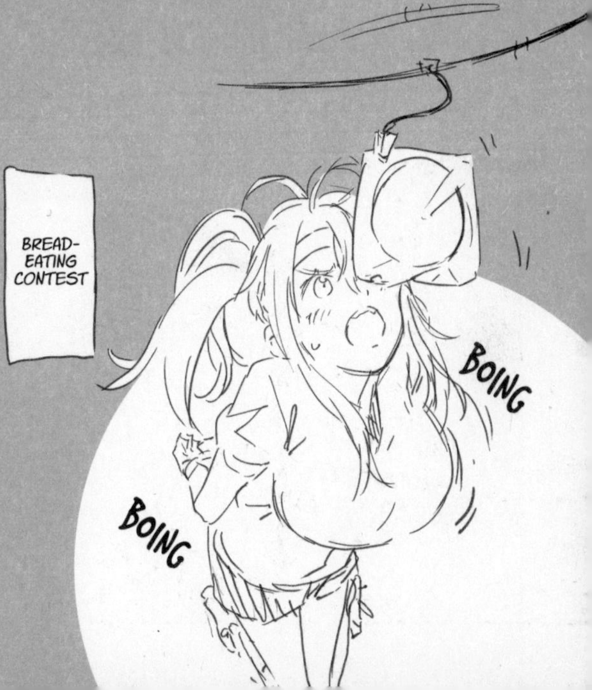
BREAD-EATING CONTEST
BOING
BOING

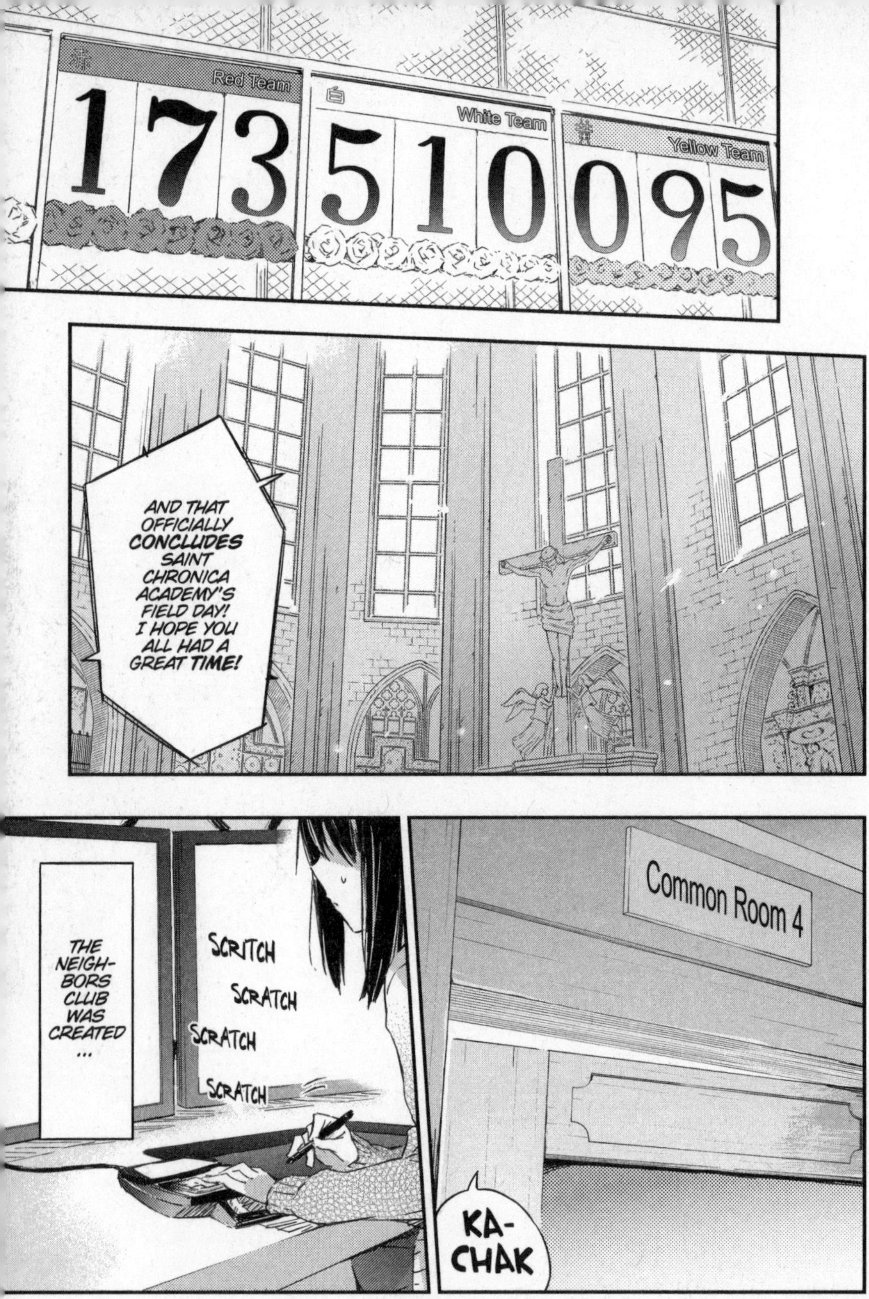
Yellow Team
095
白
White Team
510
赤
Red Team
173
AND THAT OFFICIALLY CONCLUDES SAINT CHRONICA ACADEMY'S FIELD DAY! I HOPE YOU ALL HAD A GREAT TIME!
Common Room 4
KA-CHAK
THE NEIGH-BORS CLUB WAS CREATED ...
SCRITCH
SCRATCH
SCRATCH
SCRATCH

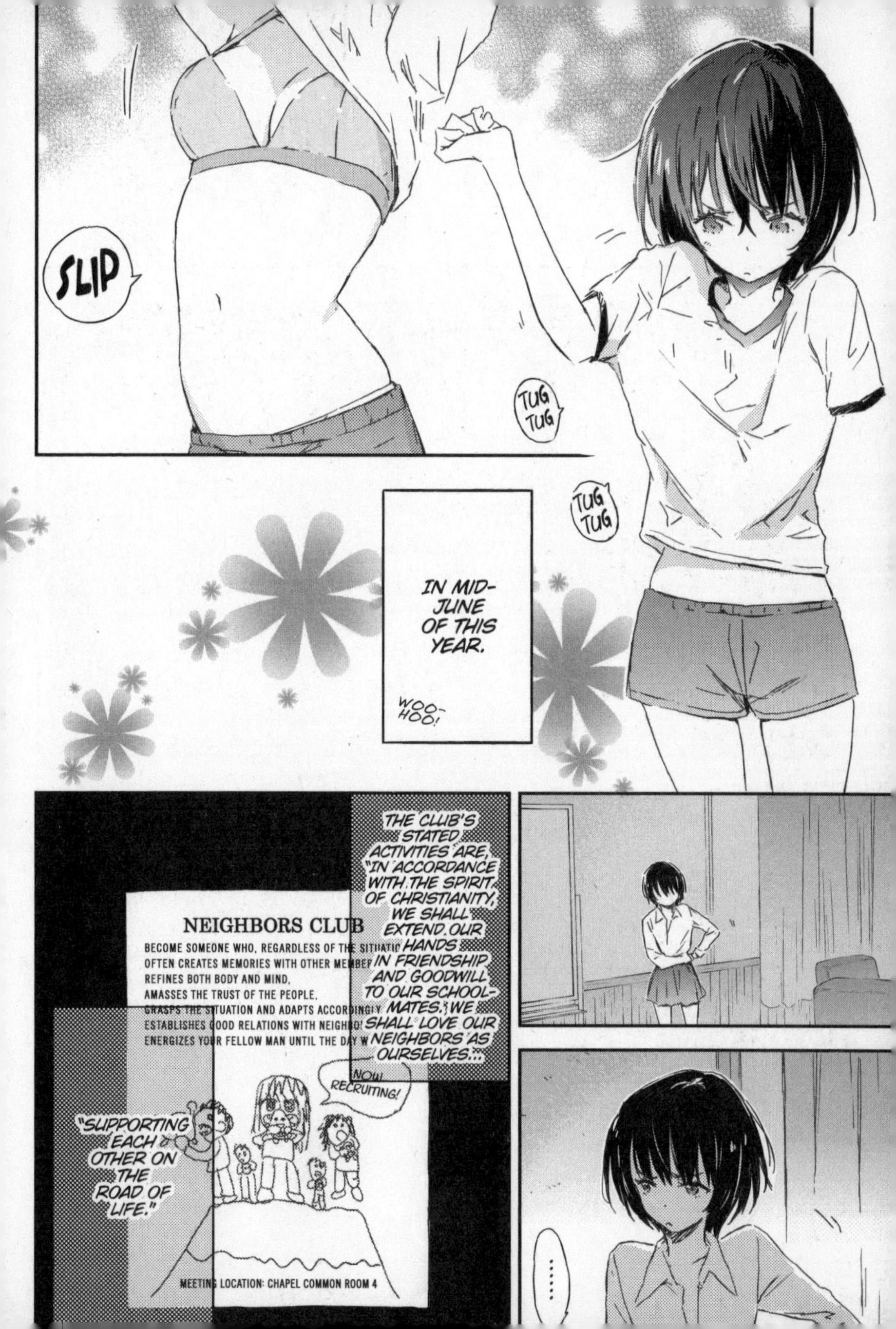
TUG TUG
SLIP
TUG TUG
IN MID-JUNE OF THIS YEAR.
WOO-HOO!
......
THE CLUB'S STATED ACTIVITIES ARE, "IN ACCORDANCE WITH THE SPIRIT OF CHRISTIANITY, WE SHALL EXTEND OUR HANDS IN FRIENDSHIP AND GOODWILL TO OUR SCHOOLMATES. WE SHALL LOVE OUR NEIGHBORS AS OURSELVES..."
NEIGHBORS CLUB
BECOME SOMEONE WHO, REGARDLESS OF THE SITUATIO
OFTEN CREATES MEMORIES WITH OTHER MEMBER
REFINES BOTH BODY AND MIND,
AMASSES THE TRUST OF THE PEOPLE,
GRASPS THE SITUATION AND ADAPTS ACCORDINGLY
ESTABLISHES GOOD RELATIONS WITH NEIGHBO
ENERGIZES YOUR FELLOW MAN UNTIL THE DAY W
NOW RECRUITING!
MEETING LOCATION: CHAPEL COMMON ROOM 4
"SUPPORTING EACH OTHER ON THE ROAD OF LIFE."

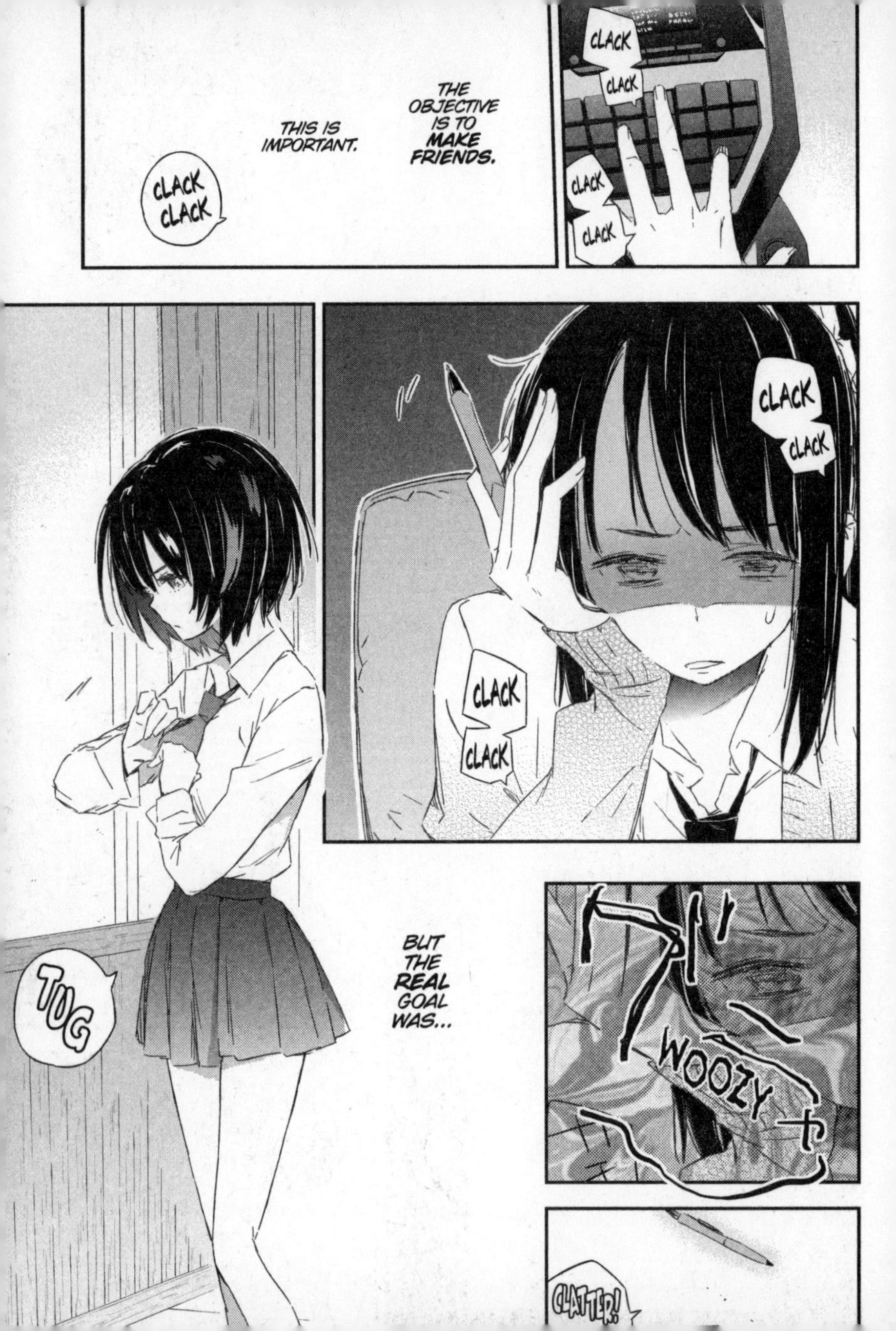
CLACK
CLACK
CLACK
CLACK
THE OBJECTIVE IS TO MAKE FRIENDS.
THIS IS IMPORTANT.
CLACK CLACK
CLACK
CLACK
CLACK
CLACK
WOOZY
CLATTER!
BUT THE REAL GOAL WAS...
TUG

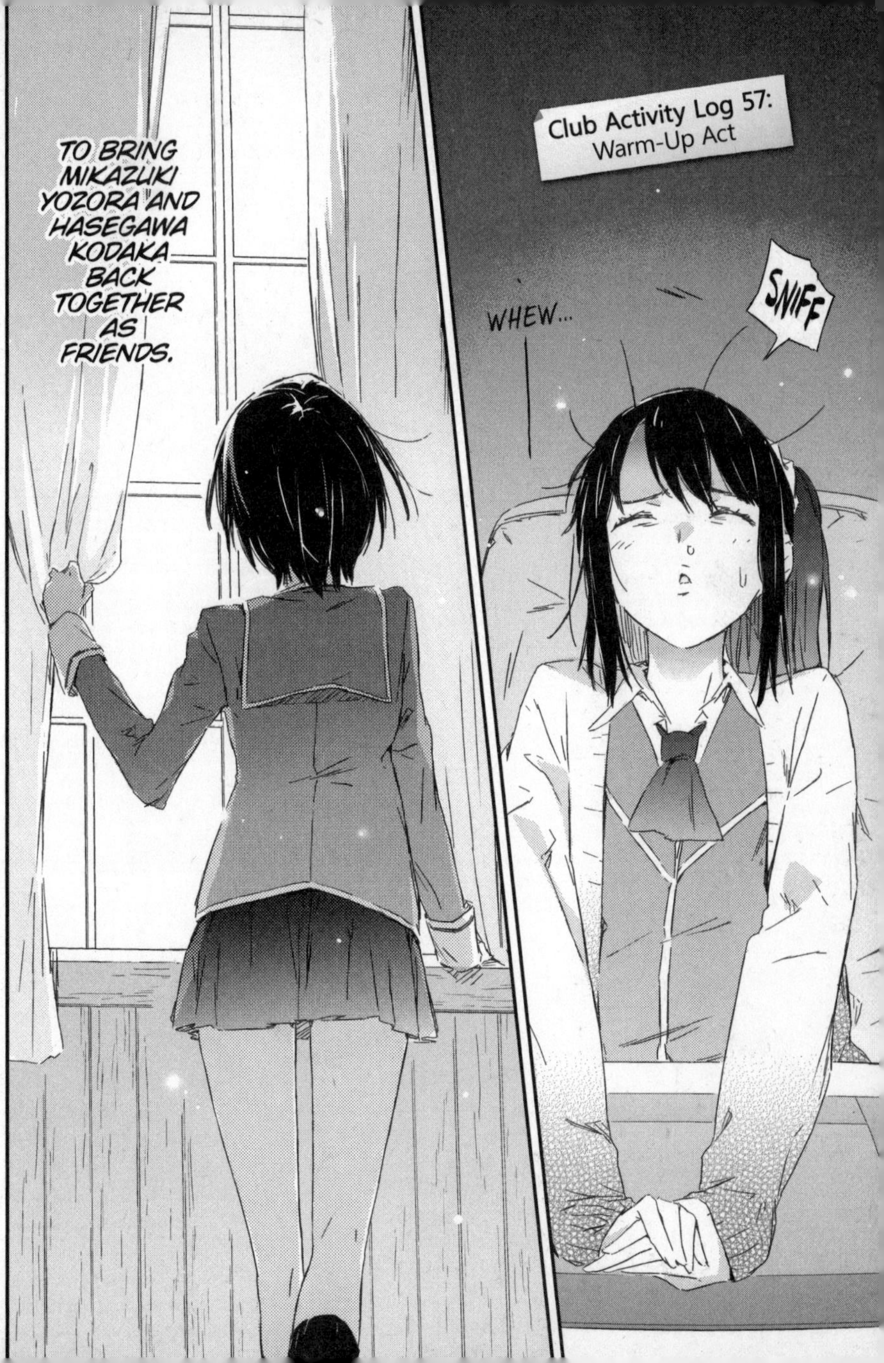
Club Activity Log 57:
Warm-Up Act
SNIFF
WHEW...
TO BRING MIKAZUKI YOZORA AND HASEGAWA KODAKA BACK TOGETHER AS FRIENDS.

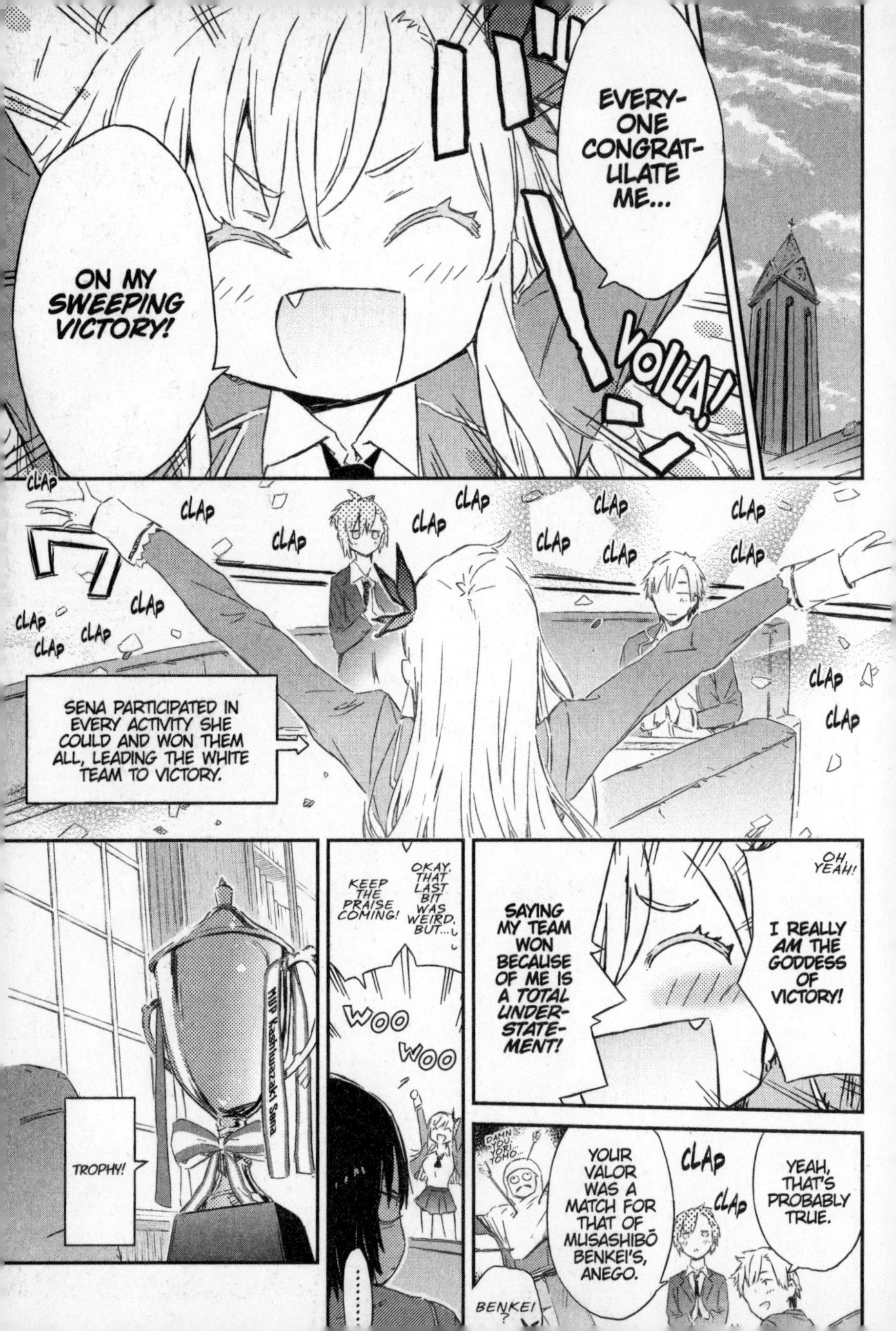
EVERY-ONE CONGRAT-ULATE ME...
VOILA!
ON MY SWEEPING VICTORY!
CLAP
CLAP
CLAP
CLAP
CLAP
SENA PARTICIPATED IN EVERY ACTIVITY SHE COULD AND WON THEM ALL, LEADING THE WHITE TEAM TO VICTORY.
OH, YEAH!
I REALLY AM THE GODDESS OF VICTORY!
SAYING MY TEAM WON BECAUSE OF ME IS A TOTAL UNDER-STATE-MENT!
OKAY, THAT LAST BIT WAS WEIRD, BUT...
KEEP THE PRAISE COMING!
WOO
WOO
MVP Kashiwazaki Sena
TROPHY!
YEAH, THAT'S PROBABLY TRUE.
CLAP
CLAP
YOUR VALOR WAS A MATCH FOR THAT OF MUSASHIBŌ BENKEI'S, ANEGO.
DAMN YOU, YORI-TOMO...
BENKEI?
...

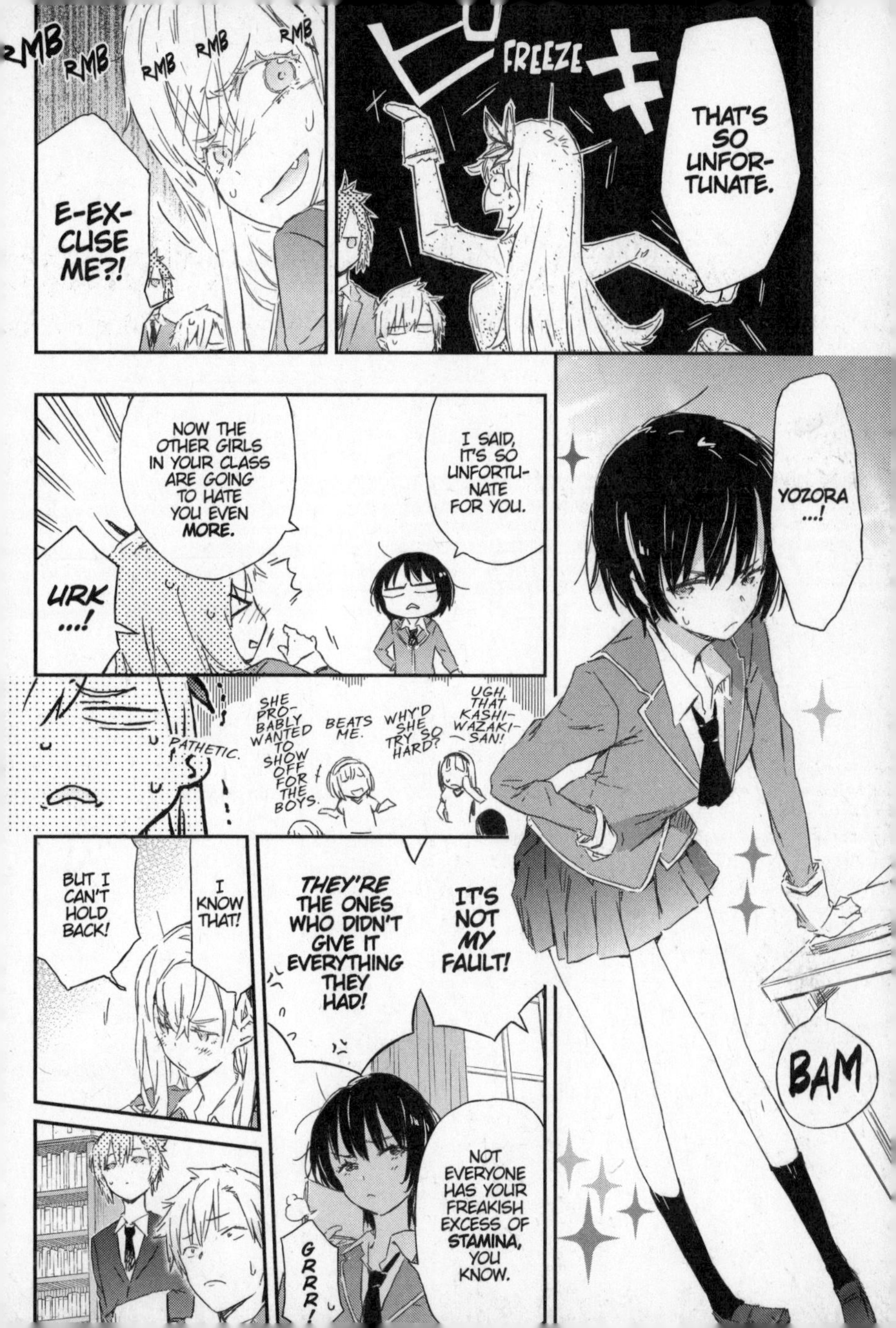
FREEZE
THAT'S SO UNFORTUNATE.
RMB RMB RMB RMB RMB
E-EX-CUSE ME?!
YOZORA ...!
BAM
I SAID, IT'S SO UNFORTUNATE FOR YOU.
NOW THE OTHER GIRLS IN YOUR CLASS ARE GOING TO HATE YOU EVEN MORE.
URK ...!
UGH, THAT KASHIWAZAKI-SAN!
WHY'D SHE TRY SO HARD?
BEATS ME.
SHE PROBABLY WANTED TO SHOW OFF FOR THE BOYS.
PATHETIC.
IT'S NOT MY FAULT!
THEY'RE THE ONES WHO DIDN'T GIVE IT EVERYTHING THEY HAD!
I KNOW THAT!
BUT I CAN'T HOLD BACK!
NOT EVERYONE HAS YOUR FREAKISH EXCESS OF STAMINA, YOU KNOW.
GRRR!

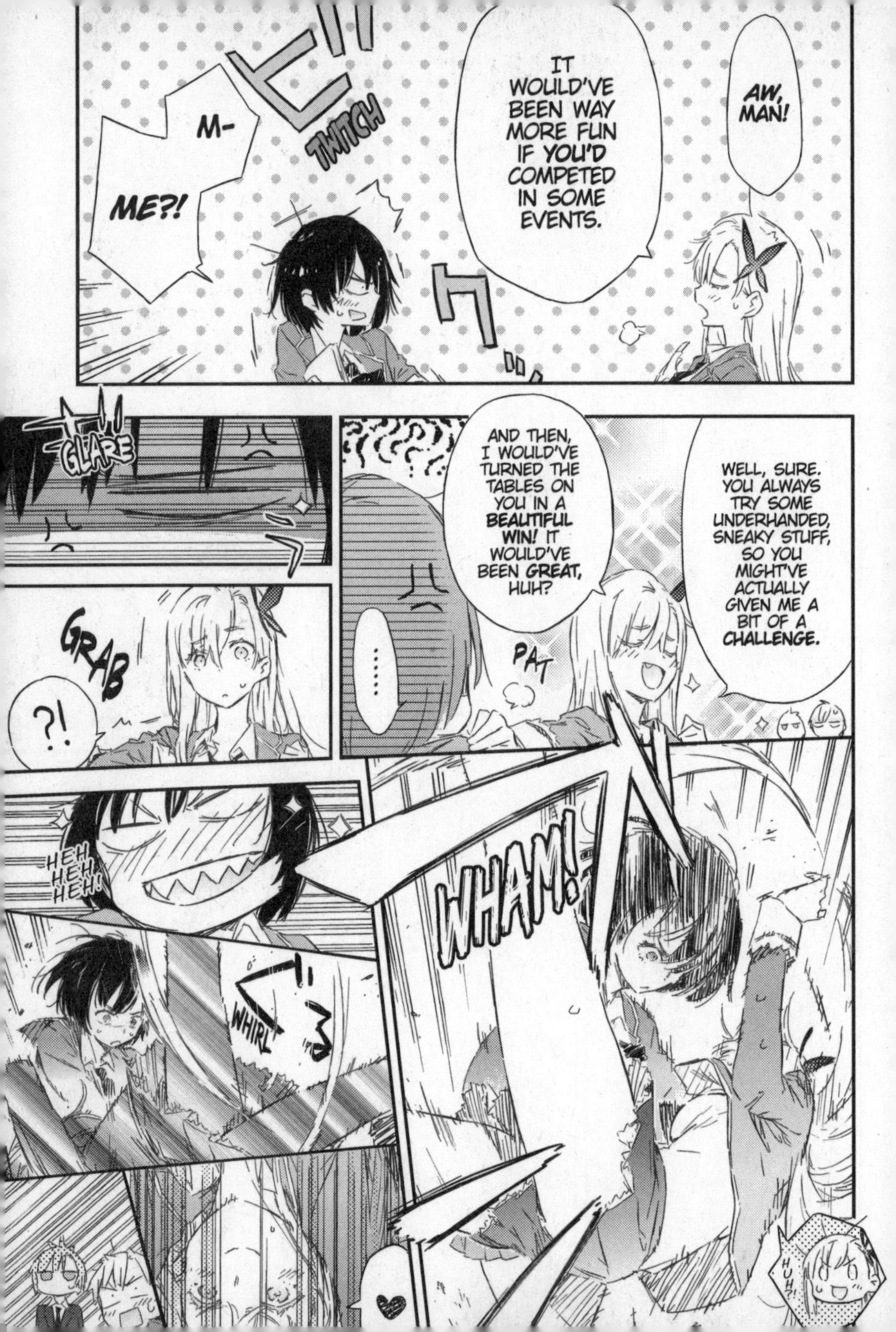
AW, MAN!
IT WOULD'VE BEEN WAY MORE FUN IF YOU'D COMPETED IN SOME EVENTS.
TWITCH
M-
ME?!
WELL, SURE. YOU ALWAYS TRY SOME UNDERHANDED, SNEAKY STUFF, SO YOU MIGHT'VE ACTUALLY GIVEN ME A BIT OF A CHALLENGE.
AND THEN, I WOULD'VE TURNED THE TABLES ON YOU IN A BEAUTIFUL WIN! IT WOULD'VE BEEN GREAT, HUH?
PAT
......
GLARE
GRAB
?!
HEH HEH HEH!
WHAM!
WHIRL
HUH?!

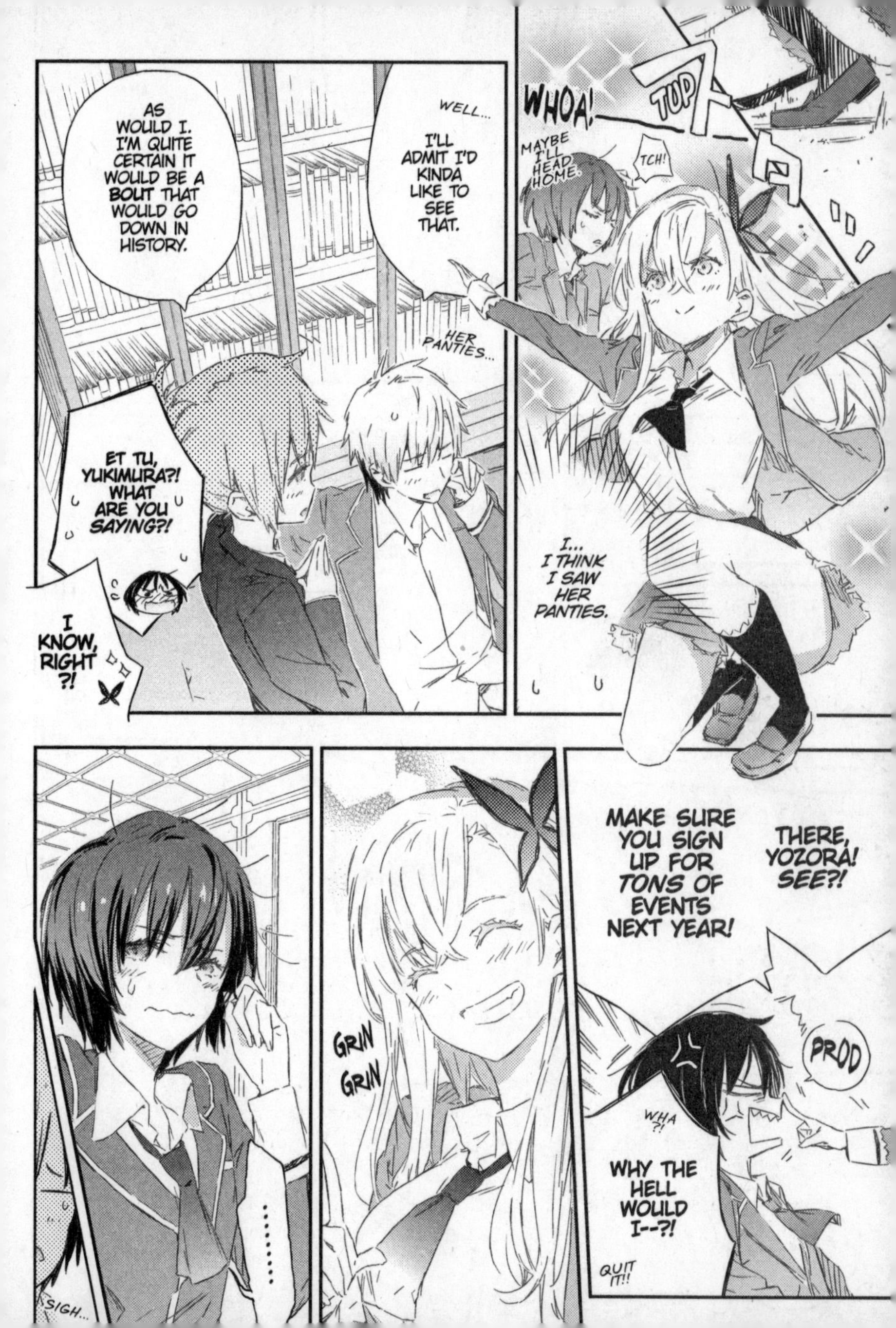
WHOA!
TUP
TCH!
MAYBE I'LL HEAD HOME.
I... I THINK I SAW HER PANTIES.
WELL...
I'LL ADMIT I'D KINDA LIKE TO SEE THAT.
AS WOULD I. I'M QUITE CERTAIN IT WOULD BE A BOUT THAT WOULD GO DOWN IN HISTORY.
HER PANTIES...
ET TU, YUKIMURA?! WHAT ARE YOU SAYING?!
I KNOW, RIGHT?!
THERE, YOZORA! SEE?!
MAKE SURE YOU SIGN UP FOR TONS OF EVENTS NEXT YEAR!
PROD
WHA?!
WHY THE HELL WOULD I--?!
QUIT IT!!
GRIN GRIN
......
SIGH...

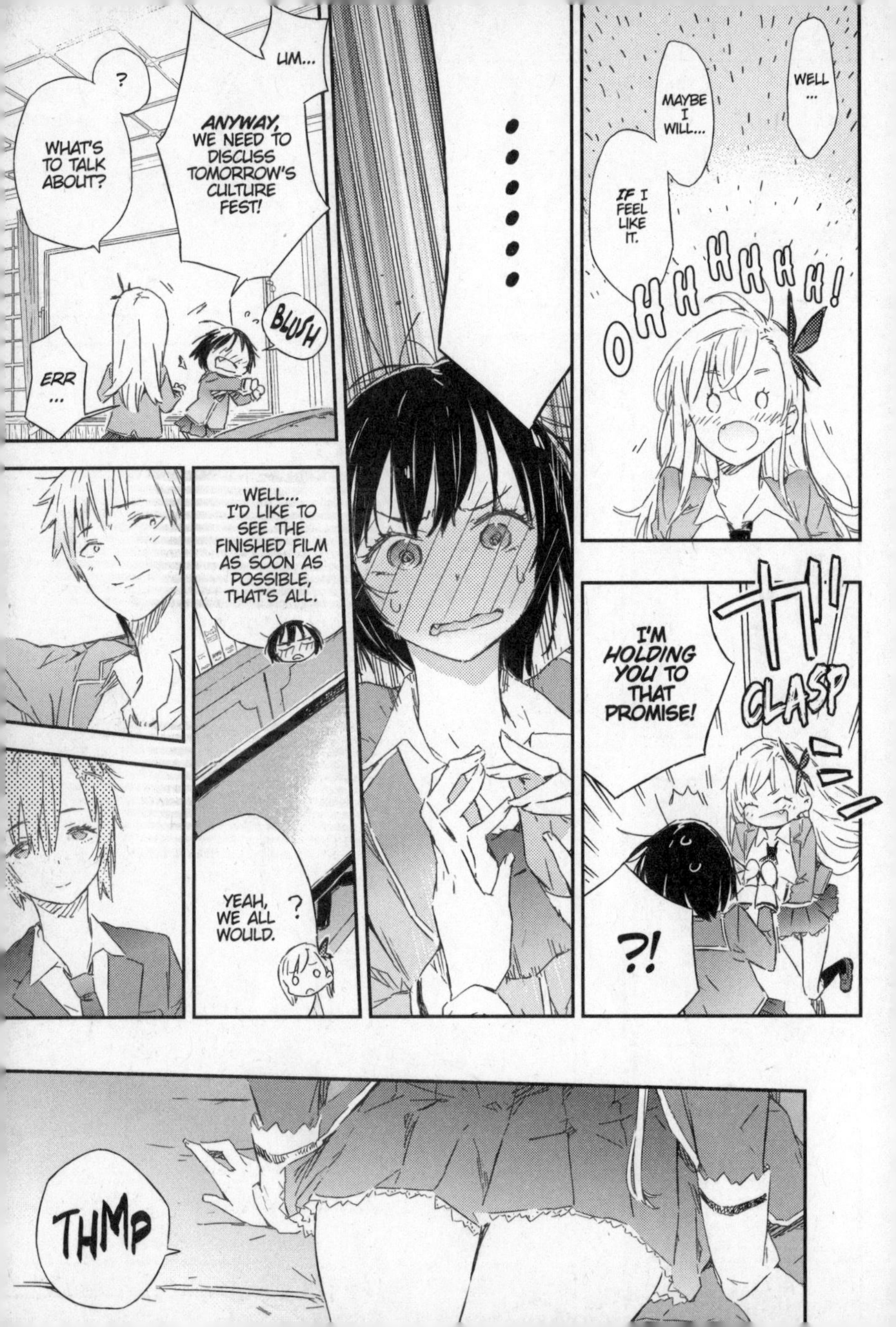
UM...
?
ANYWAY, WE NEED TO DISCUSS TOMORROW'S CULTURE FEST!
WHAT'S TO TALK ABOUT?
BLUSH
ERR ...
WELL... I'D LIKE TO SEE THE FINISHED FILM AS SOON AS POSSIBLE, THAT'S ALL.
YEAH, WE ALL WOULD.
?
......
WELL ...
MAYBE I WILL...
IF I FEEL LIKE IT.
OHHHHHHH!
I'M HOLDING YOU TO THAT PROMISE!
CLASP
?!
THMP

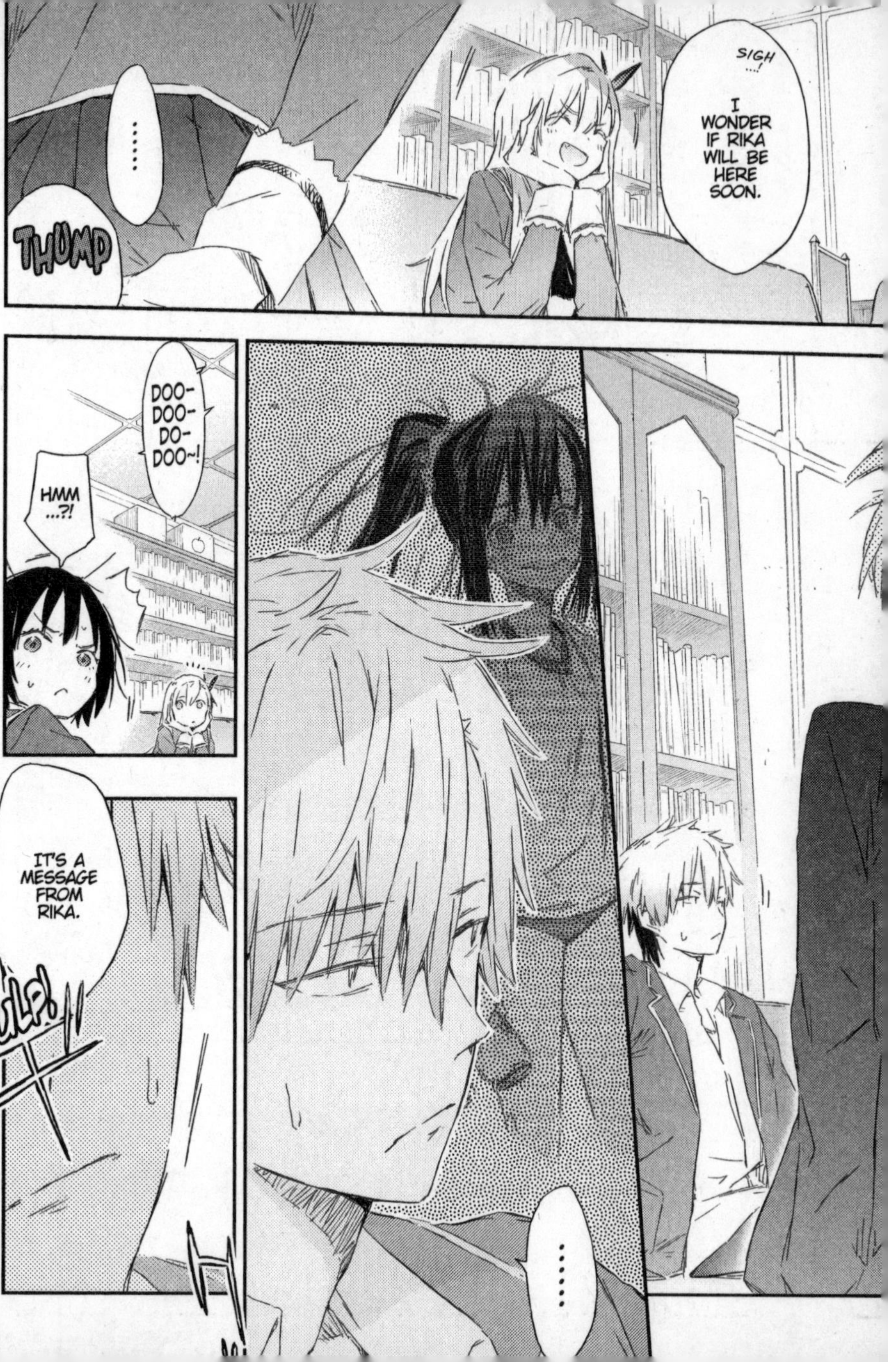
SIGH ...!
I WONDER IF RIKA WILL BE HERE SOON.
......
THUMP
......
DOO-DOO-DO-DOO~!
HMM ...?!
IT'S A MESSAGE FROM RIKA.
GULP!

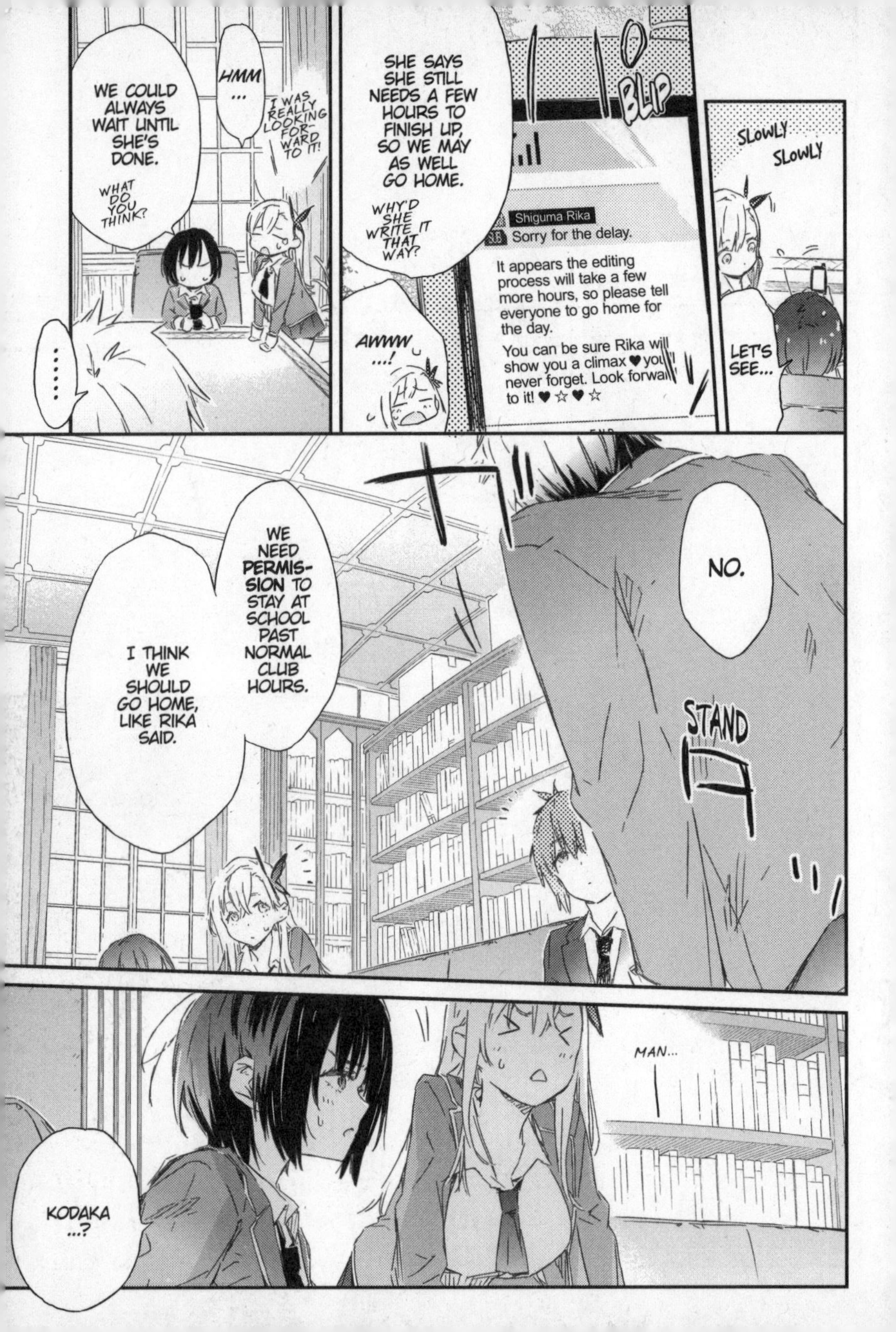
SLOWLY
SLOWLY
LET'S SEE...
BLIP
Shiguma Rika
Sorry for the delay.
It appears the editing process will take a few more hours, so please tell everyone to go home for the day.
You can be sure Rika will show you a climax ♥ you'll never forget. Look forwa to it! ♥ ☆ ♥ ☆
SHE SAYS SHE STILL NEEDS A FEW HOURS TO FINISH UP, SO WE MAY AS WELL GO HOME.
WHY'D SHE WRITE IT THAT WAY?
AWWW ...!
HMM ...
I WAS REALLY LOOKING FORWARD TO IT!
WE COULD ALWAYS WAIT UNTIL SHE'S DONE.
WHAT DO YOU THINK?
......
NO.
STAND
WE NEED PERMISSION TO STAY AT SCHOOL PAST NORMAL CLUB HOURS.
I THINK WE SHOULD GO HOME, LIKE RIKA SAID.
MAN...
KODAKA ...?

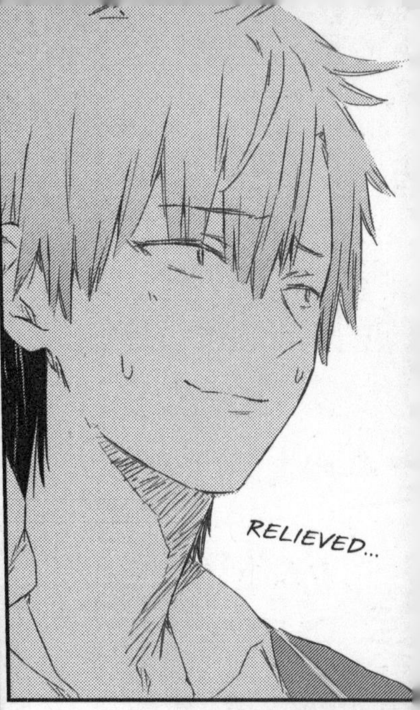
RELIEVED...
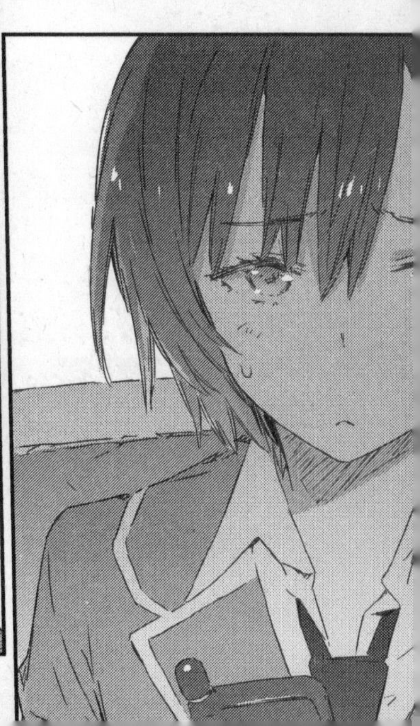
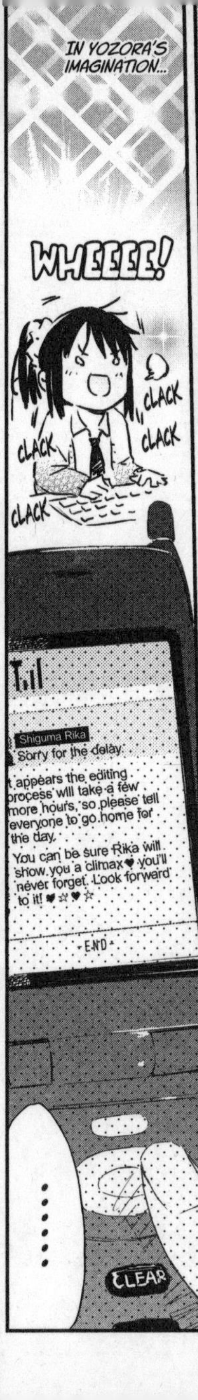
IN YOZORA'S IMAGINATION...
WHEEEE!
CLACK
CLACK
CLACK
CLACK
Shiguma Rika
Sorry for the delay.
t appears the editing process will take a few more hours, so please tell everyone to go home for the day.
You can be sure Rika will show you a climax♥ you'll never forget. Look forward to it! ♥☆♥☆
-END-
......
CLEAR
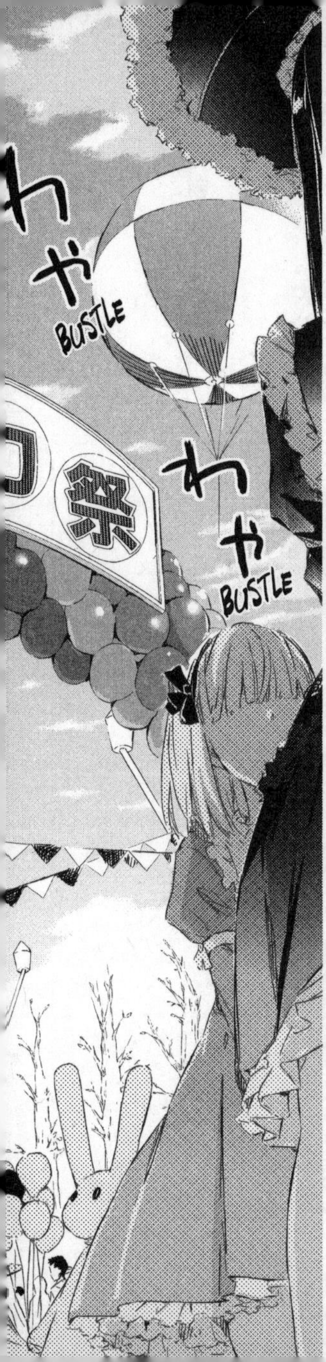
わ
や
BUSTLE
わ
や
BUSTLE
祭

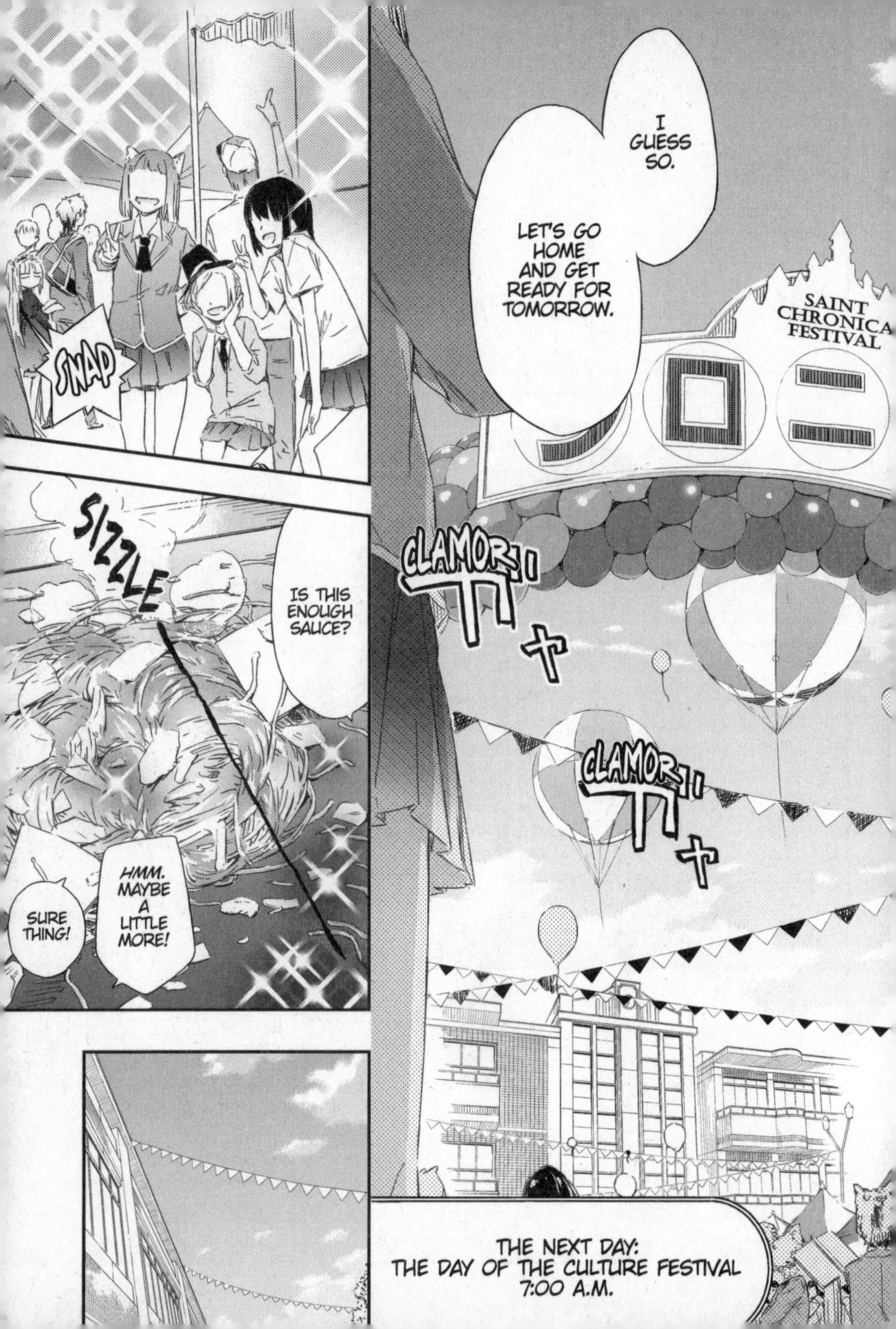
I GUESS SO.
LET'S GO HOME AND GET READY FOR TOMORROW.
SAINT CHRONICA FESTIVAL
CLAMOR
CLAMOR
THE NEXT DAY: THE DAY OF THE CULTURE FESTIVAL 7:00 A.M.
SNAP
SIZZLE
IS THIS ENOUGH SAUCE?
HMM. MAYBE A LITTLE MORE!
SURE THING!

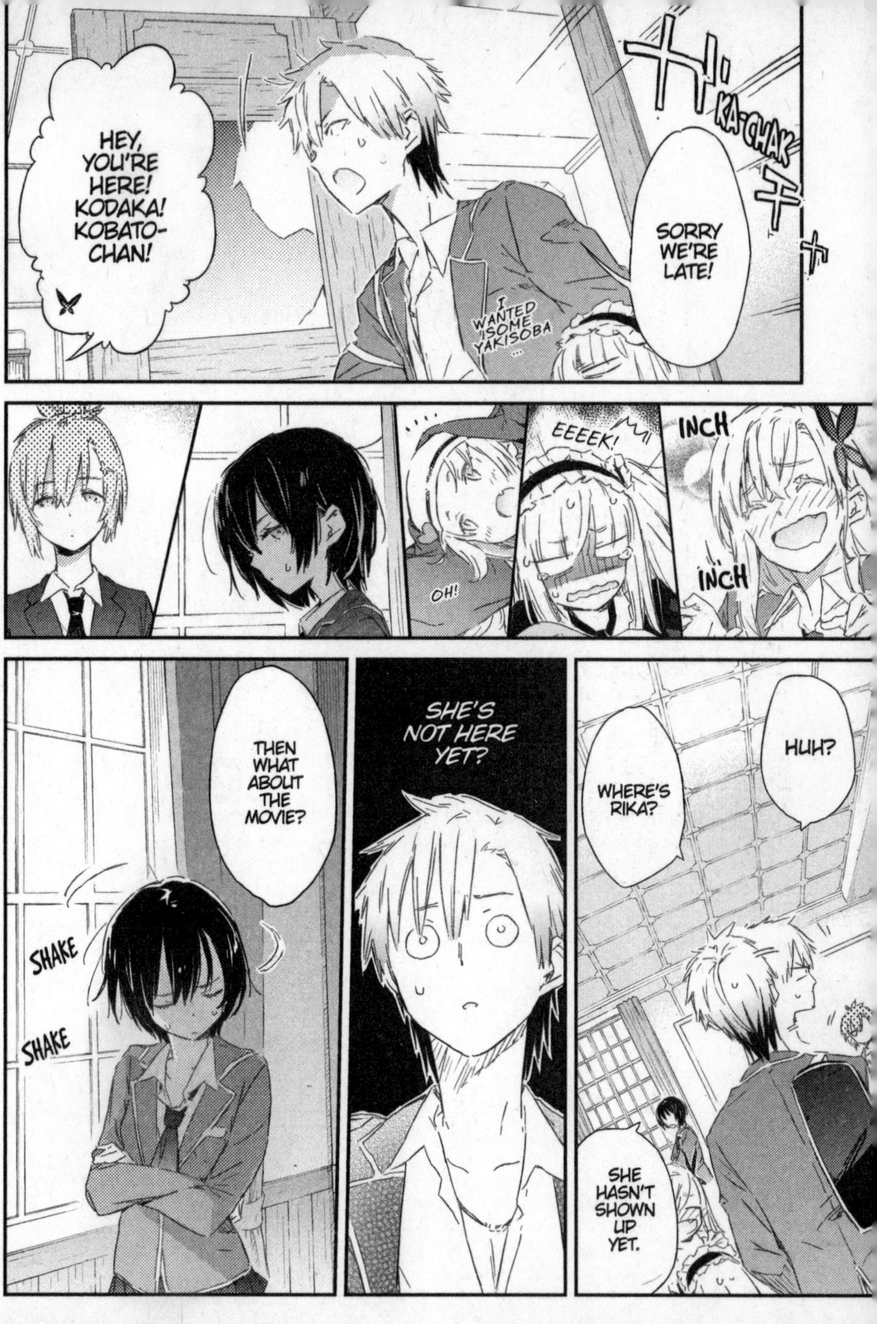
KA-CHAK
SORRY WE'RE LATE!
I WANTED SOME YAKISOBA...
HEY, YOU'RE HERE! KODAKA! KOBATO-CHAN!
INCH
INCH
EEEEK!
OH!
HUH?
WHERE'S RIKA?
SHE HASN'T SHOWN UP YET.
SHE'S NOT HERE YET?
THEN WHAT ABOUT THE MOVIE?
SHAKE
SHAKE

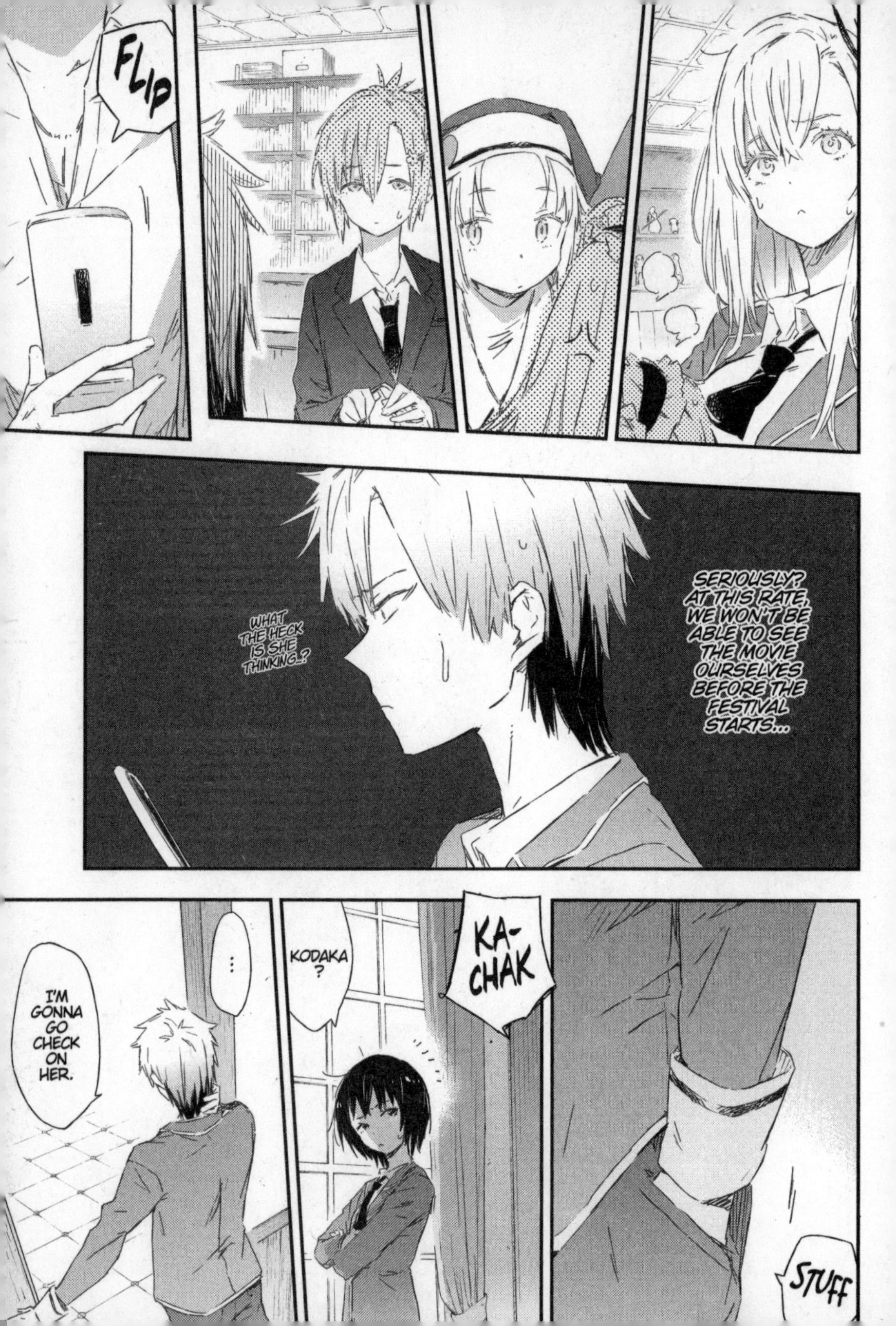
FLIP
SERIOUSLY? AT THIS RATE, WE WON'T BE ABLE TO SEE THE MOVIE OURSELVES BEFORE THE FESTIVAL STARTS...
WHAT THE HECK IS SHE THINKING...?
STUFF
KA-CHAK
KODAKA?
...
I'M GONNA GO CHECK ON HER.

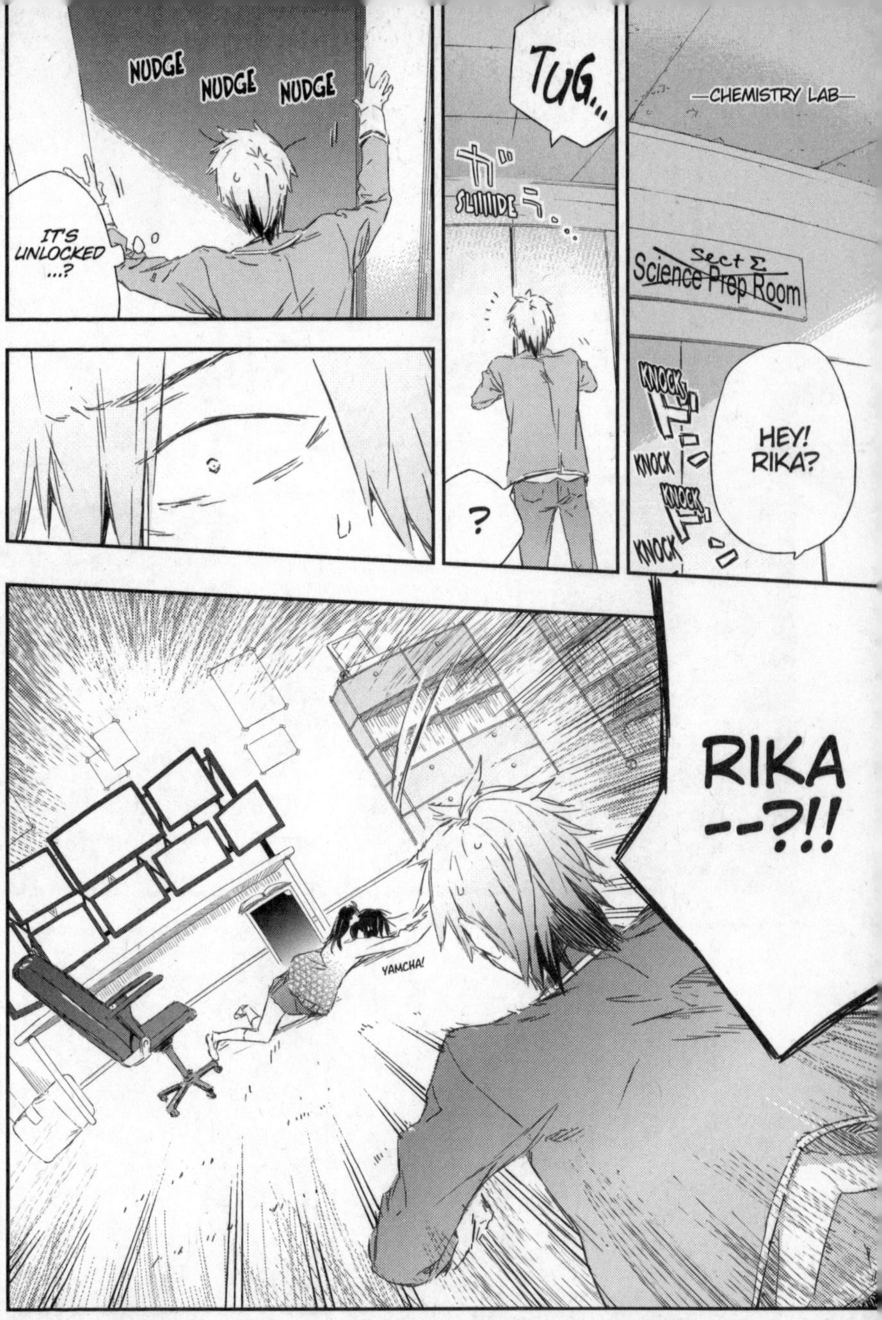
—CHEMISTRY LAB—
Sect Σ
Science Prep Room
HEY! RIKA?
KNOCK KNOCK KNOCK KNOCK
TUG...
SLIIIIDE
?
NUDGE NUDGE NUDGE
IT'S UNLOCKED ...?
RIKA --?!!
YAMCHA!

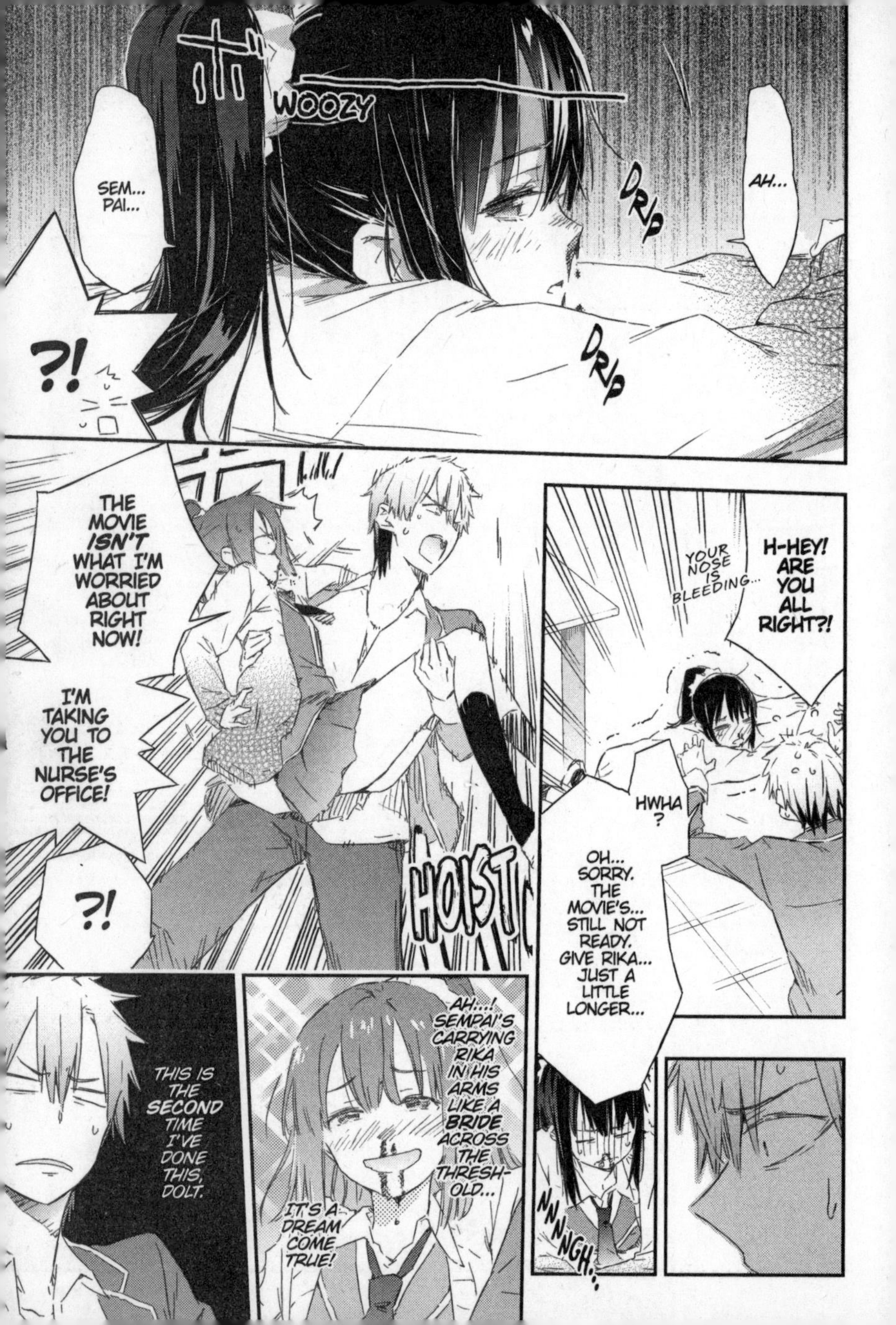
AH...
DRIP
DRIP
WOOZY
SEM... PAI...
?!
H-HEY! ARE YOU ALL RIGHT?!
YOUR NOSE IS BLEEDING...
HWHA?
OH... SORRY. THE MOVIE'S... STILL NOT READY. GIVE RIKA... JUST A LITTLE LONGER...
THE MOVIE ISN'T WHAT I'M WORRIED ABOUT RIGHT NOW!
I'M TAKING YOU TO THE NURSE'S OFFICE!
HOIST
?!
NNNNGH...
AH...! SEMPAI'S CARRYING RIKA IN HIS ARMS LIKE A BRIDE ACROSS THE THRESH-OLD...
IT'S A DREAM COME TRUE!
THIS IS THE SECOND TIME I'VE DONE THIS, DOLT.

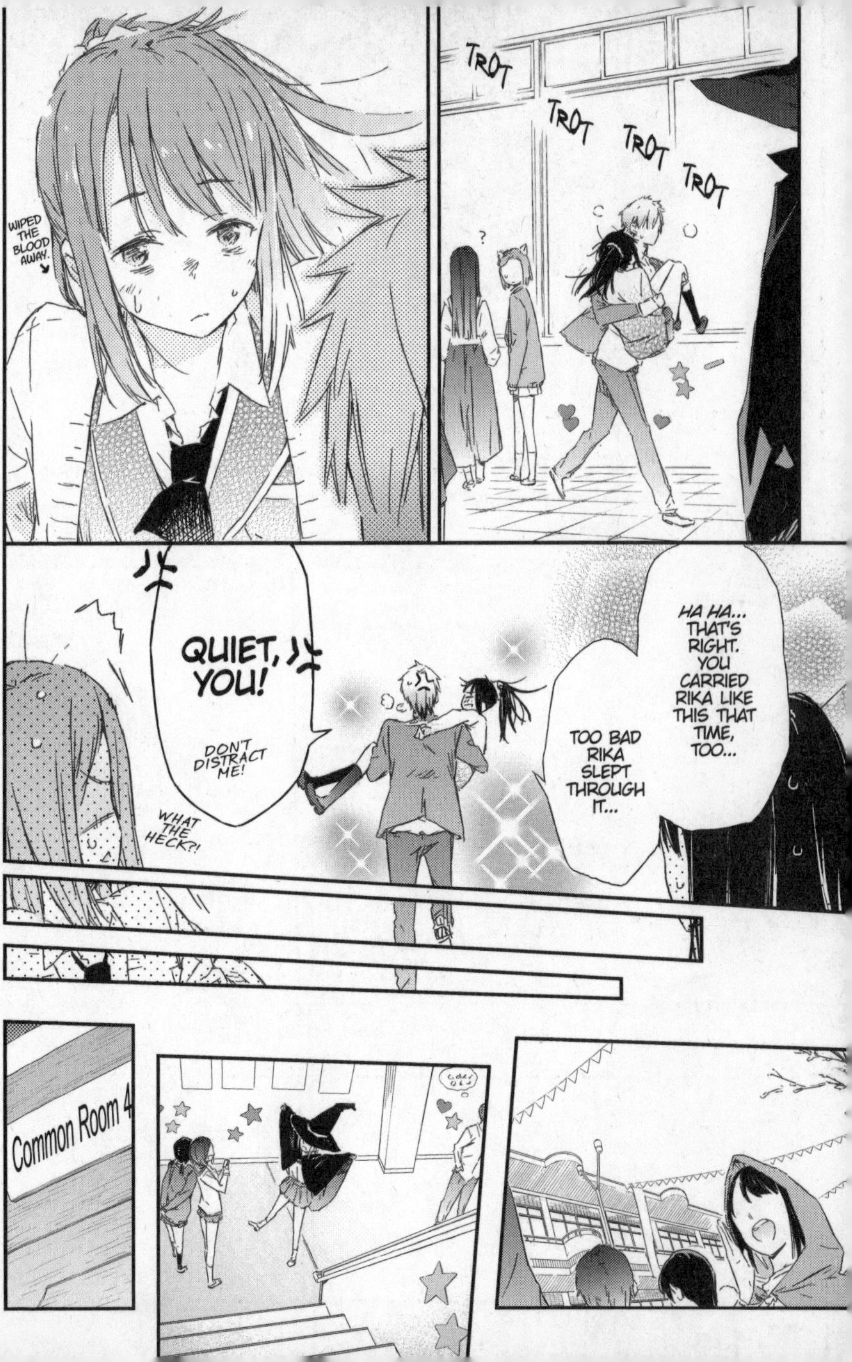
TROT
TROT
TROT
TROT
WIPED THE BLOOD AWAY.
HA HA... THAT'S RIGHT. YOU CARRIED RIKA LIKE THIS THAT TIME, TOO...
TOO BAD RIKA SLEPT THROUGH IT...
QUIET, YOU!
DON'T DISTRACT ME!
WHAT THE HECK?!
Common Room 4

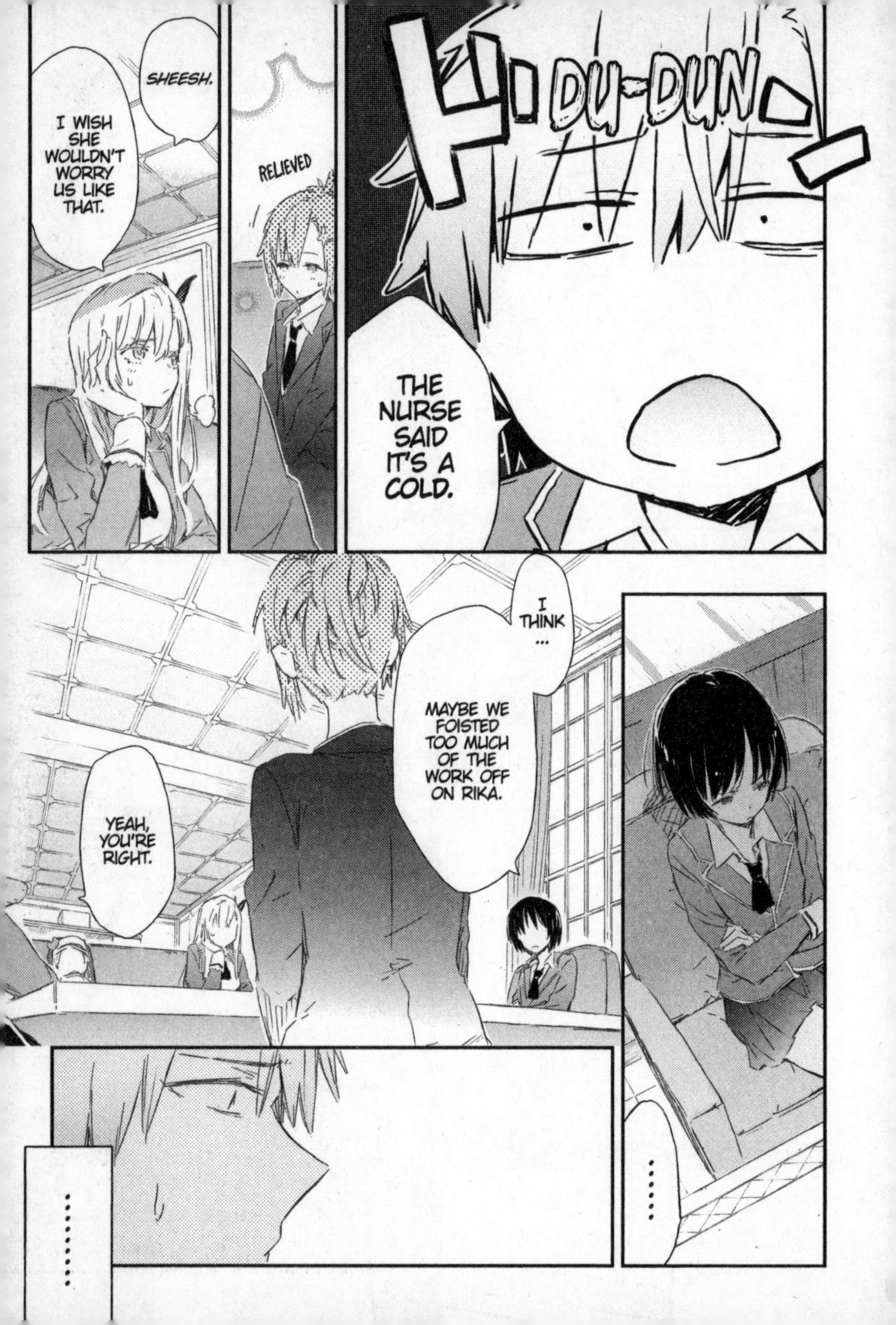
DU-DUN
THE NURSE SAID IT'S A COLD.
RELIEVED
SHEESH.
I WISH SHE WOULDN'T WORRY US LIKE THAT.
I THINK ...
MAYBE WE FOISTED TOO MUCH OF THE WORK OFF ON RIKA.
YEAH, YOU'RE RIGHT.
......
......

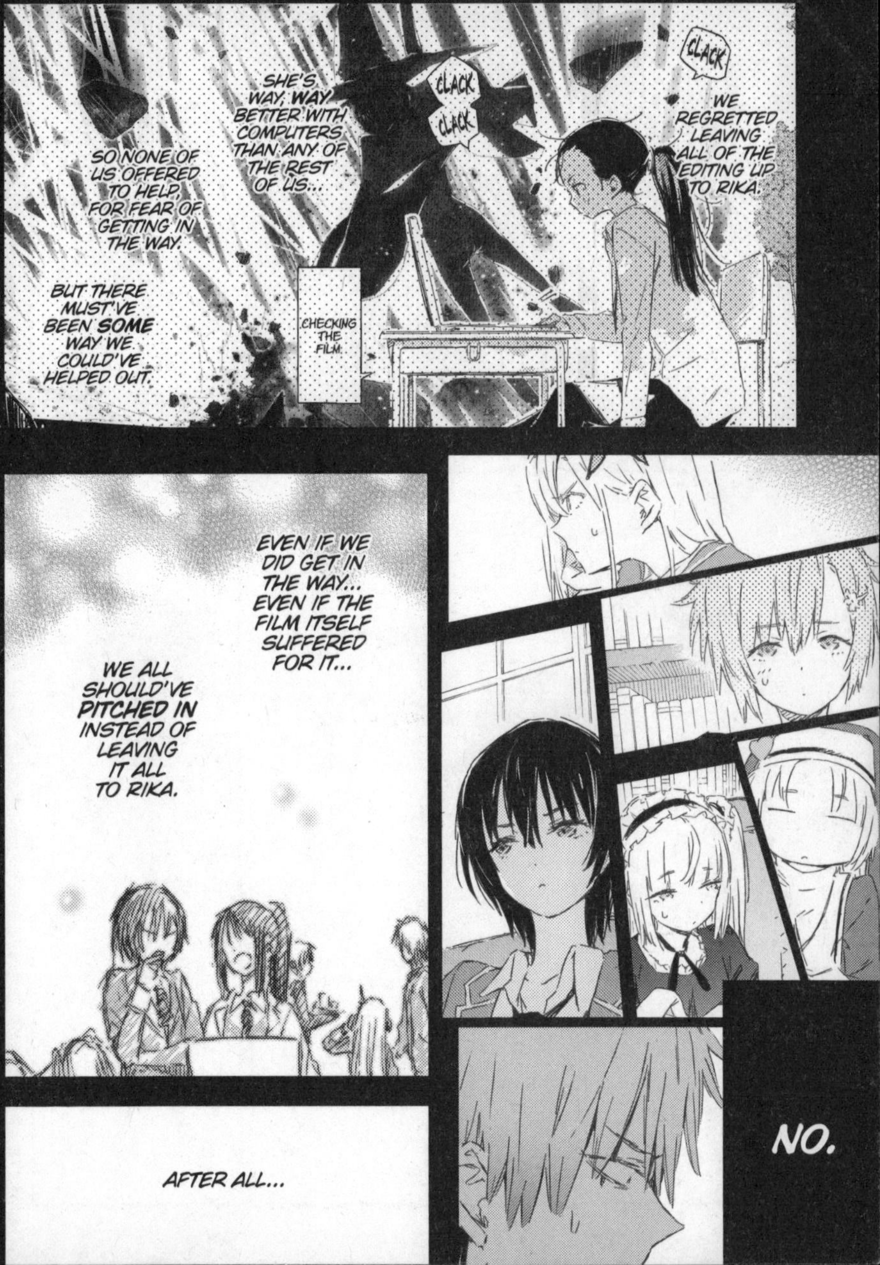
CLACK
WE REGRETTED LEAVING ALL OF THE EDITING UP TO RIKA.
CLACK CLACK
SHE'S WAY, WAY BETTER WITH COMPUTERS THAN ANY OF THE REST OF US...
SO NONE OF US OFFERED TO HELP, FOR FEAR OF GETTING IN THE WAY.
CHECKING THE FILM.
BUT THERE MUST'VE BEEN SOME WAY WE COULD'VE HELPED OUT.
EVEN IF WE DID GET IN THE WAY... EVEN IF THE FILM ITSELF SUFFERED FOR IT...
WE ALL SHOULD'VE PITCHED IN INSTEAD OF LEAVING IT ALL TO RIKA.
NO.
AFTER ALL...

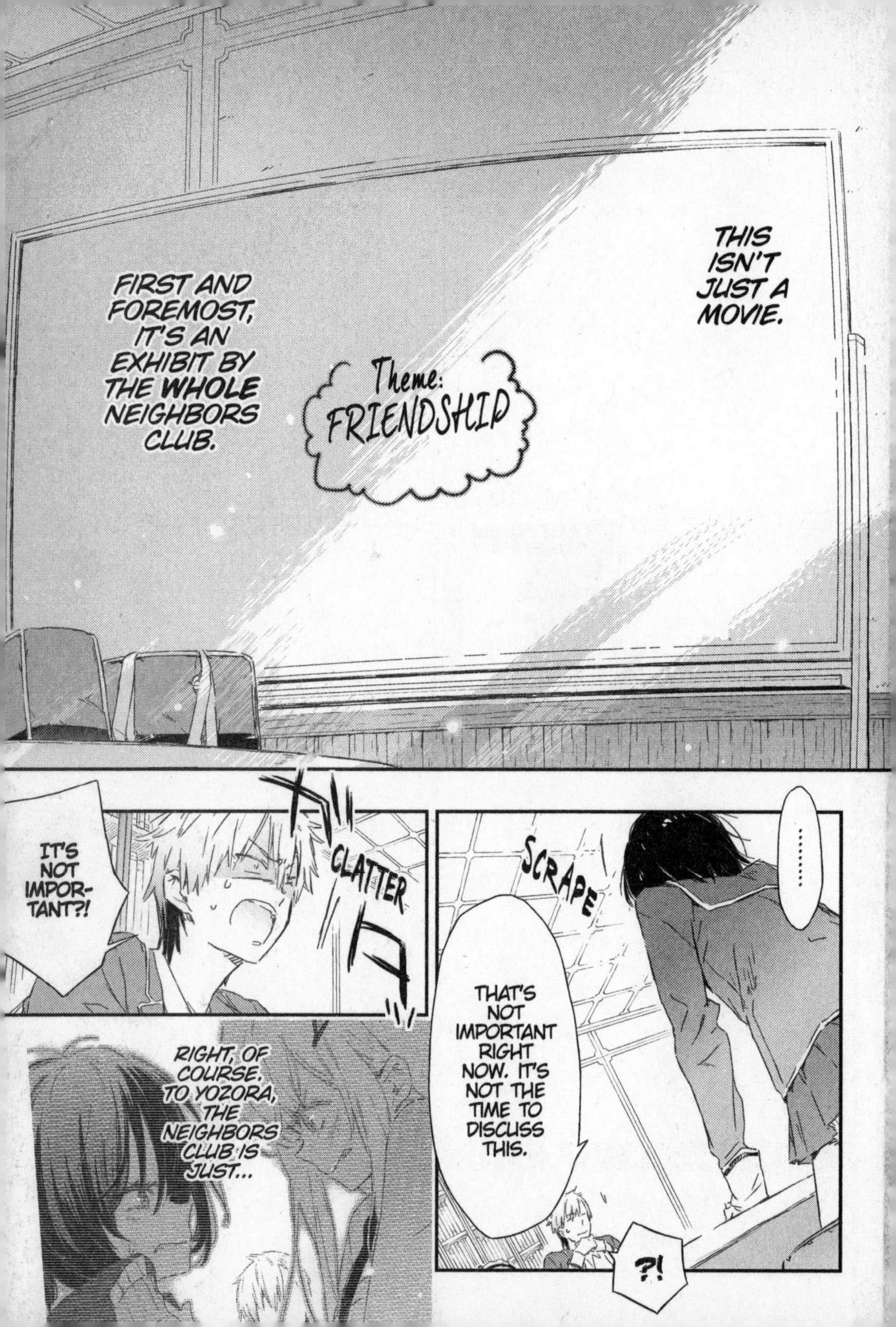
THIS ISN'T JUST A MOVIE.
Theme: FRIENDSHIP
FIRST AND FOREMOST, IT'S AN EXHIBIT BY THE **WHOLE** NEIGHBORS CLUB.
......
SCRAPE
THAT'S NOT IMPORTANT RIGHT NOW. IT'S NOT THE TIME TO DISCUSS THIS.
?!
CLATTER
IT'S NOT IMPORTANT?!
RIGHT, OF COURSE. TO YOZORA, THE NEIGHBORS CLUB IS JUST...

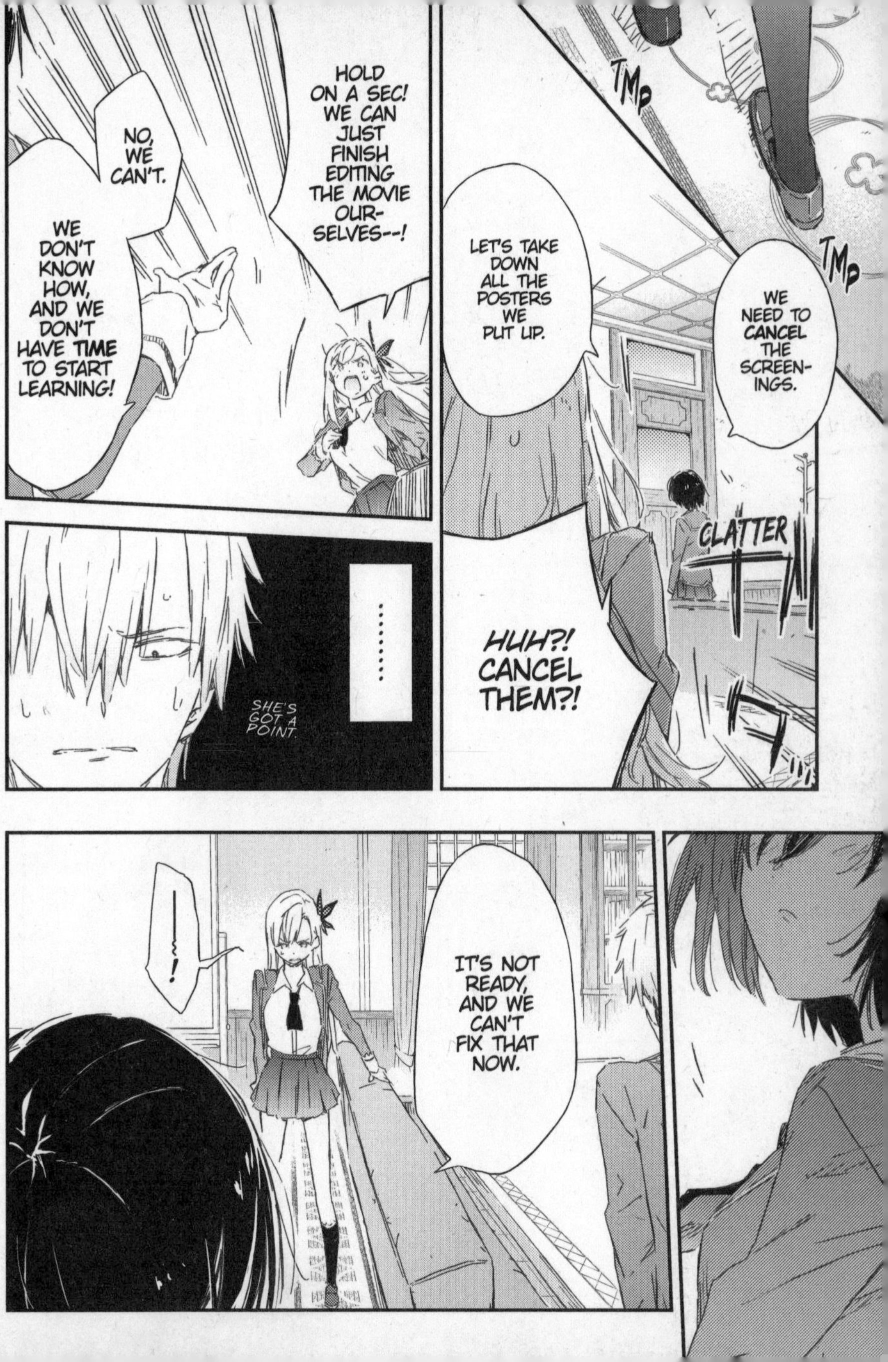
TMP
TMP
WE NEED TO CANCEL THE SCREEN-INGS.
LET'S TAKE DOWN ALL THE POSTERS WE PUT UP.
CLATTER
HUH?! CANCEL THEM?!
HOLD ON A SEC! WE CAN JUST FINISH EDITING THE MOVIE OUR-SELVES--!
NO, WE CAN'T.
WE DON'T KNOW HOW, AND WE DON'T HAVE TIME TO START LEARNING!
......
SHE'S GOT A POINT.
IT'S NOT READY, AND WE CAN'T FIX THAT NOW.
--!

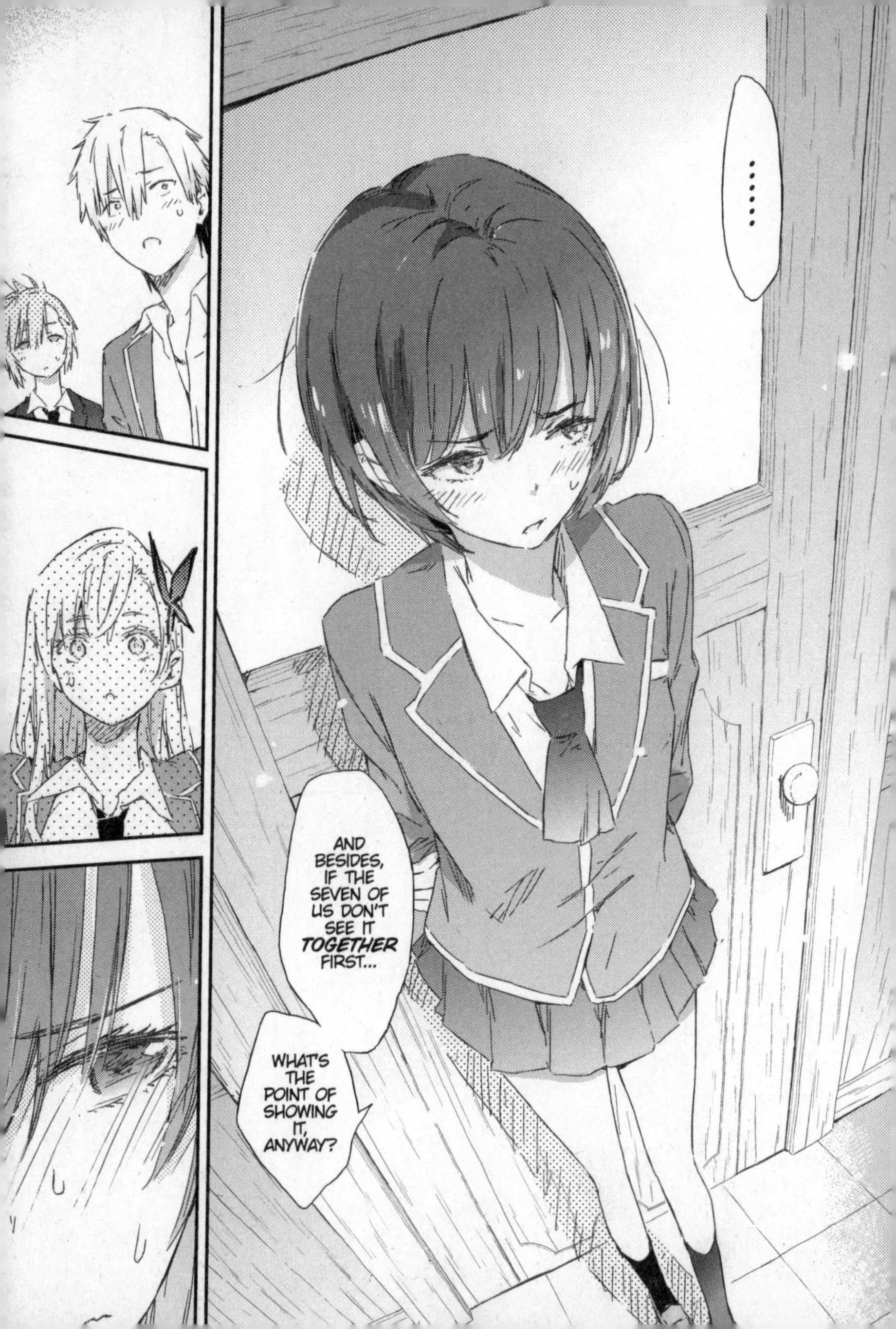
......
AND BESIDES, IF THE SEVEN OF US DON'T SEE IT ***TOGETHER*** FIRST...
WHAT'S THE POINT OF SHOWING IT, ANYWAY?

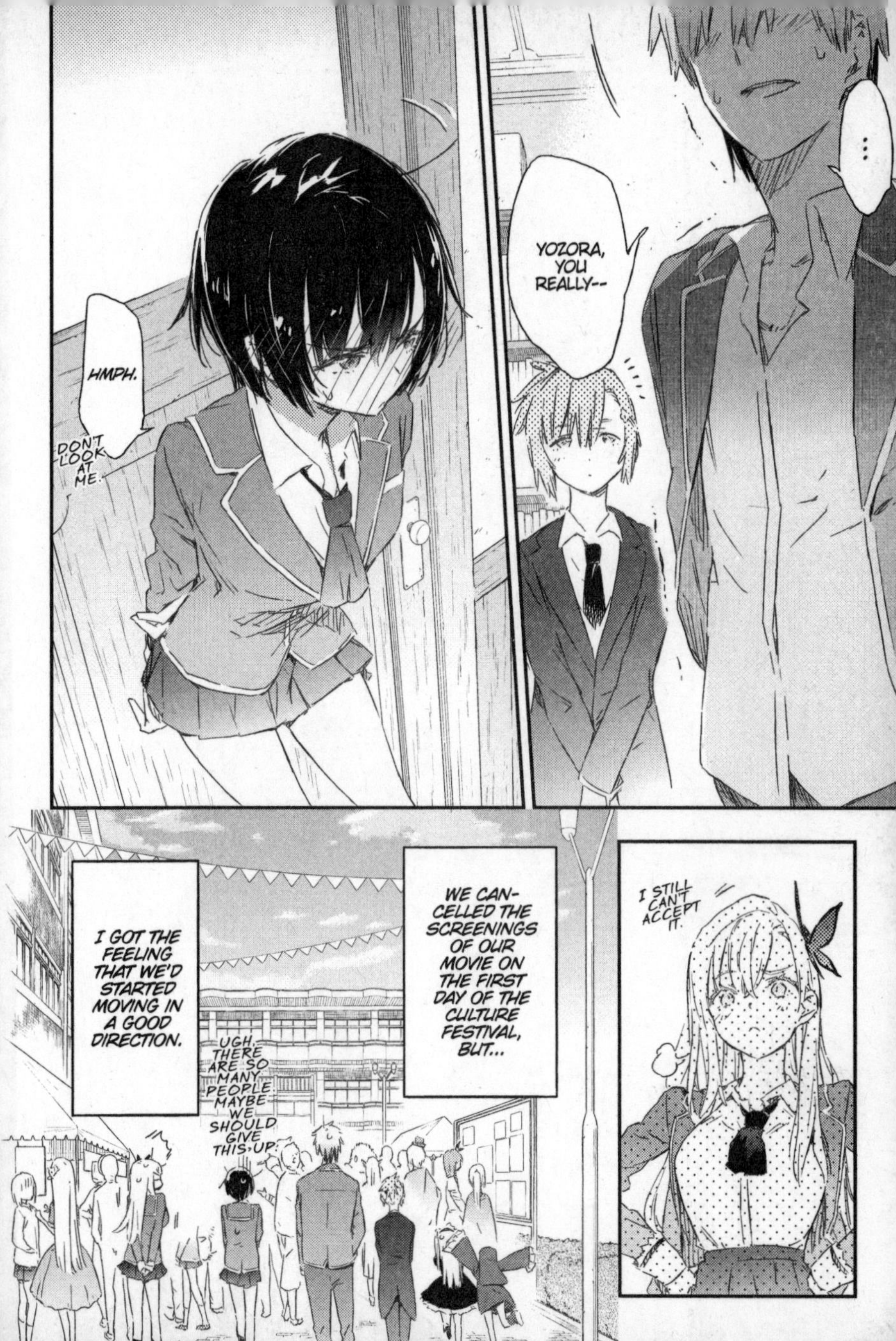
...
YOZORA, YOU REALLY--
HMPH.
DON'T LOOK AT ME.
I STILL CAN'T ACCEPT IT.
WE CAN-CELLED THE SCREENINGS OF OUR MOVIE ON THE FIRST DAY OF THE CULTURE FESTIVAL, BUT...
I GOT THE FEELING THAT WE'D STARTED MOVING IN A GOOD DIRECTION.
UGH, THERE ARE SO MANY PEOPLE. MAYBE WE SHOULD GIVE THIS UP.

FACTOID: MUSASHIBŌ BENKEI WAS A 12TH CENTURY WARRIOR WHO WAS KILLED BY THE ARMY CONTROLLED BY HIS LORD'S BROTHER (MINAMOTO NO YORITOMO). IT IS SAID THAT BENKEI, WHILE TRYING TO PROTECT HIS LORD, WAS KILLED BY A RAIN OF ARROWS, BUT STAYED ON HIS FEET EVEN AFTER HIS DEATH.

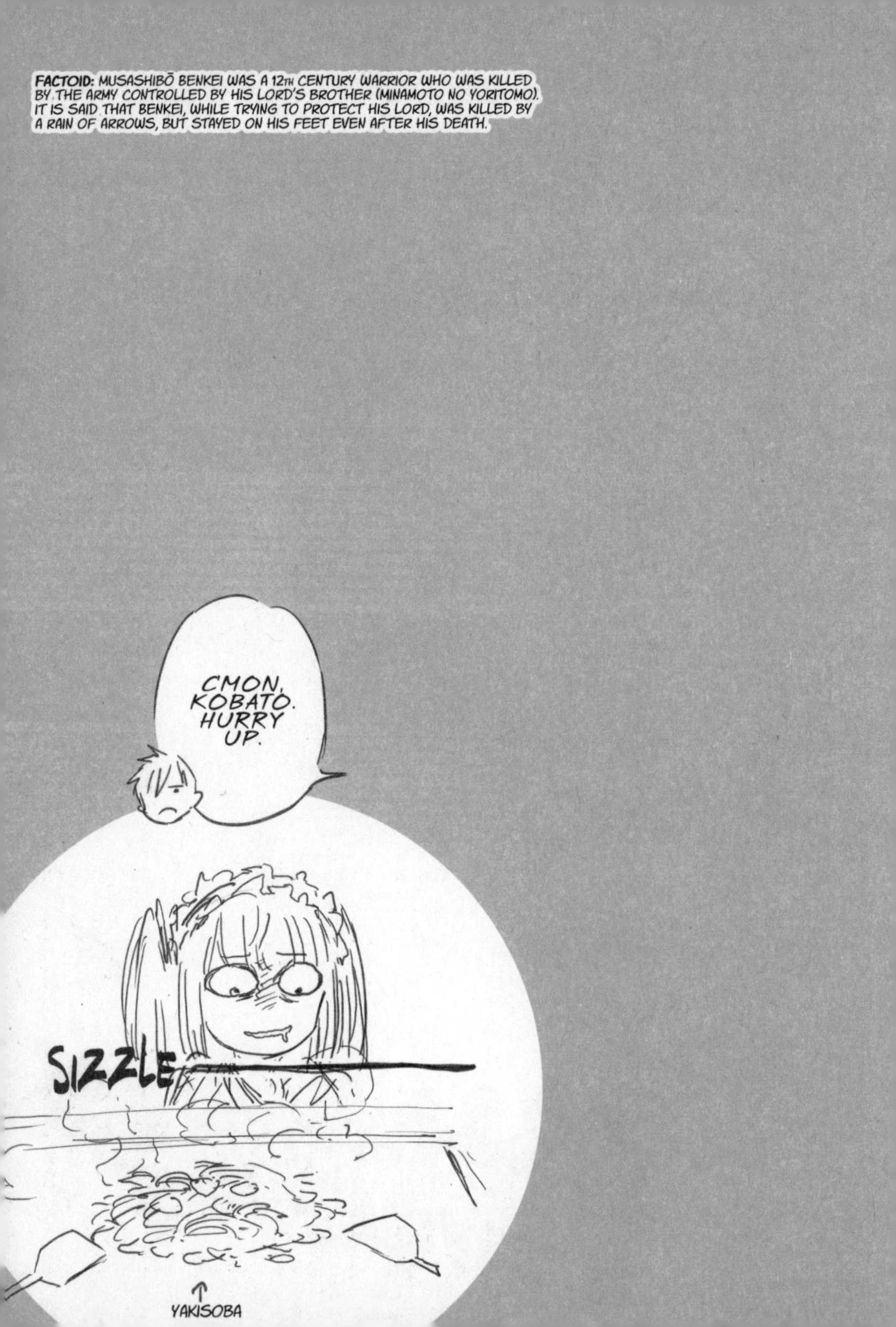
CMON, KOBATO. HURRY UP.
SIZZLE
YAKISOBA

Haganai
I don't have many friends

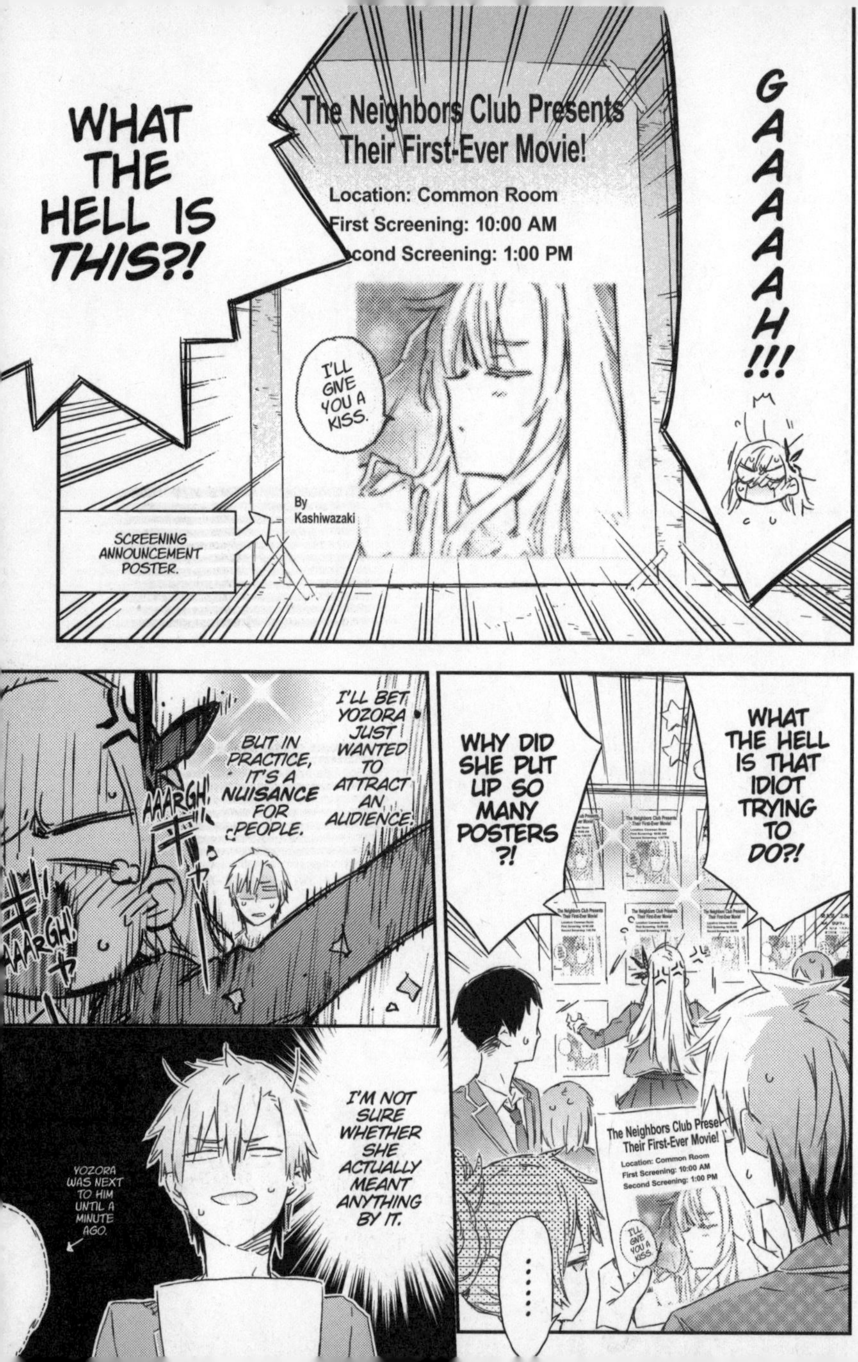
GAAAAAAH!!!
The Neighbors Club Presents
Their First-Ever Movie!
Location: Common Room
First Screening: 10:00 AM
Second Screening: 1:00 PM
WHAT THE HELL IS THIS?!
I'LL GIVE YOU A KISS.
By Kashiwazaki
SCREENING ANNOUNCEMENT POSTER.
WHAT THE HELL IS THAT IDIOT TRYING TO DO?!
WHY DID SHE PUT UP SO MANY POSTERS ?!
The Neighbors Club Prese
Their First-Ever Movie!
Location: Common Room
First Screening: 10:00 AM
Second Screening: 1:00 PM
I'LL GIVE YOU A KISS.
......
I'LL BET YOZORA JUST WANTED TO ATTRACT AN AUDIENCE.
BUT IN PRACTICE, IT'S A NUISANCE FOR PEOPLE.
AAARGH!
AAARGH!
I'M NOT SURE WHETHER SHE ACTUALLY MEANT ANYTHING BY IT.
YOZORA WAS NEXT TO HIM UNTIL A MINUTE AGO.

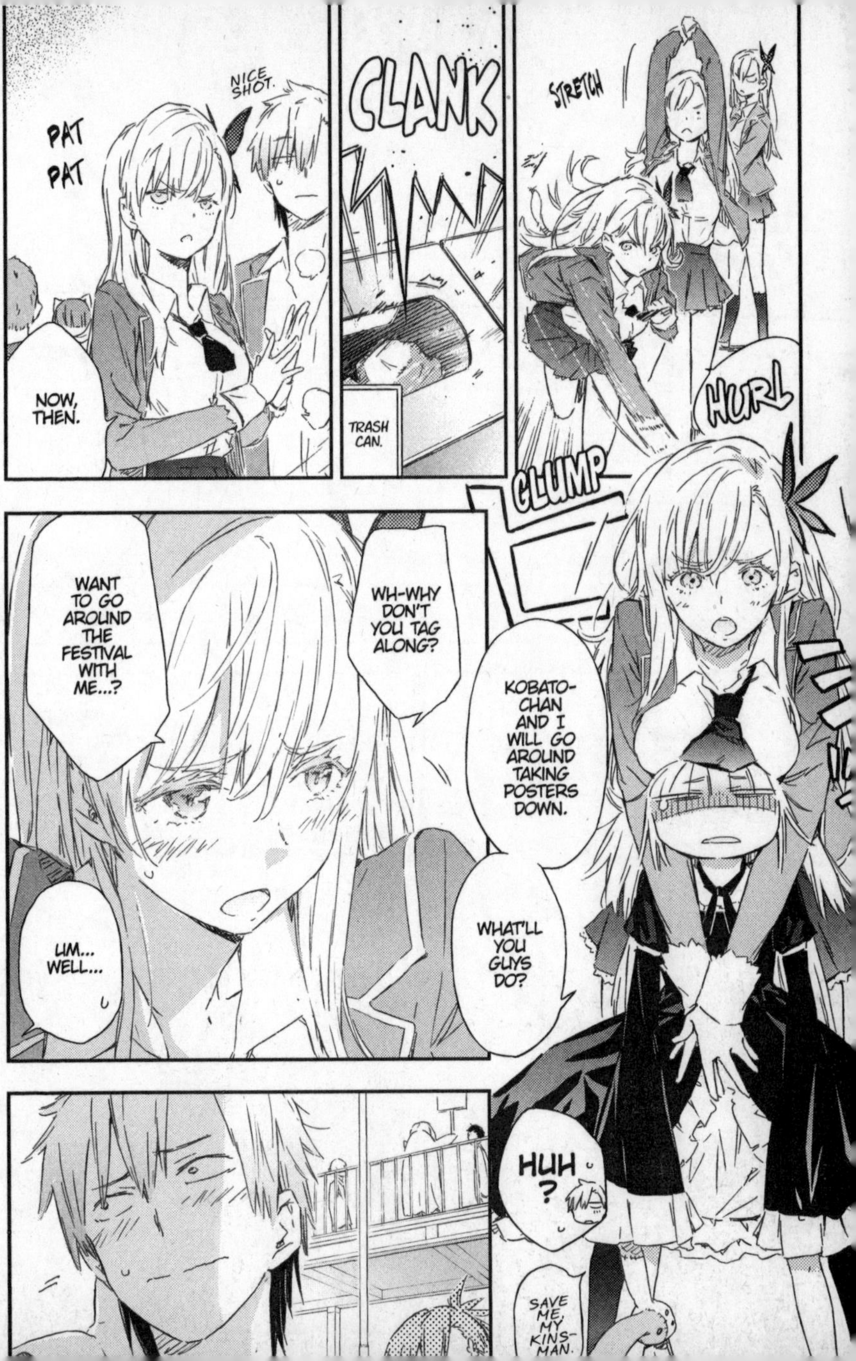
STRETCH
HURL
CLANK
TRASH CAN.
PAT PAT
NICE SHOT.
NOW, THEN.
CLUMP
KOBATO-CHAN AND I WILL GO AROUND TAKING POSTERS DOWN.
WHAT'LL YOU GUYS DO?
HUH?
SAVE ME, MY KINS-MAN.
WH-WHY DON'T YOU TAG ALONG?
WANT TO GO AROUND THE FESTIVAL WITH ME...?
UM... WELL...

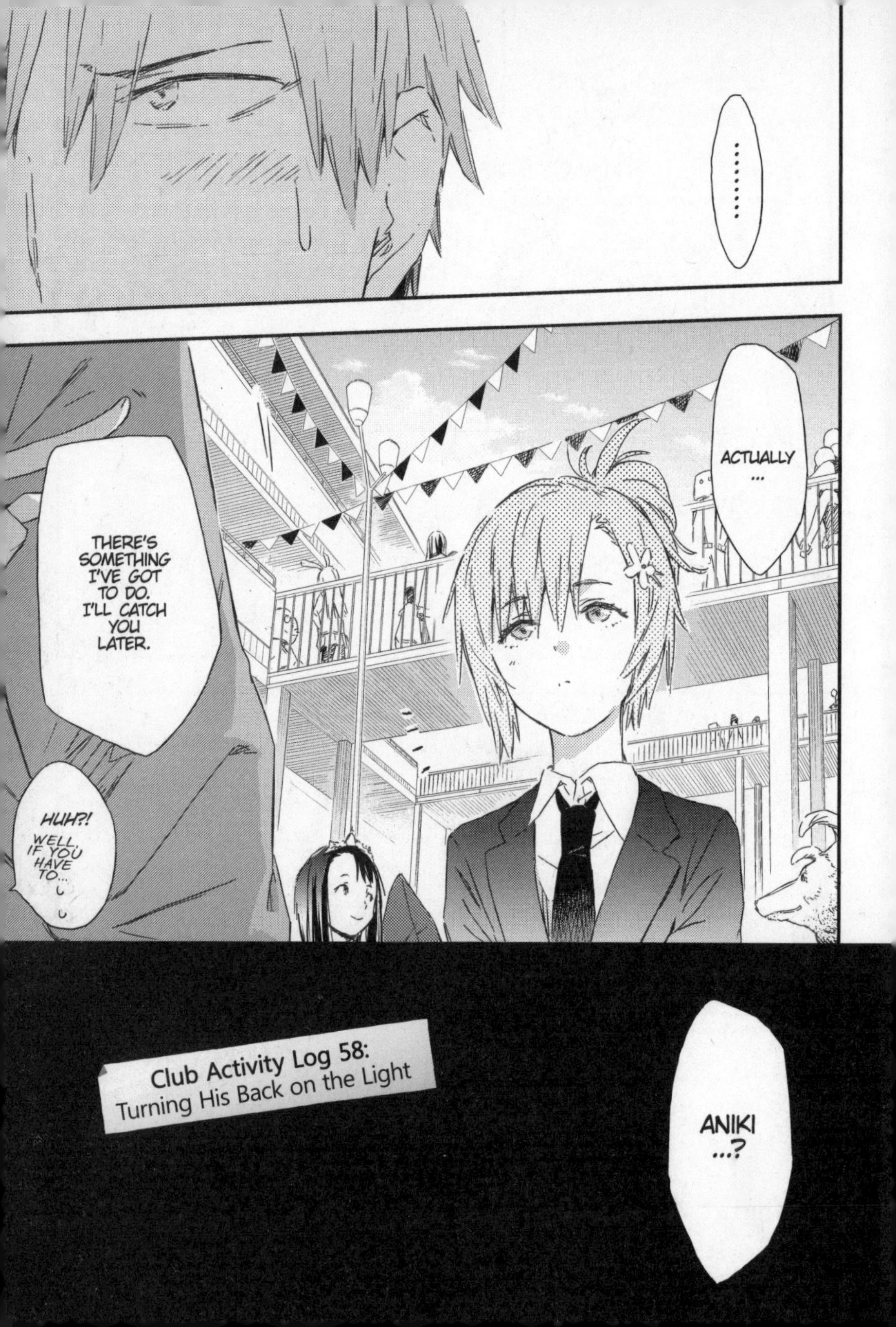
....
ACTUALLY...
THERE'S SOMETHING I'VE GOT TO DO. I'LL CATCH YOU LATER.
HUH?! WELL, IF YOU HAVE TO...
ANIKI...?
Club Activity Log 58: Turning His Back on the Light

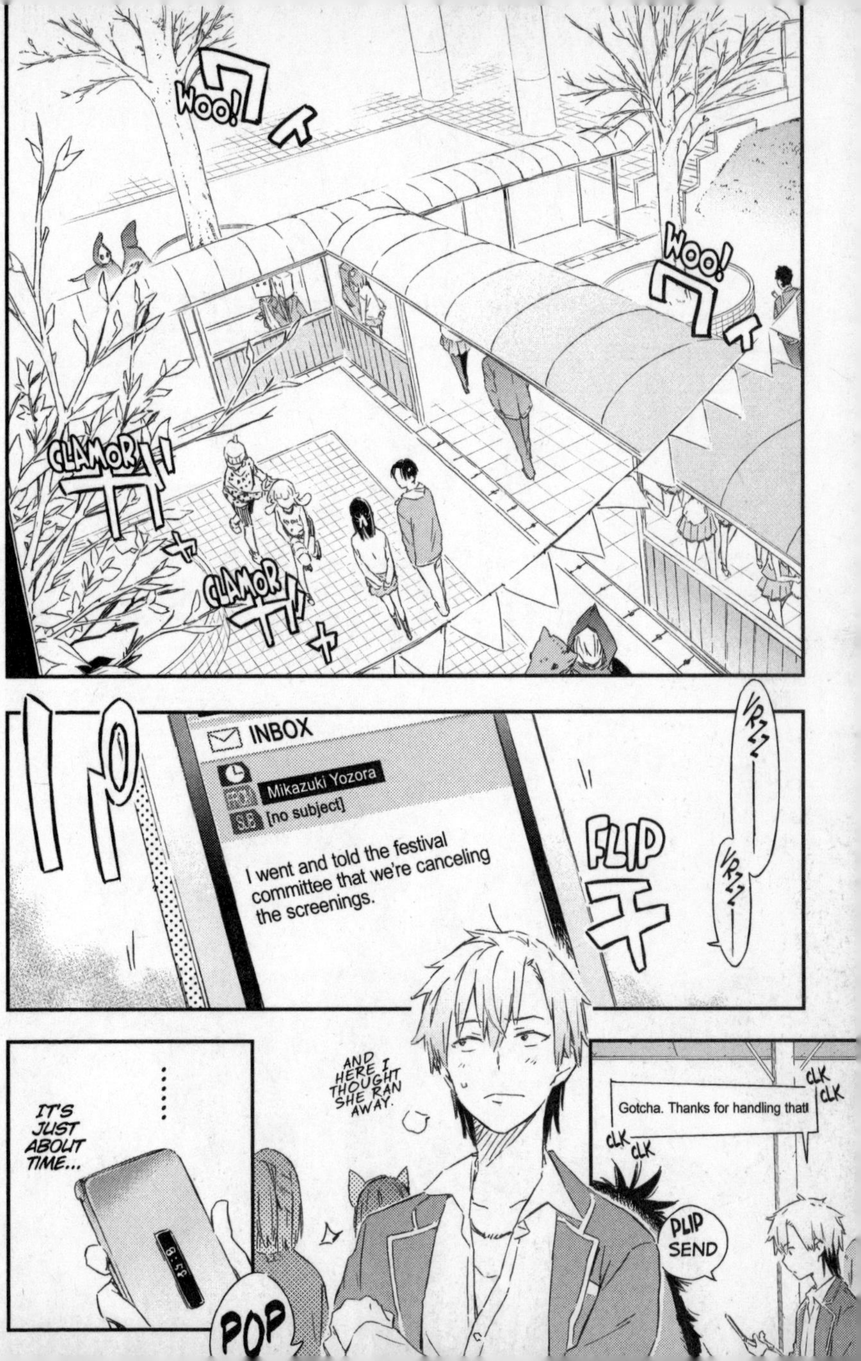
WOO!
WOO!
CLAMOR
CLAMOR
VRZZ——
VRZZ——
FLIP
INBOX
Mikazuki Yozora
[no subject]
I went and told the festival committee that we're canceling the screenings.
CLK CLK
Gotcha. Thanks for handling that!
CLK CLK
PLIP SEND
AND HERE I THOUGHT SHE RAN AWAY.
......
IT'S JUST ABOUT TIME...
8:55
POP

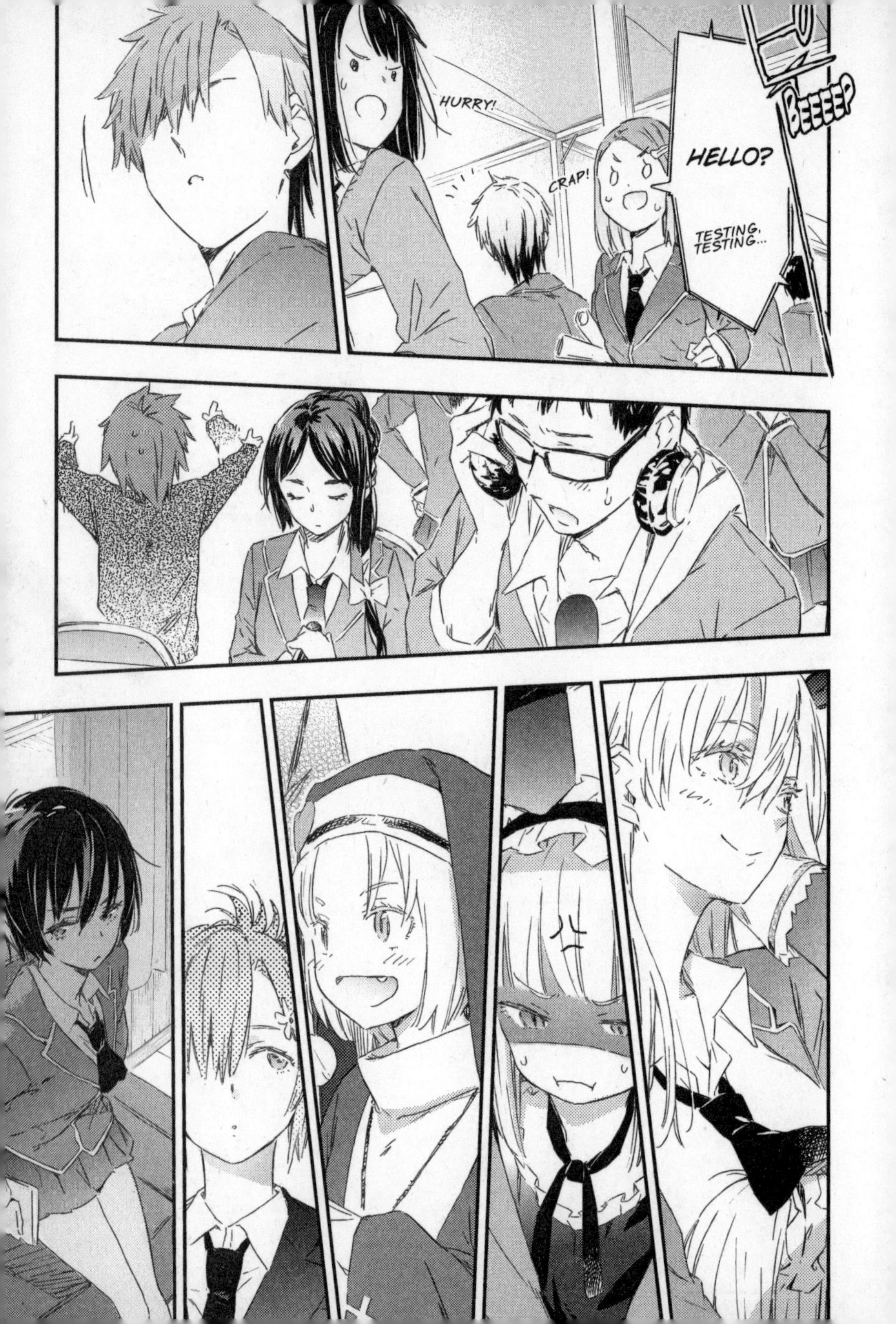
BEEEEP
HELLO?
TESTING, TESTING...
CRAP!
HURRY!

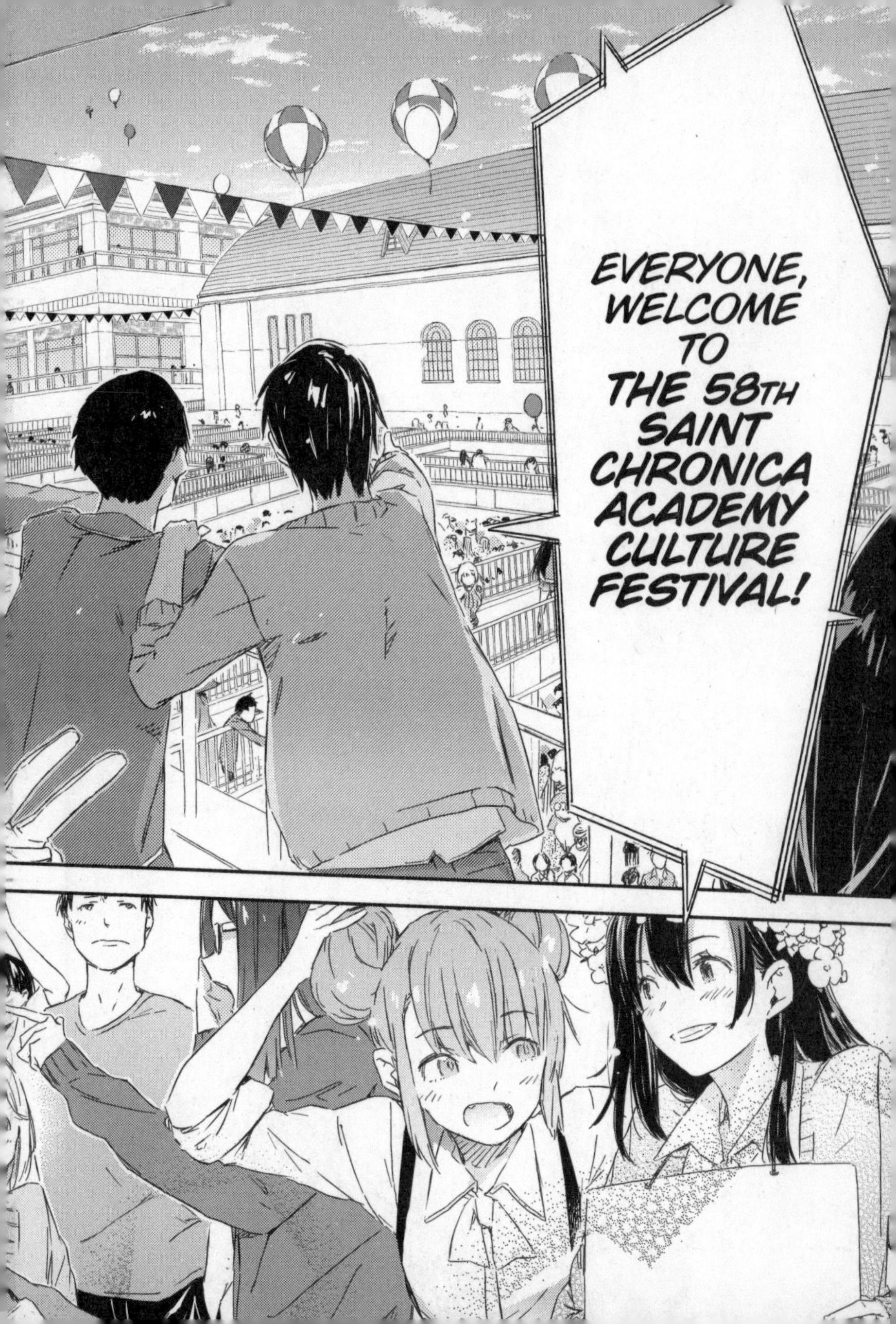
EVERYONE, WELCOME TO THE 58TH SAINT CHRONICA ACADEMY CULTURE FESTIVAL!

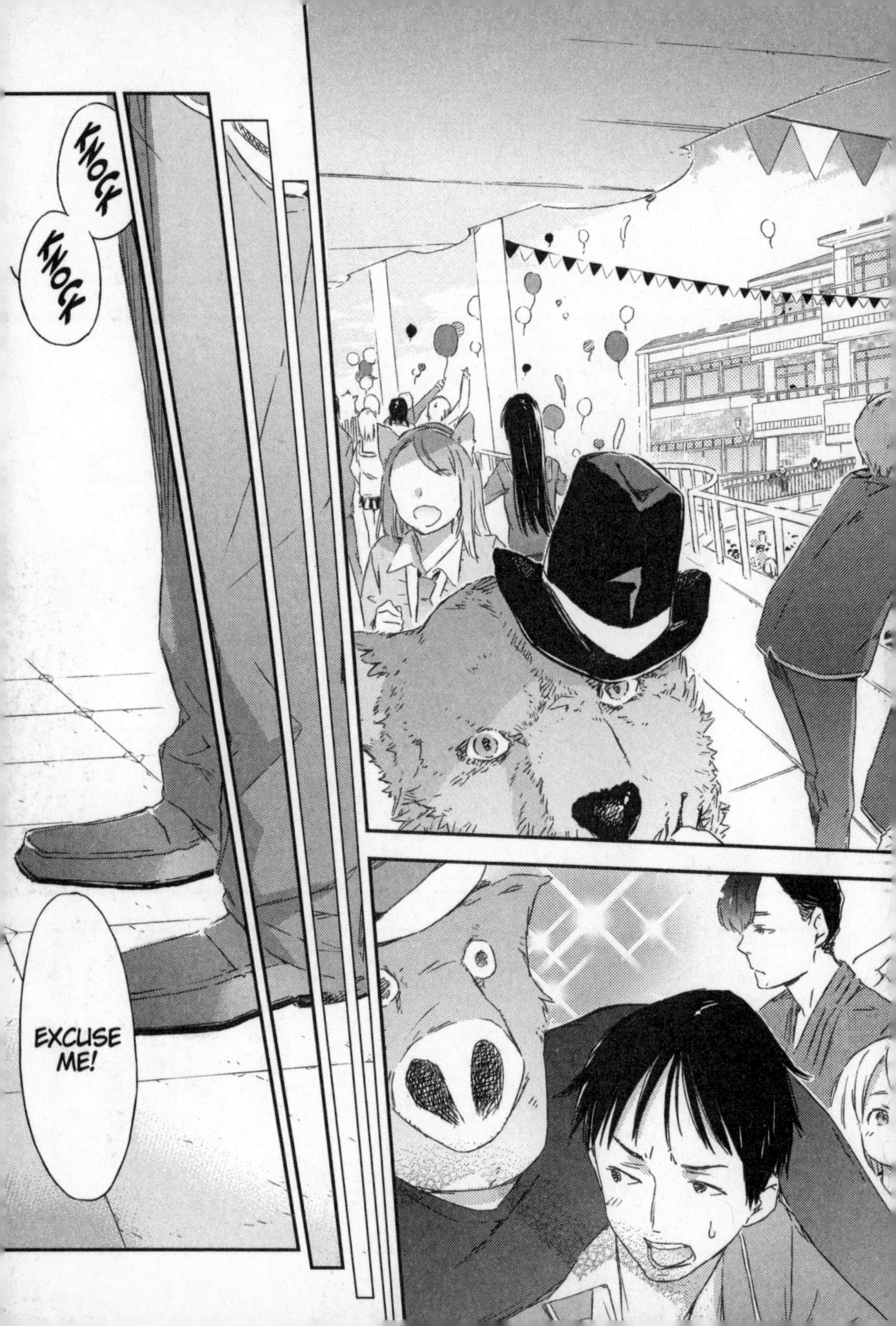
KNOCK
KNOCK
EXCUSE ME!

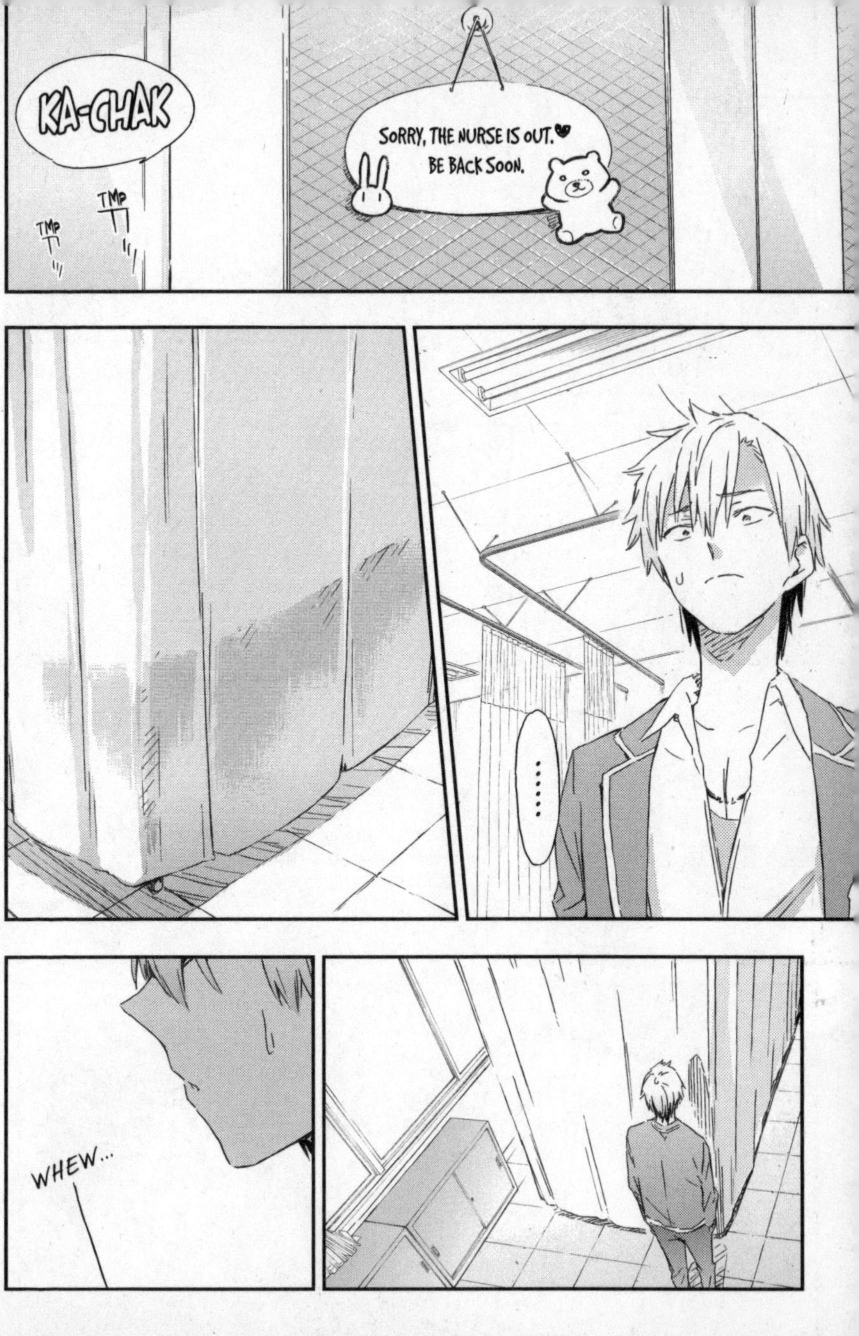
SORRY, THE NURSE IS OUT.
BE BACK SOON.
KA-CHAK
TMP
TMP
......
WHEW...

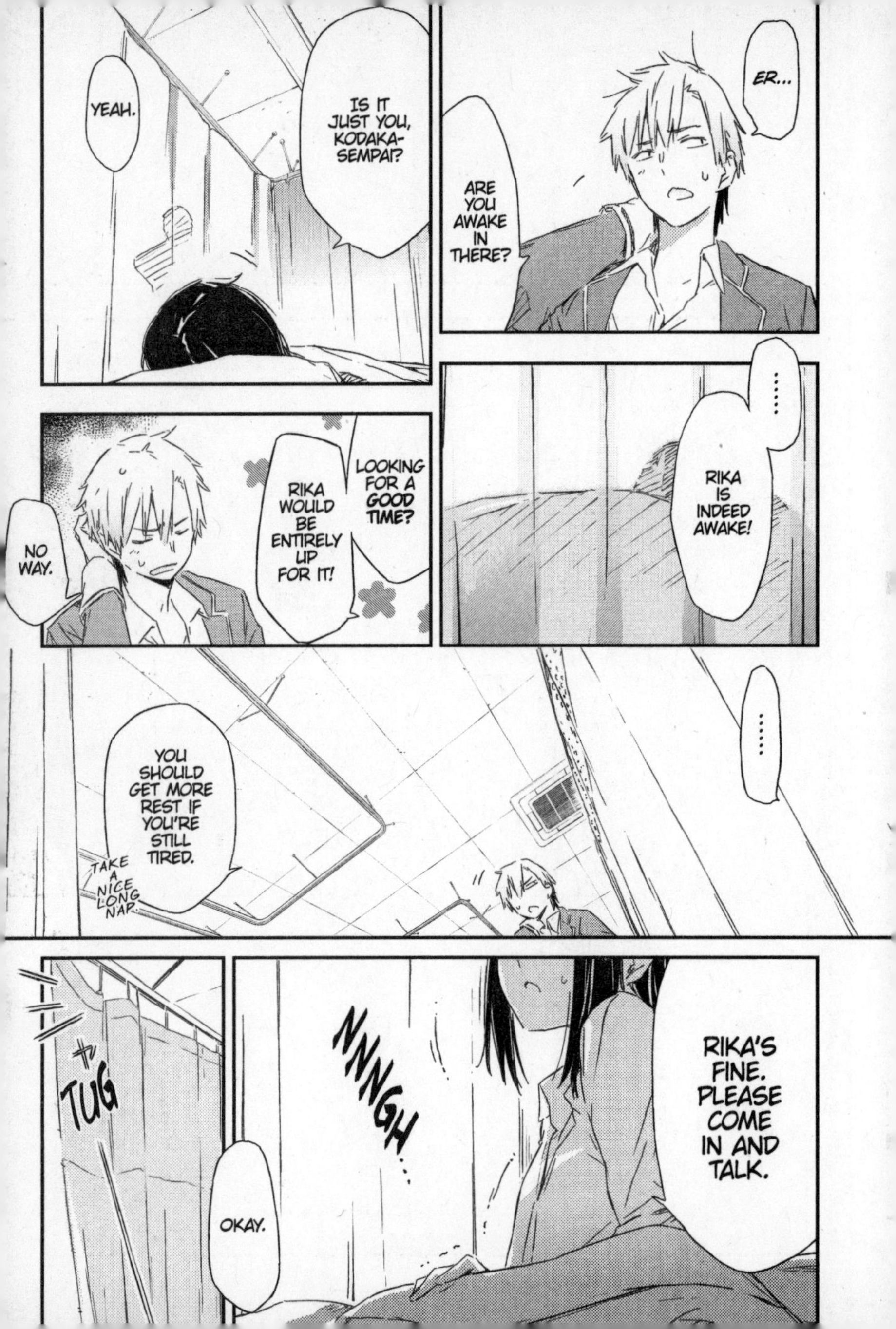
ER...
ARE YOU AWAKE IN THERE?
IS IT JUST YOU, KODAKA-SEMPAI?
YEAH.
......
RIKA IS INDEED AWAKE!
LOOKING FOR A GOOD TIME?
RIKA WOULD BE ENTIRELY UP FOR IT!
NO WAY.
......
YOU SHOULD GET MORE REST IF YOU'RE STILL TIRED.
TAKE A NICE LONG NAP.
RIKA'S FINE. PLEASE COME IN AND TALK.
NNNGH...
OKAY.
TUG

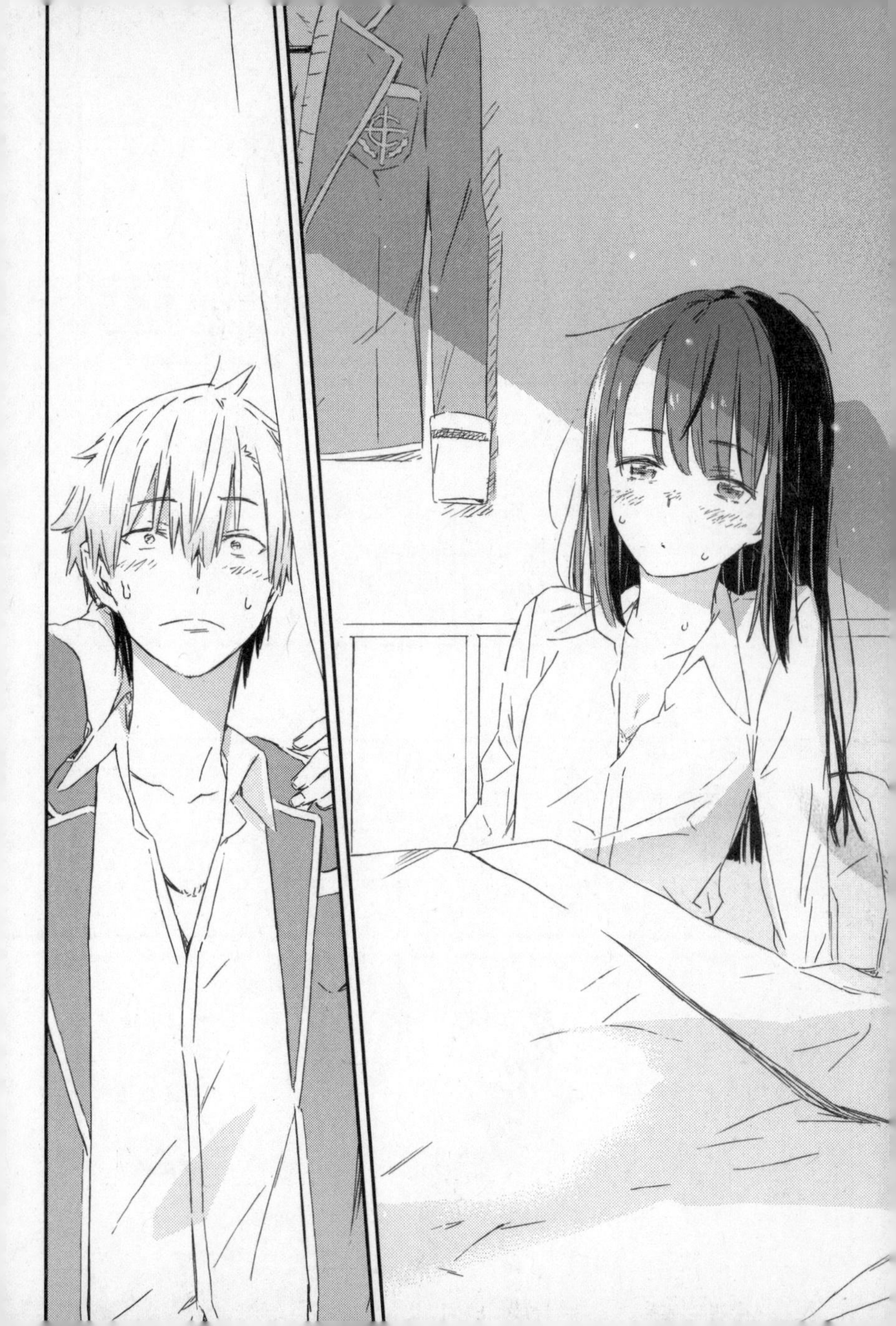

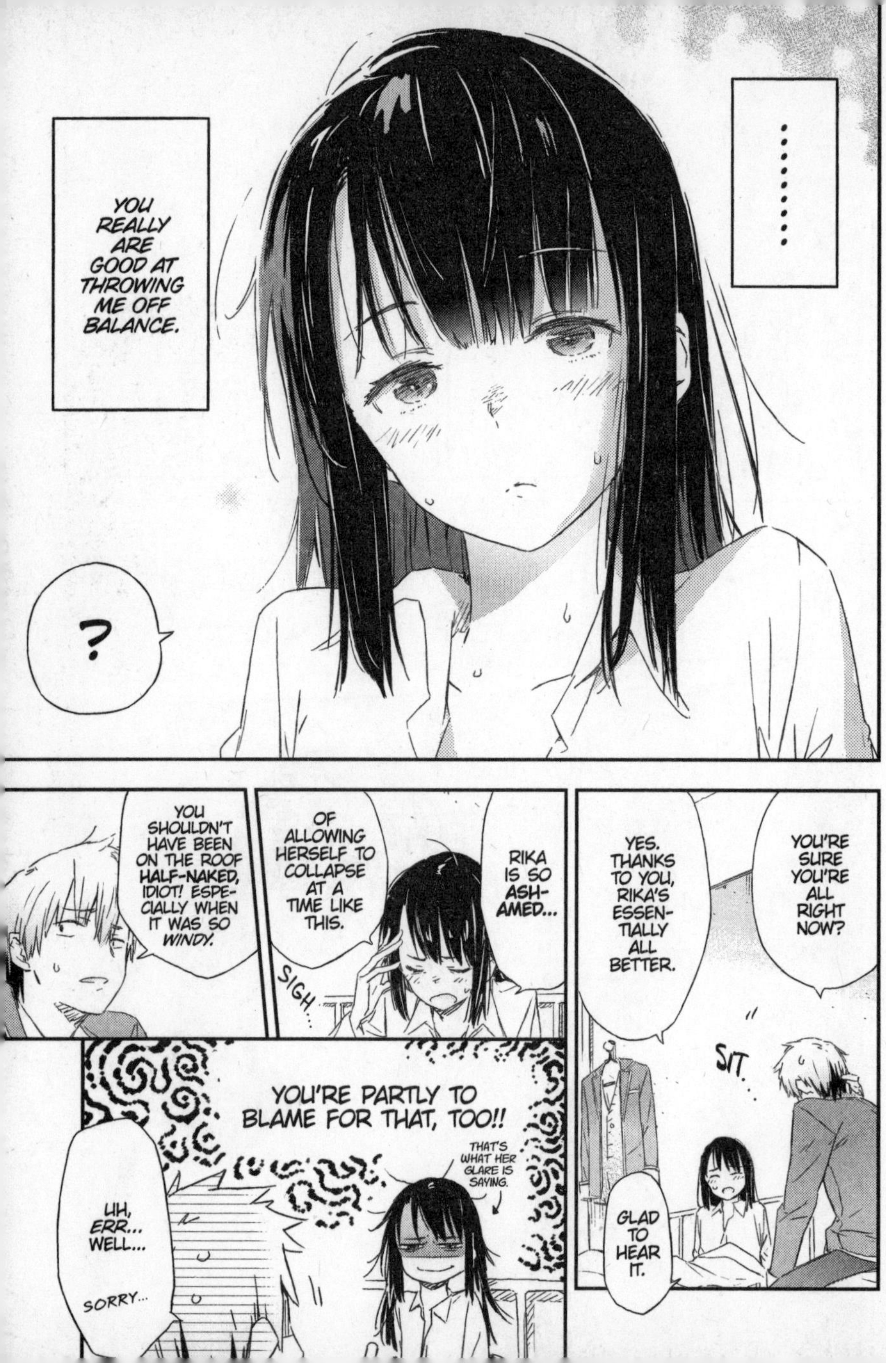
......
YOU REALLY ARE GOOD AT THROWING ME OFF BALANCE.
?
YOU'RE SURE YOU'RE ALL RIGHT NOW?
YES. THANKS TO YOU, RIKA'S ESSENTIALLY ALL BETTER.
RIKA IS SO ASHAMED...
OF ALLOWING HERSELF TO COLLAPSE AT A TIME LIKE THIS.
SIGH...
YOU SHOULDN'T HAVE BEEN ON THE ROOF HALF-NAKED, IDIOT! ESPECIALLY WHEN IT WAS SO WINDY.
SIT...
GLAD TO HEAR IT.
YOU'RE PARTLY TO BLAME FOR THAT, TOO!!
THAT'S WHAT HER GLARE IS SAYING.
UH, ERR... WELL...
SORRY...

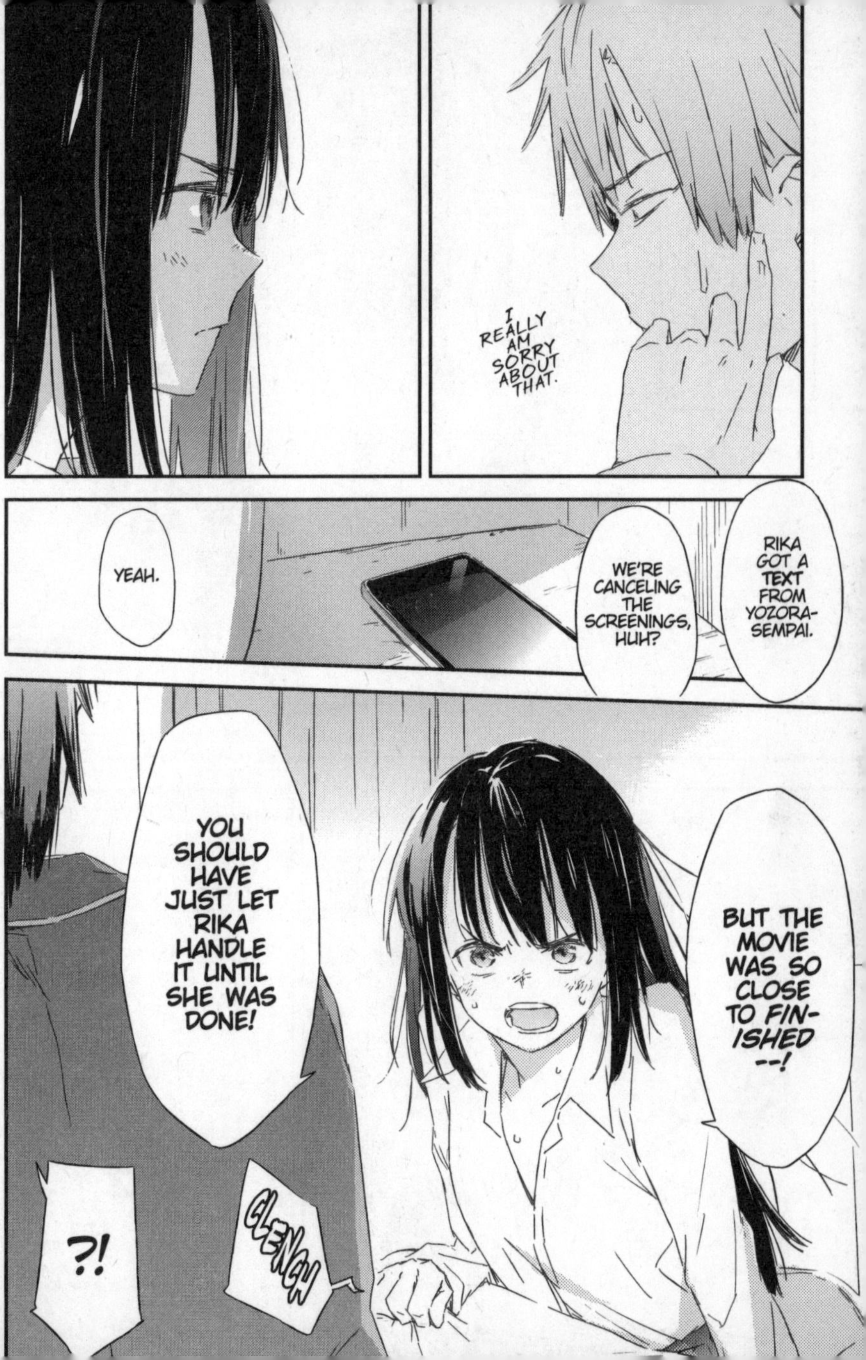
I REALLY AM SORRY ABOUT THAT.
RIKA GOT A TEXT FROM YOZORA-SEMPAI.
WE'RE CANCELING THE SCREENINGS, HUH?
YEAH.
BUT THE MOVIE WAS SO CLOSE TO *FIN-ISHED* --!
YOU SHOULD HAVE JUST LET RIKA HANDLE IT UNTIL SHE WAS DONE!
CLENCH
?!

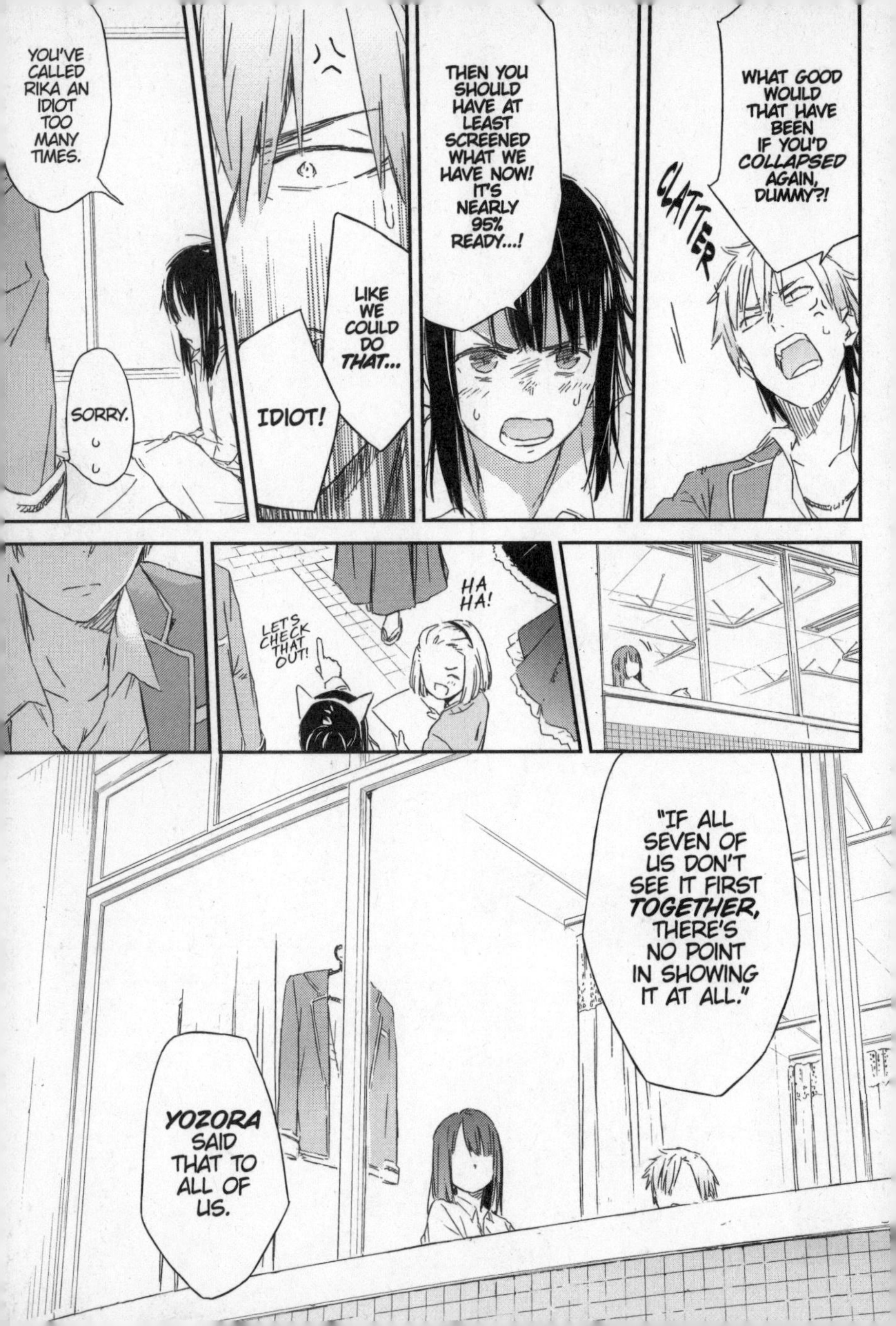
WHAT GOOD WOULD THAT HAVE BEEN IF YOU'D COLLAPSED AGAIN, DUMMY?!
CLATTER
THEN YOU SHOULD HAVE AT LEAST SCREENED WHAT WE HAVE NOW! IT'S NEARLY 95% READY...!
LIKE WE COULD DO THAT...
IDIOT!
YOU'VE CALLED RIKA AN IDIOT TOO MANY TIMES.
SORRY.
HA HA!
LET'S CHECK THAT OUT!
"IF ALL SEVEN OF US DON'T SEE IT FIRST TOGETHER, THERE'S NO POINT IN SHOWING IT AT ALL."
YOZORA SAID THAT TO ALL OF US.

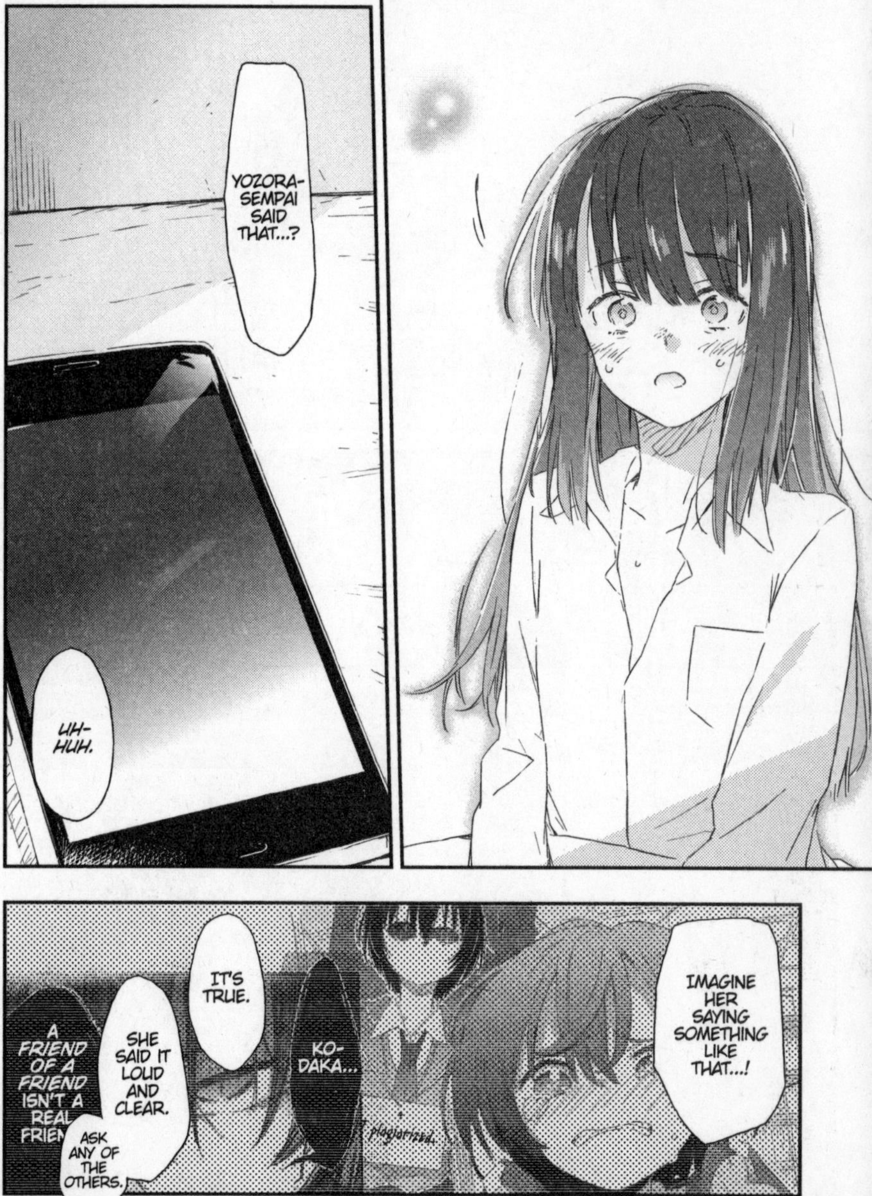
YOZORA-SEMPAI SAID THAT...?
UH-HUH.
IMAGINE HER SAYING SOMETHING LIKE THAT...!
IT'S TRUE.
KO-DAKA...
plagiarized.
SHE SAID IT LOUD AND CLEAR.
A FRIEND OF A FRIEND ISN'T A REAL FRIEN
ASK ANY OF THE OTHERS.

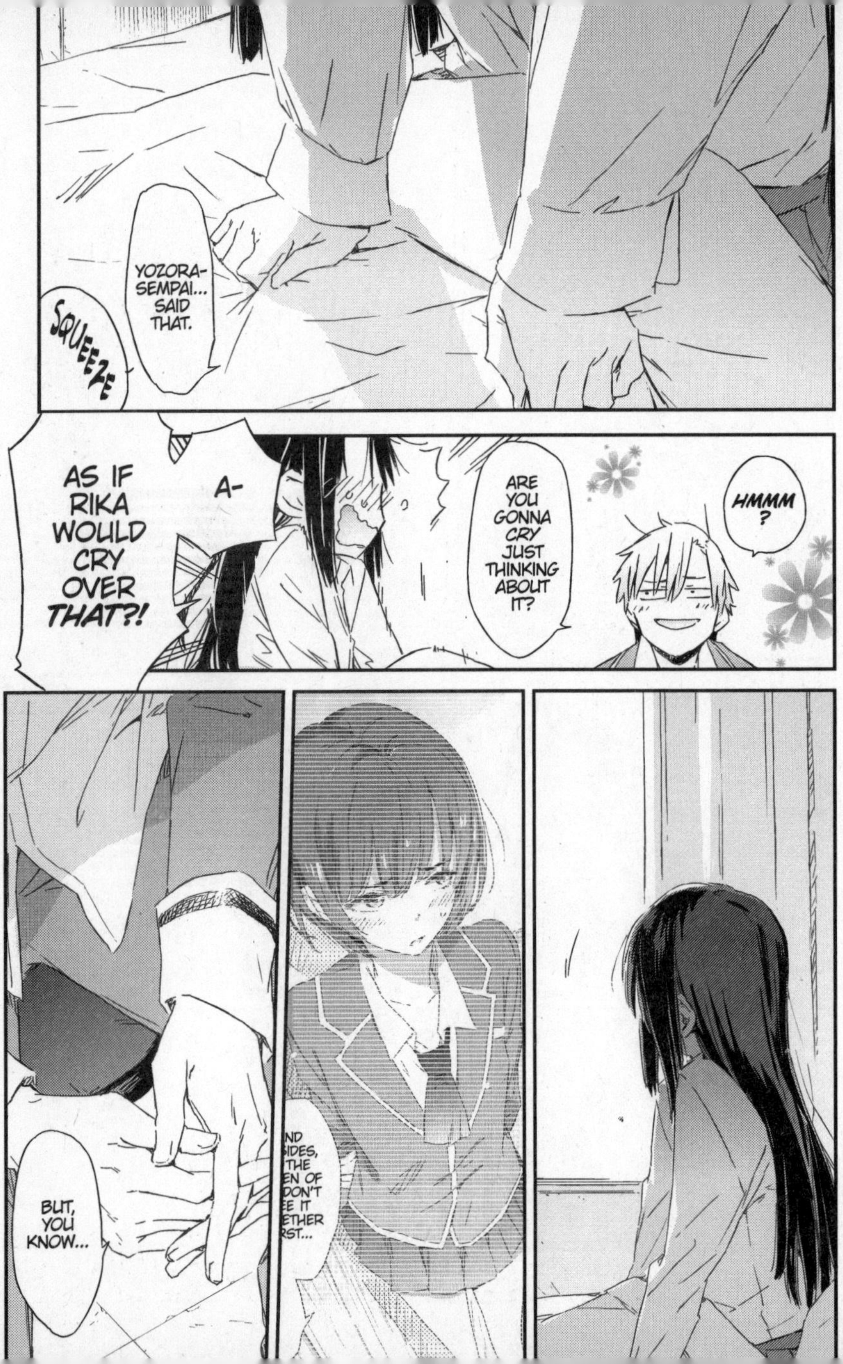
YOZORA-SEMPAI... SAID THAT.
SQUEEZE
HMMM?
ARE YOU GONNA CRY JUST THINKING ABOUT IT?
A-
AS IF RIKA WOULD CRY OVER THAT?!
ND SIDES, THE EN OF DON'T EE IT ETHER RST...
BUT, YOU KNOW...

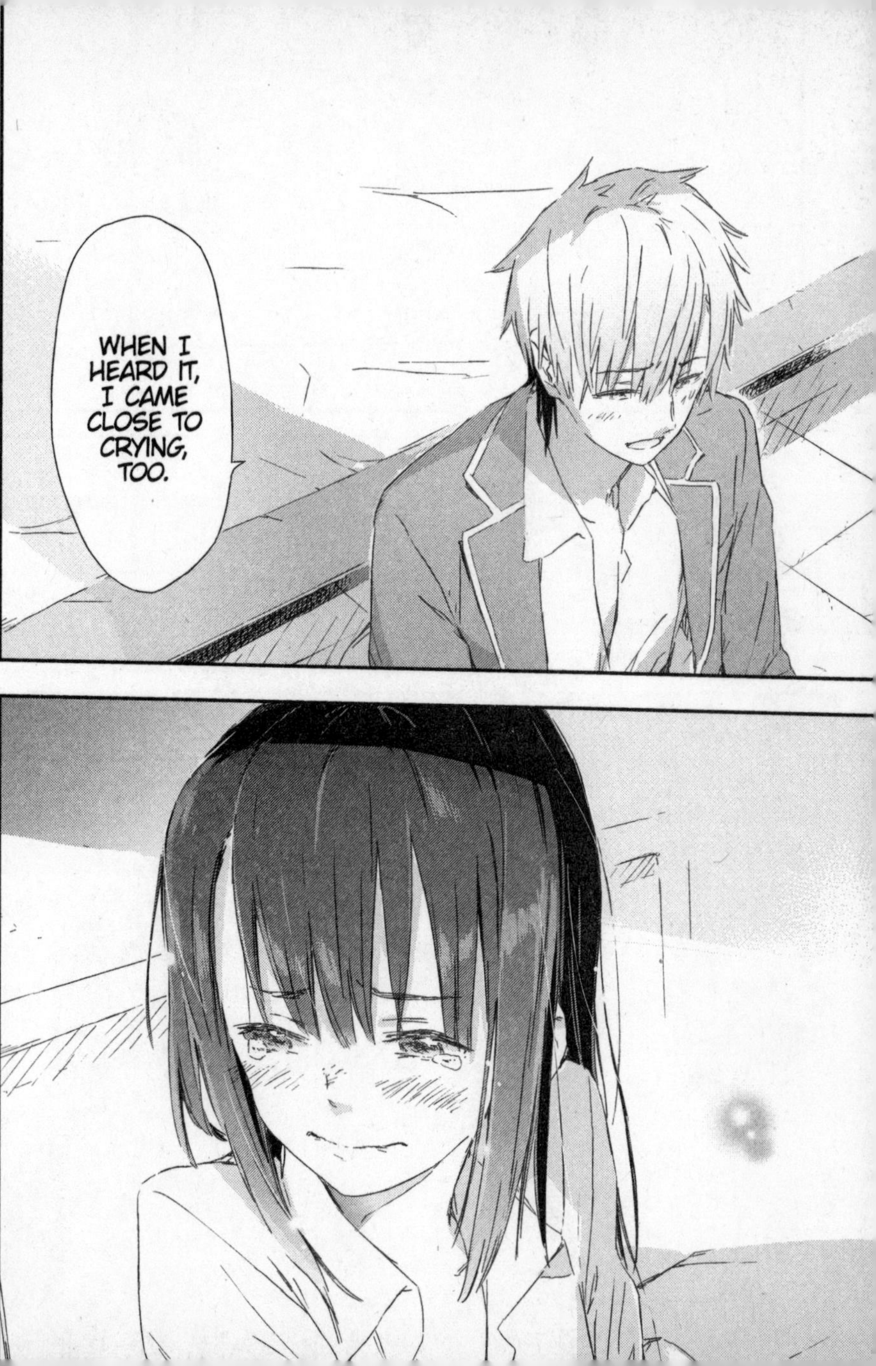
WHEN I HEARD IT, I CAME CLOSE TO CRYING, TOO.

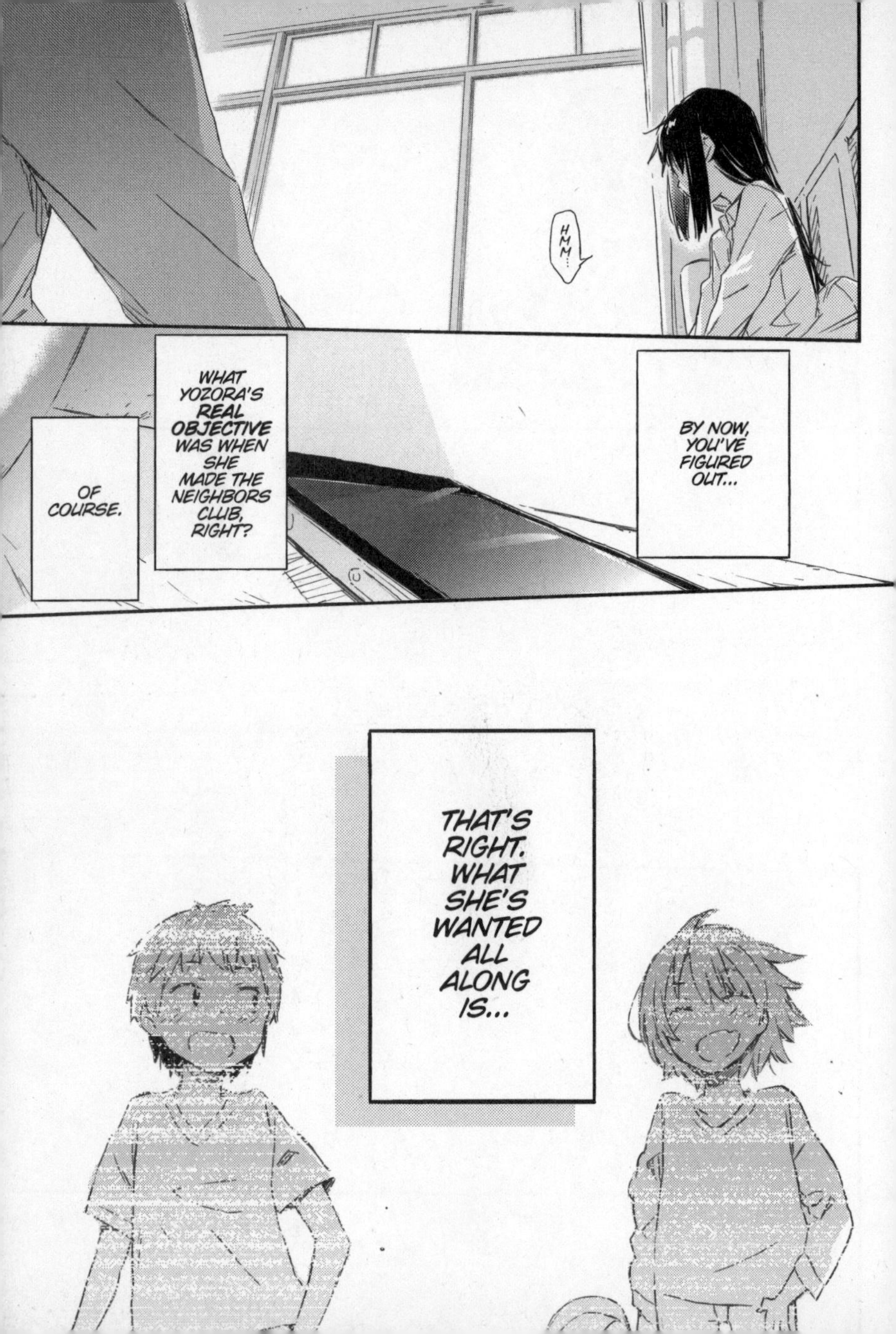
HMM...
BY NOW, YOU'VE FIGURED OUT...
WHAT YOZORA'S REAL OBJECTIVE WAS WHEN SHE MADE THE NEIGHBORS CLUB, RIGHT?
OF COURSE.
THAT'S RIGHT. WHAT SHE'S WANTED ALL ALONG IS...

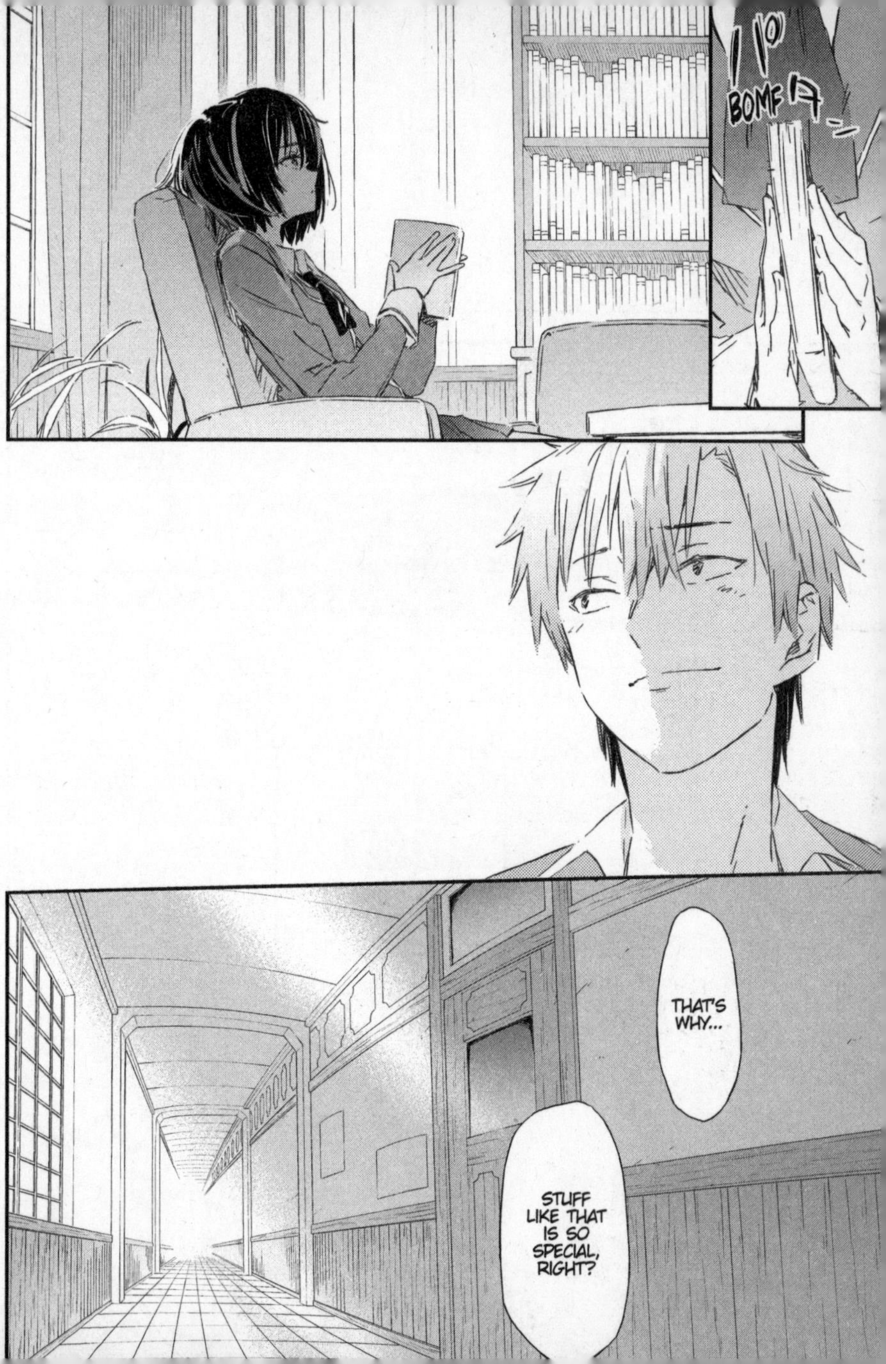
BOMF !?
THAT'S WHY...
STUFF LIKE THAT IS SO SPECIAL, RIGHT?

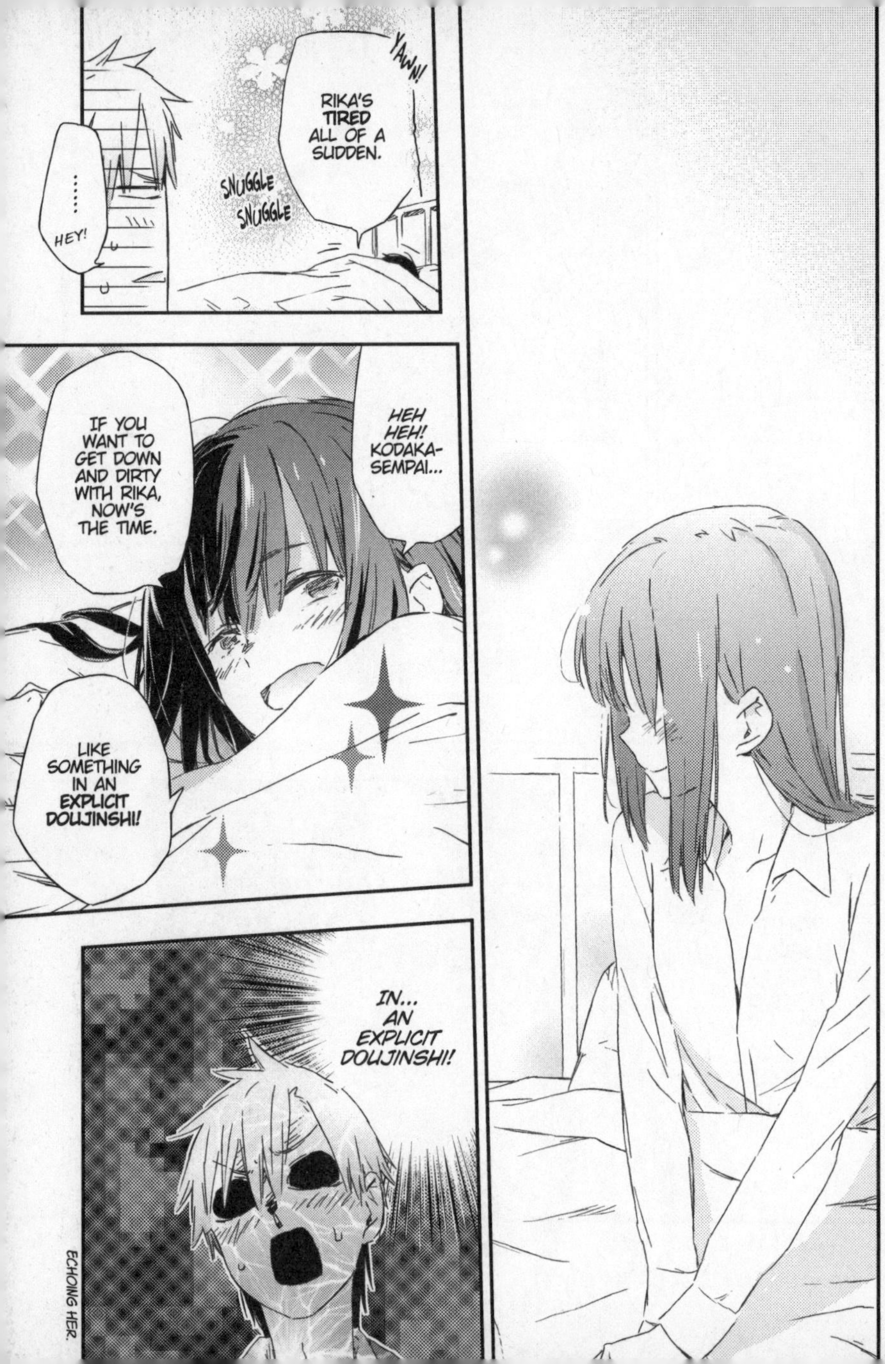
YAWN!
RIKA'S TIRED ALL OF A SUDDEN.
SNUGGLE SNUGGLE
......
HEY!
HEH HEH! KODAKA-SEMPAI...
IF YOU WANT TO GET DOWN AND DIRTY WITH RIKA, NOW'S THE TIME.
LIKE SOMETHING IN AN EXPLICIT DOUJINSHI!
IN... AN EXPLICIT DOUJINSHI!
ECHOING HER.

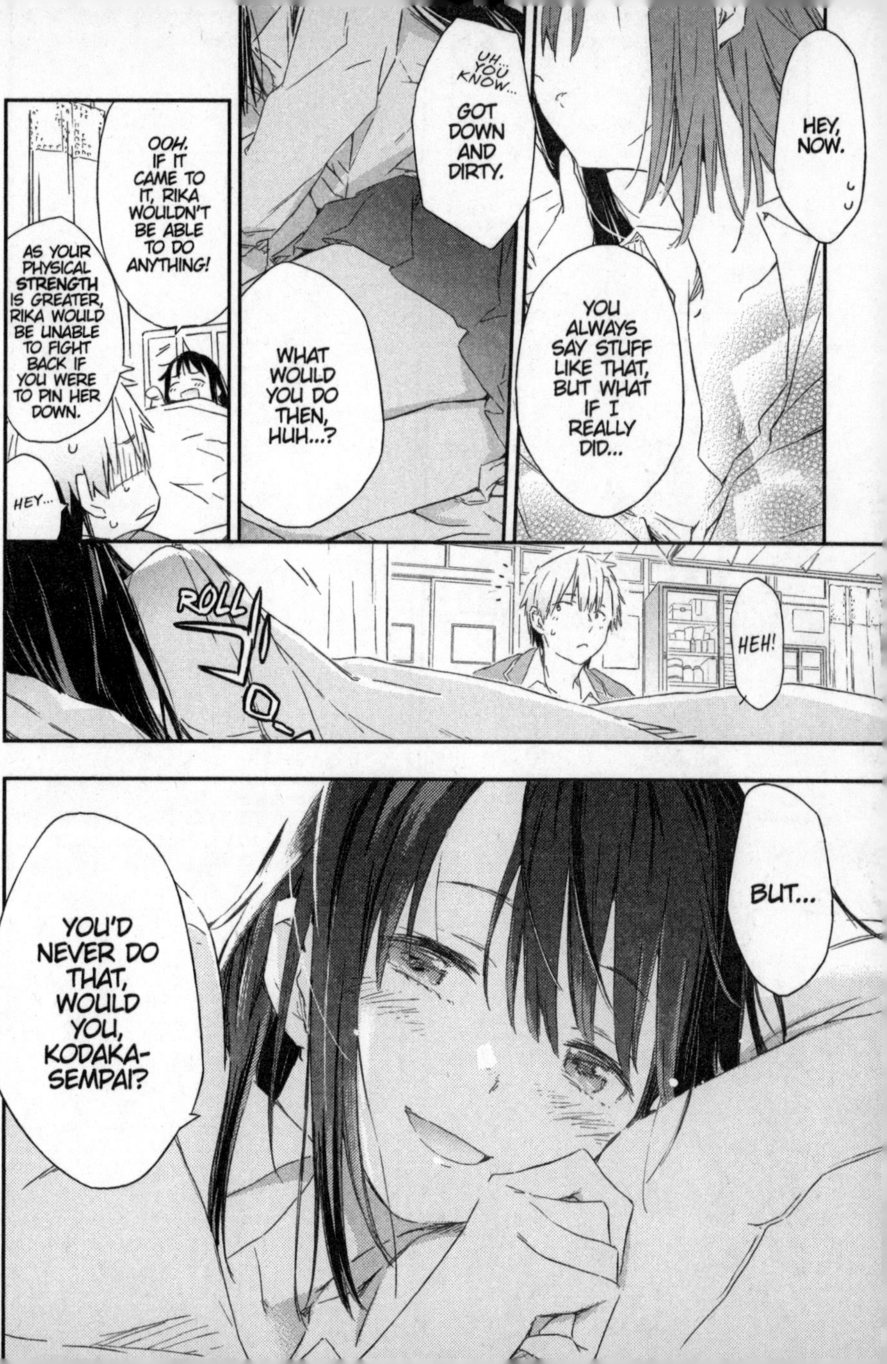
HEY, NOW.
UH... YOU KNOW...
GOT DOWN AND DIRTY.
YOU ALWAYS SAY STUFF LIKE THAT, BUT WHAT IF I REALLY DID...
WHAT WOULD YOU DO THEN, HUH...?
OOH. IF IT CAME TO IT, RIKA WOULDN'T BE ABLE TO DO ANYTHING!
AS YOUR PHYSICAL STRENGTH IS GREATER, RIKA WOULD BE UNABLE TO FIGHT BACK IF YOU WERE TO PIN HER DOWN.
HEY...
HEH!
ROLL
BUT...
YOU'D NEVER DO THAT, WOULD YOU, KODAKA-SEMPAI?

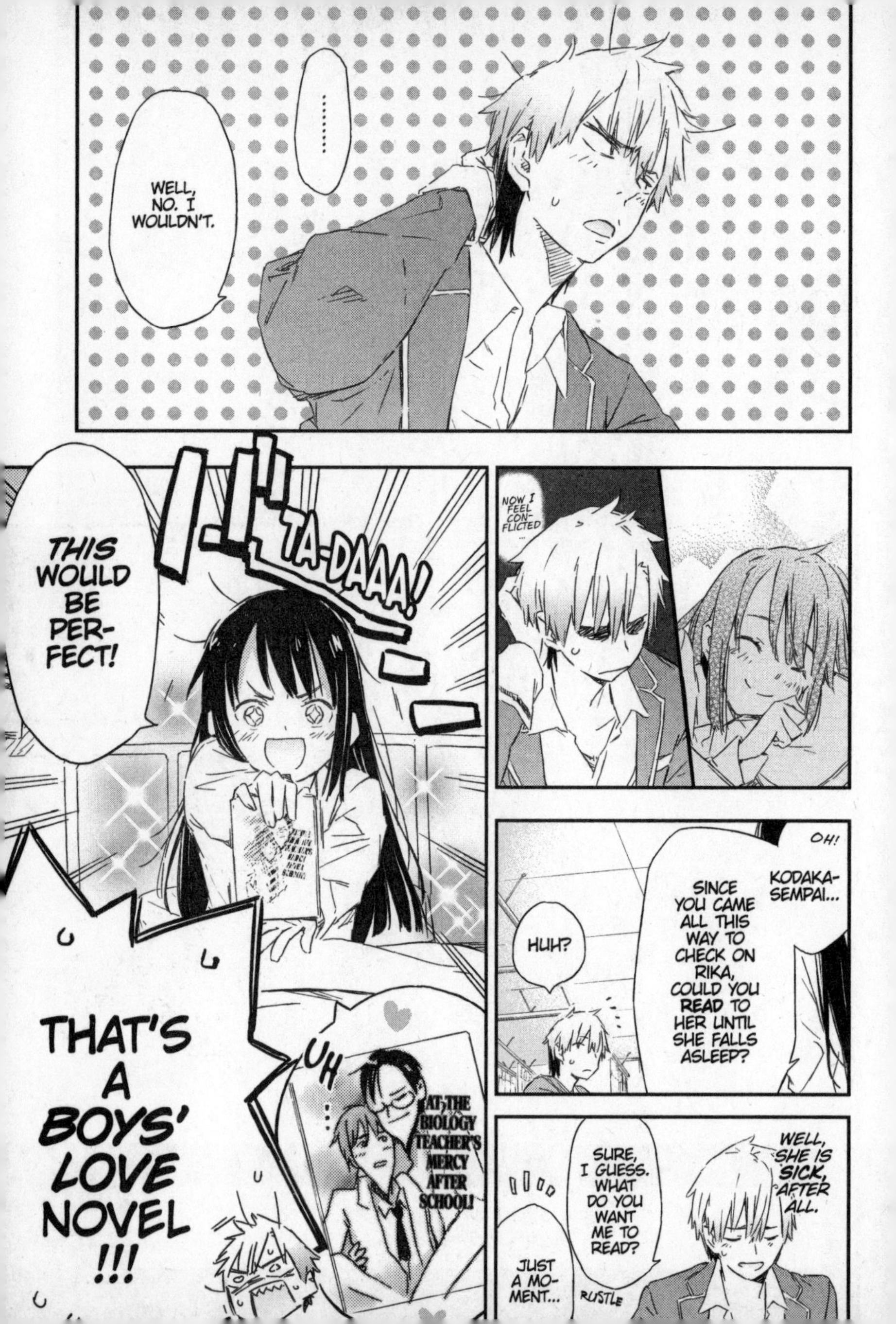
......
WELL, NO. I WOULDN'T.
NOW I FEEL CONFLICTED...
OH!
KODAKA-SEMPAI...
SINCE YOU CAME ALL THIS WAY TO CHECK ON RIKA, COULD YOU READ TO HER UNTIL SHE FALLS ASLEEP?
HUH?
WELL, SHE IS SICK, AFTER ALL.
SURE, I GUESS. WHAT DO YOU WANT ME TO READ?
JUST A MOMENT...
RUSTLE
TA-DAAA!
THIS WOULD BE PERFECT!
UH
EAT: THE BIOLOGY TEACHER'S MERCY AFTER SCHOOL!
THAT'S A BOYS' LOVE NOVEL!!!

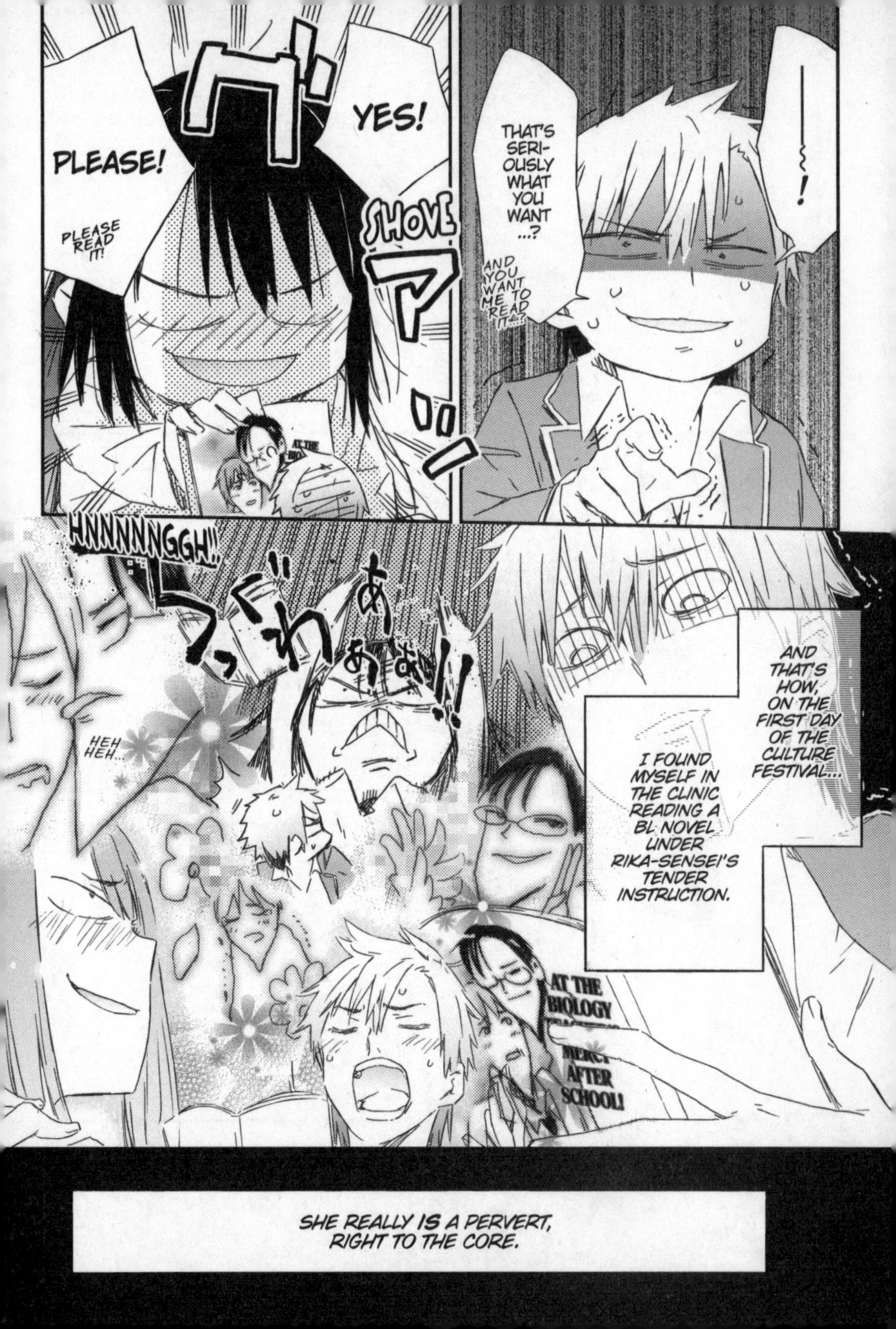—!
THAT'S SERI-OUSLY WHAT YOU WANT ...?
AND YOU WANT ME TO READ IT...?
YES!
PLEASE!
PLEASE READ IT!
SHOVE
AND THAT'S HOW, ON THE FIRST DAY OF THE CULTURE FESTIVAL...
I FOUND MYSELF IN THE CLINIC READING A BL NOVEL UNDER RIKA-SENSEI'S TENDER INSTRUCTION.
HNNNNNGGH!!
HEH HEH...
AT THE BIOLOGY
MERCY AFTER SCHOOL!
SHE REALLY IS A PERVERT, RIGHT TO THE CORE.

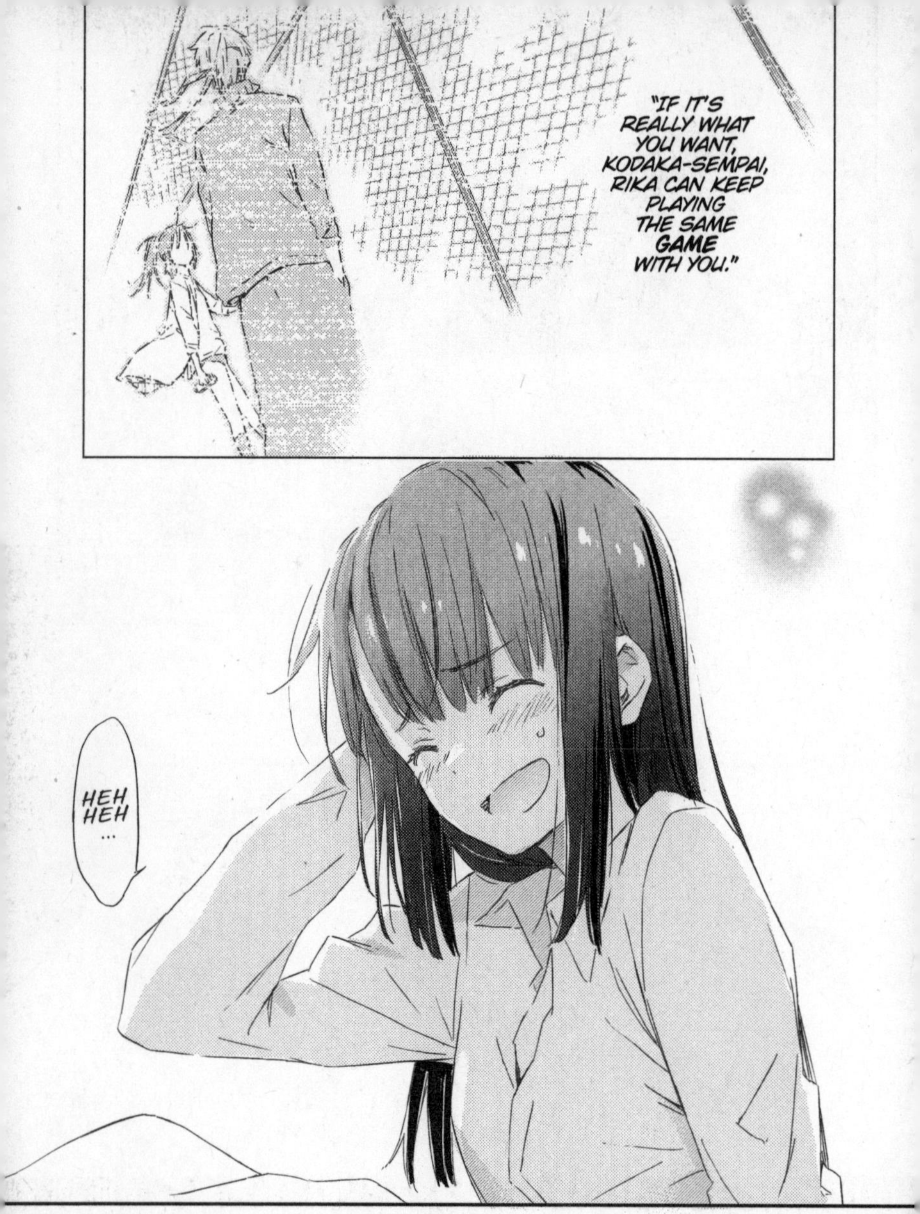
"IF IT'S REALLY WHAT YOU WANT, KODAKA-SEMPAI, RIKA CAN KEEP PLAYING THE SAME GAME WITH YOU."
HEH HEH ...

BUT SHE'S ALSO INCREDIBLY CONSIDERATE.

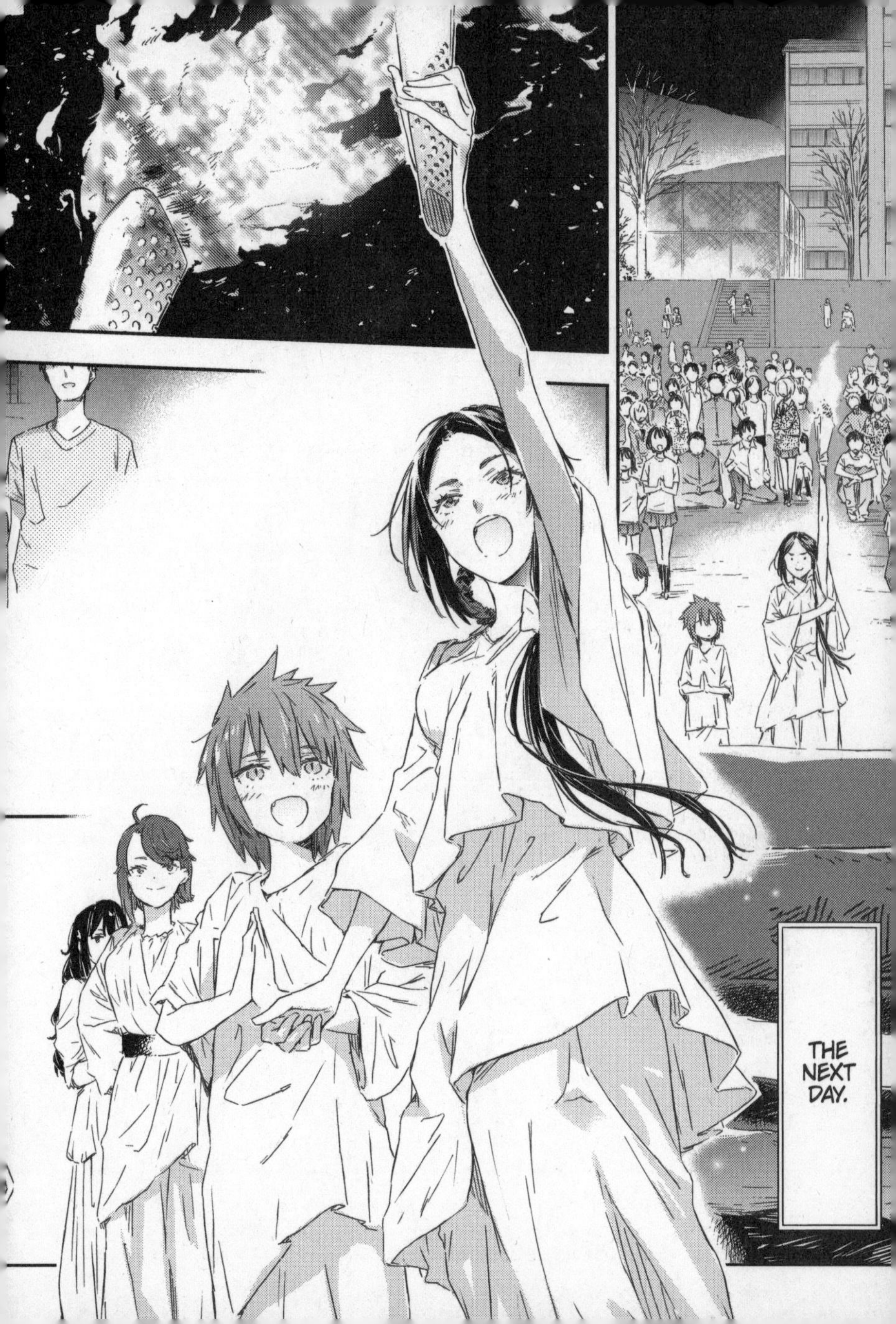
THE NEXT DAY.

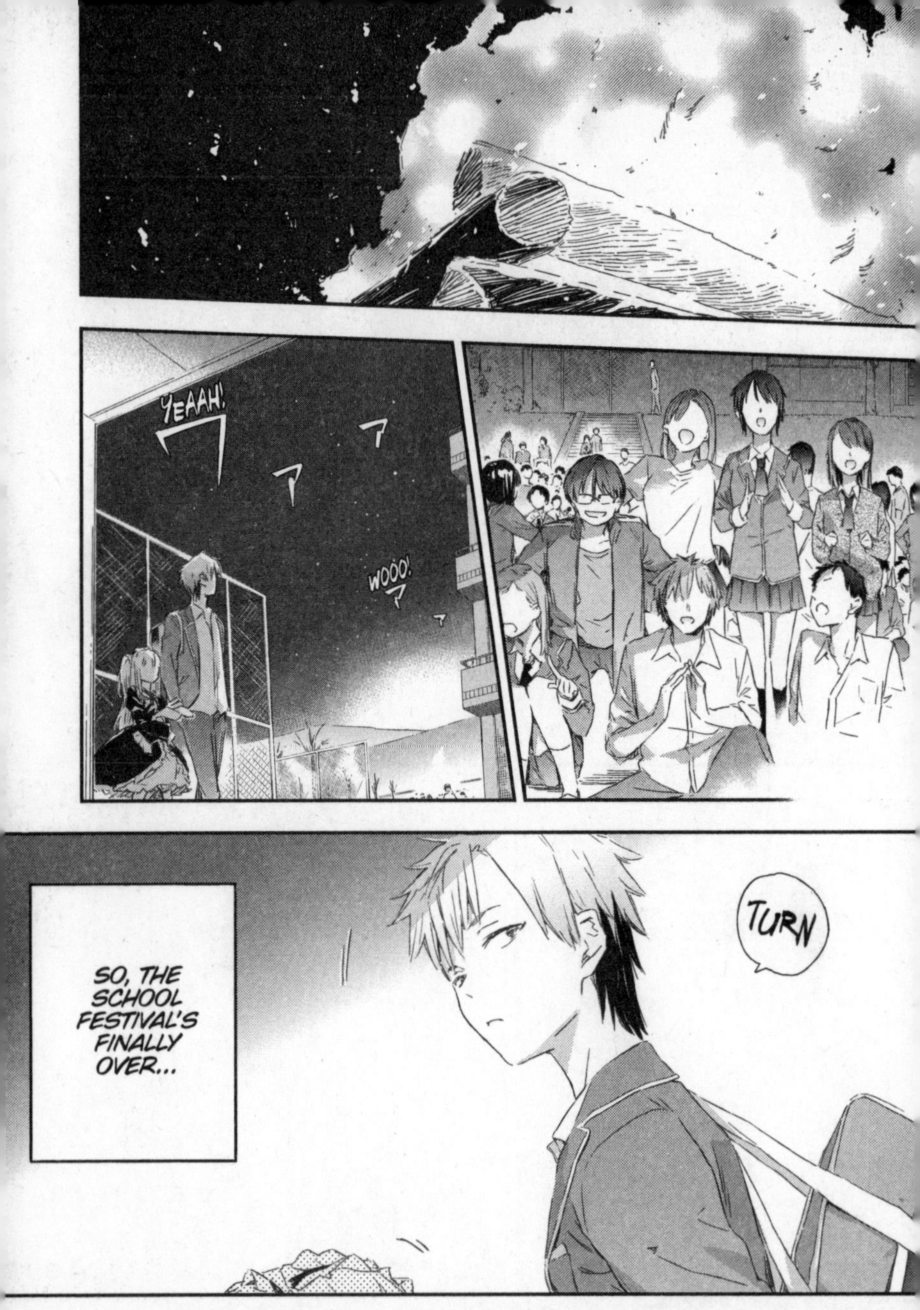
YEAAH!
WOOO!
TURN
SO, THE SCHOOL FESTIVAL'S FINALLY OVER...

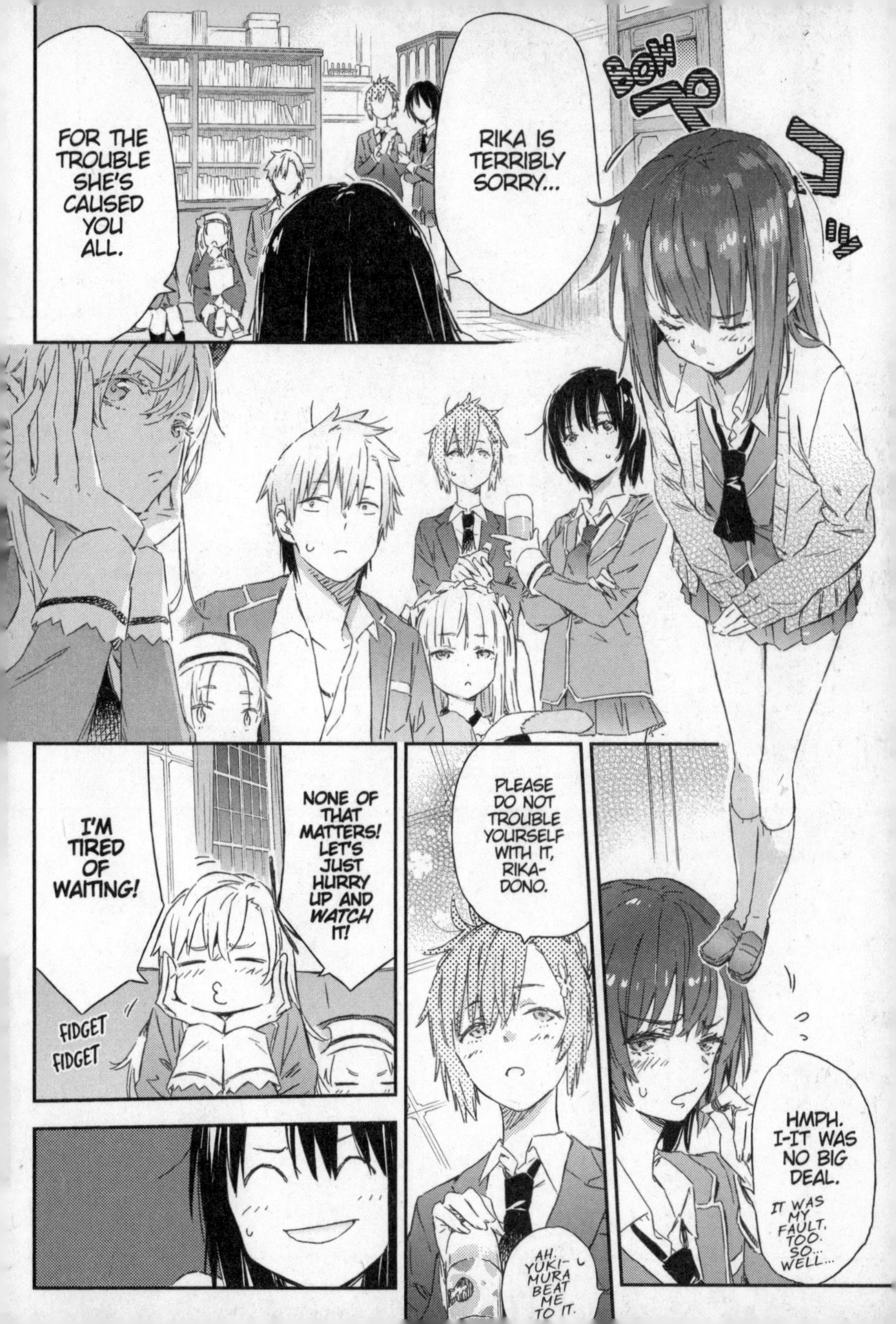
BOW
RIKA IS TERRIBLY SORRY...
FOR THE TROUBLE SHE'S CAUSED YOU ALL.
PLEASE DO NOT TROUBLE YOURSELF WITH IT, RIKA-DONO.
NONE OF THAT MATTERS! LET'S JUST HURRY UP AND WATCH IT!
I'M TIRED OF WAITING!
FIDGET FIDGET
HMPH. I-IT WAS NO BIG DEAL.
IT WAS MY FAULT, TOO. SO... WELL...
AH. YUKIMURA BEAT ME TO IT.

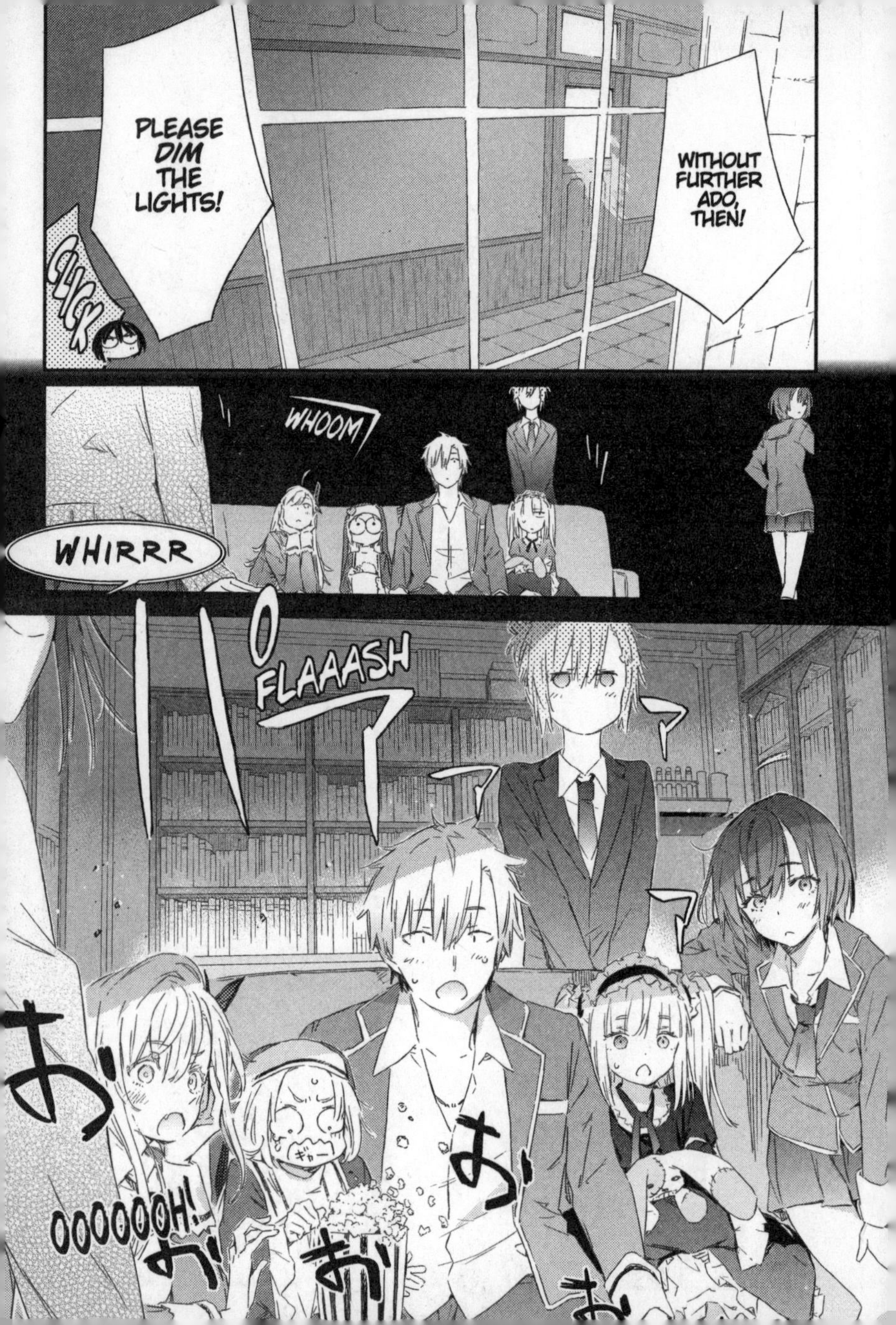
WITHOUT FURTHER ADO, THEN!
PLEASE DIM THE LIGHTS!
CLICK
WHOOM
WHIRRR
FLAAASH
ギャー
OOOOOOH!

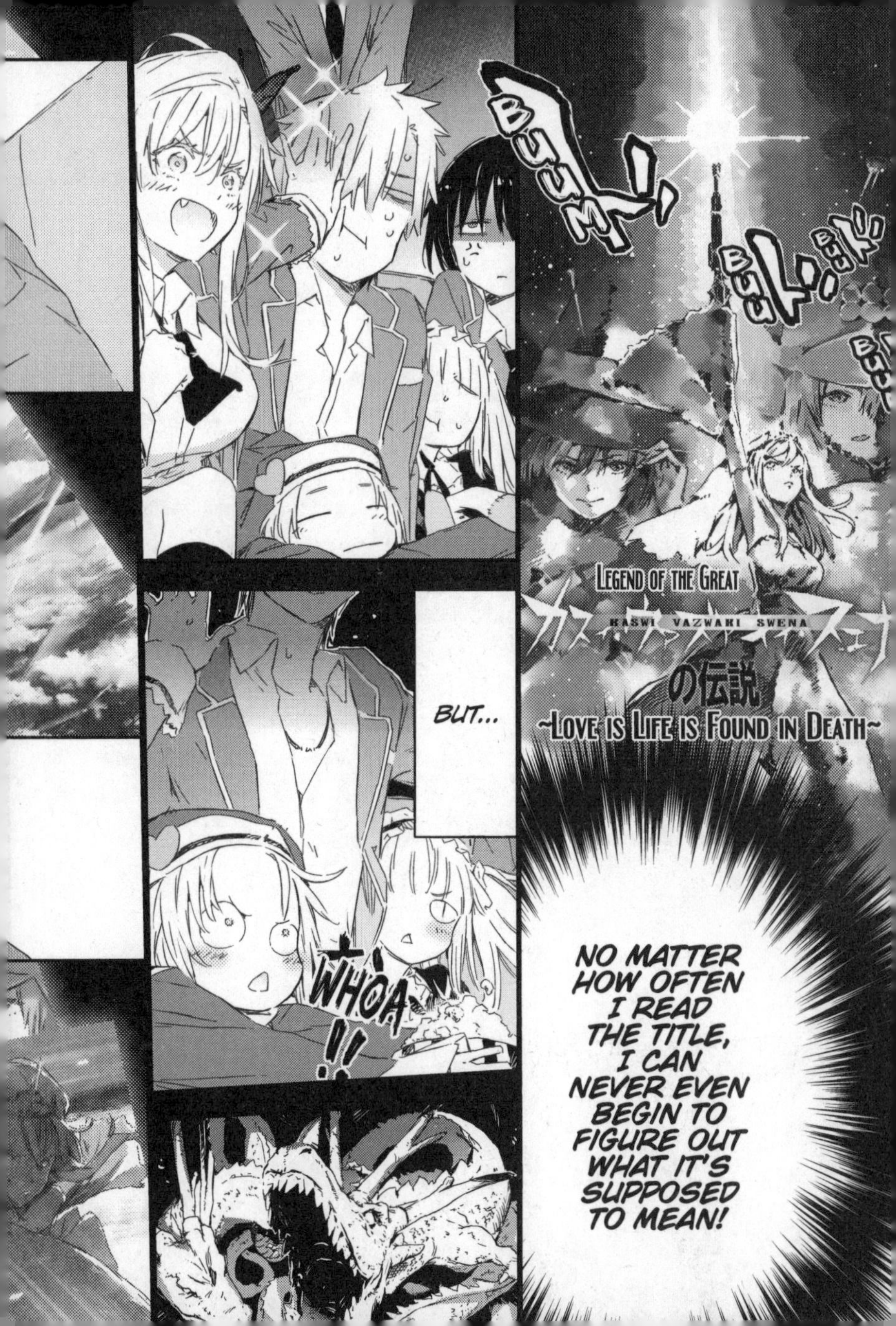
BUUUM
Buu
Buu
Buu
Legend of the Great
KASWI VAZWARI SWENA
の伝説
~Love is Life is Found in Death~
NO MATTER HOW OFTEN I READ THE TITLE, I CAN NEVER EVEN BEGIN TO FIGURE OUT WHAT IT'S SUPPOSED TO MEAN!
BUT...
WHOA!!

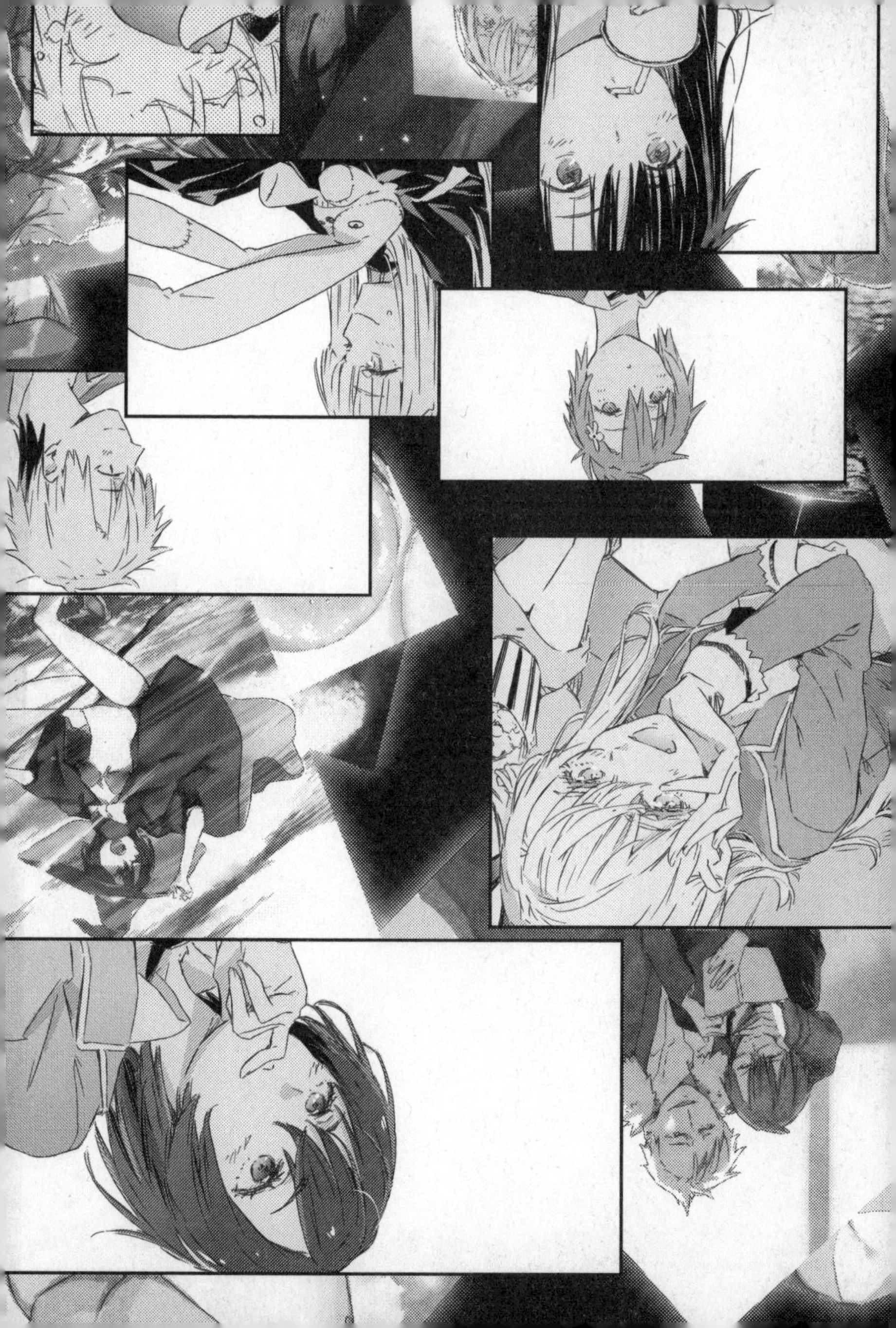

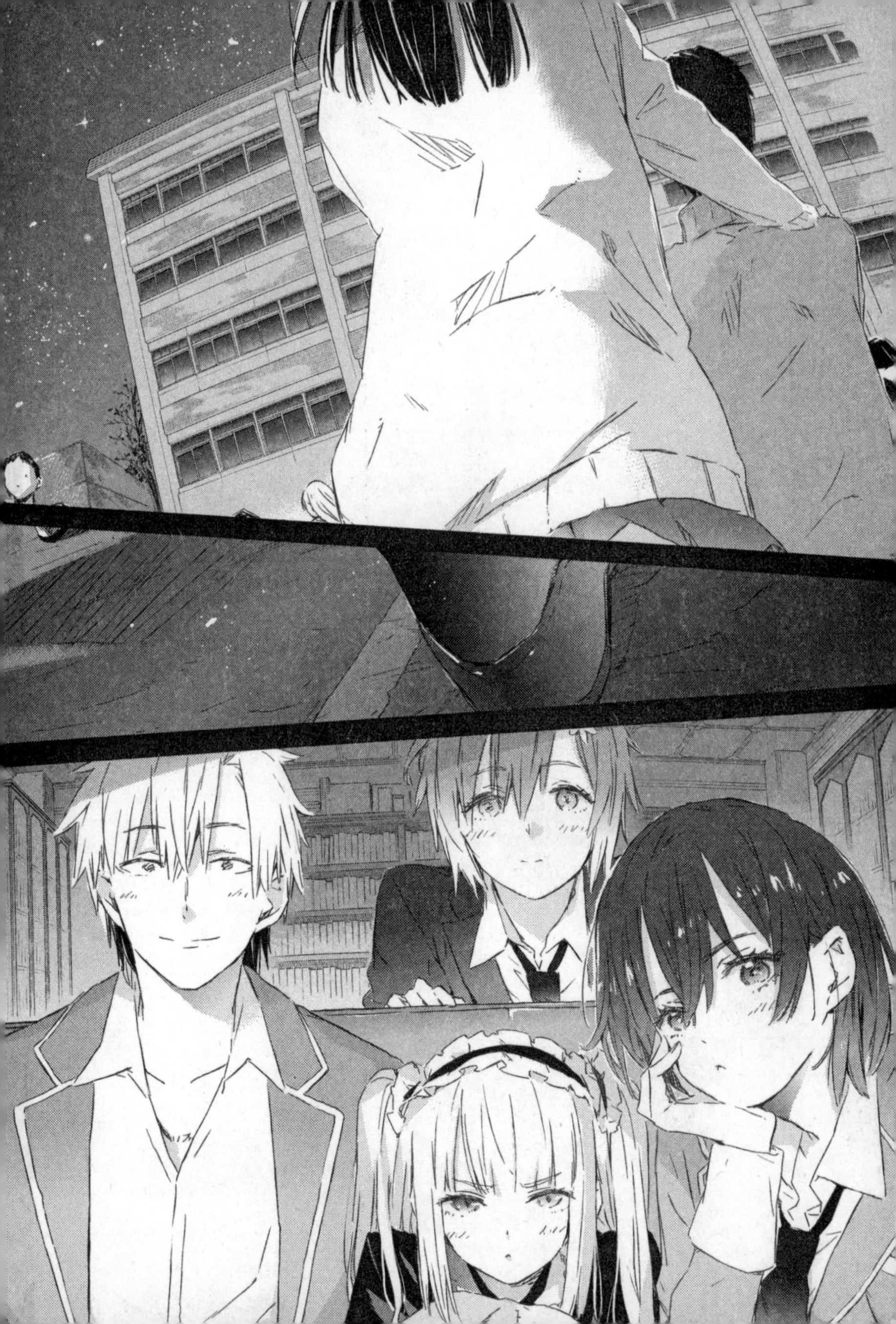

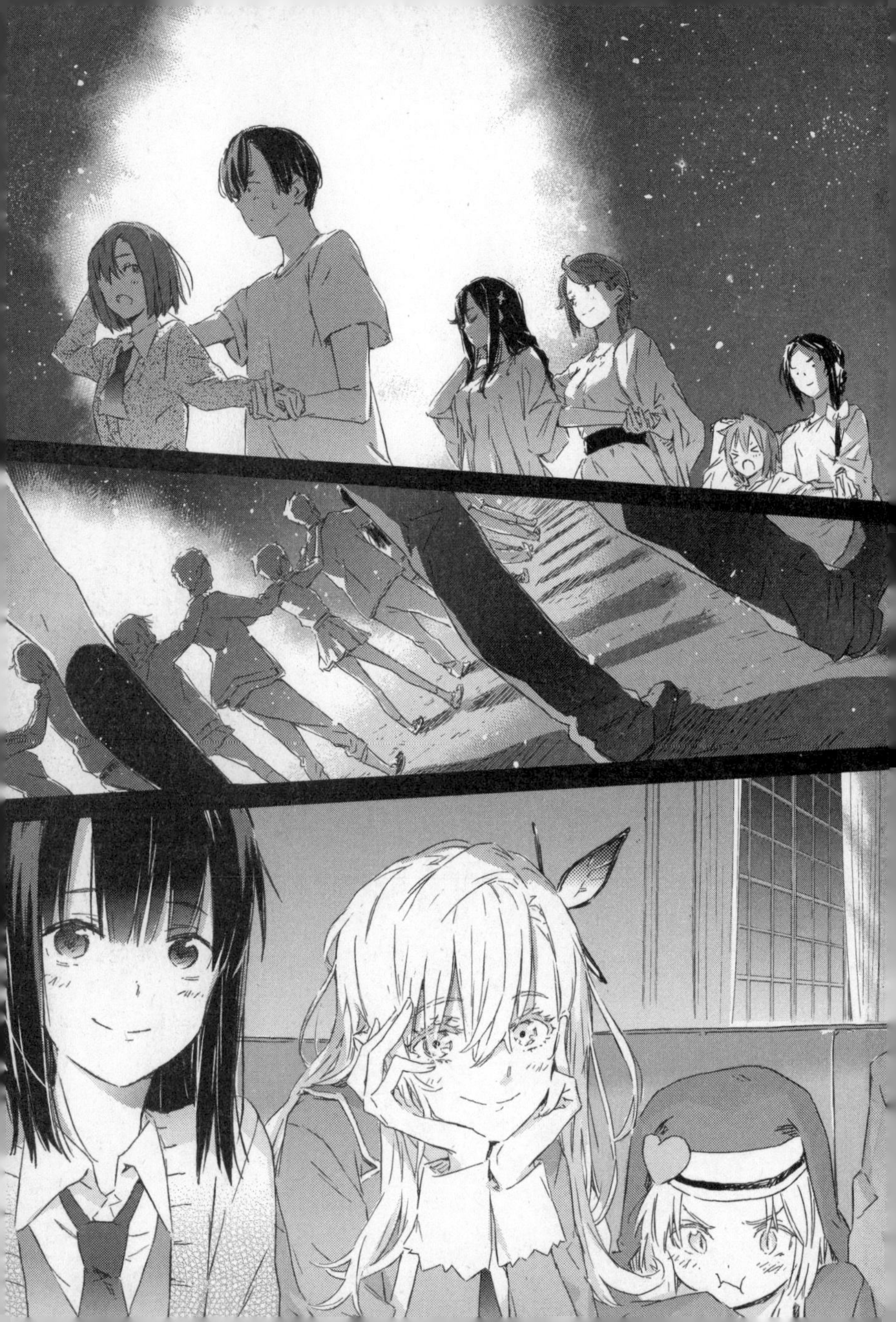

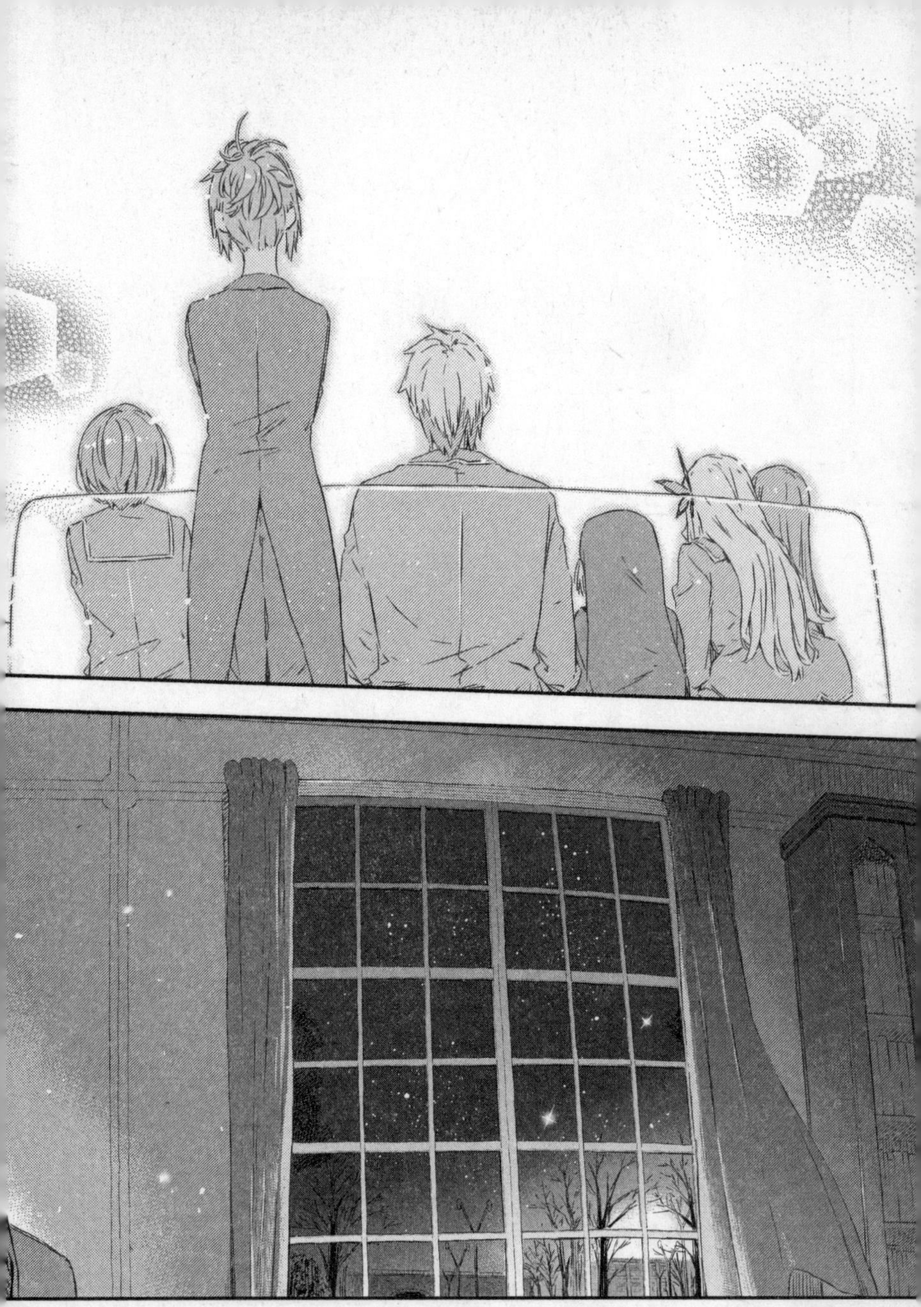

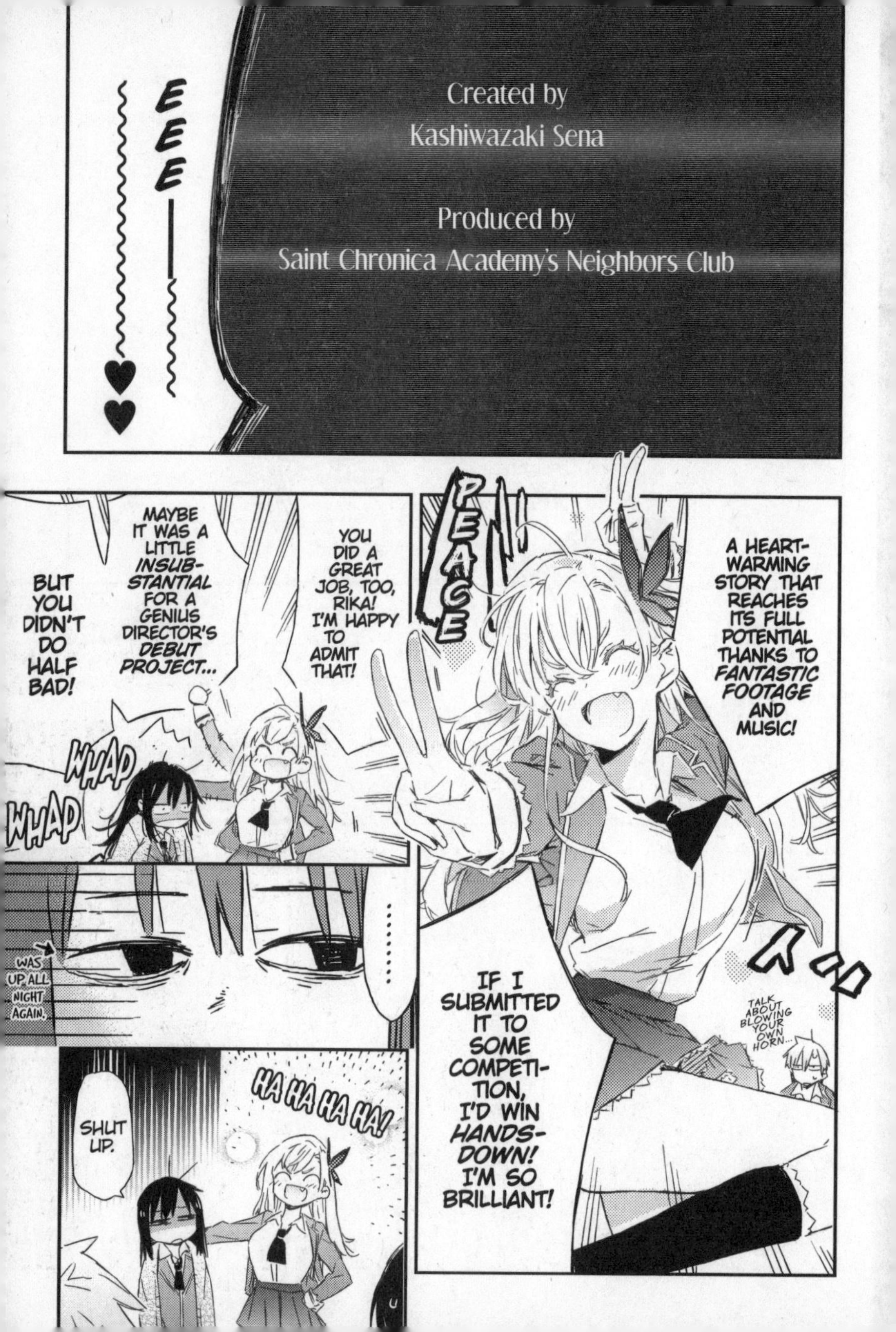
EEE—
Created by
Kashiwazaki Sena
Produced by
Saint Chronica Academy's Neighbors Club
PEACE
A HEART-WARMING STORY THAT REACHES ITS FULL POTENTIAL THANKS TO FANTASTIC FOOTAGE AND MUSIC!
IF I SUBMITTED IT TO SOME COMPETITION, I'D WIN HANDS-DOWN! I'M SO BRILLIANT!
TALK ABOUT BLOWING YOUR OWN HORN...
YOU DID A GREAT JOB, TOO, RIKA! I'M HAPPY TO ADMIT THAT!
MAYBE IT WAS A LITTLE INSUBSTANTIAL FOR A GENIUS DIRECTOR'S DEBUT PROJECT...
BUT YOU DIDN'T DO HALF BAD!
WHAP
WHAP
......
WAS UP ALL NIGHT AGAIN.
HA HA HA HA!
SHUT UP.

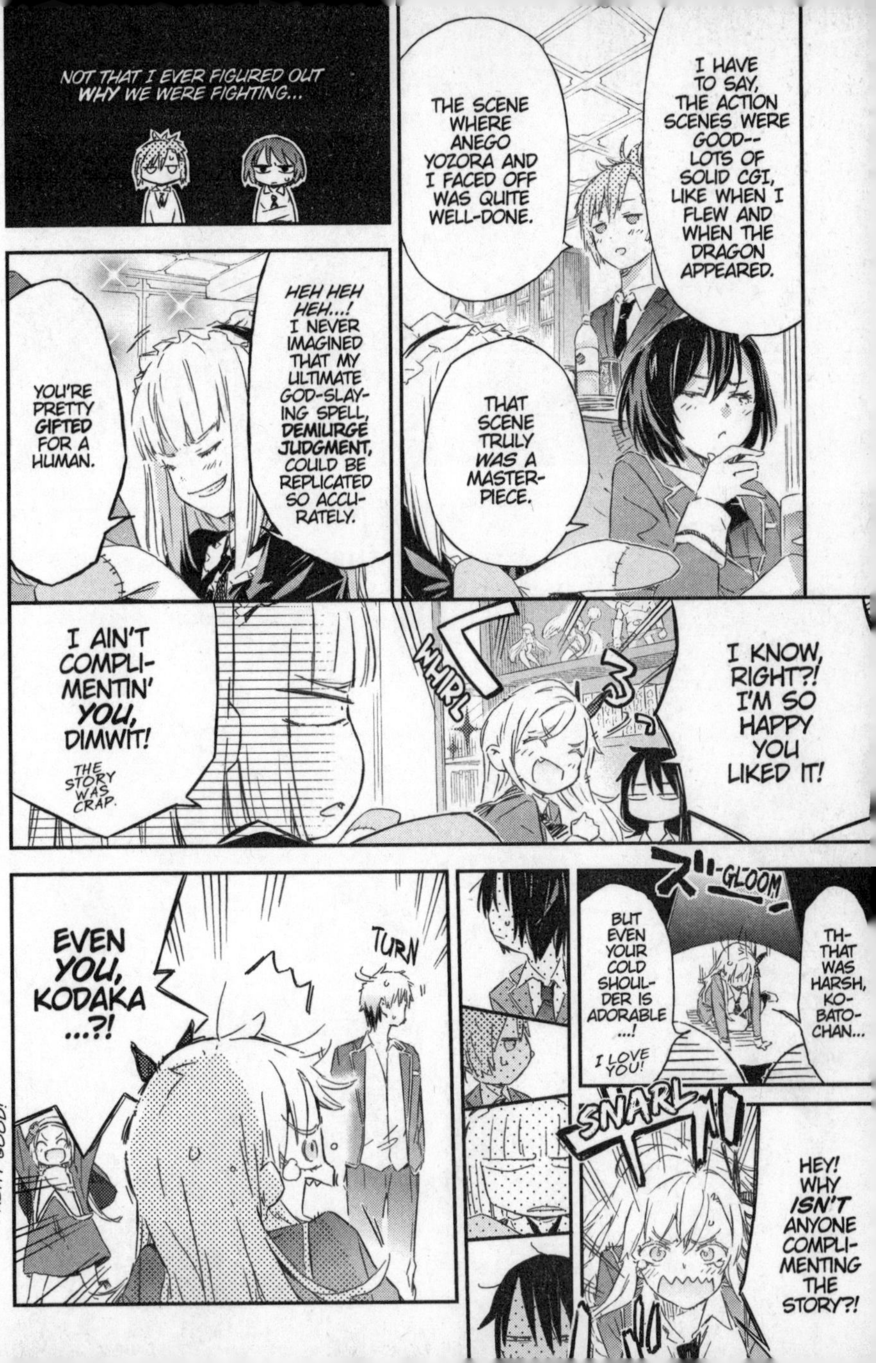
I HAVE TO SAY, THE ACTION SCENES WERE GOOD--LOTS OF SOLID CGI, LIKE WHEN I FLEW AND WHEN THE DRAGON APPEARED.
THE SCENE WHERE ANEGO YOZORA AND I FACED OFF WAS QUITE WELL-DONE.
NOT THAT I EVER FIGURED OUT WHY WE WERE FIGHTING...
THAT SCENE TRULY WAS A MASTERPIECE.
HEH HEH HEH...! I NEVER IMAGINED THAT MY ULTIMATE GOD-SLAYING SPELL, DEMIURGE JUDGMENT, COULD BE REPLICATED SO ACCURATELY.
YOU'RE PRETTY GIFTED FOR A HUMAN.
I KNOW, RIGHT?! I'M SO HAPPY YOU LIKED IT!
WHIRL
I AIN'T COMPLIMENTIN' YOU, DIMWIT!
THE STORY WAS CRAP.
TH-THAT WAS HARSH, KOBATO-CHAN...
GLOOM
BUT EVEN YOUR COLD SHOULDER IS ADORABLE...!
I LOVE YOU!
HEY! WHY ISN'T ANYONE COMPLIMENTING THE STORY?!
SNARL
TURN
EVEN YOU, KODAKA...?!
I THOUGHT IT WAS PRETTY GOOD!

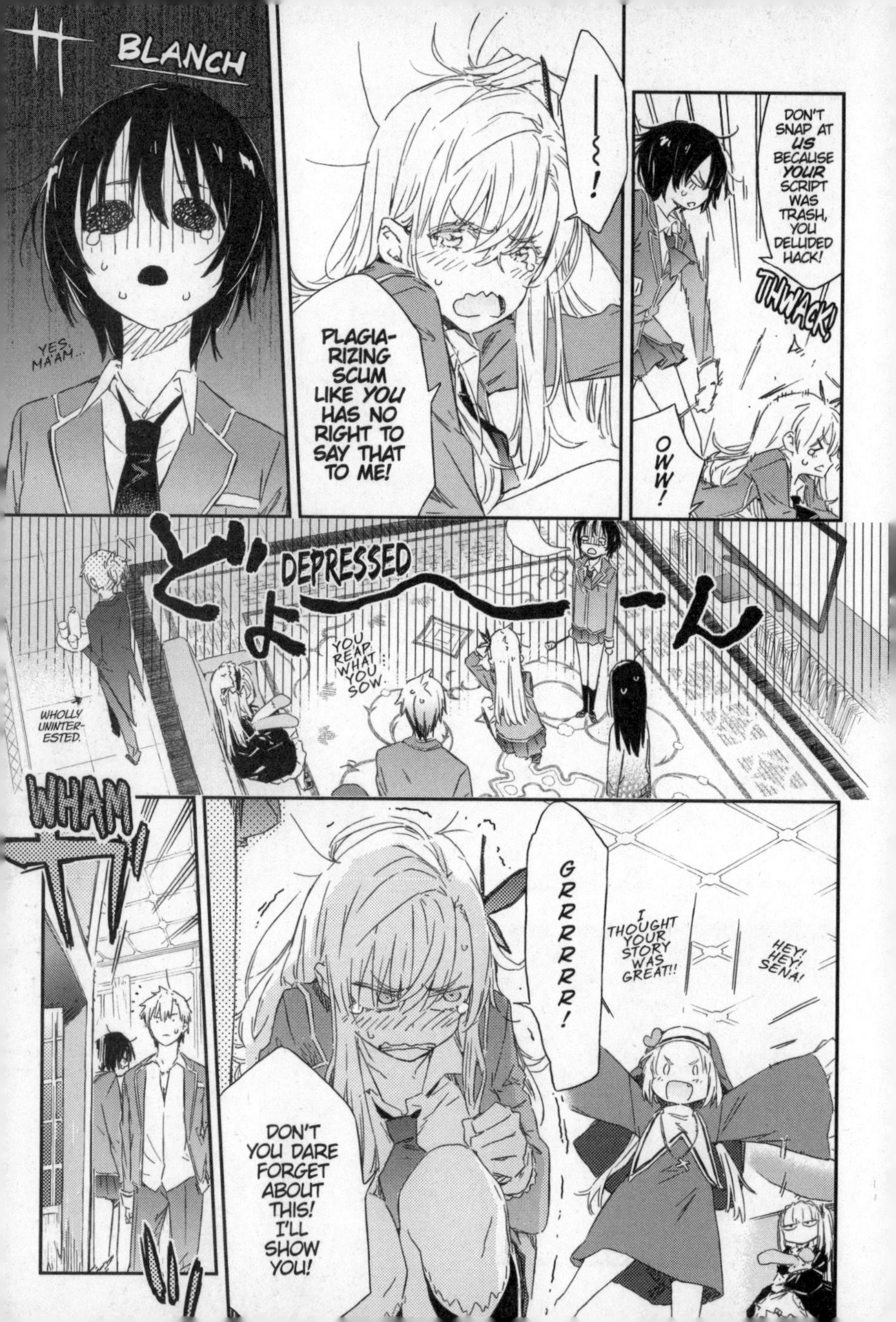
DON'T SNAP AT US BECAUSE YOUR SCRIPT WAS TRASH, YOU DELUDED HACK!
THWACK!
OWW!
~!
PLAGIA-RIZING SCUM LIKE YOU HAS NO RIGHT TO SAY THAT TO ME!
BLANCH
YES, MA'AM...
どよ〜〜ん
DEPRESSED
YOU REAP WHAT YOU SOW.
WHOLLY UNINTER-ESTED.
HEY! HEY! SENA!
I THOUGHT YOUR STORY WAS GREAT!!
GRRRRRR!
DON'T YOU DARE FORGET ABOUT THIS! I'LL SHOW YOU!
WHAM

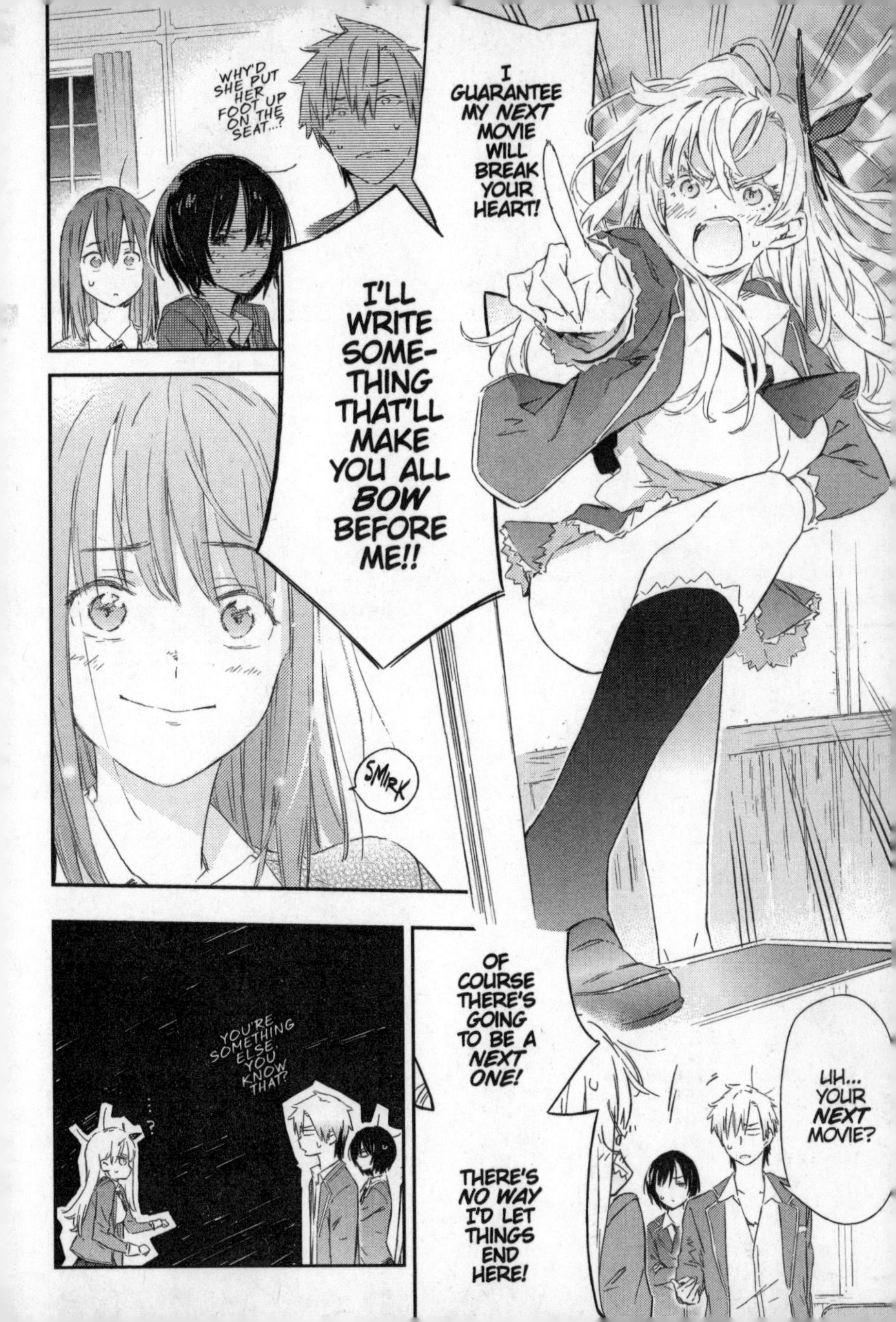
I GUARANTEE MY NEXT MOVIE WILL BREAK YOUR HEART!
I'LL WRITE SOME-THING THAT'LL MAKE YOU ALL BOW BEFORE ME!!
WHY'D SHE PUT HER FOOT UP ON THE SEAT...?
SMIRK
UH... YOUR NEXT MOVIE?
OF COURSE THERE'S GOING TO BE A NEXT ONE!
THERE'S NO WAY I'D LET THINGS END HERE!
YOU'RE SOMETHING ELSE, YOU KNOW THAT?
...?

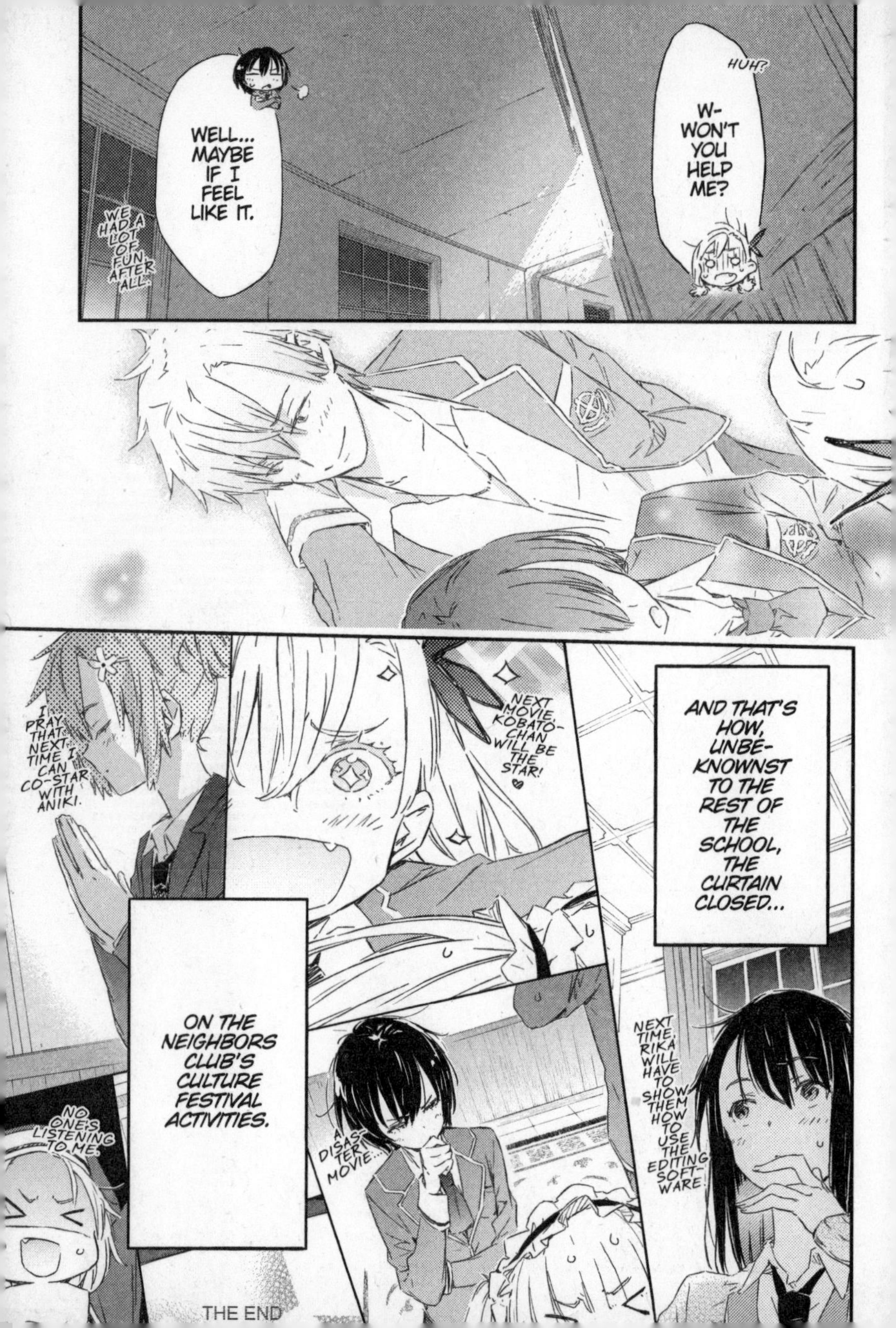
HUH?
W-WON'T YOU HELP ME?
WELL... MAYBE IF I FEEL LIKE IT.
WE HAD A LOT OF FUN AFTER ALL.
AND THAT'S HOW, UNBE-KNOWNST TO THE REST OF THE SCHOOL, THE CURTAIN CLOSED...
NEXT MOVIE, KOBATO-CHAN WILL BE THE STAR!
I PRAY THAT NEXT TIME I CAN CO-STAR WITH ANIKI.
NEXT TIME, RIKA WILL HAVE TO SHOW THEM HOW TO USE THE EDITING SOFT-WARE.
A DISAS-TER MOVIE...
ON THE NEIGHBORS CLUB'S CULTURE FESTIVAL ACTIVITIES.
NO ONE'S LISTENING TO ME.
THE END

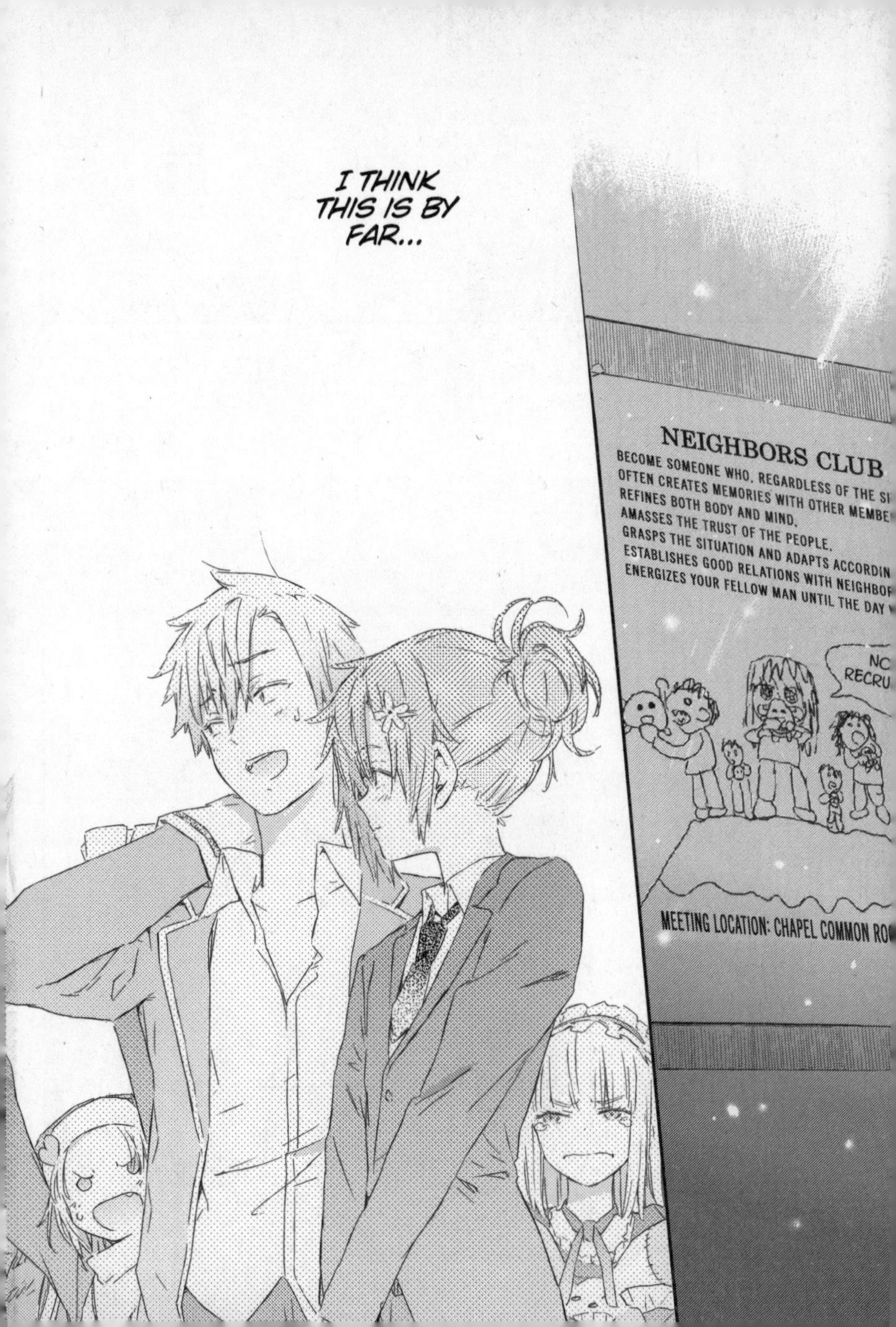
I THINK THIS IS BY FAR...
NEIGHBORS CLUB
BECOME SOMEONE WHO, REGARDLESS OF THE SI
OFTEN CREATES MEMORIES WITH OTHER MEMBE
REFINES BOTH BODY AND MIND,
AMASSES THE TRUST OF THE PEOPLE,
GRASPS THE SITUATION AND ADAPTS ACCORDIN
ESTABLISHES GOOD RELATIONS WITH NEIGHBOR
ENERGIZES YOUR FELLOW MAN UNTIL THE DAY
NO RECRU
MEETING LOCATION: CHAPEL COMMON RO

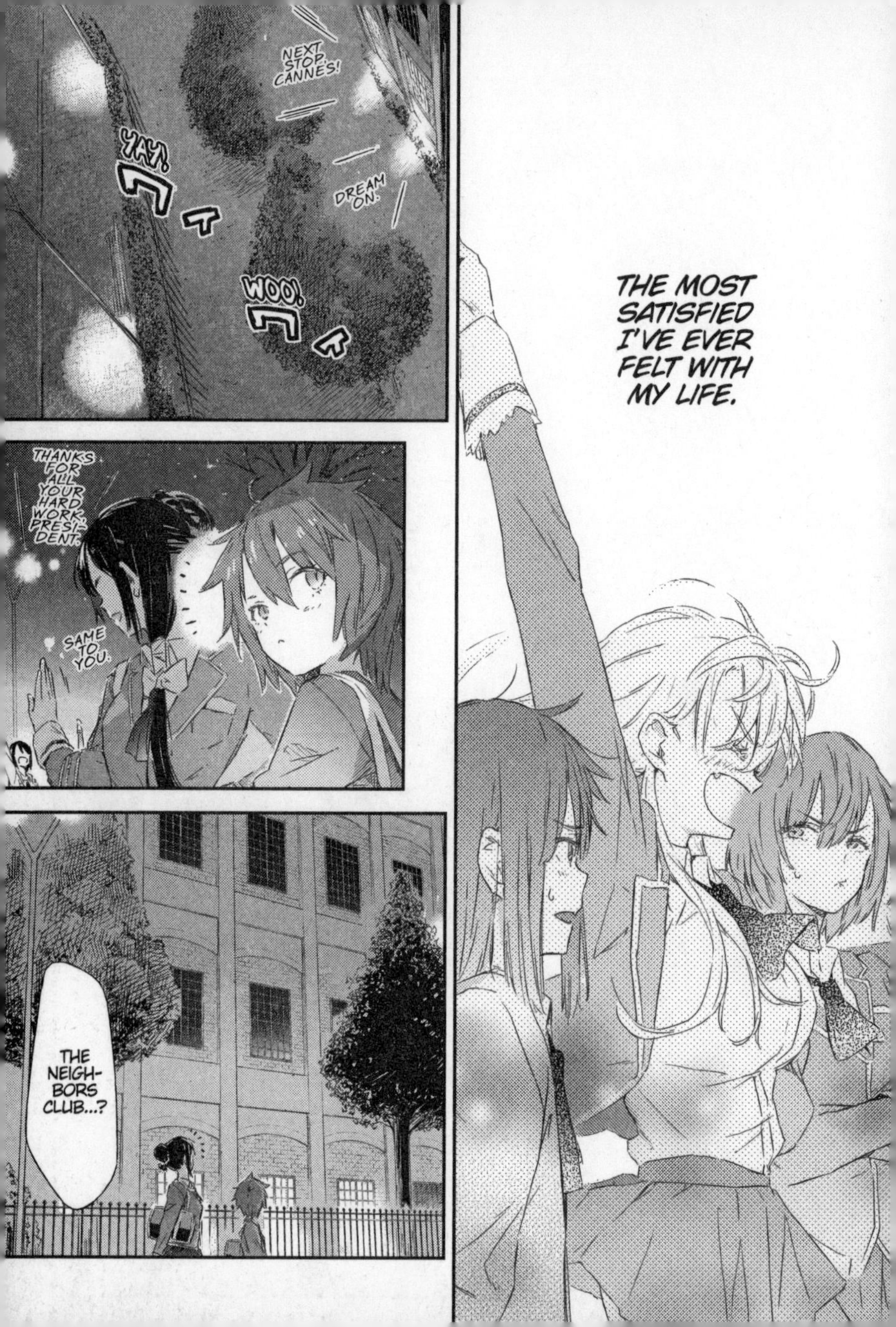
THE MOST SATISFIED I'VE EVER FELT WITH MY LIFE.
NEXT STOP, CANNES!
YAY! ♪
DREAM ON.
WOO! ♪
THANKS FOR ALL YOUR HARD WORK, PRESIDENT.
SAME TO YOU.
THE NEIGHBORS CLUB...?

BL

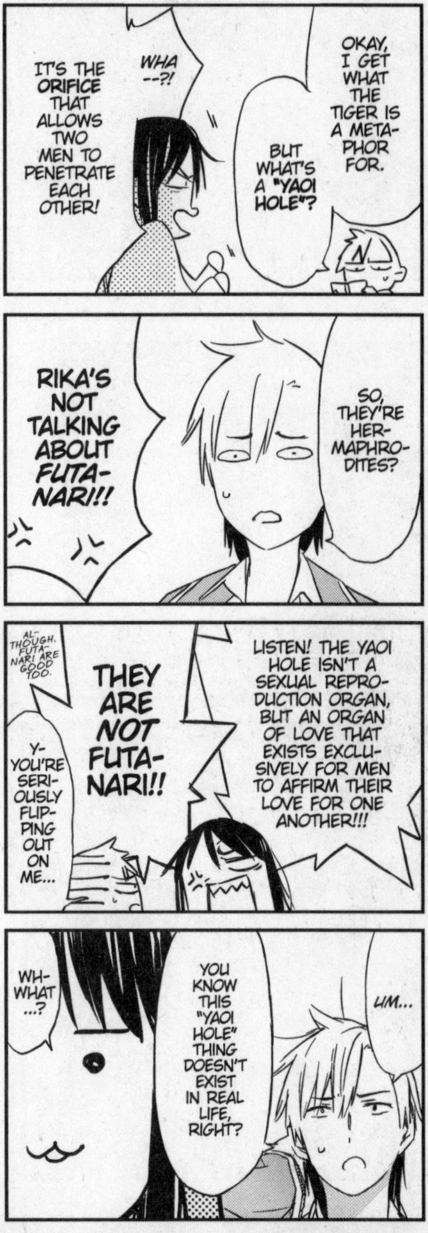
OKAY, I GET WHAT THE TIGER IS A METAPHOR FOR.
BUT WHAT'S A "YAOI HOLE"?
WHA--?!
IT'S THE ORIFICE THAT ALLOWS TWO MEN TO PENETRATE EACH OTHER!
SO, THEY'RE HERMAPHRODITES?
RIKA'S NOT TALKING ABOUT FUTANARI!!
LISTEN! THE YAOI HOLE ISN'T A SEXUAL REPRODUCTION ORGAN, BUT AN ORGAN OF LOVE THAT EXISTS EXCLUSIVELY FOR MEN TO AFFIRM THEIR LOVE FOR ONE ANOTHER!!!
THEY ARE NOT FUTANARI!!
ALTHOUGH, FUTANARI ARE GOOD TOO.
Y-YOU'RE SERIOUSLY FLIPPING OUT ON ME...
UM...
YOU KNOW THIS "YAOI HOLE" THING DOESN'T EXIST IN REAL LIFE, RIGHT?
WH-WHAT...?

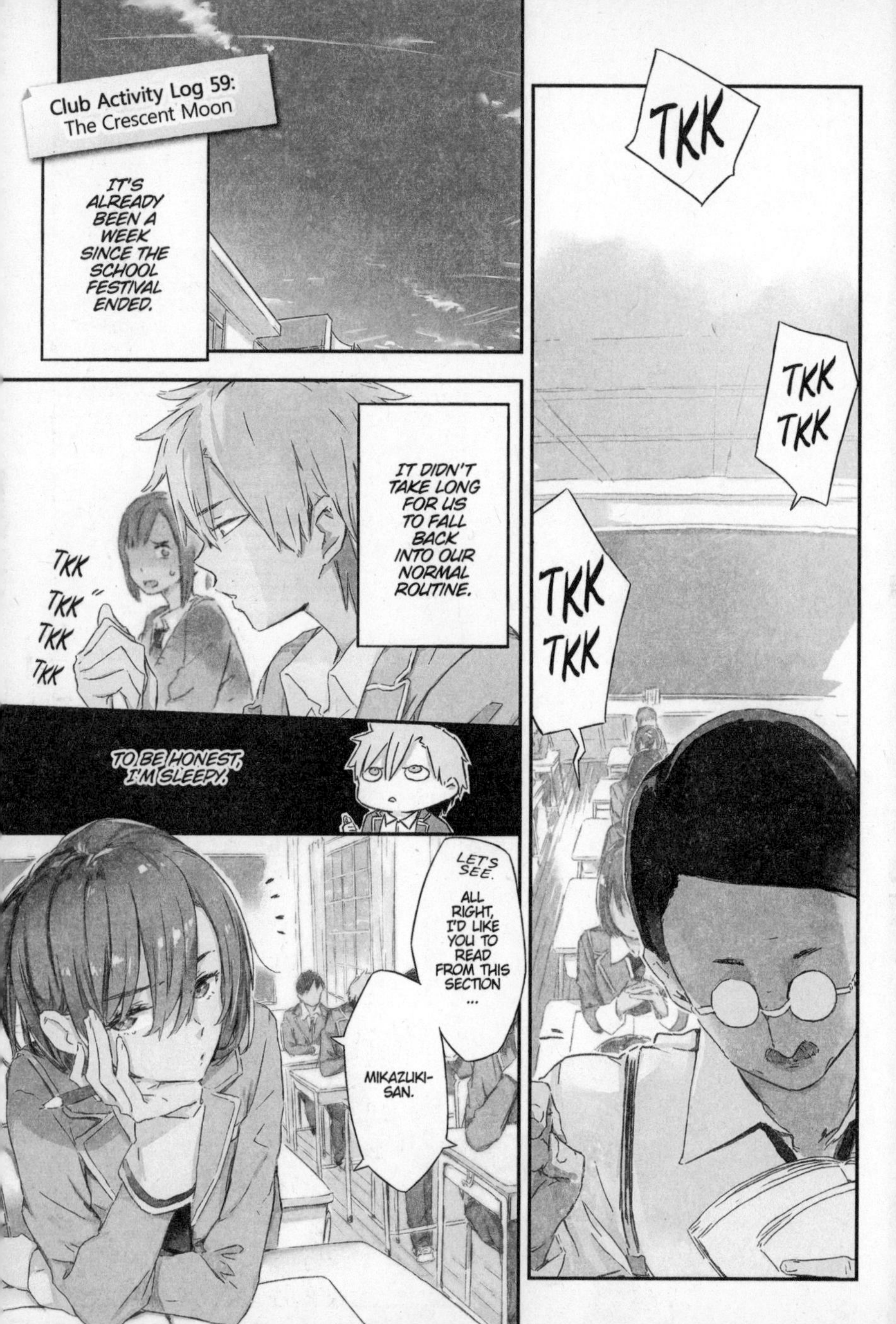
TKK
TKK TKK
TKK TKK
Club Activity Log 59: The Crescent Moon
IT'S ALREADY BEEN A WEEK SINCE THE SCHOOL FESTIVAL ENDED.
IT DIDN'T TAKE LONG FOR US TO FALL BACK INTO OUR NORMAL ROUTINE.
TKK TKK TKK TKK
TO BE HONEST, I'M SLEEPY.
LET'S SEE.
ALL RIGHT, I'D LIKE YOU TO READ FROM THIS SECTION ...
MIKAZUKI-SAN.

Haganai

I don't have many friends

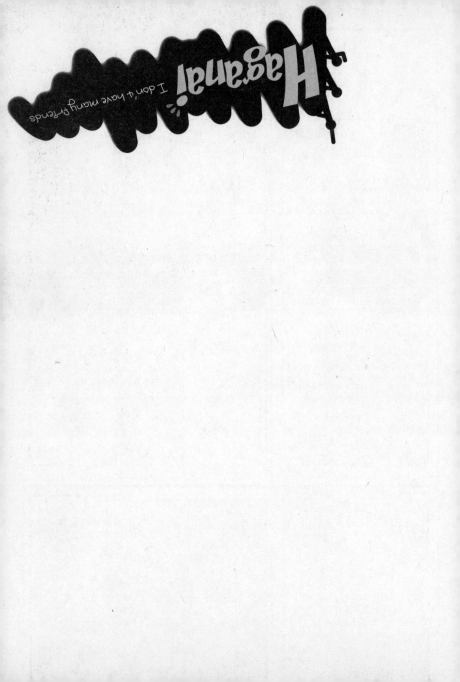

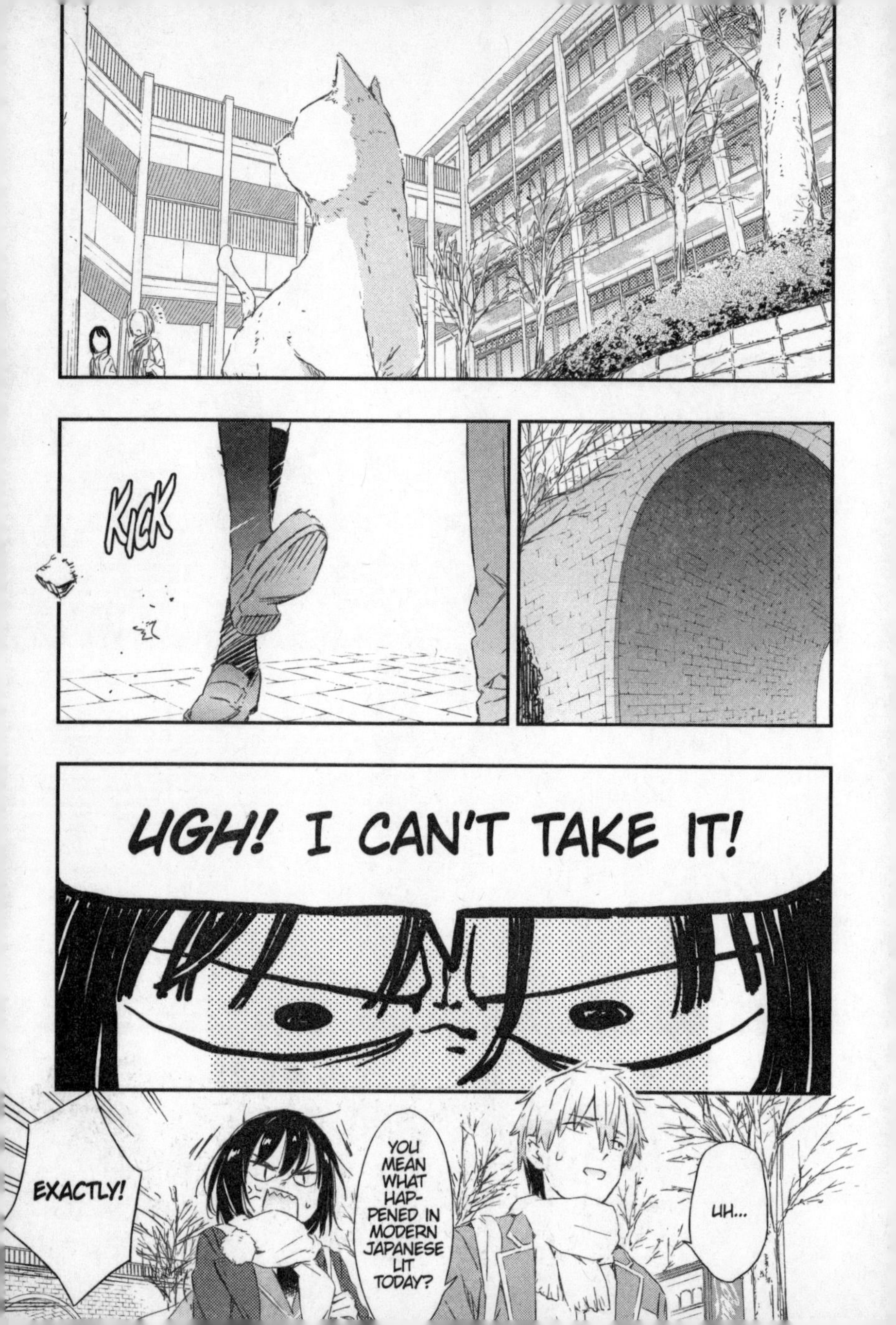
KICK
UGH! I CAN'T TAKE IT!
UH...
YOU MEAN WHAT HAP-PENED IN MODERN JAPANESE LIT TODAY?
EXACTLY!

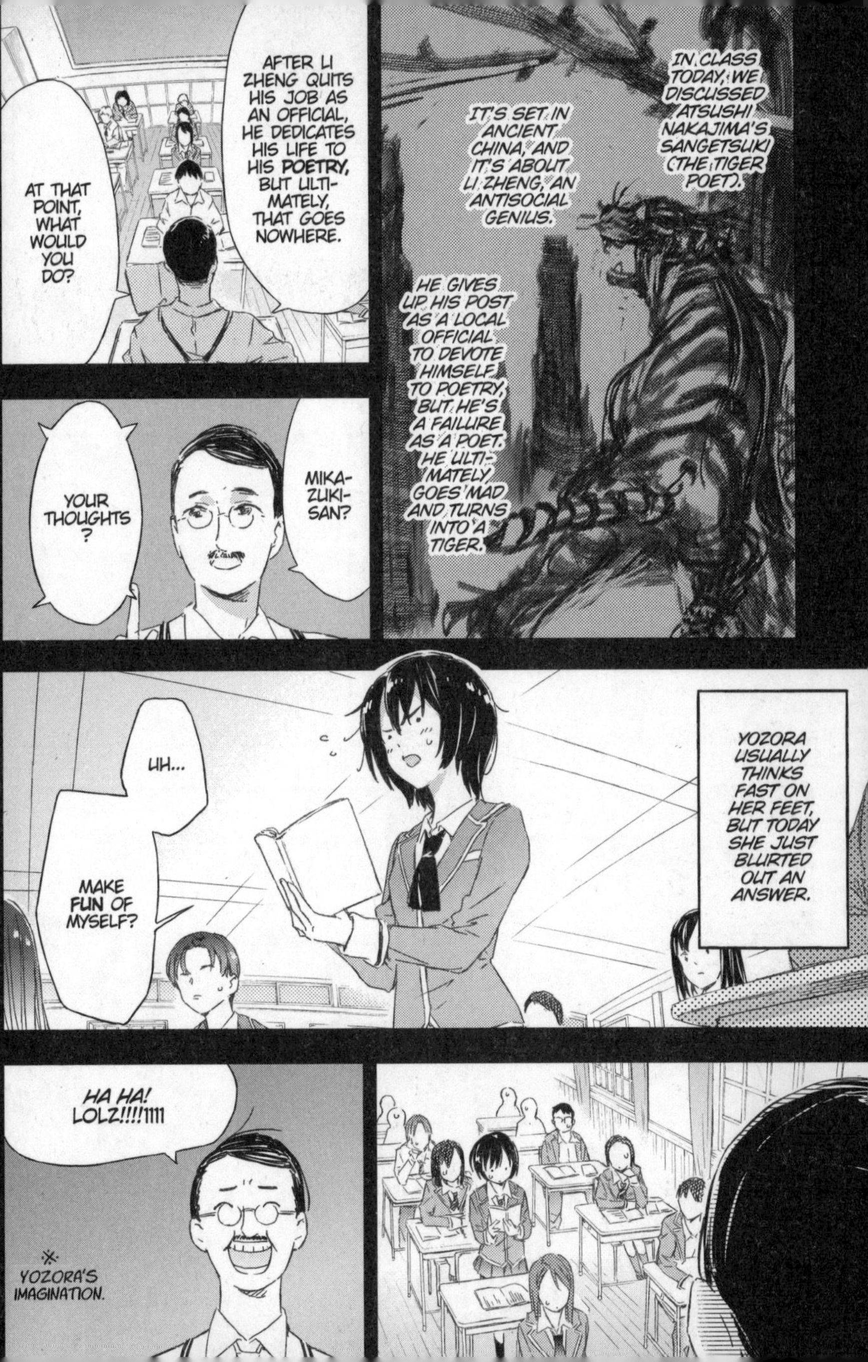
IN CLASS TODAY, WE DISCUSSED ATSUSHI NAKAJIMA'S SANGETSUKI (THE TIGER POET).
IT'S SET IN ANCIENT CHINA, AND IT'S ABOUT LI ZHENG, AN ANTISOCIAL GENIUS.
HE GIVES UP HIS POST AS A LOCAL OFFICIAL TO DEVOTE HIMSELF TO POETRY, BUT HE'S A FAILURE AS A POET. HE ULTI-MATELY GOES MAD AND TURNS INTO A TIGER.
AFTER LI ZHENG QUITS HIS JOB AS AN OFFICIAL, HE DEDICATES HIS LIFE TO HIS **POETRY**, BUT ULTI-MATELY, THAT GOES NOWHERE.
AT THAT POINT, WHAT WOULD YOU DO?
MIKA-ZUKI-SAN?
YOUR THOUGHTS ?
YOZORA USUALLY THINKS FAST ON HER FEET, BUT TODAY SHE JUST BLURTED OUT AN ANSWER.
UH...
MAKE **FUN** OF MYSELF?
HA HA! LOLZ!!!!1111
※ YOZORA'S IMAGINATION.

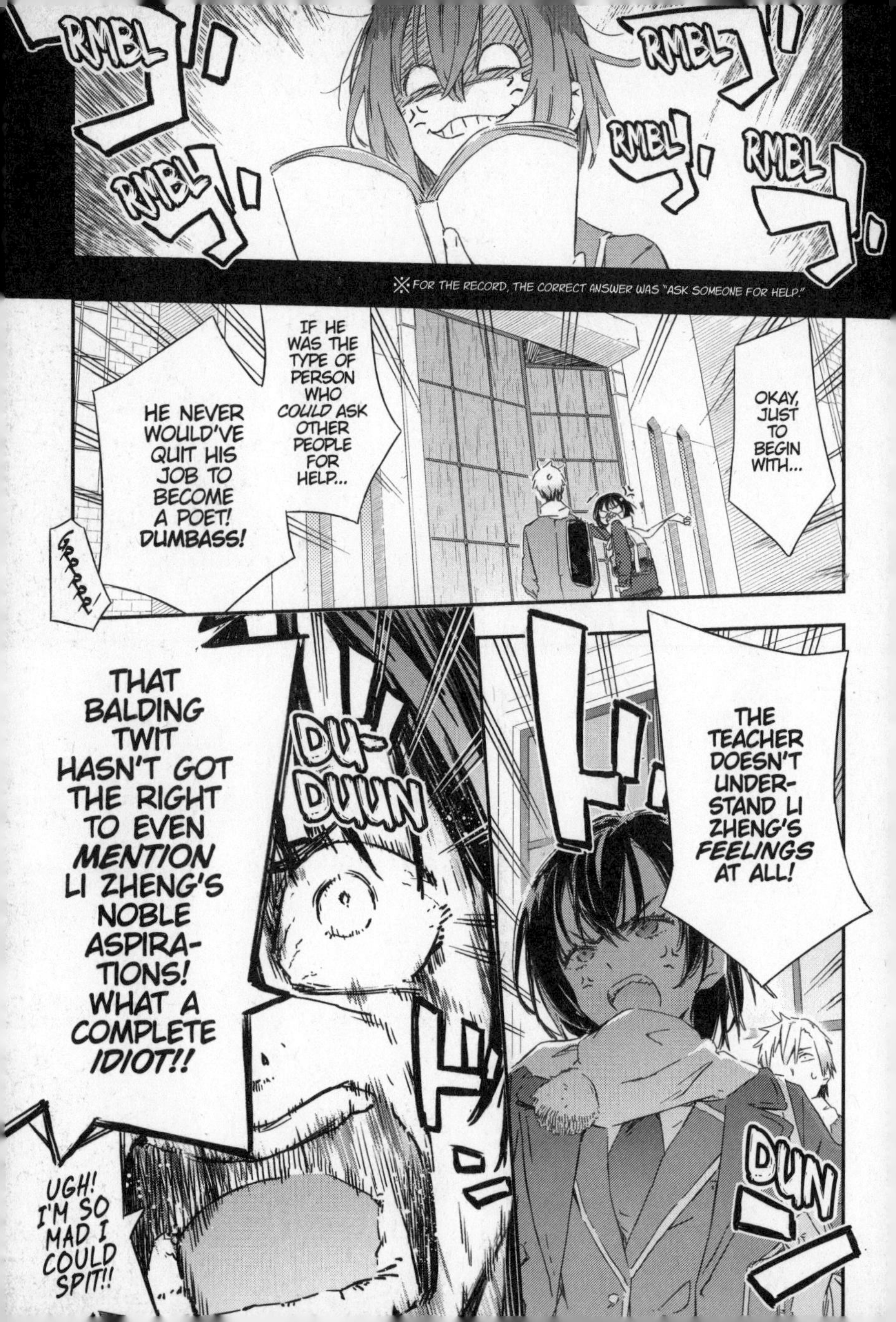
RMBL
RMBL
RMBL
RMBL
RMBL
※FOR THE RECORD, THE CORRECT ANSWER WAS "ASK SOMEONE FOR HELP."
OKAY, JUST TO BEGIN WITH...
IF HE WAS THE TYPE OF PERSON WHO *COULD* ASK OTHER PEOPLE FOR HELP...
HE NEVER WOULD'VE QUIT HIS JOB TO BECOME A POET! DUMBASS!
GRRRRR!
THE TEACHER DOESN'T UNDER-STAND LI ZHENG'S *FEELINGS* AT ALL!
DUN
DU-DUUN
THAT BALDING TWIT HASN'T GOT THE RIGHT TO EVEN *MENTION* LI ZHENG'S NOBLE ASPIRA-TIONS! WHAT A COMPLETE *IDIOT*!!
UGH! I'M SO MAD I COULD SPIT!!

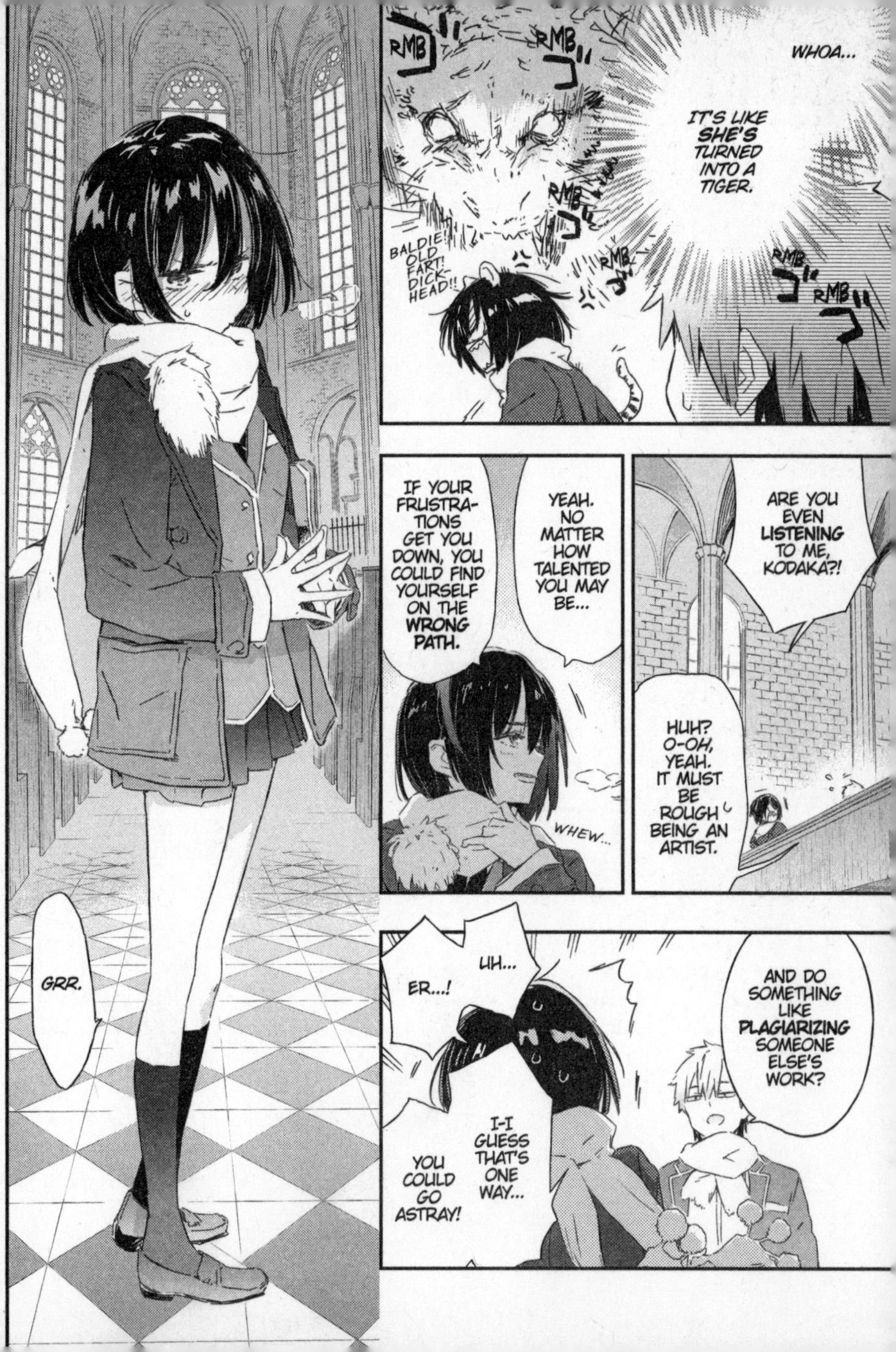
WHOA...
IT'S LIKE SHE'S TURNED INTO A TIGER.
RMB
RMB
RMB
RMB
RMB
RMB
BALDIE! OLD FART! DICK-HEAD!!
ARE YOU EVEN LISTENING TO ME, KODAKA?!
HUH? O-OH, YEAH. IT MUST BE ROUGH BEING AN ARTIST.
YEAH. NO MATTER HOW TALENTED YOU MAY BE...
IF YOUR FRUSTRATIONS GET YOU DOWN, YOU COULD FIND YOURSELF ON THE WRONG PATH.
WHEW...
AND DO SOMETHING LIKE PLAGIARIZING SOMEONE ELSE'S WORK?
UH...
ER...!
I-I GUESS THAT'S ONE WAY...
YOU COULD GO ASTRAY!
GRR.

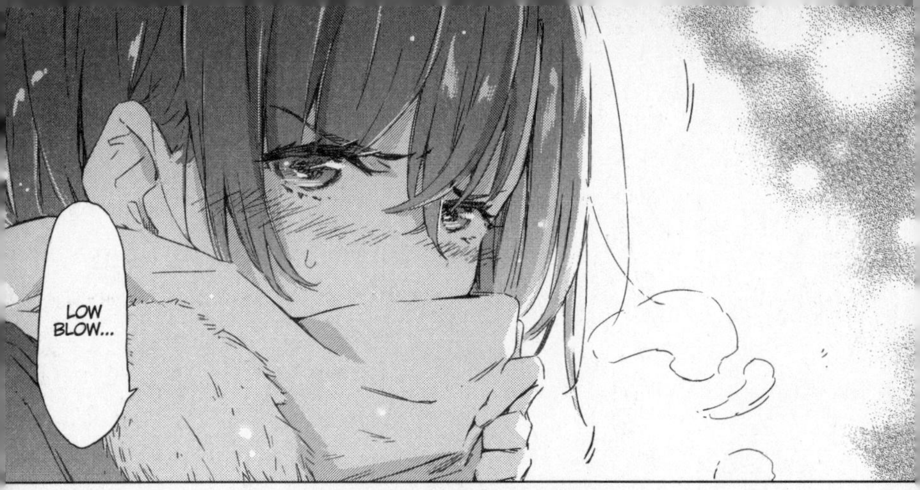
LOW BLOW...
ASKING PEOPLE FOR HELP IS WAY EASIER SAID THAN DONE.
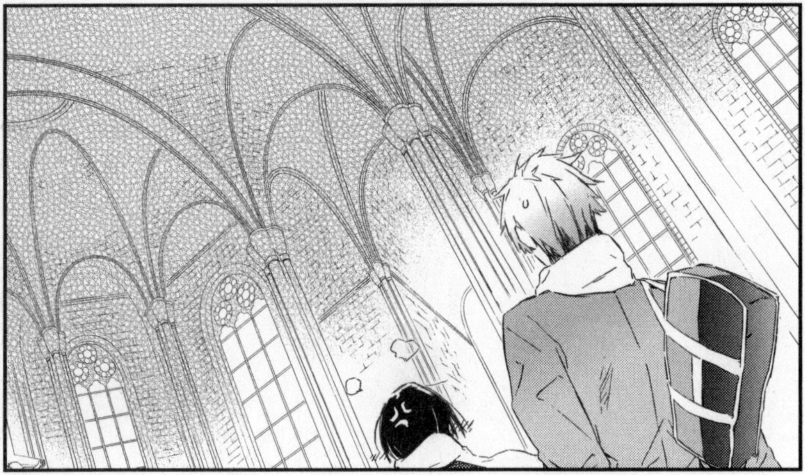
ANYWAY, THINGS WENT BACK TO NORMAL BRIEFLY...
BUT IT WAS ONLY A TEMPORARY LULL.

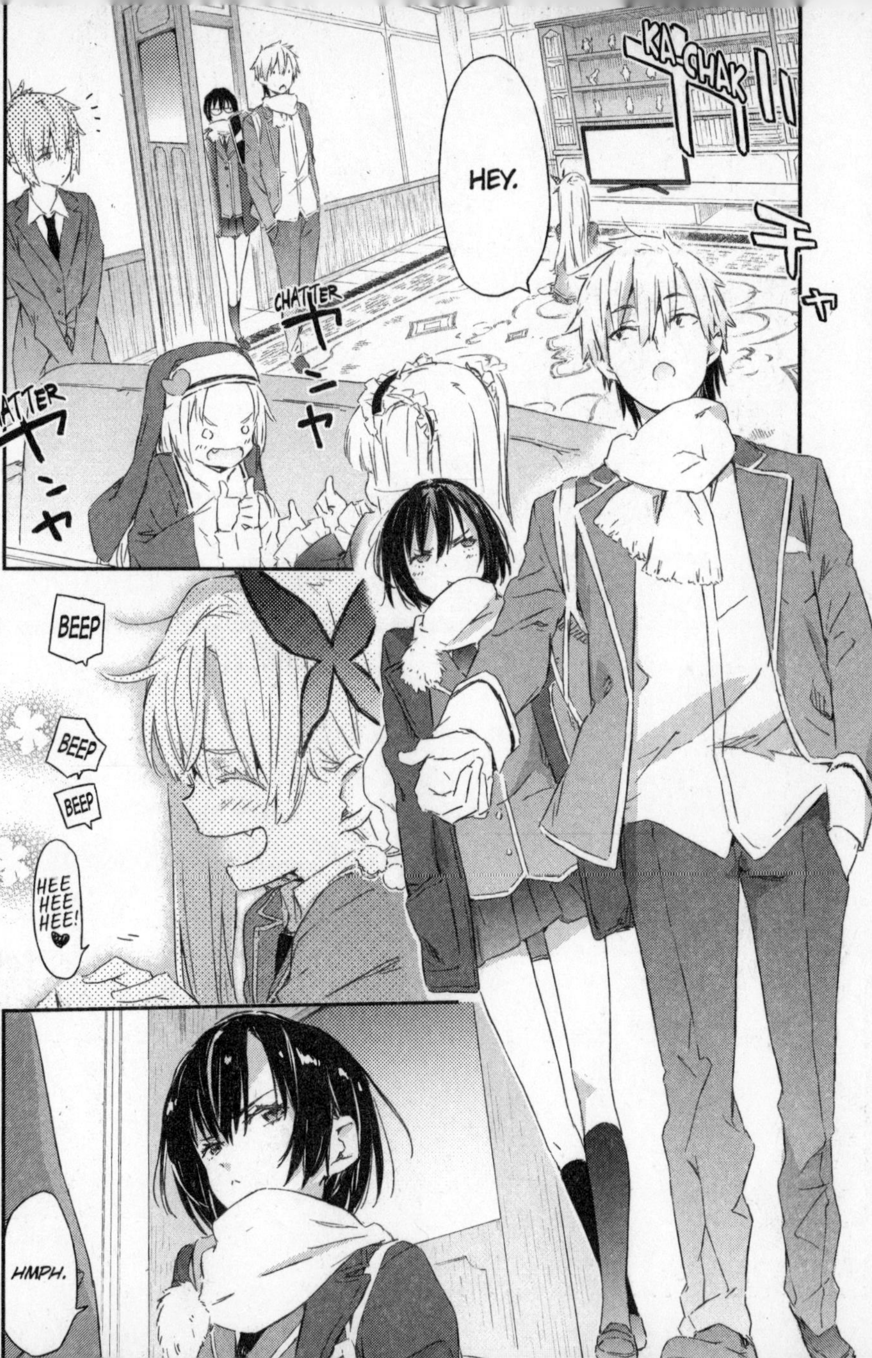
KA-CHAK チャ
HEY.
CHATTER ヤニャ
CHATTER ヤニャ
BEEP
BEEP
BEEP
HEE HEE HEE!
HMPH.

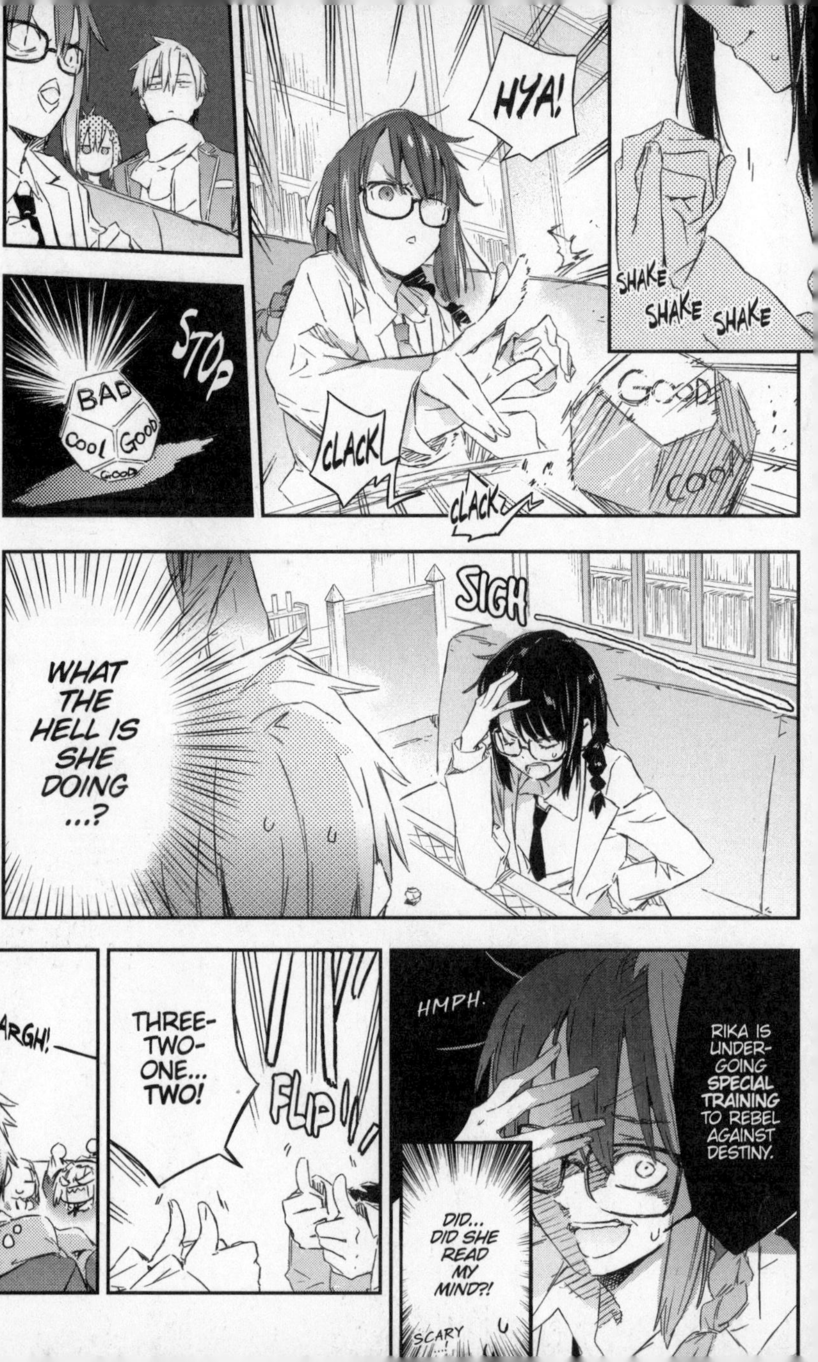
SHAKE
SHAKE
SHAKE
HYA!
GOOD
CLACK
CLACK
STOP
BAD
COOL
GOOD
GOOD
SIGH
WHAT THE HELL IS SHE DOING ...?
RIKA IS UNDERGOING SPECIAL TRAINING TO REBEL AGAINST DESTINY.
HMPH.
DID... DID SHE READ MY MIND?!
SCARY ...!
FLIP
THREE-TWO-ONE... TWO!
AAARGH!
ANOTHER PEACEFUL DAY IN THE NEIGHBORS CLUB...

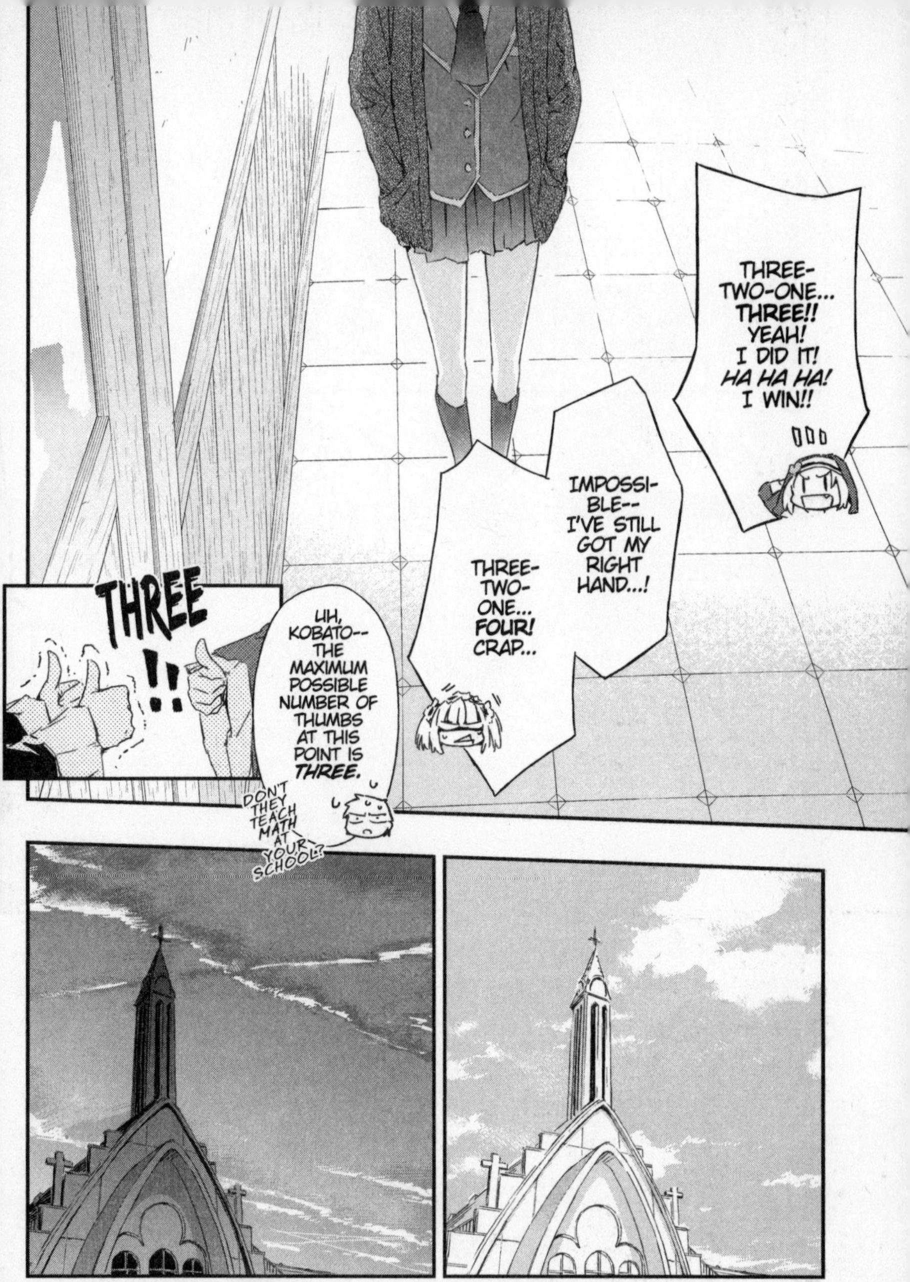
THREE-TWO-ONE... THREE!! YEAH! I DID IT! HA HA HA! I WIN!!
IMPOSSIBLE-- I'VE STILL GOT MY RIGHT HAND...!
THREE-TWO-ONE... FOUR! CRAP...
THREE!!
UH, KOBATO-- THE MAXIMUM POSSIBLE NUMBER OF THUMBS AT THIS POINT IS THREE.
DON'T THEY TEACH MATH AT YOUR SCHOOL?

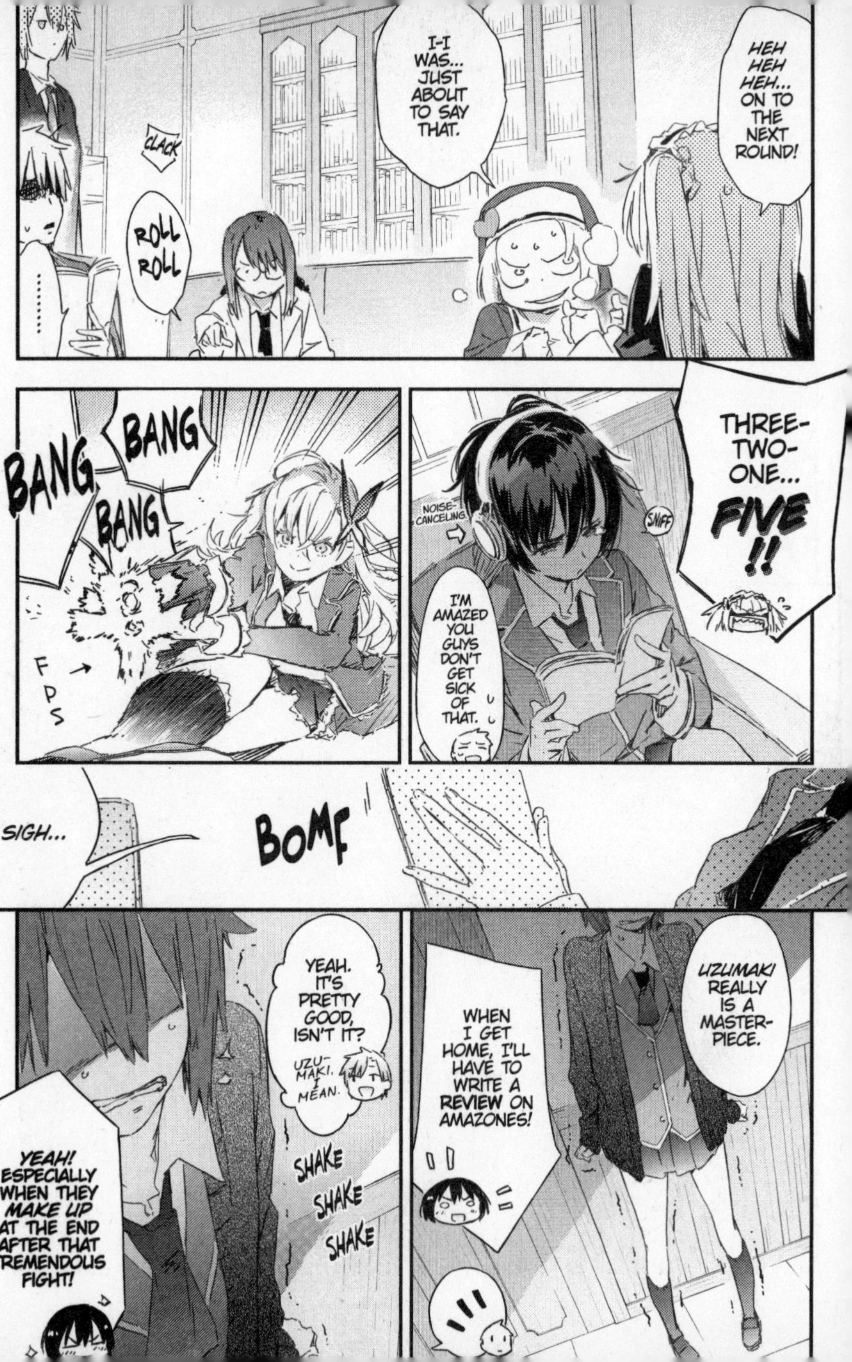
HEH HEH HEH... ON TO THE NEXT ROUND!
I-I WAS... JUST ABOUT TO SAY THAT.
CLACK
ROLL ROLL
......
THREE-TWO-ONE... FIVE!!
SNIFF
NOISE-CANCELING
I'M AMAZED YOU GUYS DON'T GET SICK OF THAT.
BANG
BANG
BANG
F P S
BOMF
SIGH...
UZUMAKI REALLY IS A MASTER-PIECE.
WHEN I GET HOME, I'LL HAVE TO WRITE A REVIEW ON AMAZONES!
YEAH. IT'S PRETTY GOOD, ISN'T IT?
UZU-MAKI, I MEAN.
SHAKE
SHAKE
SHAKE
YEAH! ESPECIALLY WHEN THEY MAKE UP AT THE END AFTER THAT TREMENDOUS FIGHT!

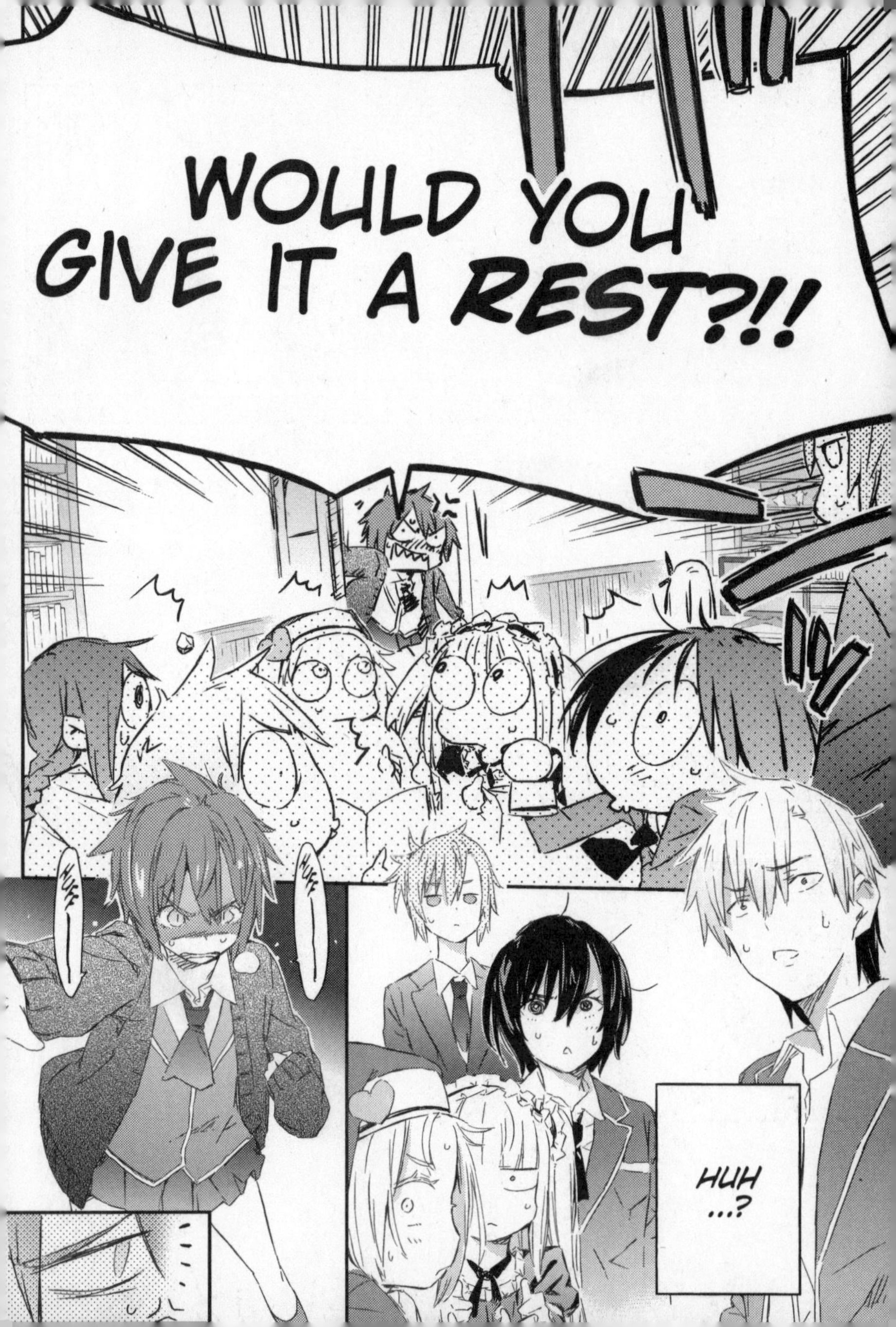
WOULD YOU GIVE IT A REST?!!
HUFF
HUFF
HUH ...?

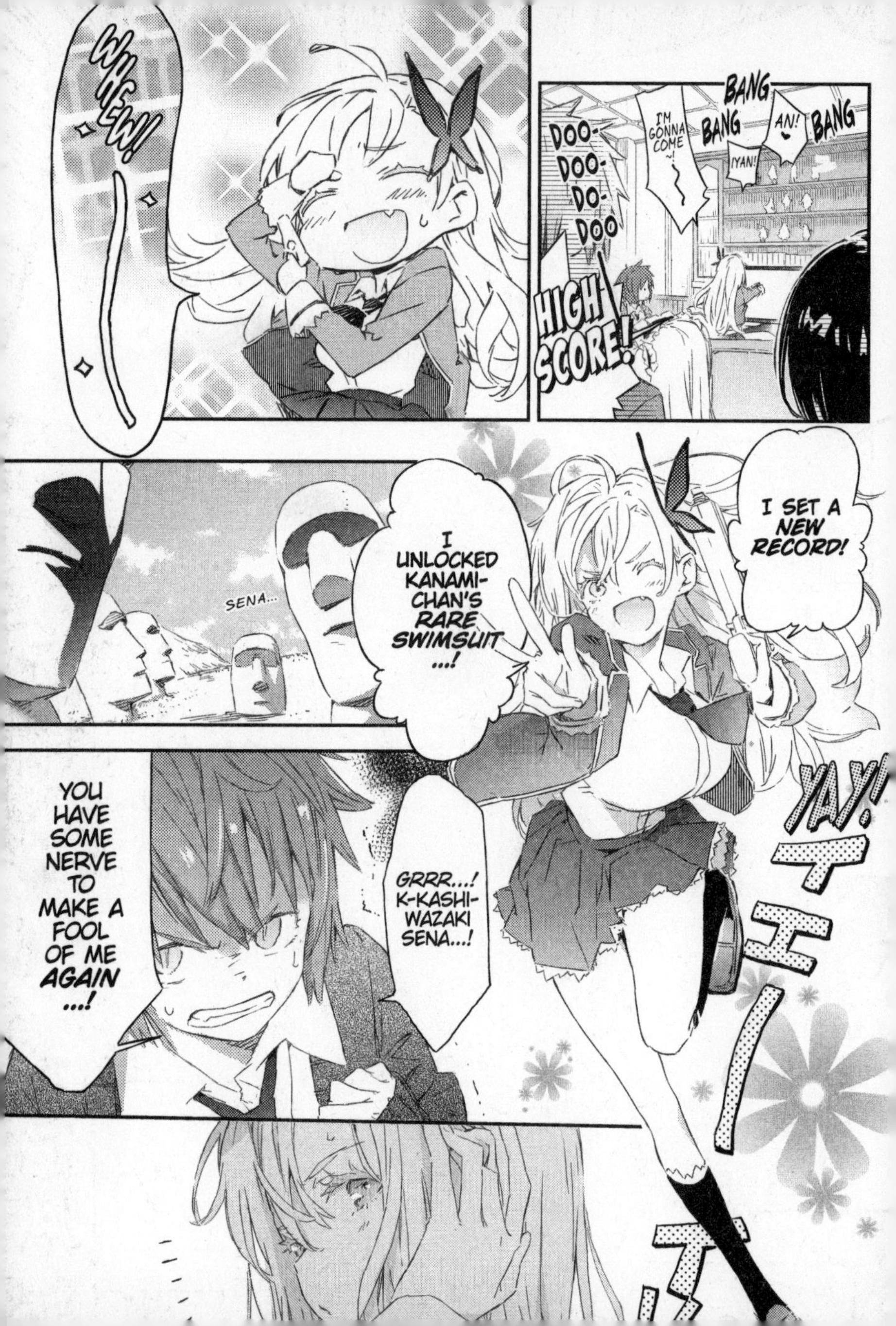
BANG
BANG
AN!
BANG
I'M GONNA COME ~!
IYAN!
DOO-DOO-DO-DOO
HIGH SCORE!
WHEW!
I SET A NEW RECORD!
I UNLOCKED KANAMI-CHAN'S RARE SWIMSUIT ...!
SENA...
YAY!!
GRRR...! K-KASHI-WAZAKI SENA...!
YOU HAVE SOME NERVE TO MAKE A FOOL OF ME AGAIN ...!

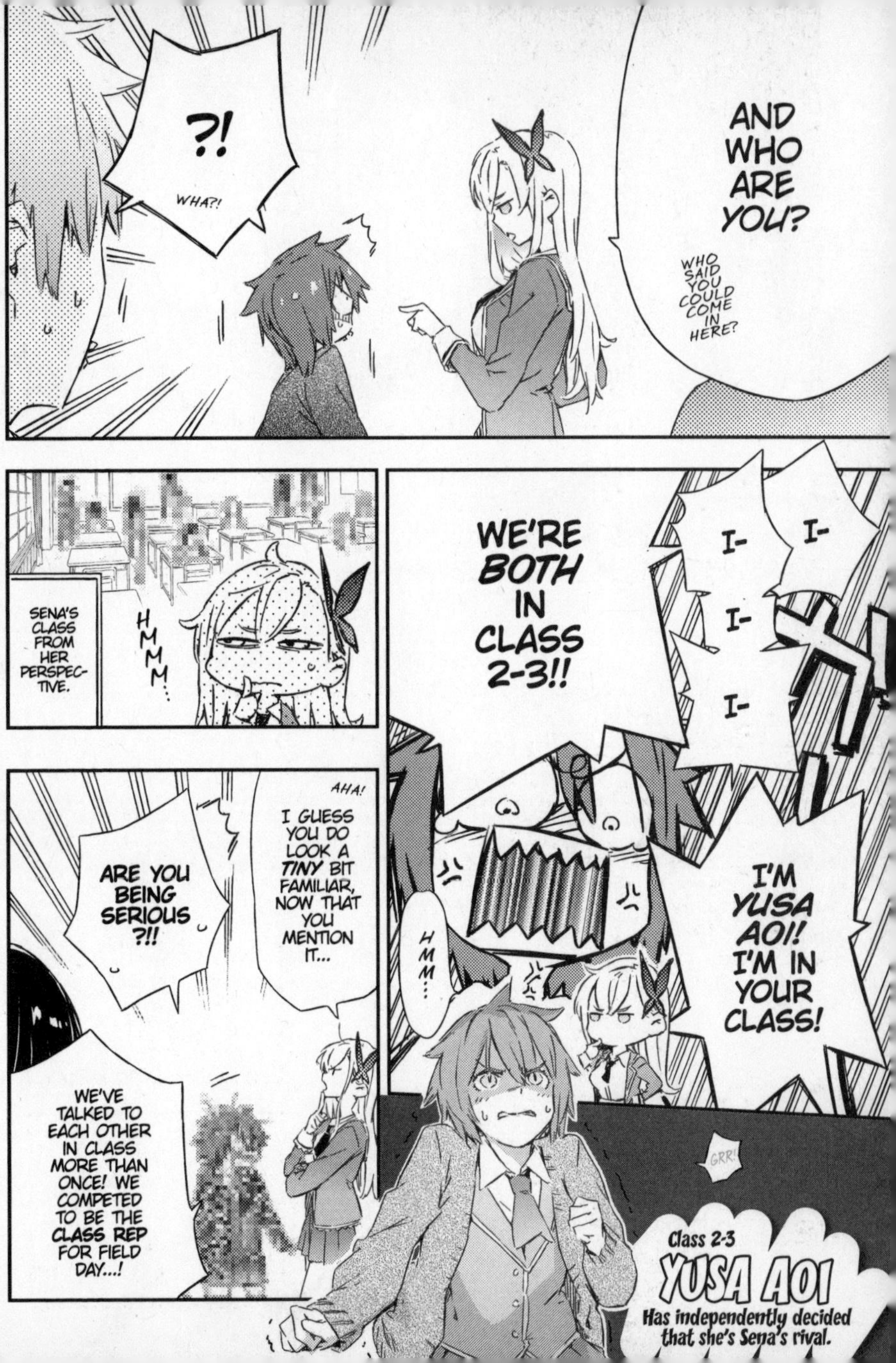
AND WHO ARE YOU?
WHO SAID YOU COULD COME IN HERE?
?!
WHA?!
WE'RE *BOTH* IN CLASS 2-3!!
I- I- I- I-
I'M *YUSA AOI!* I'M IN YOUR CLASS!
HMM...
GRR!
Class 2-3
YUSA AOI
Has independently decided that she's Sena's rival.
SENA'S CLASS FROM HER PERSPECTIVE.
HMMM...
AHA!
I GUESS YOU DO LOOK A *TINY* BIT FAMILIAR, NOW THAT YOU MENTION IT...
ARE YOU BEING SERIOUS ?!!
WE'VE TALKED TO EACH OTHER IN CLASS MORE THAN ONCE! WE COMPETED TO BE THE **CLASS REP** FOR FIELD DAY...!

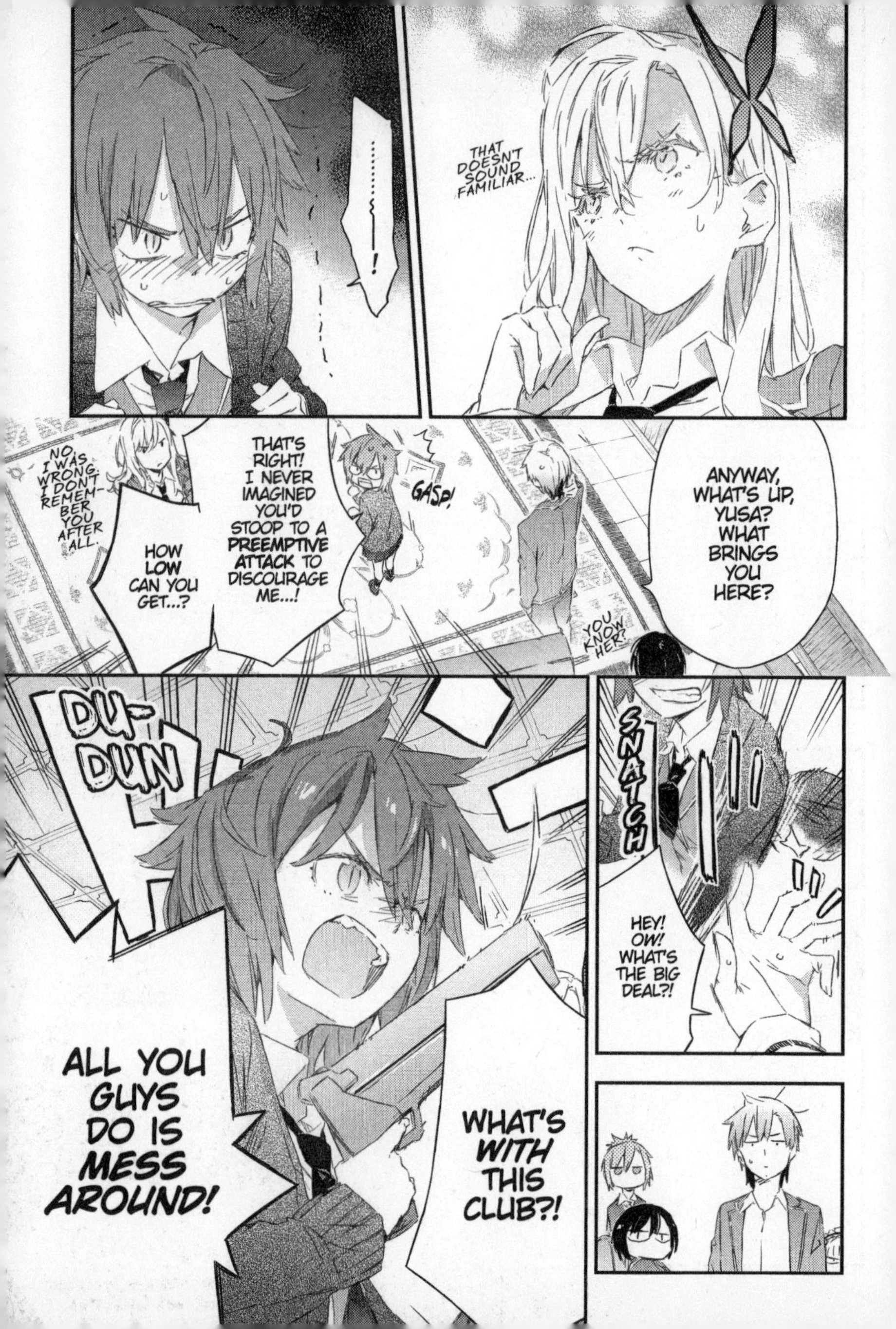
THAT DOESN'T SOUND FAMILIAR...
......!
ANYWAY, WHAT'S UP, YUSA? WHAT BRINGS YOU HERE?
YOU KNOW HER?
GASP!
THAT'S RIGHT! I NEVER IMAGINED YOU'D STOOP TO A PREEMPTIVE ATTACK TO DISCOURAGE ME...!
HOW LOW CAN YOU GET...?
NO, I WAS WRONG. I DON'T REMEMBER YOU AFTER ALL.
SNATCH
HEY! OW! WHAT'S THE BIG DEAL?!
DU-DUN
ALL YOU GUYS DO IS MESS AROUND!
WHAT'S WITH THIS CLUB?!

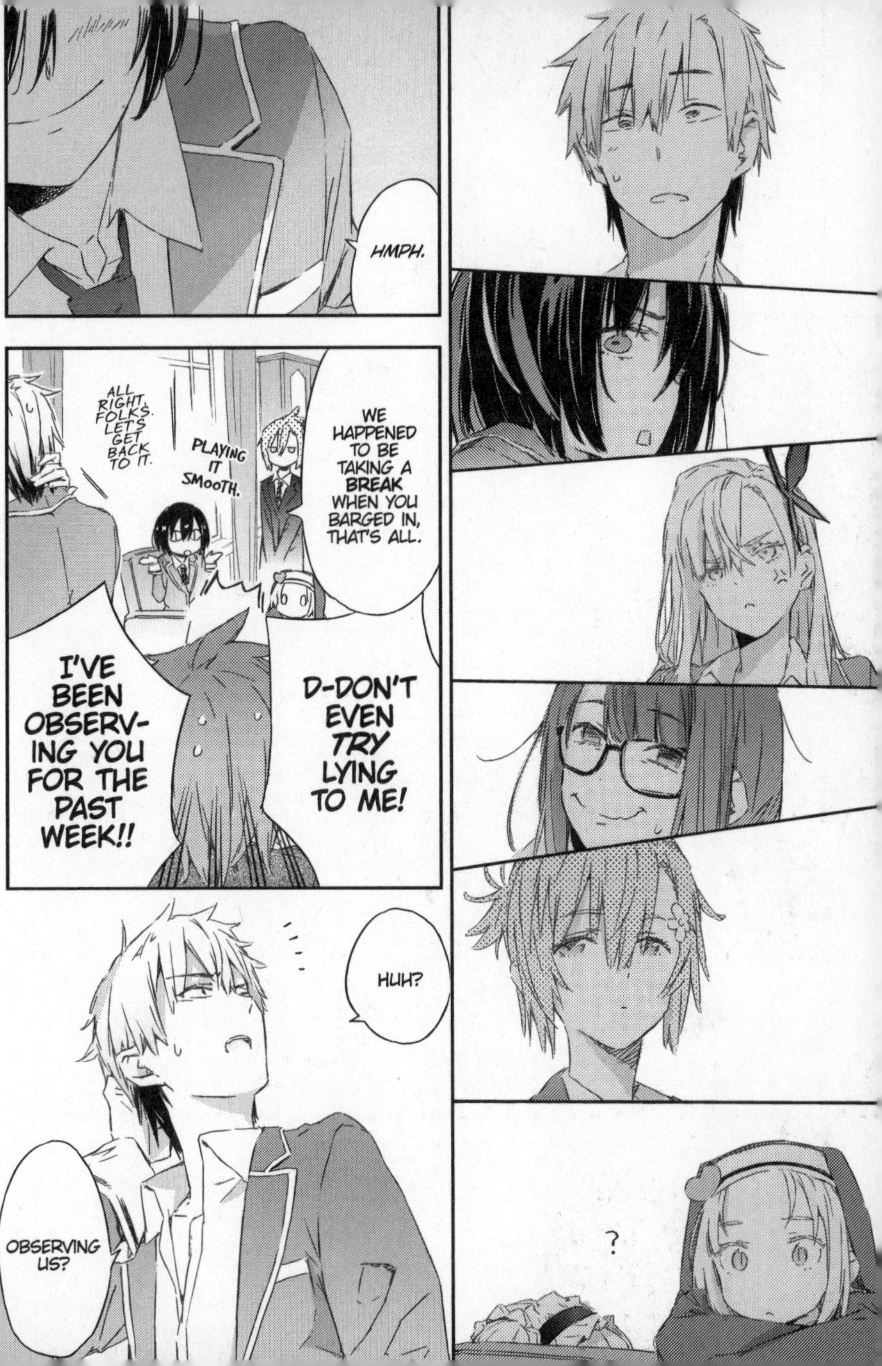
HMPH.
WE HAPPENED TO BE TAKING A BREAK WHEN YOU BARGED IN, THAT'S ALL.
ALL RIGHT, FOLKS. LET'S GET BACK TO IT.
PLAYING IT SMOOTH.
D-DON'T EVEN TRY LYING TO ME!
I'VE BEEN OBSERV-ING YOU FOR THE PAST WEEK!!
HUH?
OBSERVING US?
?

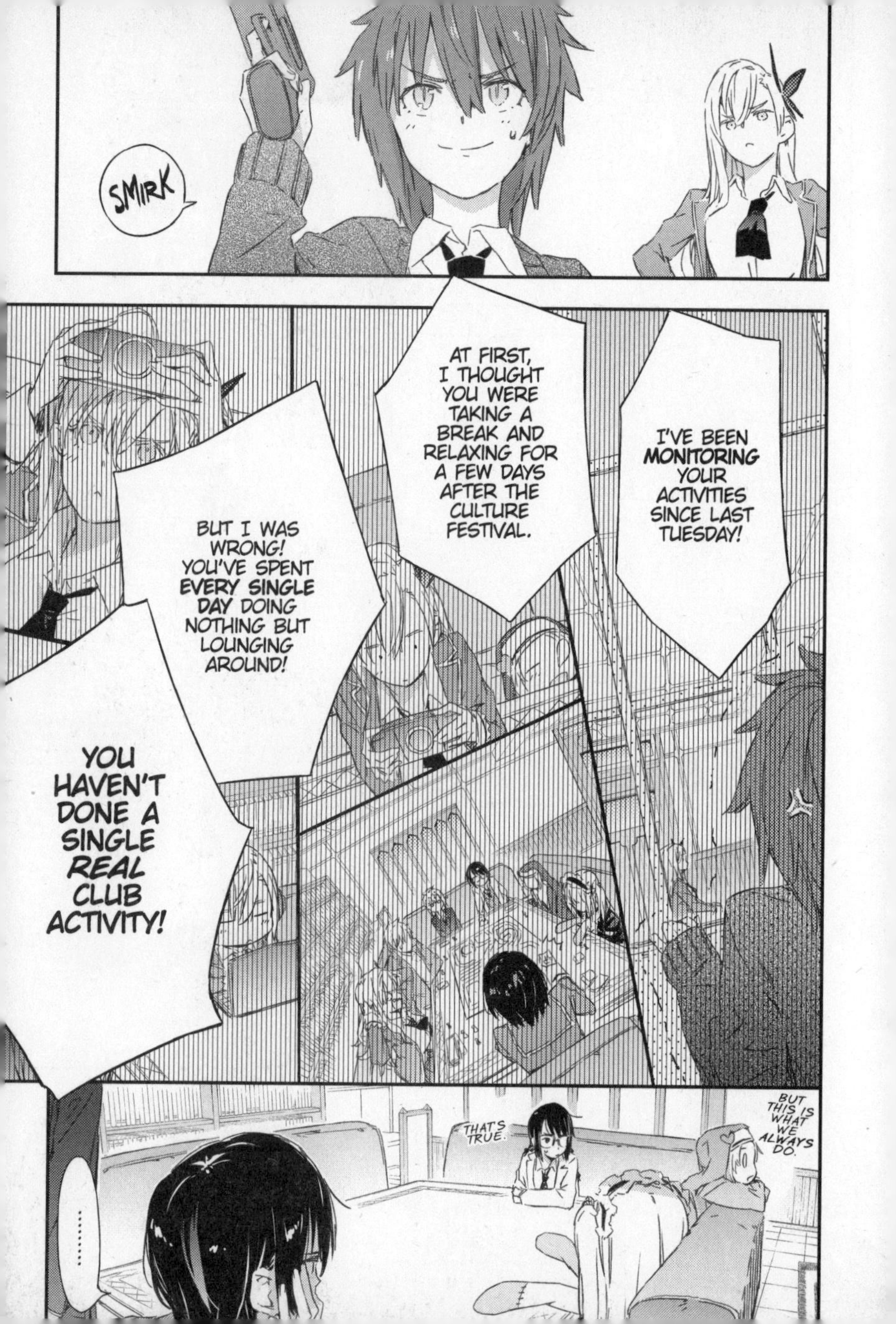
SMIRK
I'VE BEEN MONITORING YOUR ACTIVITIES SINCE LAST TUESDAY!
AT FIRST, I THOUGHT YOU WERE TAKING A BREAK AND RELAXING FOR A FEW DAYS AFTER THE CULTURE FESTIVAL.
BUT I WAS WRONG! YOU'VE SPENT EVERY SINGLE DAY DOING NOTHING BUT LOUNGING AROUND!
YOU HAVEN'T DONE A SINGLE REAL CLUB ACTIVITY!
BUT THIS IS WHAT WE ALWAYS DO.
THAT'S TRUE.
......

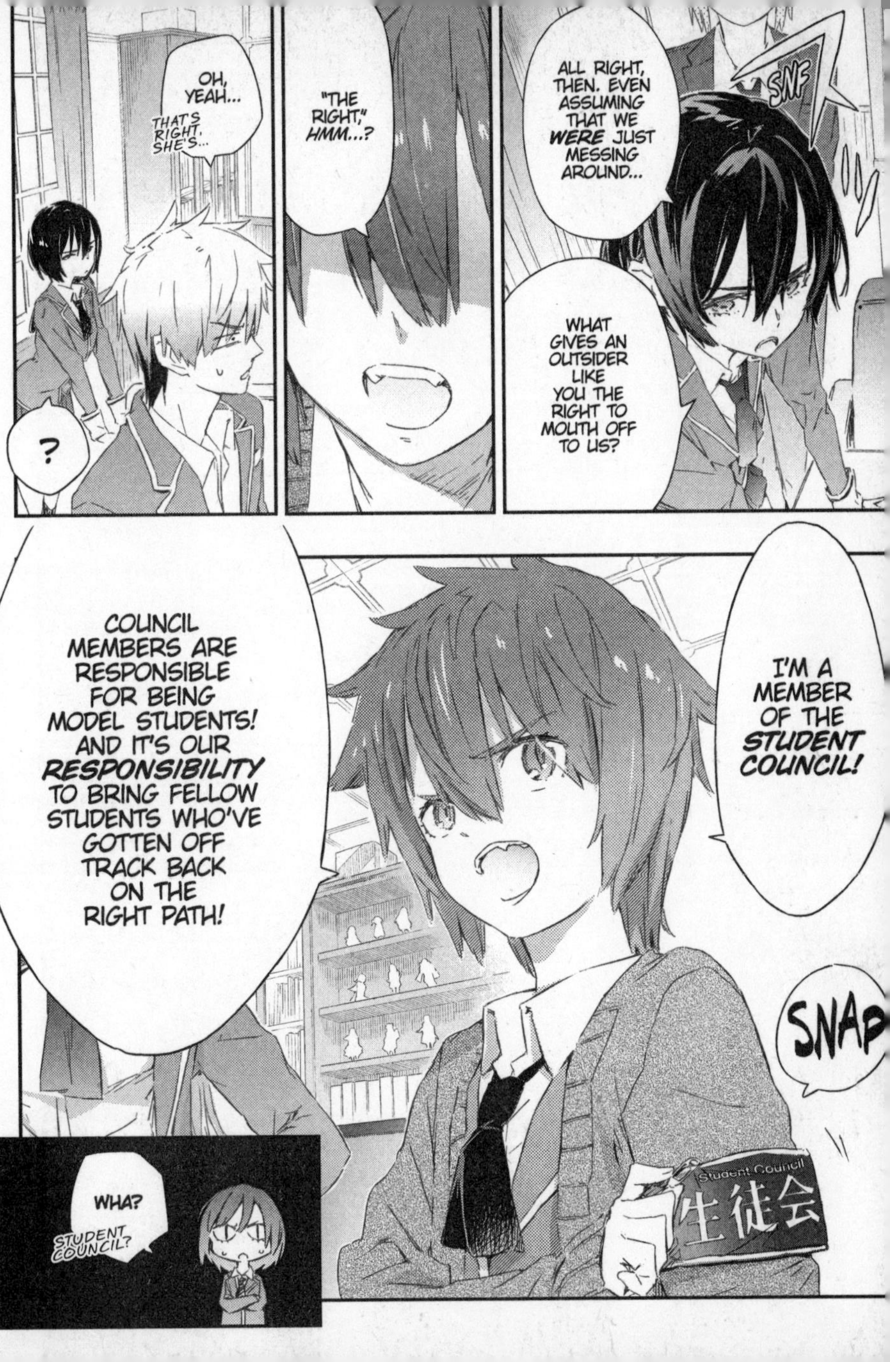
SNF
ALL RIGHT, THEN. EVEN ASSUMING THAT WE WERE JUST MESSING AROUND...
WHAT GIVES AN OUTSIDER LIKE YOU THE RIGHT TO MOUTH OFF TO US?
"THE RIGHT," HMM...?
OH, YEAH...
THAT'S RIGHT. SHE'S...
?
I'M A MEMBER OF THE STUDENT COUNCIL!
SNAP
Student Council
生徒会
COUNCIL MEMBERS ARE RESPONSIBLE FOR BEING MODEL STUDENTS! AND IT'S OUR RESPONSIBILITY TO BRING FELLOW STUDENTS WHO'VE GOTTEN OFF TRACK BACK ON THE RIGHT PATH!
WHA?
STUDENT COUNCIL?

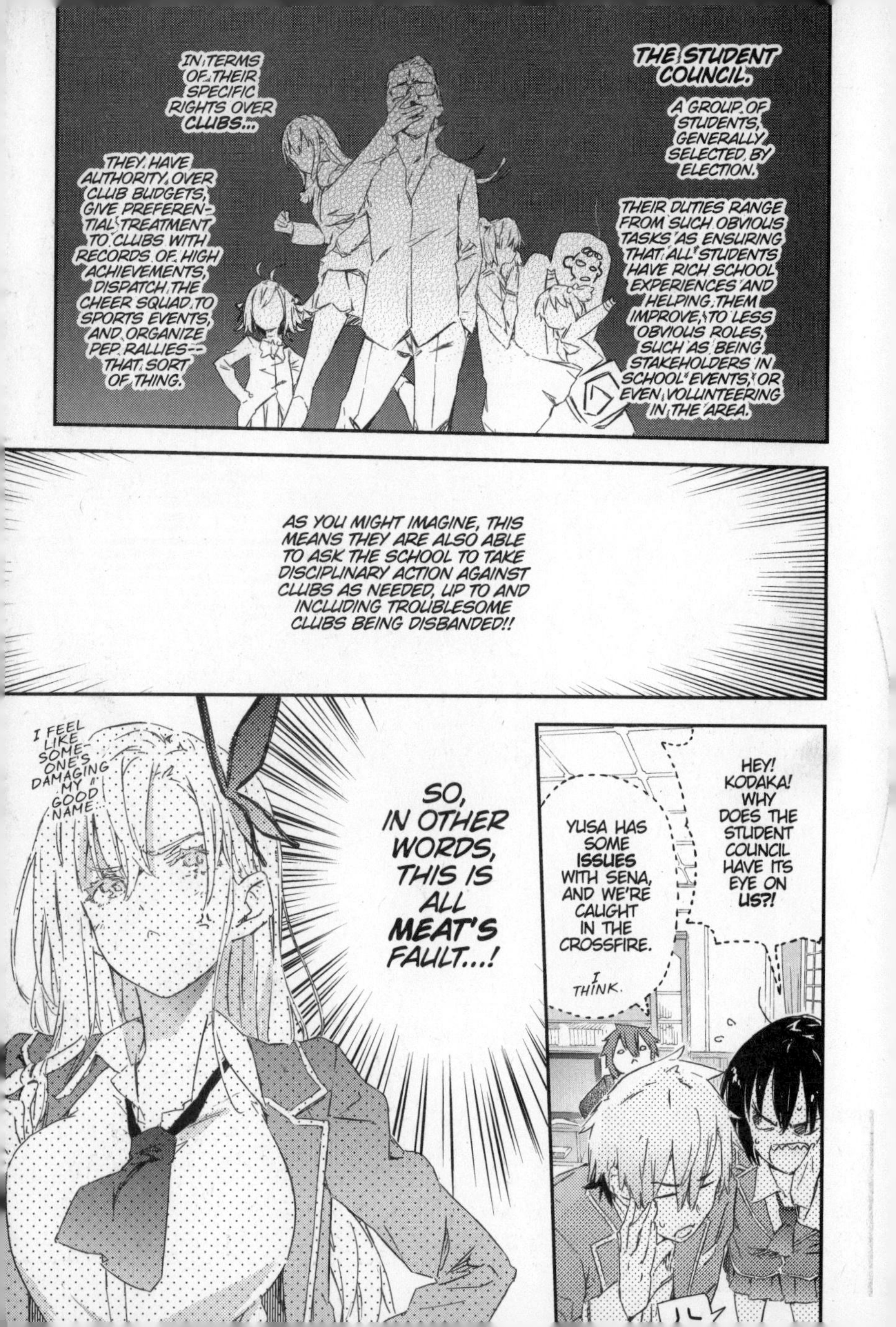
THE STUDENT COUNCIL.
A GROUP OF STUDENTS, GENERALLY SELECTED BY ELECTION.
THEIR DUTIES RANGE FROM SUCH OBVIOUS TASKS AS ENSURING THAT ALL STUDENTS HAVE RICH SCHOOL EXPERIENCES AND HELPING THEM IMPROVE, TO LESS OBVIOUS ROLES, SUCH AS BEING STAKEHOLDERS IN SCHOOL EVENTS, OR EVEN VOLUNTEERING IN THE AREA.
IN TERMS OF THEIR SPECIFIC RIGHTS OVER CLUBS...
THEY HAVE AUTHORITY OVER CLUB BUDGETS, GIVE PREFERENTIAL TREATMENT TO CLUBS WITH RECORDS OF HIGH ACHIEVEMENTS, DISPATCH THE CHEER SQUAD TO SPORTS EVENTS, AND ORGANIZE PEP RALLIES--THAT SORT OF THING.
AS YOU MIGHT IMAGINE, THIS MEANS THEY ARE ALSO ABLE TO ASK THE SCHOOL TO TAKE DISCIPLINARY ACTION AGAINST CLUBS AS NEEDED, UP TO AND INCLUDING TROUBLESOME CLUBS BEING DISBANDED!!
HEY! KODAKA! WHY DOES THE STUDENT COUNCIL HAVE ITS EYE ON US?!
YUSA HAS SOME ISSUES WITH SENA, AND WE'RE CAUGHT IN THE CROSSFIRE.
I THINK.
SO, IN OTHER WORDS, THIS IS ALL MEAT'S FAULT...!
I FEEL LIKE SOME-ONE'S DAMAGING MY GOOD NAME...

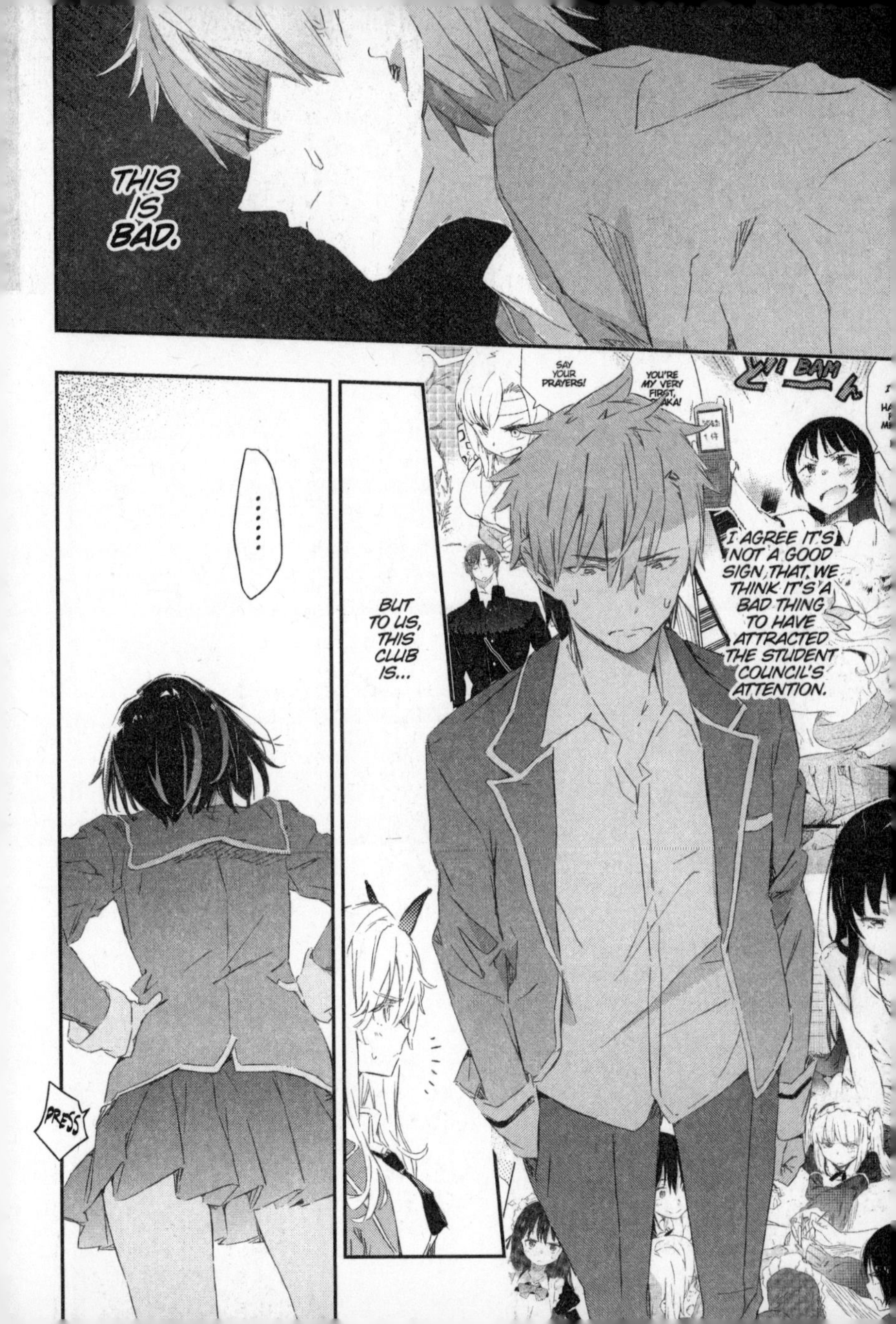
THIS IS BAD.
BAM
SAY YOUR PRAYERS!
YOU'RE MY VERY FIRST,
I AGREE IT'S NOT A GOOD SIGN THAT, WE THINK IT'S A BAD THING TO HAVE ATTRACTED THE STUDENT COUNCIL'S ATTENTION.
BUT TO US, THIS CLUB IS...
......
PRESS

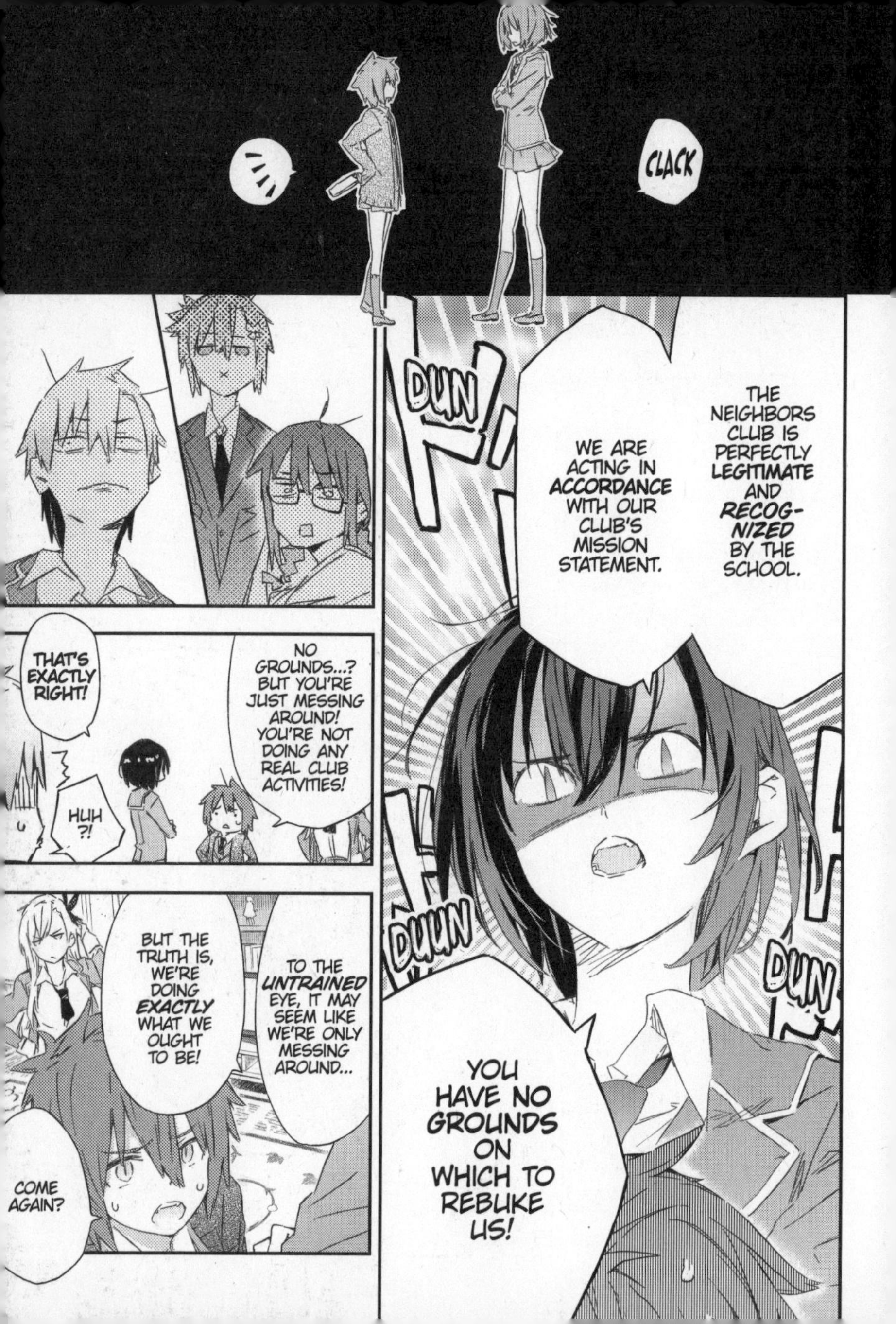
CLACK
...
DUN
THE NEIGHBORS CLUB IS PERFECTLY LEGITIMATE AND RECOGNIZED BY THE SCHOOL.
WE ARE ACTING IN ACCORDANCE WITH OUR CLUB'S MISSION STATEMENT.
DUUN
DUN
YOU HAVE NO GROUNDS ON WHICH TO REBUKE US!
NO GROUNDS...? BUT YOU'RE JUST MESSING AROUND! YOU'RE NOT DOING ANY REAL CLUB ACTIVITIES!
THAT'S EXACTLY RIGHT!
HUH ?!
TO THE UNTRAINED EYE, IT MAY SEEM LIKE WE'RE ONLY MESSING AROUND...
BUT THE TRUTH IS, WE'RE DOING EXACTLY WHAT WE OUGHT TO BE!
COME AGAIN?

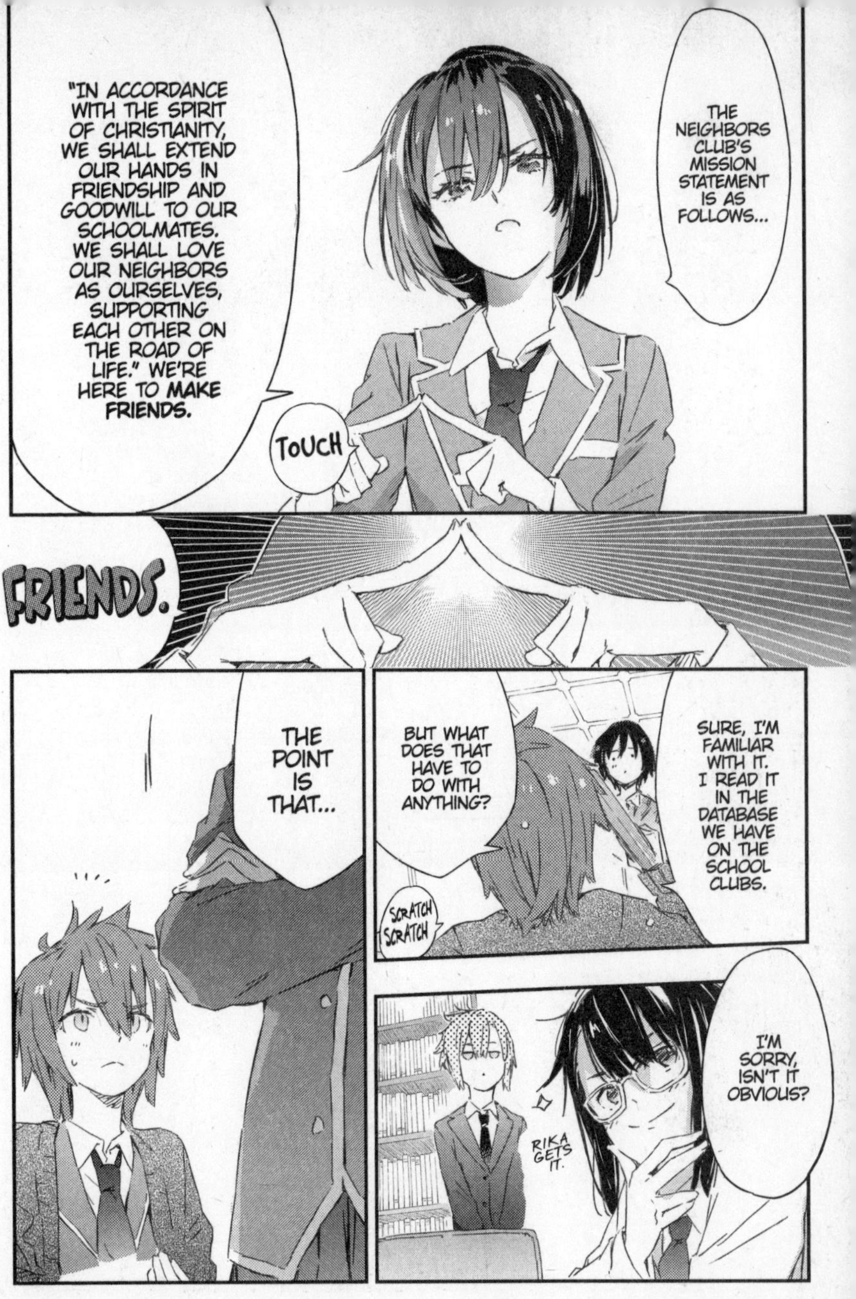
THE NEIGHBORS CLUB'S MISSION STATEMENT IS AS FOLLOWS...
"IN ACCORDANCE WITH THE SPIRIT OF CHRISTIANITY, WE SHALL EXTEND OUR HANDS IN FRIENDSHIP AND GOODWILL TO OUR SCHOOLMATES. WE SHALL LOVE OUR NEIGHBORS AS OURSELVES, SUPPORTING EACH OTHER ON THE ROAD OF LIFE." WE'RE HERE TO MAKE FRIENDS.
TOUCH
FRIENDS.
SURE, I'M FAMILIAR WITH IT. I READ IT IN THE DATABASE WE HAVE ON THE SCHOOL CLUBS.
BUT WHAT DOES THAT HAVE TO DO WITH ANYTHING?
SCRATCH SCRATCH
I'M SORRY, ISN'T IT OBVIOUS?
RIKA GETS IT.
THE POINT IS THAT...

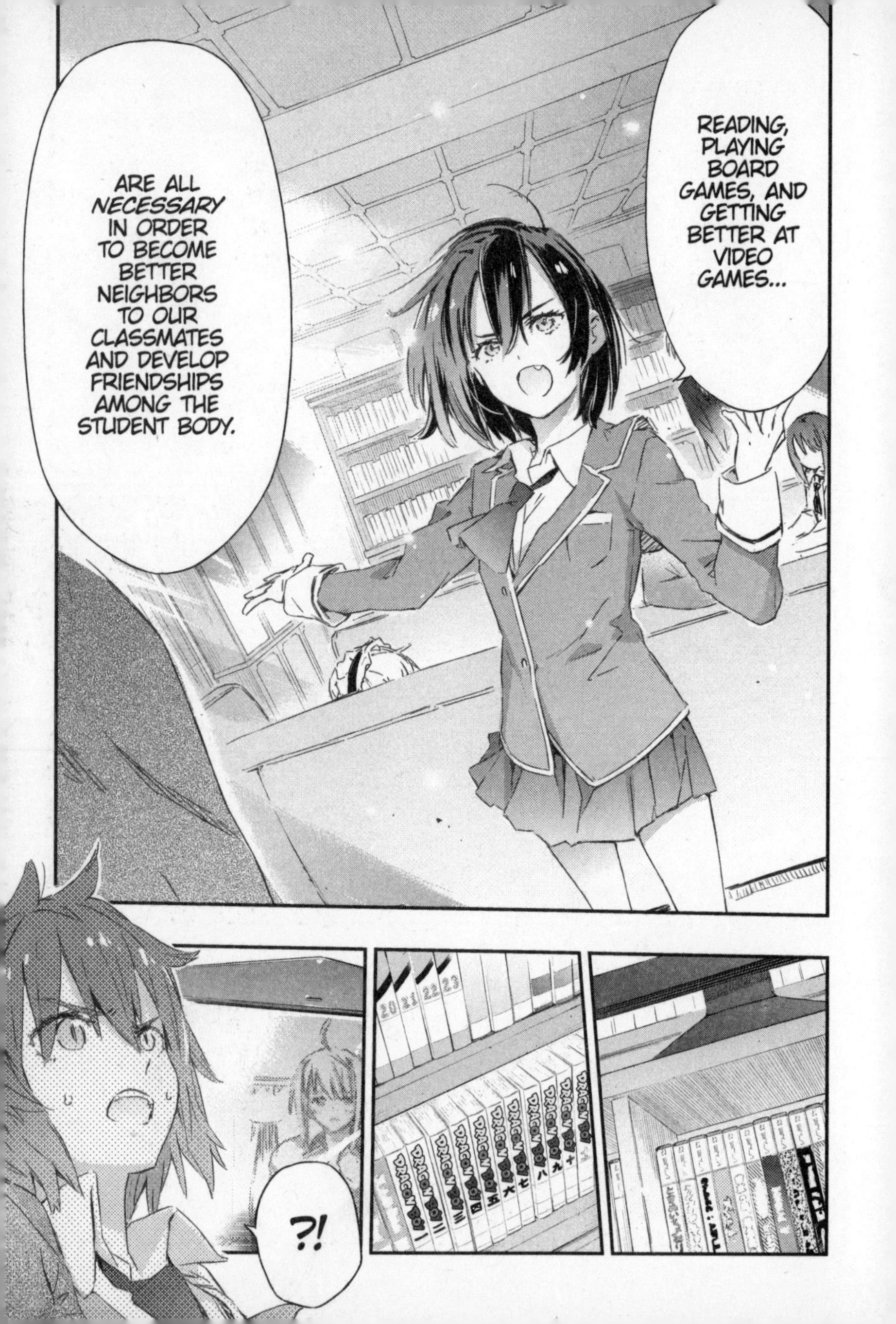
READING, PLAYING BOARD GAMES, AND GETTING BETTER AT VIDEO GAMES...
ARE ALL NECESSARY IN ORDER TO BECOME BETTER NEIGHBORS TO OUR CLASSMATES AND DEVELOP FRIENDSHIPS AMONG THE STUDENT BODY.
DRAGON BOY
?!

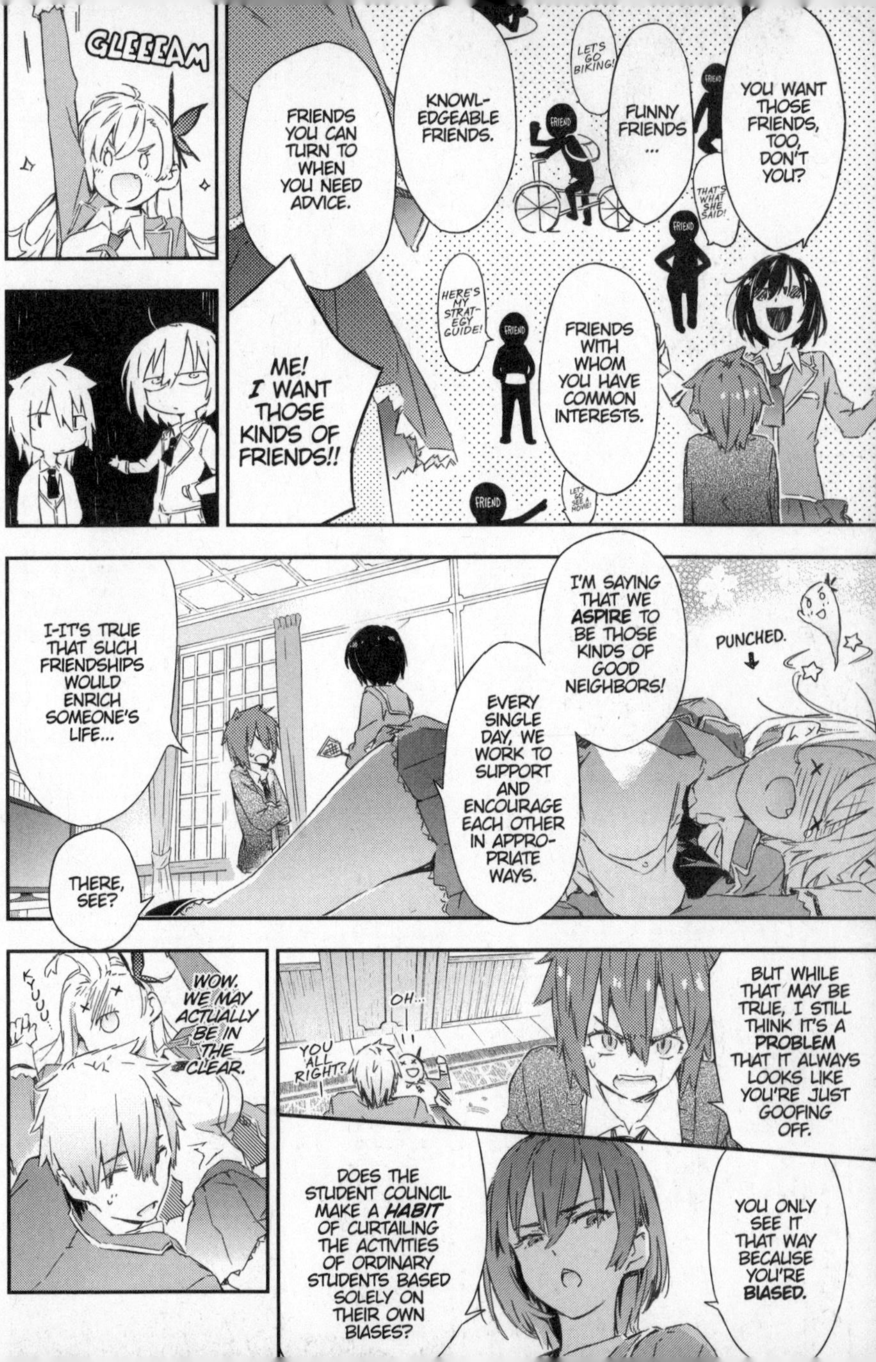
YOU WANT THOSE FRIENDS, TOO, DON'T YOU?
THAT'S WHAT SHE SAID!
FUNNY FRIENDS...
LET'S GO BIKING!
KNOWL-EDGEABLE FRIENDS.
FRIENDS YOU CAN TURN TO WHEN YOU NEED ADVICE.
FRIENDS WITH WHOM YOU HAVE COMMON INTERESTS.
HERE'S MY STRAT-EGY GUIDE!
LET'S GO SEE A MOVIE!
FRIEND
ME! I WANT THOSE KINDS OF FRIENDS!!
GLEEEAM
I'M SAYING THAT WE ASPIRE TO BE THOSE KINDS OF GOOD NEIGHBORS!
PUNCHED.
EVERY SINGLE DAY, WE WORK TO SUPPORT AND ENCOURAGE EACH OTHER IN APPRO-PRIATE WAYS.
I-IT'S TRUE THAT SUCH FRIENDSHIPS WOULD ENRICH SOMEONE'S LIFE...
THERE, SEE?
BUT WHILE THAT MAY BE TRUE, I STILL THINK IT'S A PROBLEM THAT IT ALWAYS LOOKS LIKE YOU'RE JUST GOOFING OFF.
OH...
YOU ALL RIGHT?
YOU ONLY SEE IT THAT WAY BECAUSE YOU'RE BIASED.
DOES THE STUDENT COUNCIL MAKE A HABIT OF CURTAILING THE ACTIVITIES OF ORDINARY STUDENTS BASED SOLELY ON THEIR OWN BIASES?
WOW. WE MAY ACTUALLY BE IN THE CLEAR.
KYUUU...

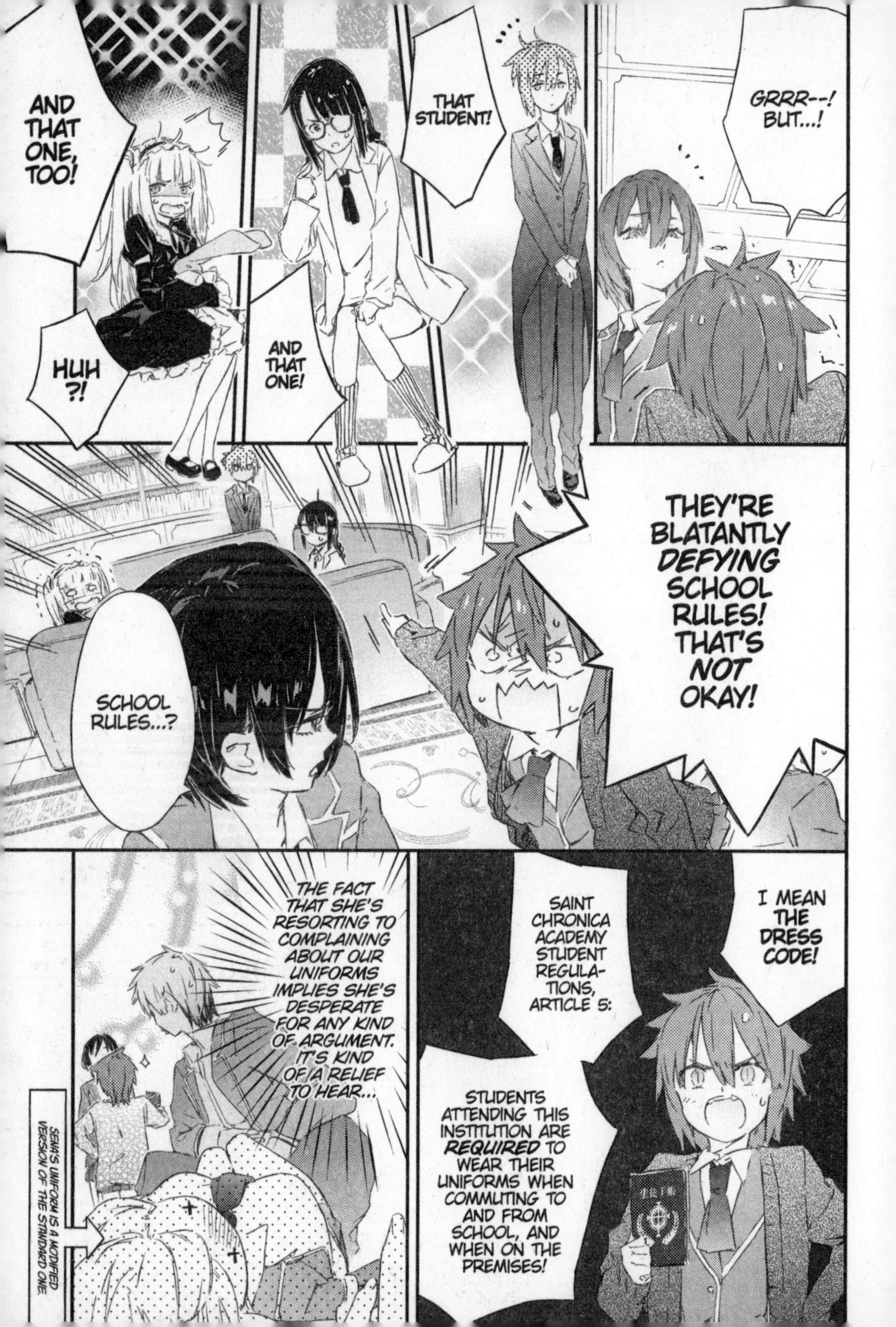
GRRR--! BUT...!
THAT STUDENT!
AND THAT ONE!
AND THAT ONE, TOO!
HUH ?!
THEY'RE BLATANTLY *DEFYING* SCHOOL RULES! THAT'S *NOT* OKAY!
SCHOOL RULES...?
I MEAN THE DRESS CODE!
SAINT CHRONICA ACADEMY STUDENT REGULATIONS, ARTICLE 5:
STUDENTS ATTENDING THIS INSTITUTION ARE ***REQUIRED*** TO WEAR THEIR UNIFORMS WHEN COMMUTING TO AND FROM SCHOOL, AND WHEN ON THE PREMISES!
THE FACT THAT SHE'S RESORTING TO COMPLAINING ABOUT OUR UNIFORMS IMPLIES SHE'S DESPERATE FOR ANY KIND OF ARGUMENT. IT'S KIND OF A RELIEF TO HEAR...
SENA'S UNIFORM IS A MODIFIED VERSION OF THE STANDARD ONE.

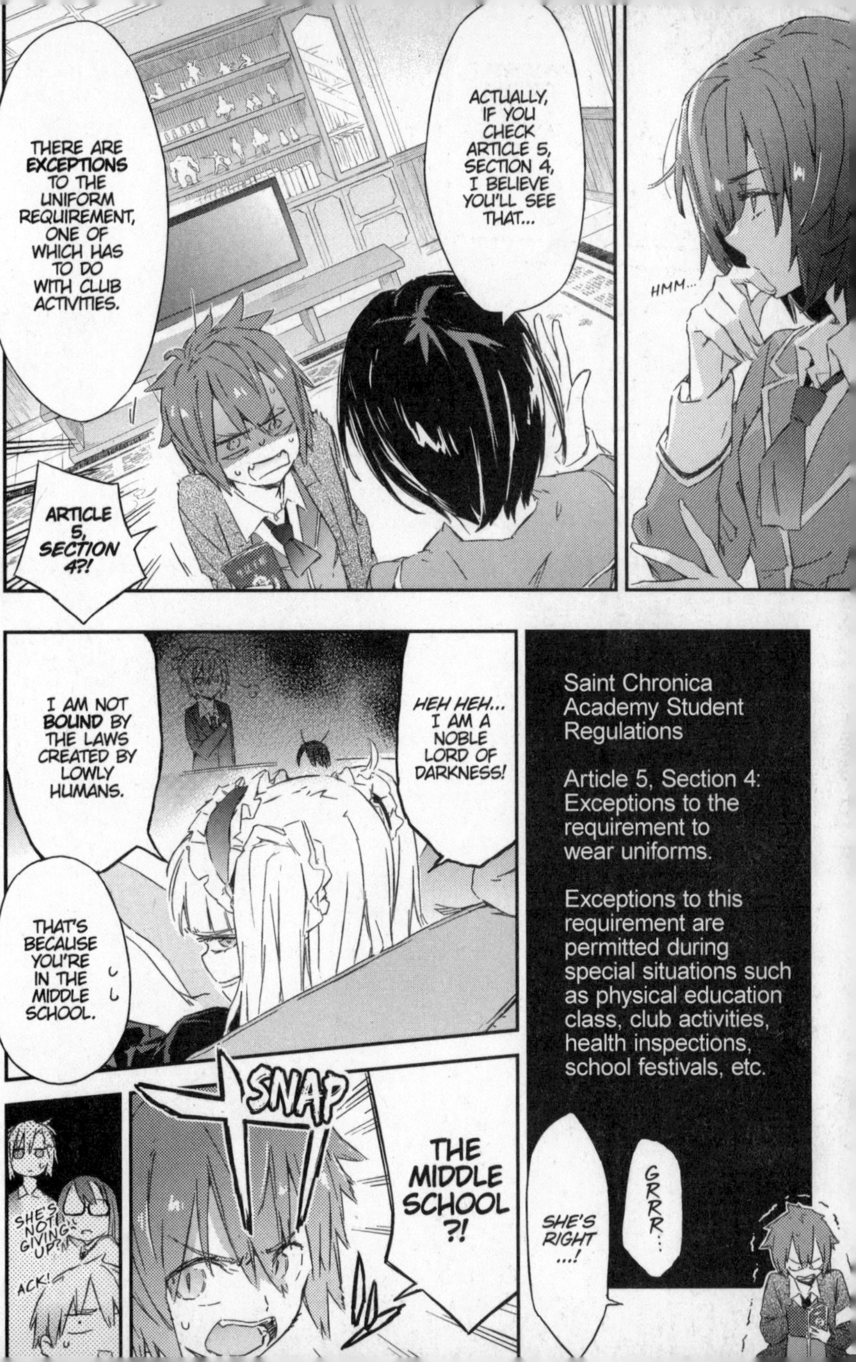
HMM...
ACTUALLY, IF YOU CHECK ARTICLE 5, SECTION 4, I BELIEVE YOU'LL SEE THAT...
THERE ARE EXCEPTIONS TO THE UNIFORM REQUIREMENT, ONE OF WHICH HAS TO DO WITH CLUB ACTIVITIES.
ARTICLE 5, SECTION 4?!
Saint Chronica Academy Student Regulations
Article 5, Section 4: Exceptions to the requirement to wear uniforms.
Exceptions to this requirement are permitted during special situations such as physical education class, club activities, health inspections, school festivals, etc.
HEH HEH... I AM A NOBLE LORD OF DARKNESS!
I AM NOT BOUND BY THE LAWS CREATED BY LOWLY HUMANS.
THAT'S BECAUSE YOU'RE IN THE MIDDLE SCHOOL.
GRRR...
SHE'S RIGHT ...!
THE MIDDLE SCHOOL ?!
SNAP
SHE'S NOT GIVING UP.
ACK!

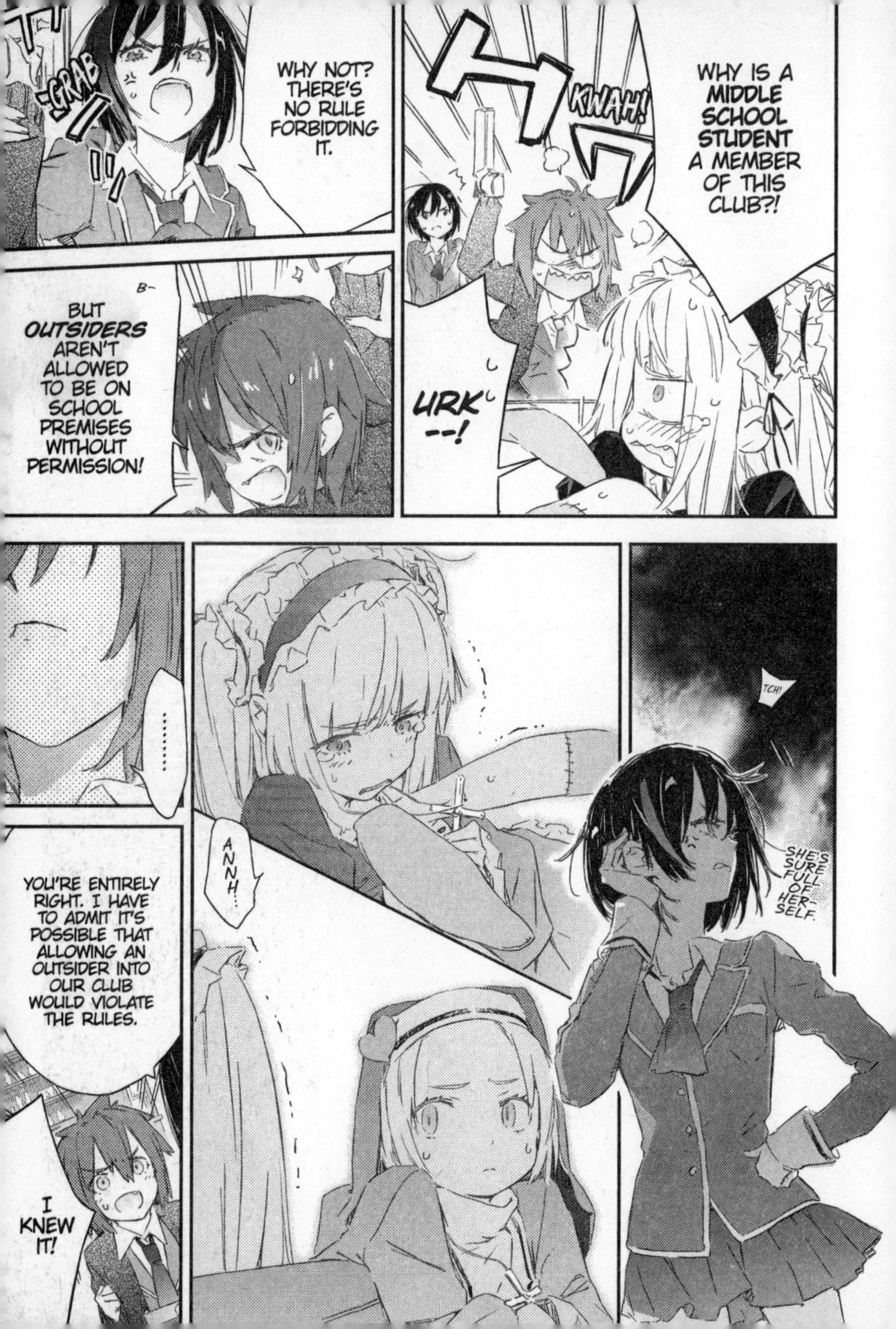

WHY IS A MIDDLE SCHOOL STUDENT A MEMBER OF THIS CLUB?!
KWAH!
URK --!
WHY NOT? THERE'S NO RULE FORBIDDING IT.
GRAB
B-
BUT OUTSIDERS AREN'T ALLOWED TO BE ON SCHOOL PREMISES WITHOUT PERMISSION!
TCH!
SHE'S SURE FULL OF HER-SELF.
ANNH...
......
YOU'RE ENTIRELY RIGHT. I HAVE TO ADMIT IT'S POSSIBLE THAT ALLOWING AN OUTSIDER INTO OUR CLUB WOULD VIOLATE THE RULES.
I KNEW IT!

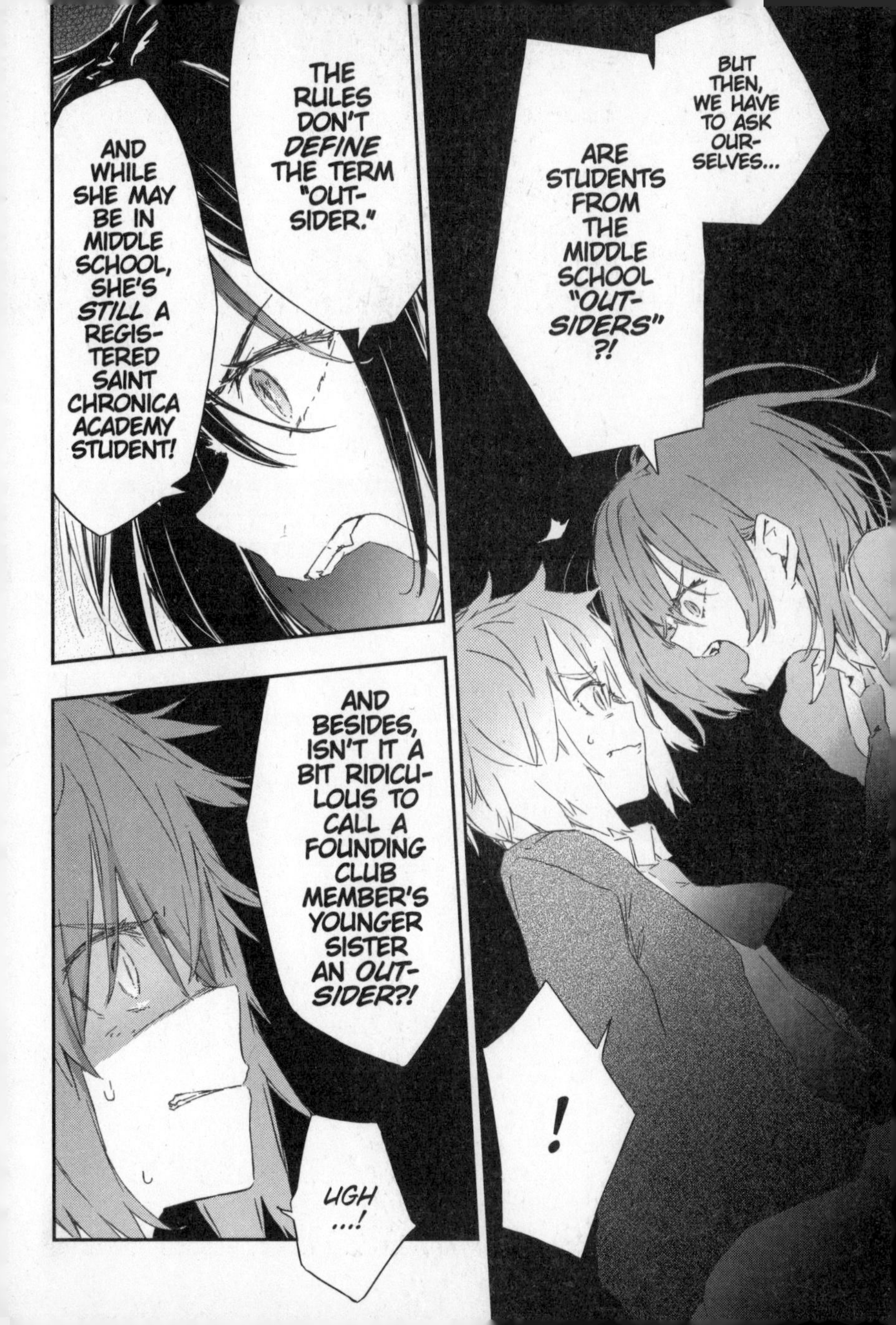
BUT THEN, WE HAVE TO ASK OURSELVES...
ARE STUDENTS FROM THE MIDDLE SCHOOL "OUTSIDERS" ?!
!
THE RULES DON'T *DEFINE* THE TERM "OUTSIDER."
AND WHILE SHE MAY BE IN MIDDLE SCHOOL, SHE'S *STILL* A REGISTERED SAINT CHRONICA ACADEMY STUDENT!
AND BESIDES, ISN'T IT A BIT RIDICULOUS TO CALL A FOUNDING CLUB MEMBER'S YOUNGER SISTER AN *OUTSIDER*?!
UGH ...!

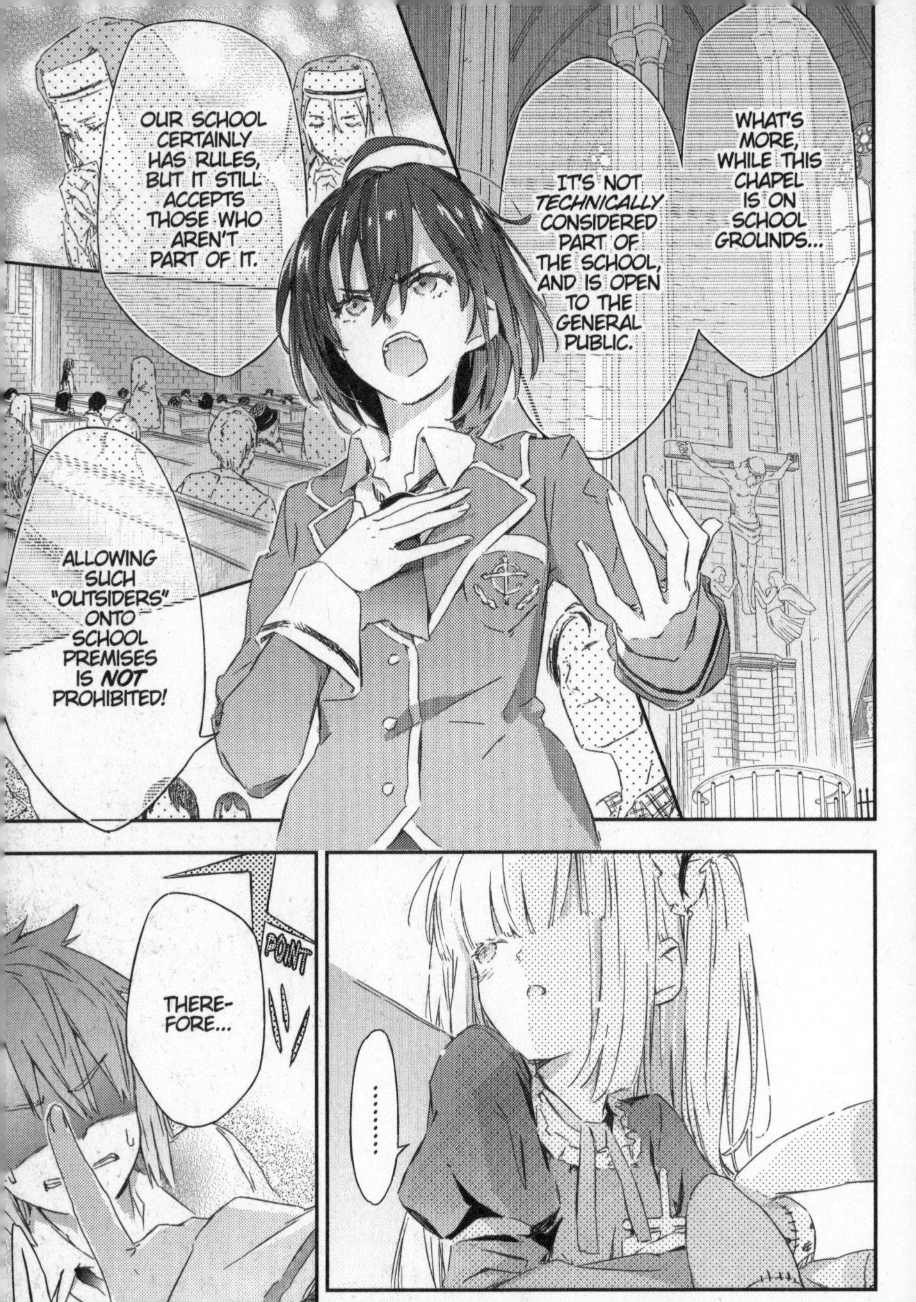
WHAT'S MORE, WHILE THIS CHAPEL IS ON SCHOOL GROUNDS...
IT'S NOT *TECHNICALLY* CONSIDERED PART OF THE SCHOOL, AND IS OPEN TO THE GENERAL PUBLIC.
OUR SCHOOL CERTAINLY HAS RULES, BUT IT STILL ACCEPTS THOSE WHO AREN'T PART OF IT.
ALLOWING SUCH "OUTSIDERS" ONTO SCHOOL PREMISES IS ***NOT*** PROHIBITED!
......
POINT
THERE-FORE...

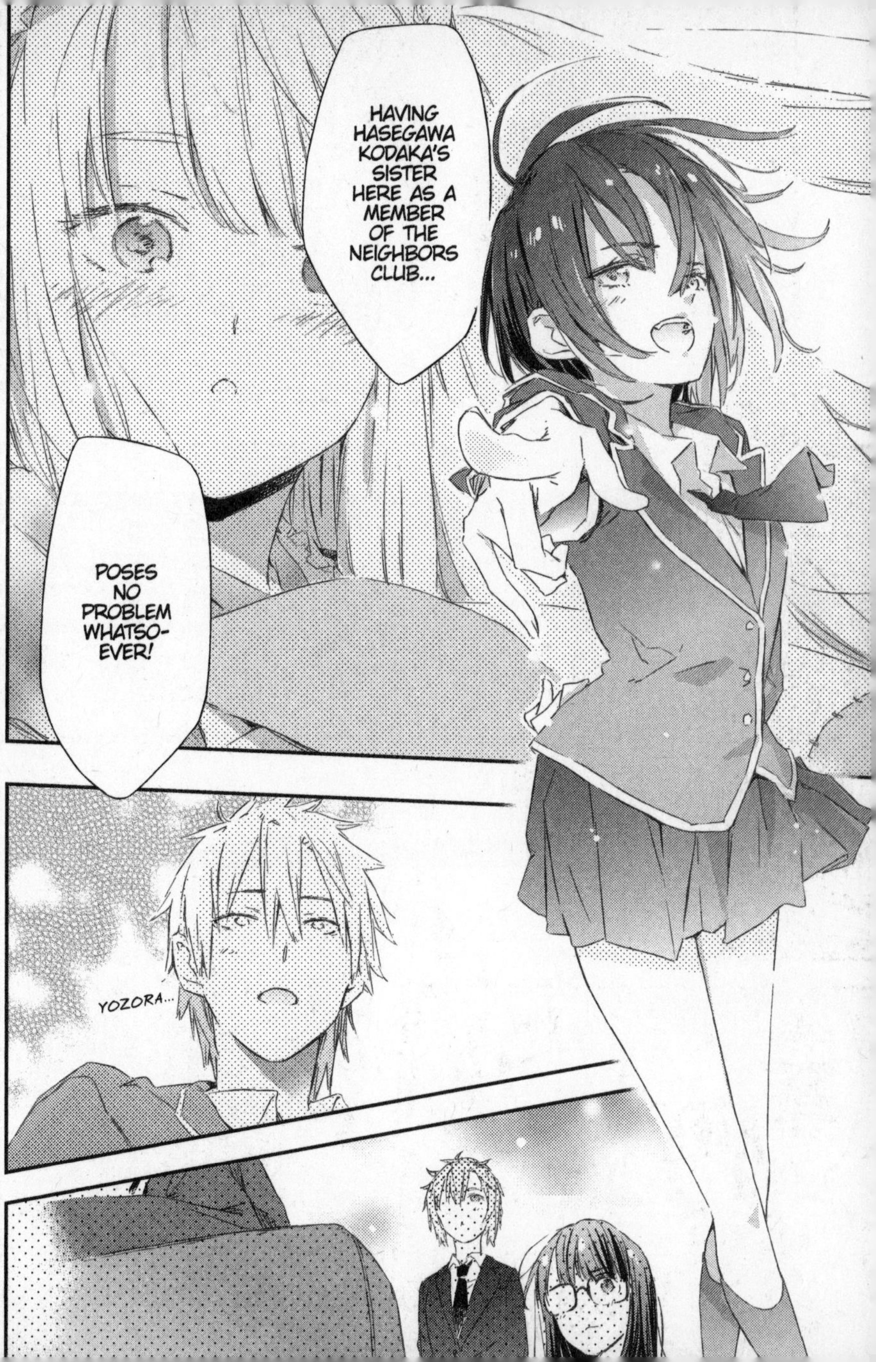
HAVING HASEGAWA KODAKA'S SISTER HERE AS A MEMBER OF THE NEIGHBORS CLUB...
POSES NO PROBLEM WHATSO-EVER!
YOZORA...

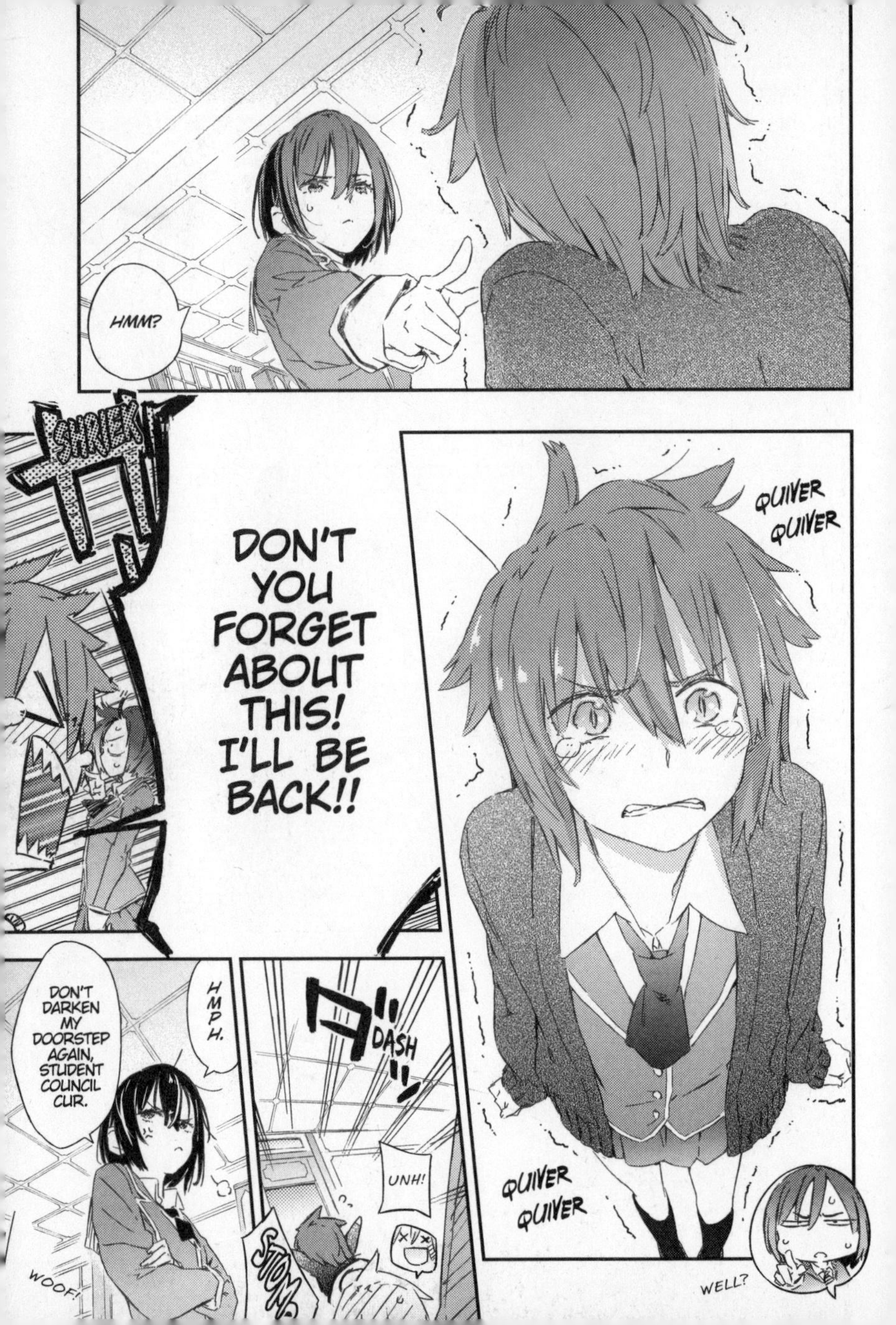
HMM?
QUIVER QUIVER
QUIVER QUIVER
WELL?
SHRIEK
DON'T YOU FORGET ABOUT THIS! I'LL BE BACK!!
DASH
UNH!
STOMP
HMPH.
DON'T DARKEN MY DOORSTEP AGAIN, STUDENT COUNCIL CUR.
WOOF!

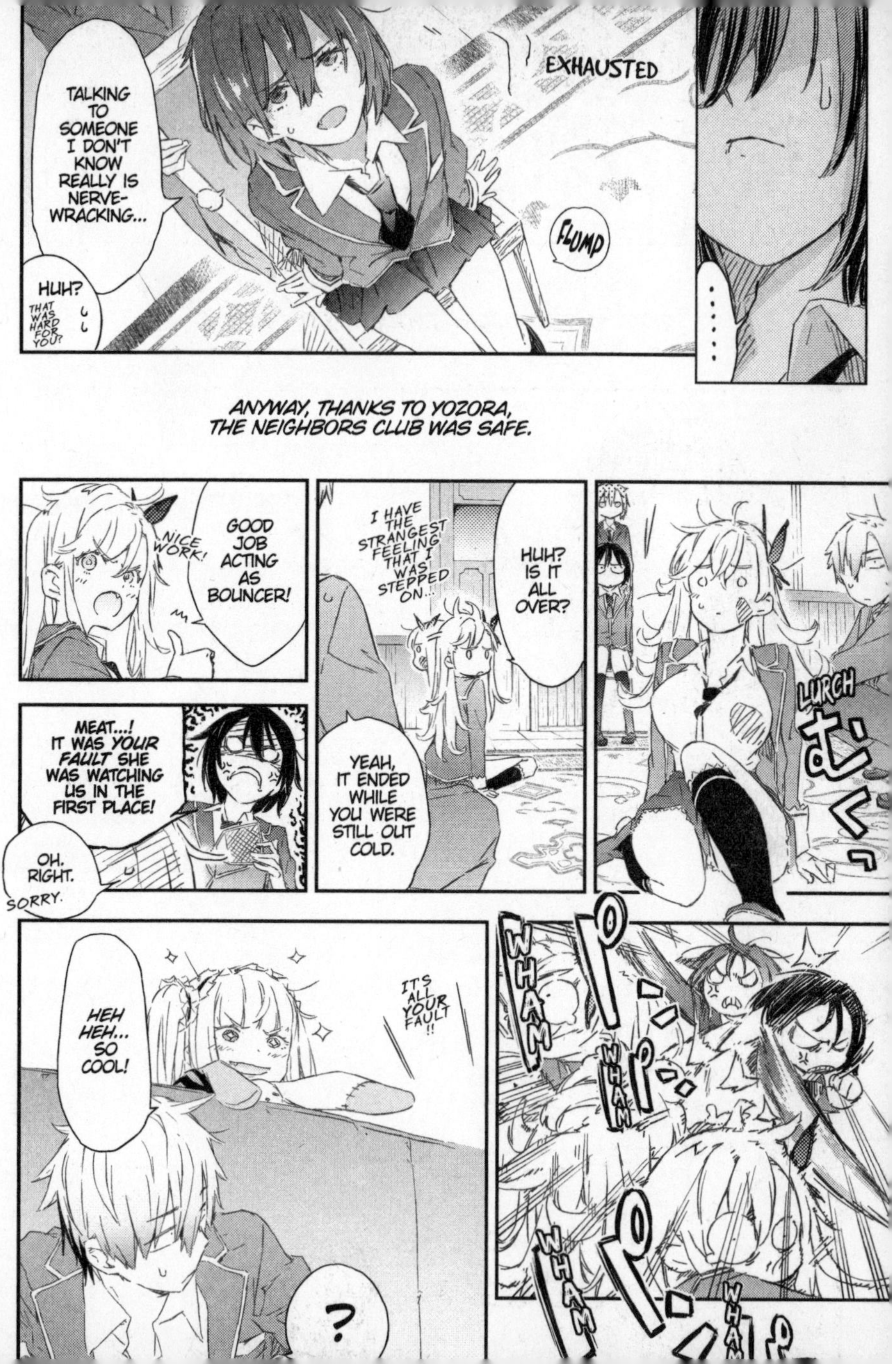
……
EXHAUSTED
TALKING TO SOMEONE I DON'T KNOW REALLY IS NERVE-WRACKING…
FLUMP
HUH?
THAT WAS HARD FOR YOU?
ANYWAY, THANKS TO YOZORA, THE NEIGHBORS CLUB WAS SAFE.
LURCH
むく
HUH? IS IT ALL OVER?
I HAVE THE STRANGEST FEELING THAT I WAS STEPPED ON…
YEAH, IT ENDED WHILE YOU WERE STILL OUT COLD.
GOOD JOB ACTING AS BOUNCER!
NICE WORK!
MEAT…! IT WAS YOUR FAULT SHE WAS WATCHING US IN THE FIRST PLACE!
OH. RIGHT.
SORRY.
WHAM
WHAM
WHAM
WHAM
IT'S ALL YOUR FAULT!!
HEH HEH… SO COOL!
?

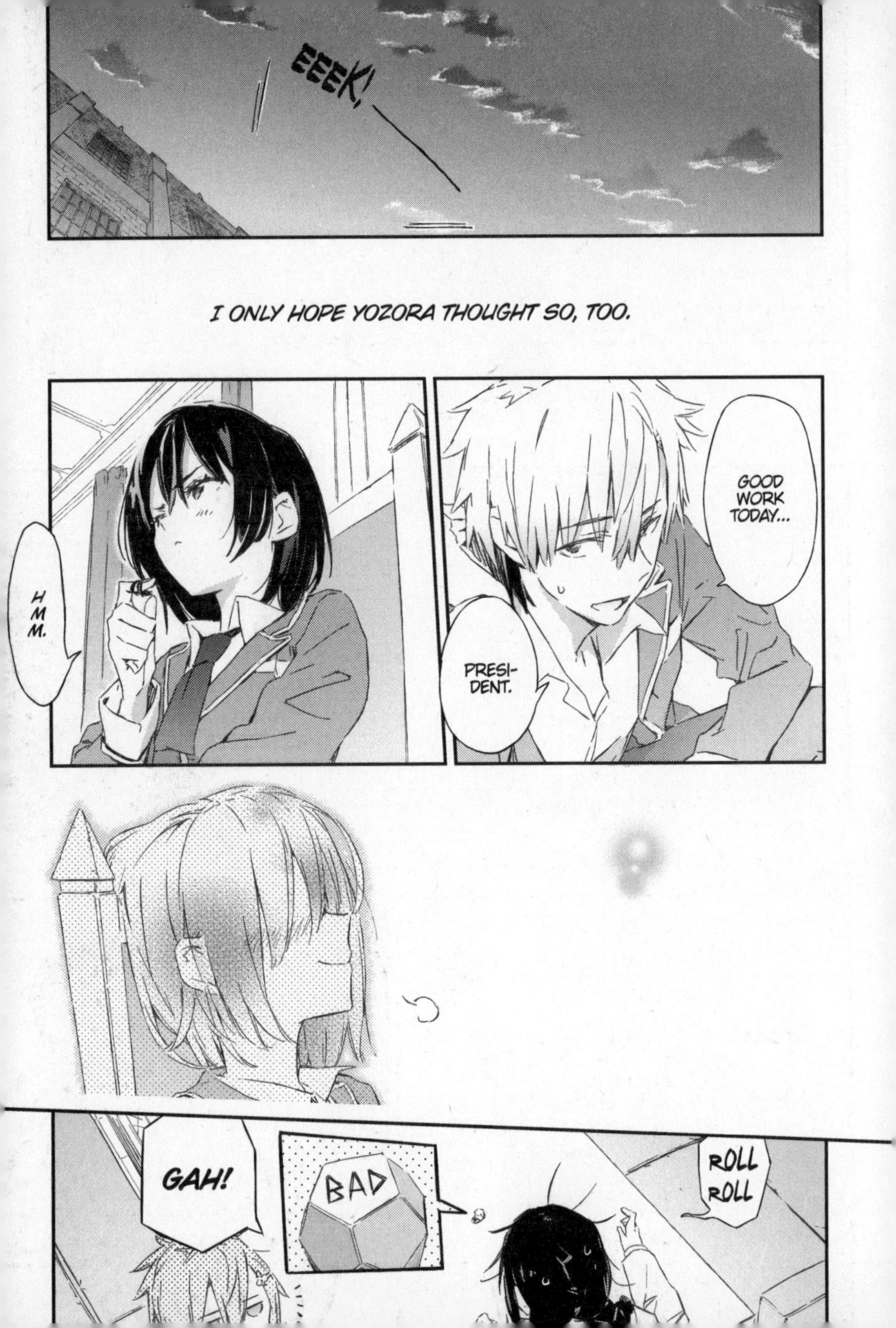
EEEK!
I ONLY HOPE YOZORA THOUGHT SO, TOO.
GOOD WORK TODAY...
PRESI-DENT.
HMM.
ROLL ROLL
BAD
GAH!

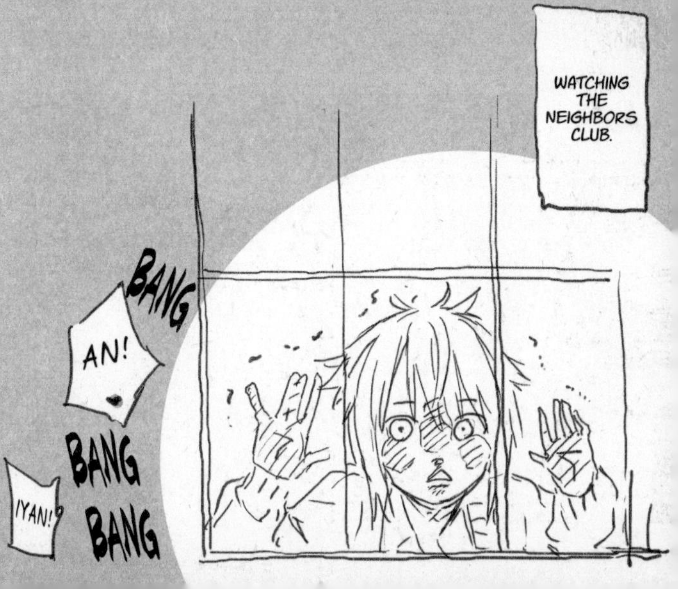
WATCHING THE NEIGHBORS CLUB.
BANG
AN! ♥
BANG
BANG
IYAN!

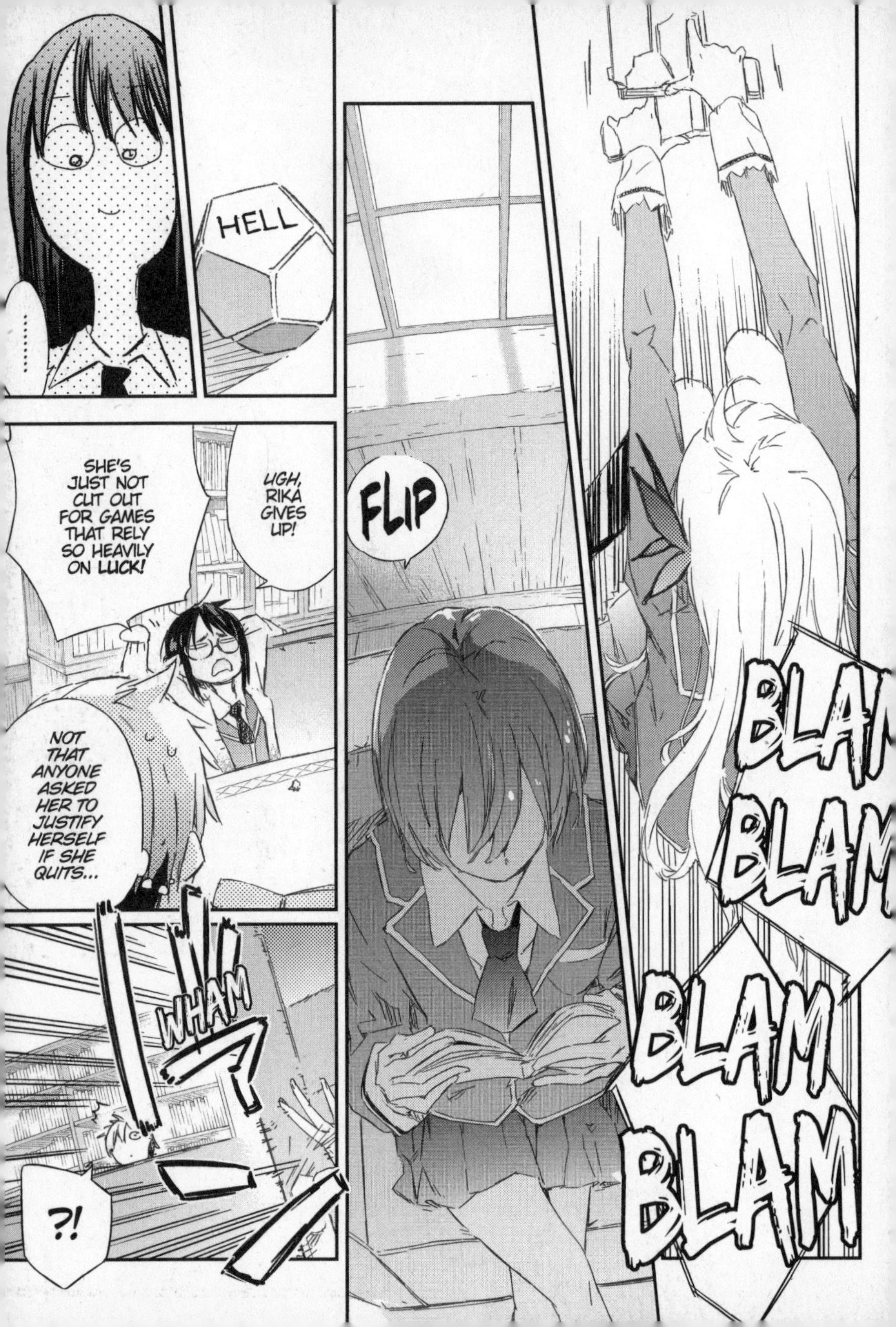
BLAM BLAM
BLAM BLAM
FLIP
HELL
......
UGH, RIKA GIVES UP!
SHE'S JUST NOT CUT OUT FOR GAMES THAT RELY SO HEAVILY ON LUCK!
NOT THAT ANYONE ASKED HER TO JUSTIFY HERSELF IF SHE QUITS...
WHAM
?!

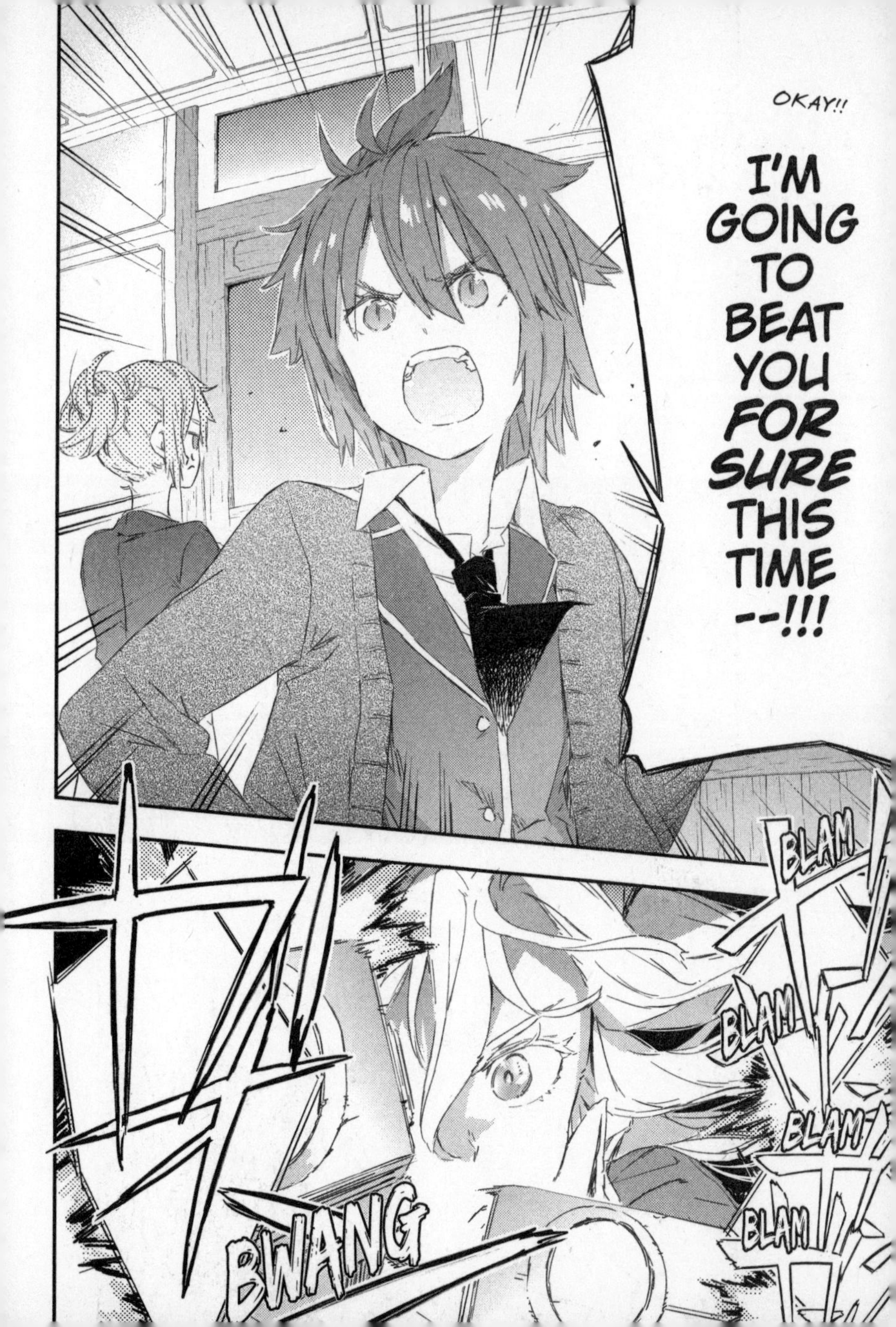
OKAY!!
I'M GOING TO BEAT YOU FOR SURE THIS TIME--!!!
BLAM
BLAM
BLAM
BLAM
BWANG

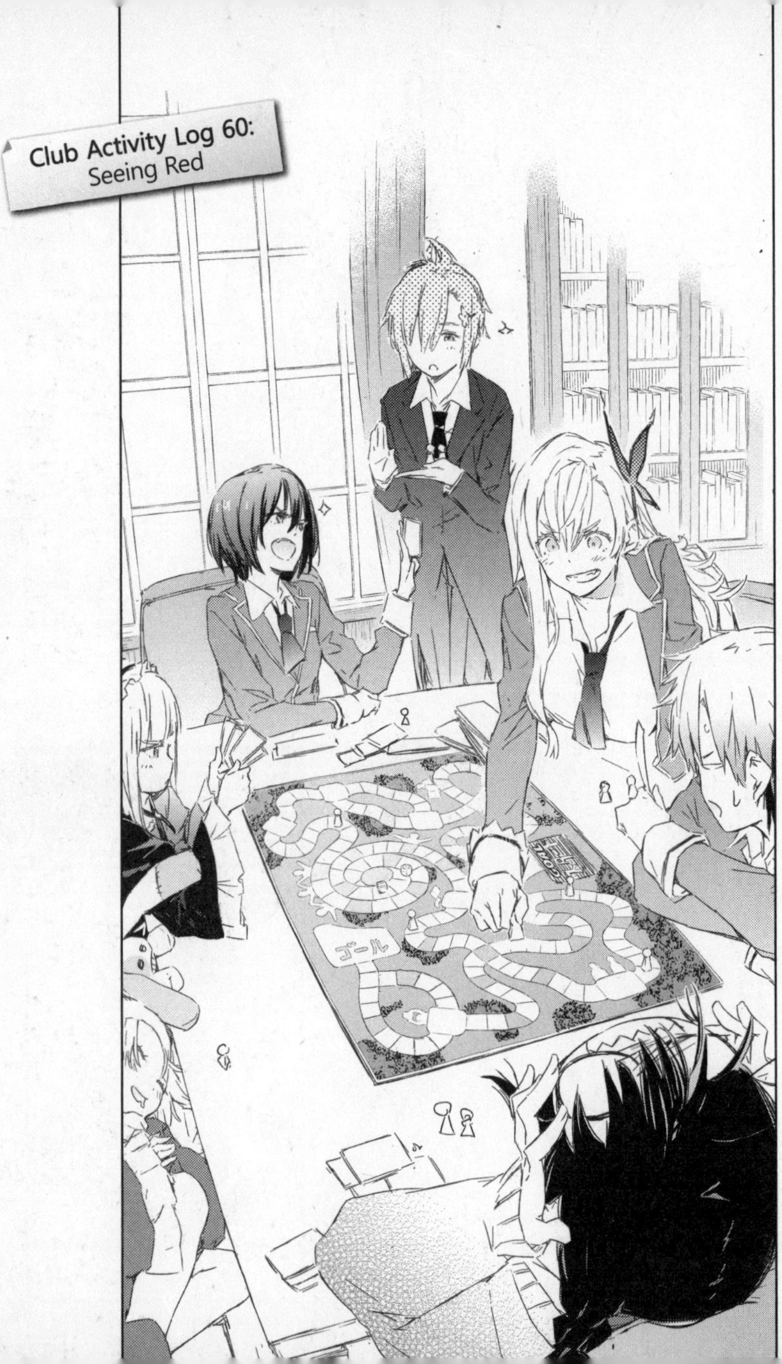
Club Activity Log 60:
Seeing Red
ゴール
GOAL

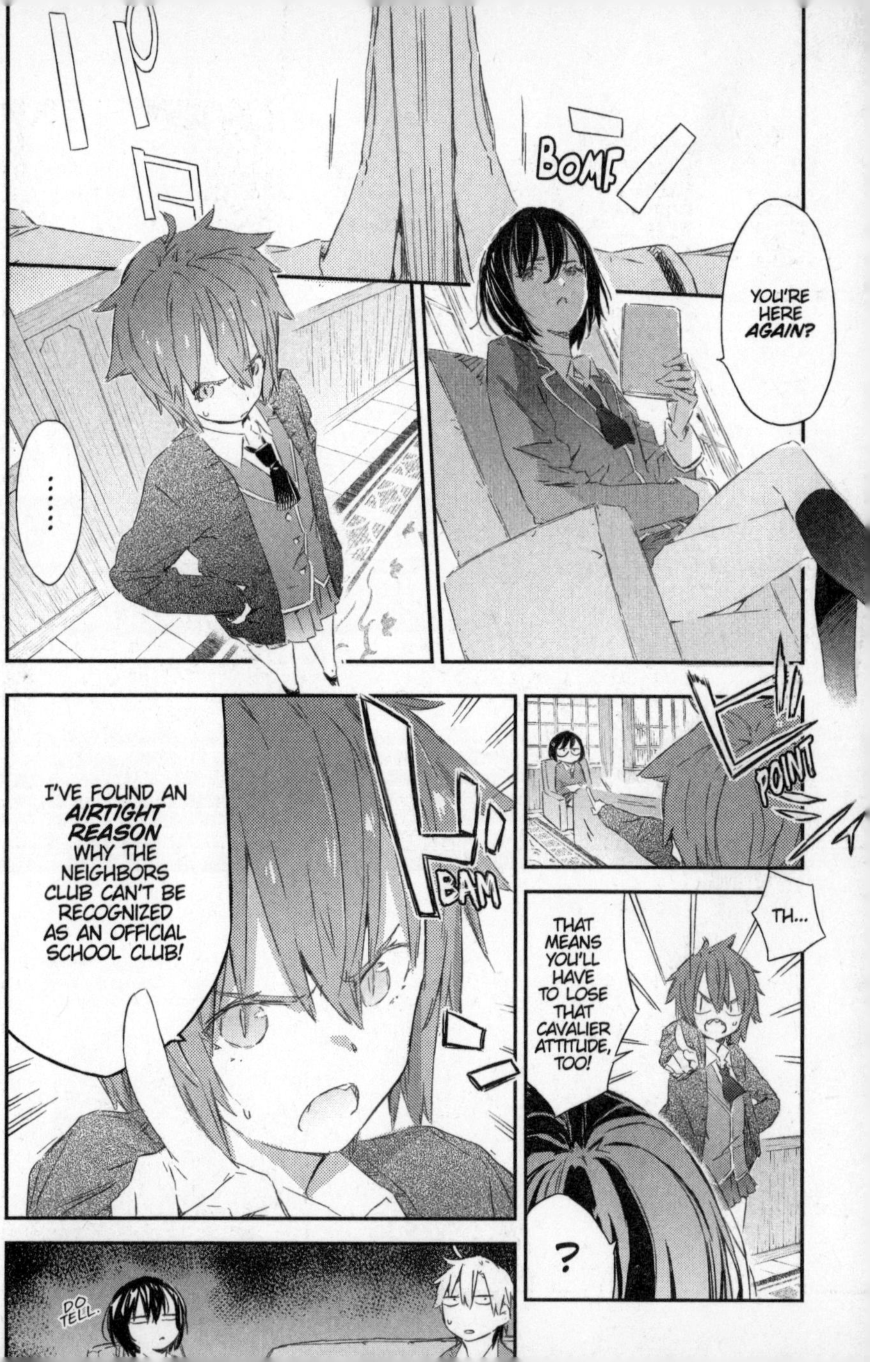
BOMF
YOU'RE HERE AGAIN?
......
POINT
BAM
I'VE FOUND AN AIRTIGHT REASON WHY THE NEIGHBORS CLUB CAN'T BE RECOGNIZED AS AN OFFICIAL SCHOOL CLUB!
TH...
THAT MEANS YOU'LL HAVE TO LOSE THAT CAVALIER ATTITUDE, TOO!
?
DO TELL.

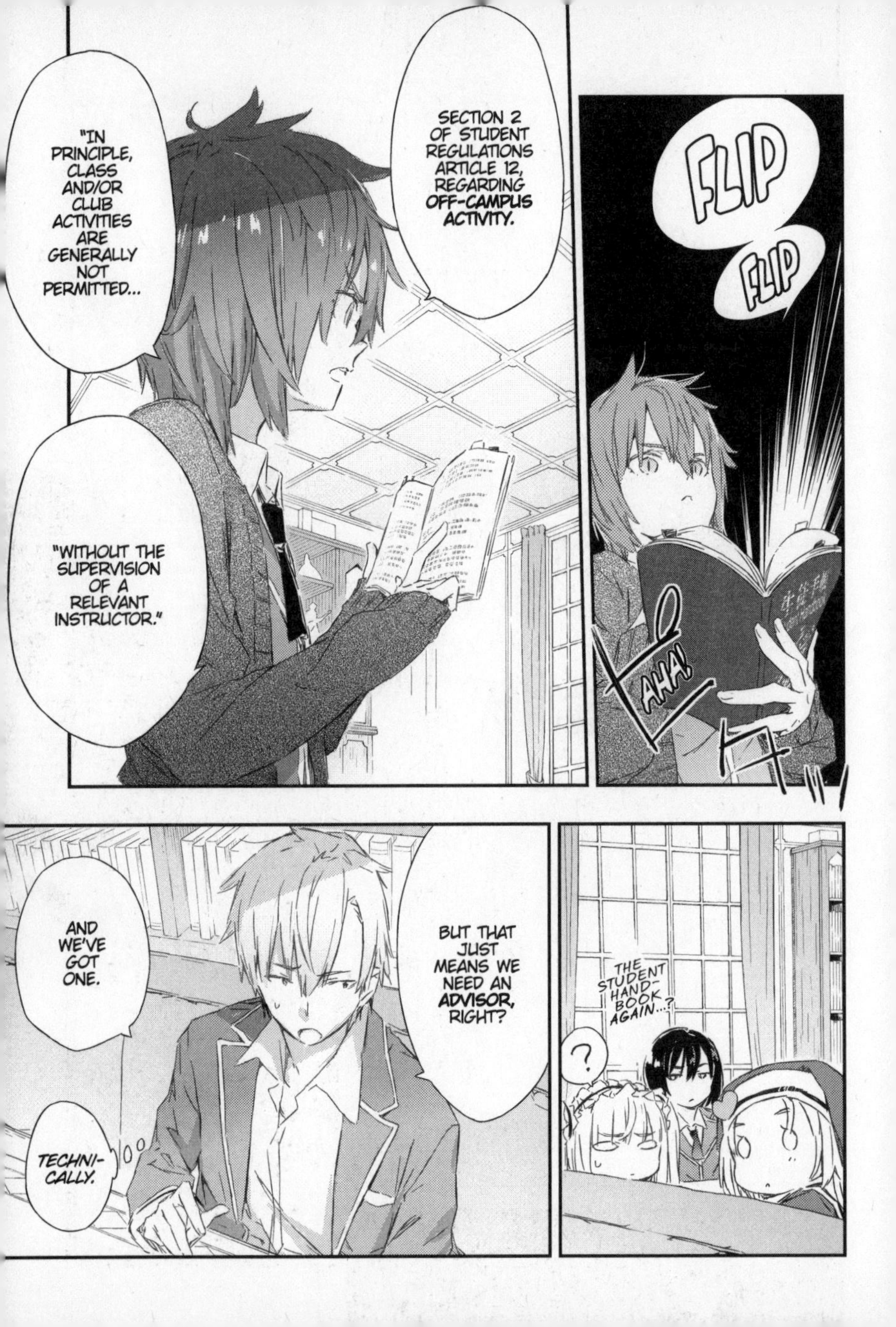
FLIP
FLIP
AHA!
SECTION 2 OF STUDENT REGULATIONS ARTICLE 12, REGARDING OFF-CAMPUS ACTIVITY.
"IN PRINCIPLE, CLASS AND/OR CLUB ACTIVITIES ARE GENERALLY NOT PERMITTED...
"WITHOUT THE SUPERVISION OF A RELEVANT INSTRUCTOR."
THE STUDENT HANDBOOK AGAIN...?
?
BUT THAT JUST MEANS WE NEED AN ADVISOR, RIGHT?
AND WE'VE GOT ONE.
TECHNICALLY.

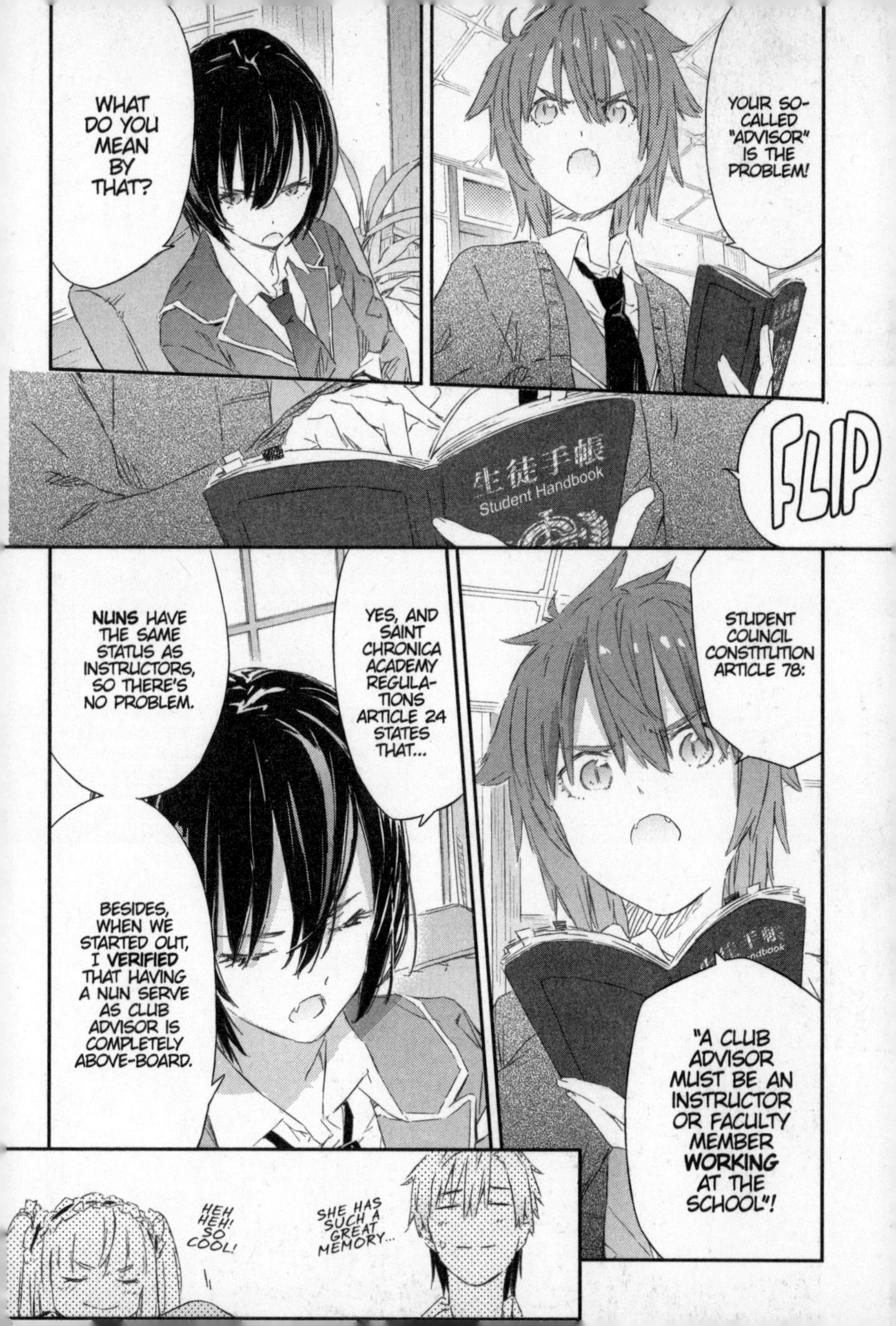
YOUR SO-CALLED "ADVISOR" IS THE PROBLEM!
WHAT DO YOU MEAN BY THAT?
FLIP
生徒手帳
Student Handbook
STUDENT COUNCIL CONSTITUTION ARTICLE 78:
"A CLUB ADVISOR MUST BE AN INSTRUCTOR OR FACULTY MEMBER WORKING AT THE SCHOOL"!
YES, AND SAINT CHRONICA ACADEMY REGULA-TIONS ARTICLE 24 STATES THAT...
NUNS HAVE THE SAME STATUS AS INSTRUCTORS, SO THERE'S NO PROBLEM.
BESIDES, WHEN WE STARTED OUT, I VERIFIED THAT HAVING A NUN SERVE AS CLUB ADVISOR IS COMPLETELY ABOVE-BOARD.
SHE HAS SUCH A GREAT MEMORY...
HEH HEH! SO COOL!

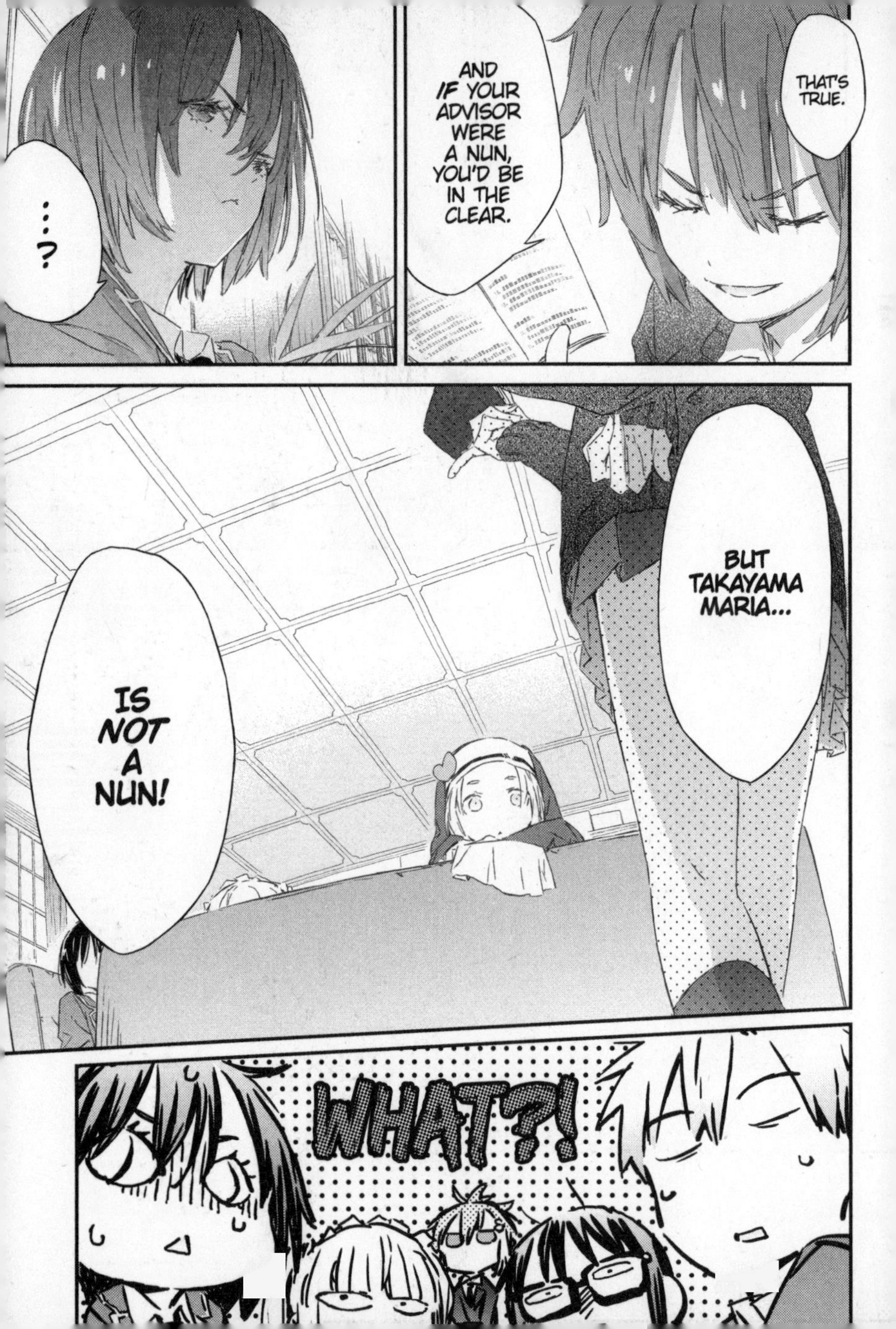
THAT'S TRUE.
AND IF YOUR ADVISOR WERE A NUN, YOU'D BE IN THE CLEAR.
...?
BUT TAKAYAMA MARIA...
IS NOT A NUN!
WHAT?!

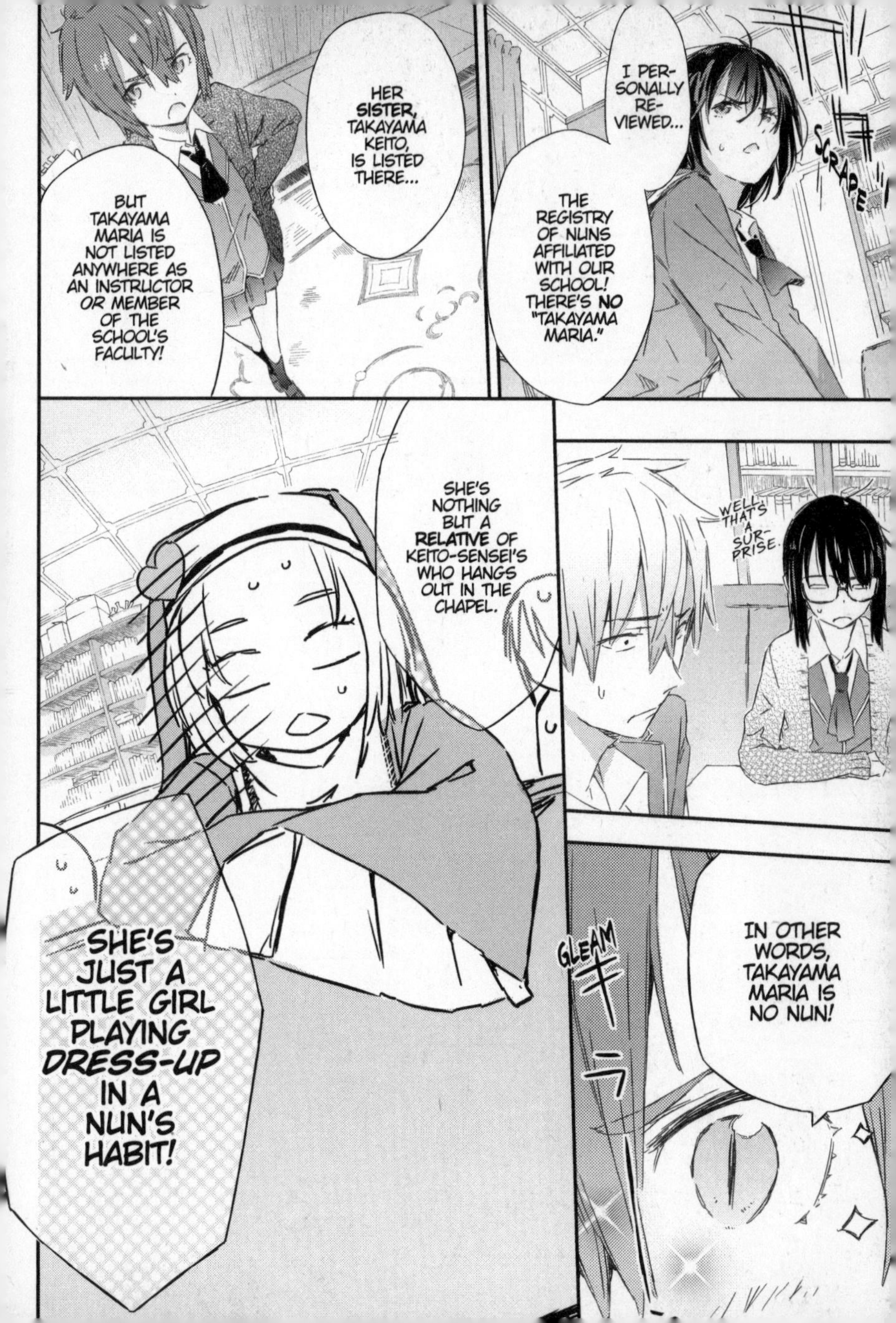
I PERSONALLY REVIEWED...
THE REGISTRY OF NUNS AFFILIATED WITH OUR SCHOOL! THERE'S NO "TAKAYAMA MARIA."
SCRAPE
HER SISTER, TAKAYAMA KEITO, IS LISTED THERE...
BUT TAKAYAMA MARIA IS NOT LISTED ANYWHERE AS AN INSTRUCTOR OR MEMBER OF THE SCHOOL'S FACULTY!
WELL THAT'S A SURPRISE.
IN OTHER WORDS, TAKAYAMA MARIA IS NO NUN!
GLEAM
SHE'S NOTHING BUT A RELATIVE OF KEITO-SENSEI'S WHO HANGS OUT IN THE CHAPEL.
SHE'S JUST A LITTLE GIRL PLAYING DRESS-UP IN A NUN'S HABIT!

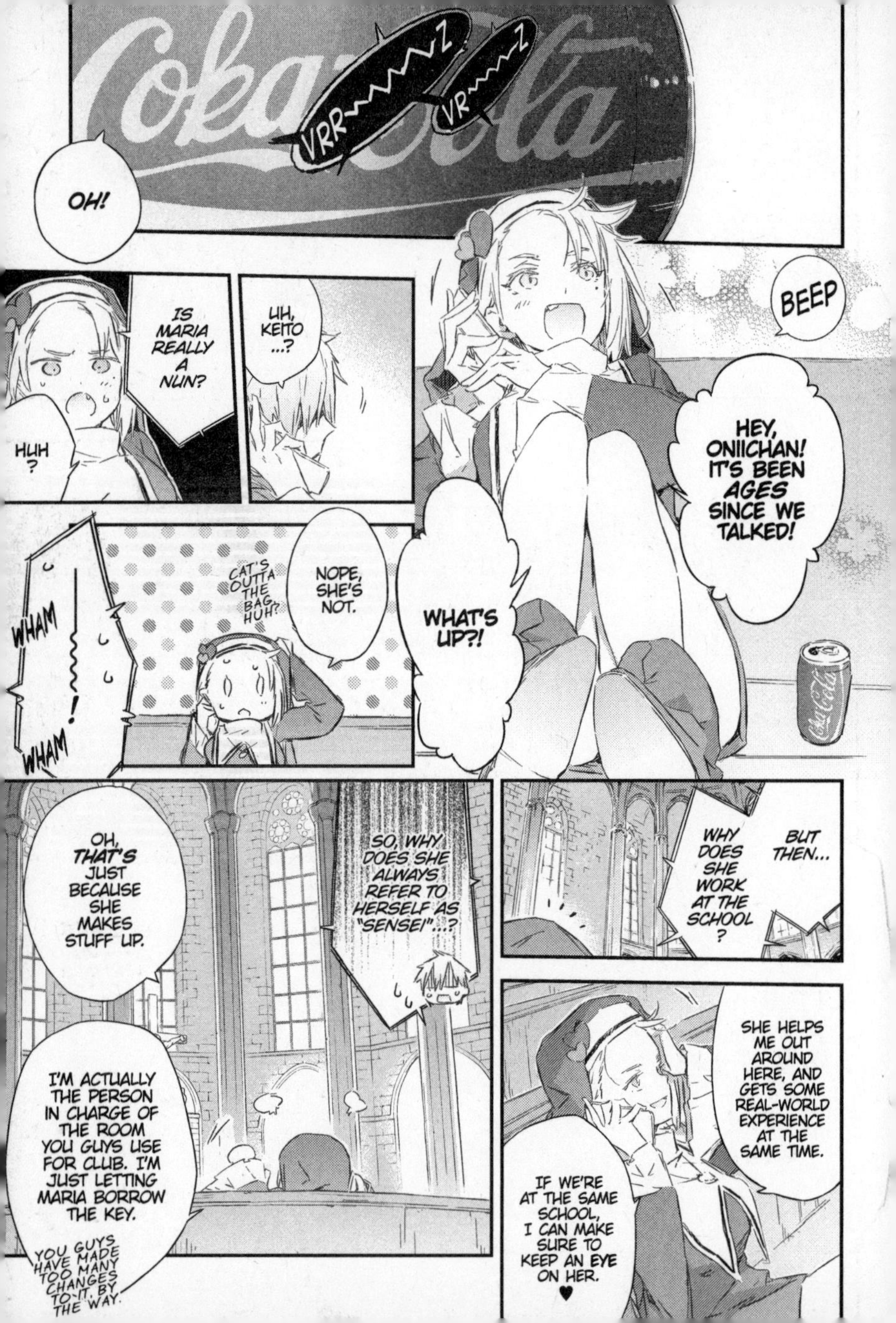
VRR~~~~~Z
VR~~~Z
OH!
BEEP
HEY, ONIICHAN! IT'S BEEN AGES SINCE WE TALKED!
WHAT'S UP?!
UH, KEITO ...?
IS MARIA REALLY A NUN?
HUH ?
NOPE, SHE'S NOT.
CAT'S OUTTA THE BAG, HUH?
WHAM ~~~~! WHAM
BUT THEN...
WHY DOES SHE WORK AT THE SCHOOL ?
SHE HELPS ME OUT AROUND HERE, AND GETS SOME REAL-WORLD EXPERIENCE AT THE SAME TIME.
IF WE'RE AT THE SAME SCHOOL, I CAN MAKE SURE TO KEEP AN EYE ON HER. ♥
SO, WHY DOES SHE ALWAYS REFER TO HERSELF AS "SENSEI"...?
OH, THAT'S JUST BECAUSE SHE MAKES STUFF UP.
I'M ACTUALLY THE PERSON IN CHARGE OF THE ROOM YOU GUYS USE FOR CLUB. I'M JUST LETTING MARIA BORROW THE KEY.
YOU GUYS HAVE MADE TOO MANY CHANGES TO IT, BY THE WAY.

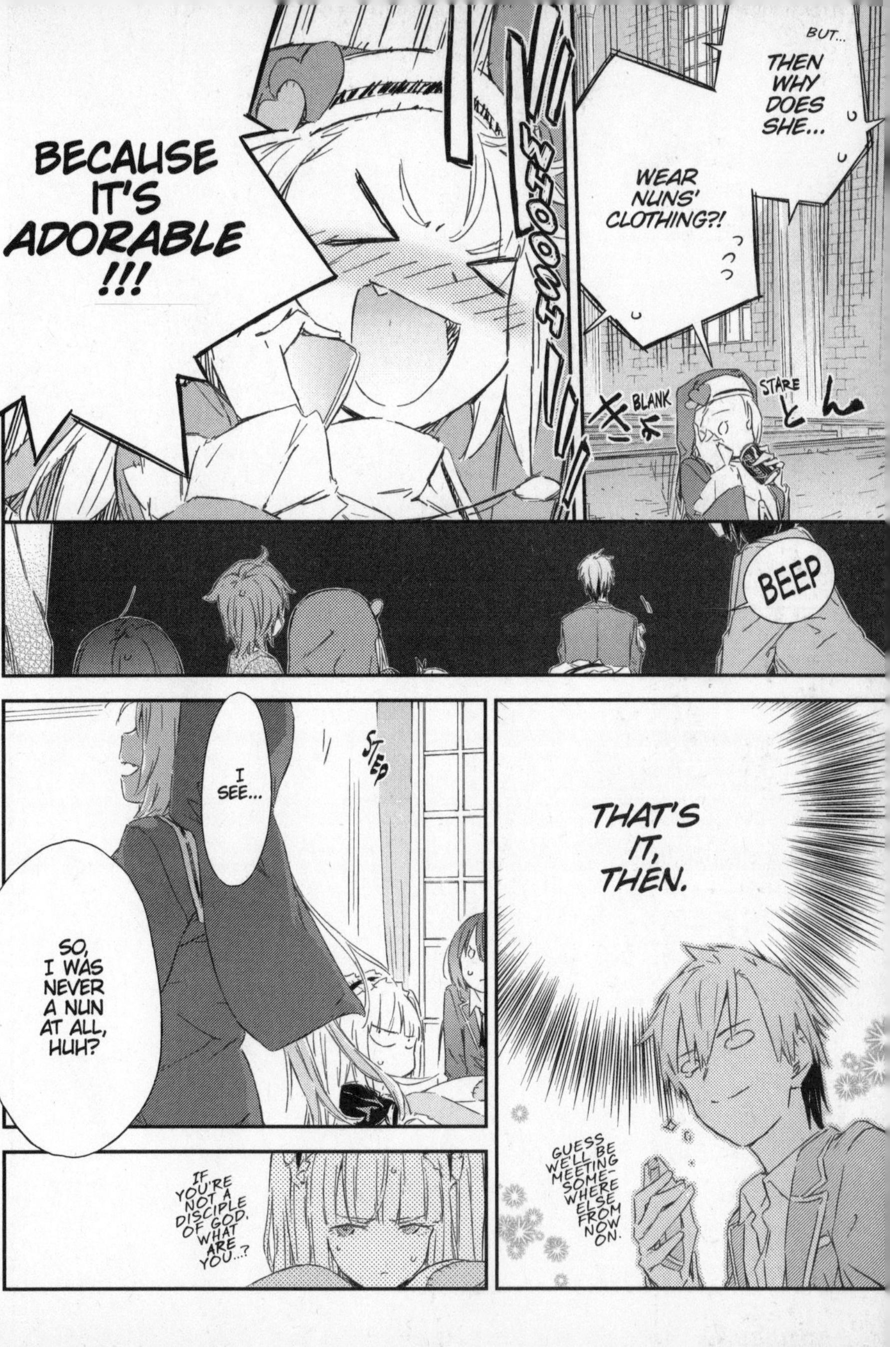
BUT...
THEN WHY DOES SHE...
WEAR NUNS' CLOTHING?!
STARE
BLANK
WHOOOSH
BECAUSE IT'S ADORABLE !!!
BEEP
THAT'S IT, THEN.
GUESS WE'LL BE MEETING SOME-WHERE ELSE FROM NOW ON.
STEP
I SEE...
SO, I WAS NEVER A NUN AT ALL, HUH?
IF YOU'RE NOT A DISCIPLE OF GOD, WHAT ARE YOU...?

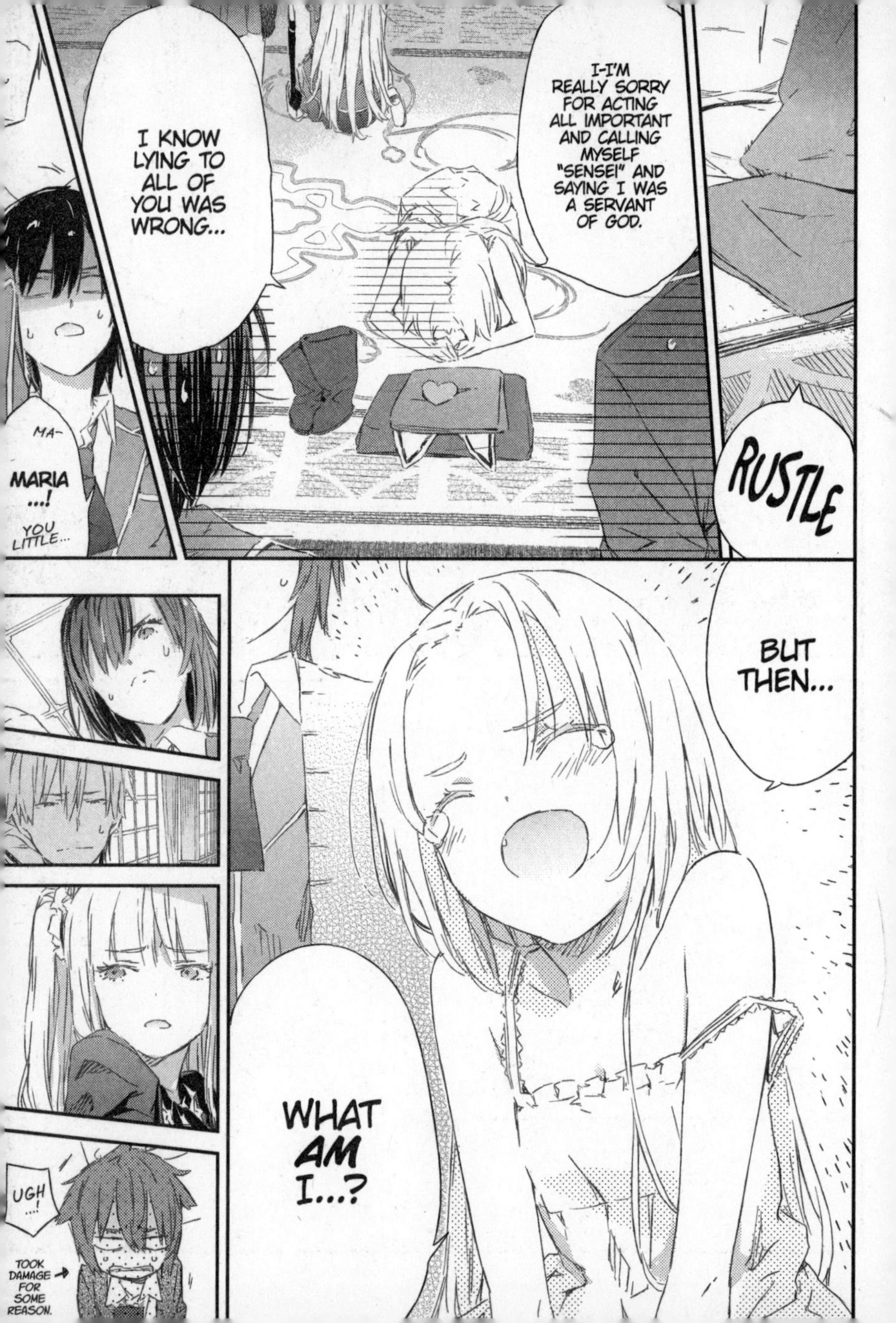
I-I'M REALLY SORRY FOR ACTING ALL IMPORTANT AND CALLING MYSELF "SENSEI" AND SAYING I WAS A SERVANT OF GOD.
I KNOW LYING TO ALL OF YOU WAS WRONG...
RUSTLE
MA- MARIA ...!
YOU LITTLE...
BUT THEN...
WHAT AM I...?
UGH ...!
TOOK DAMAGE FOR SOME REASON.

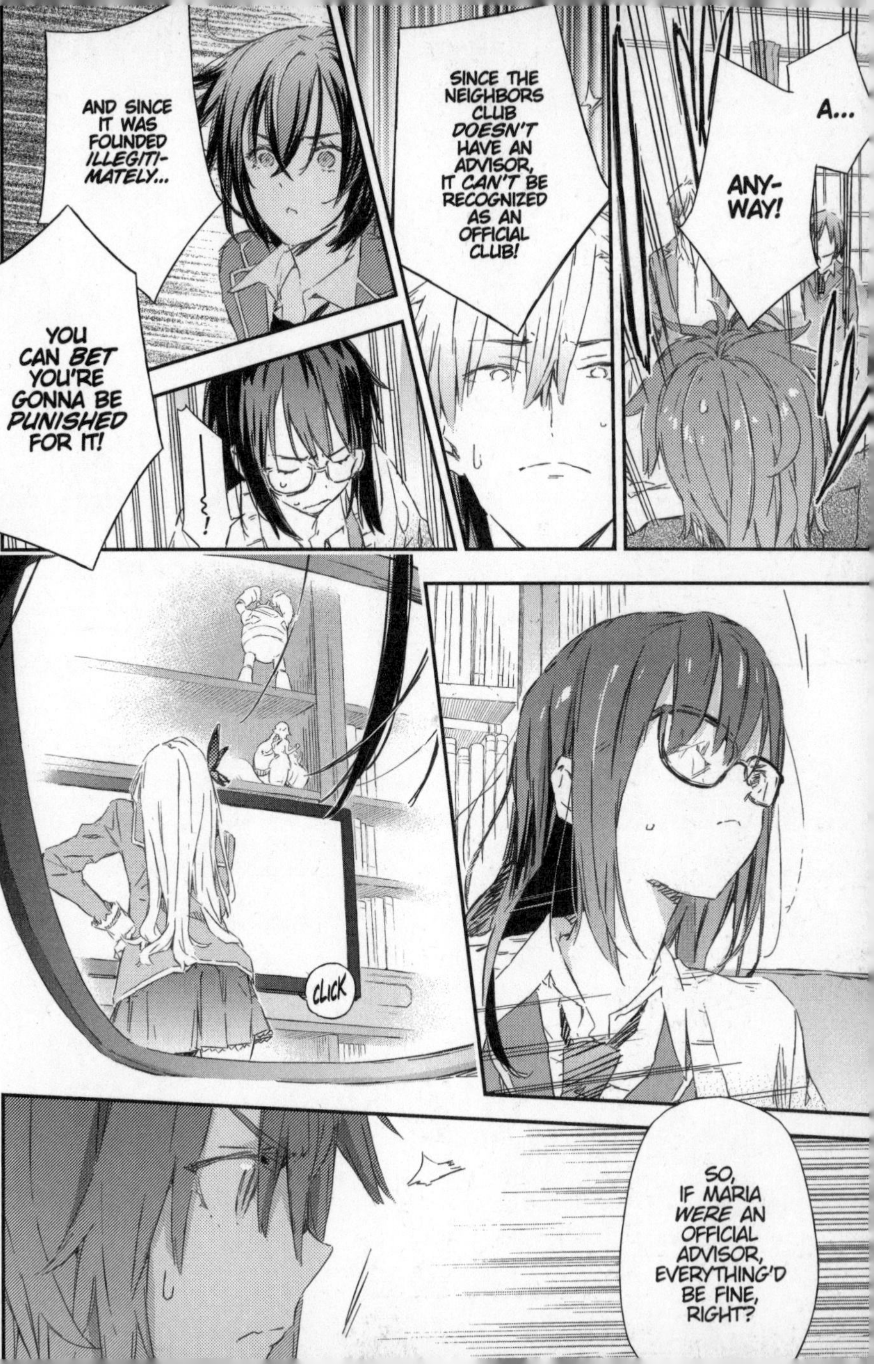
A...
ANY-WAY!
SINCE THE NEIGHBORS CLUB *DOESN'T* HAVE AN ADVISOR, IT *CAN'T* BE RECOGNIZED AS AN OFFICIAL CLUB!
AND SINCE IT WAS FOUNDED *ILLEGITI-MATELY*...
YOU CAN *BET* YOU'RE GONNA BE *PUNISHED* FOR IT!
...!
CLICK
SO, IF MARIA *WERE* AN OFFICIAL ADVISOR, EVERYTHING'D BE FINE, RIGHT?

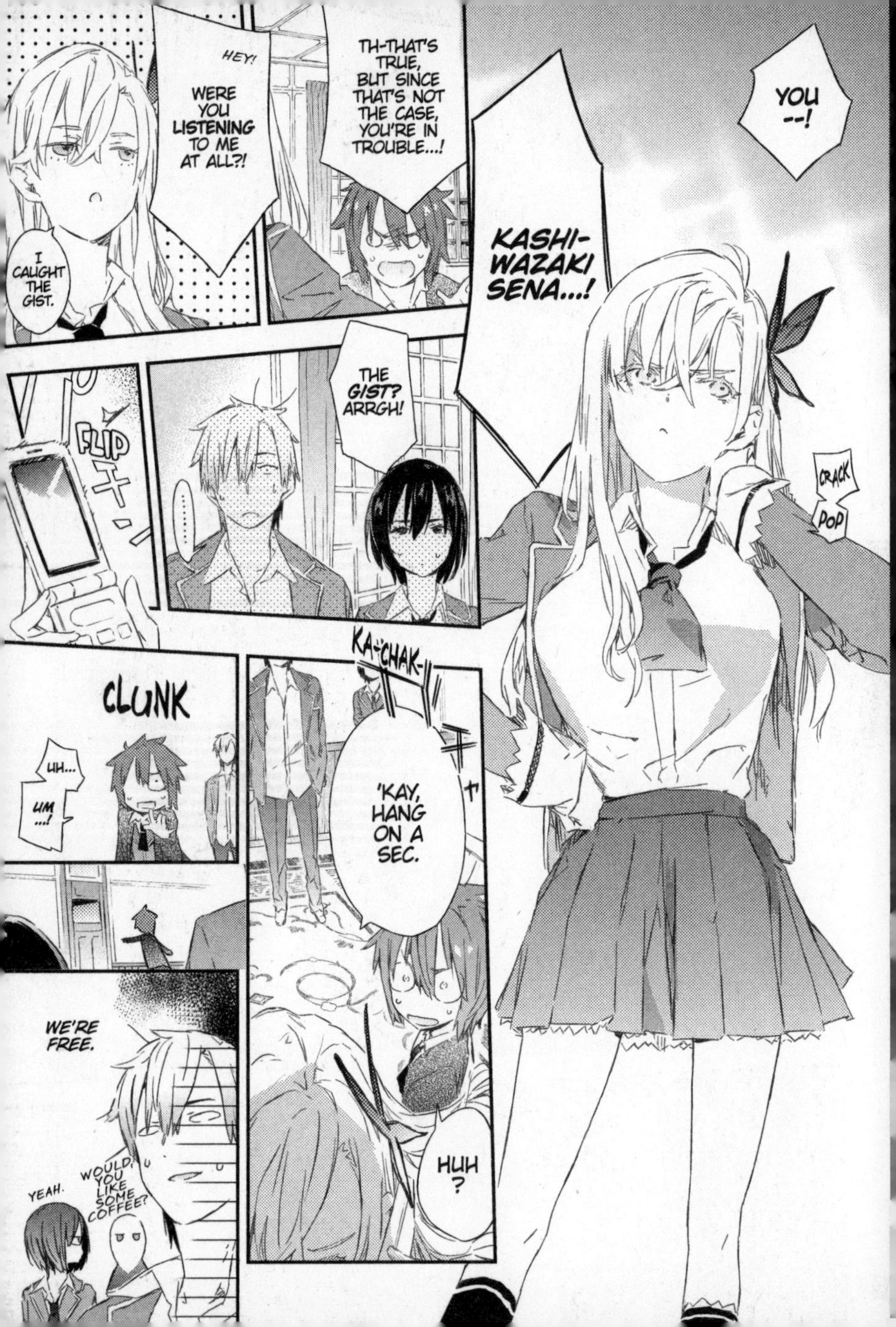
YOU --!
KASHI-WAZAKI SENA...!
CRACK
POP
TH-THAT'S TRUE, BUT SINCE THAT'S NOT THE CASE, YOU'RE IN TROUBLE...!
HEY!
WERE YOU LISTENING TO ME AT ALL?!
I CAUGHT THE GIST.
THE GIST? ARRGH!
......
FLIP
KA-CHAK-
'KAY, HANG ON A SEC.
CLUNK
UH...
UM ...!
HUH?
WE'RE FREE.
WOULD YOU LIKE SOME COFFEE?
YEAH.

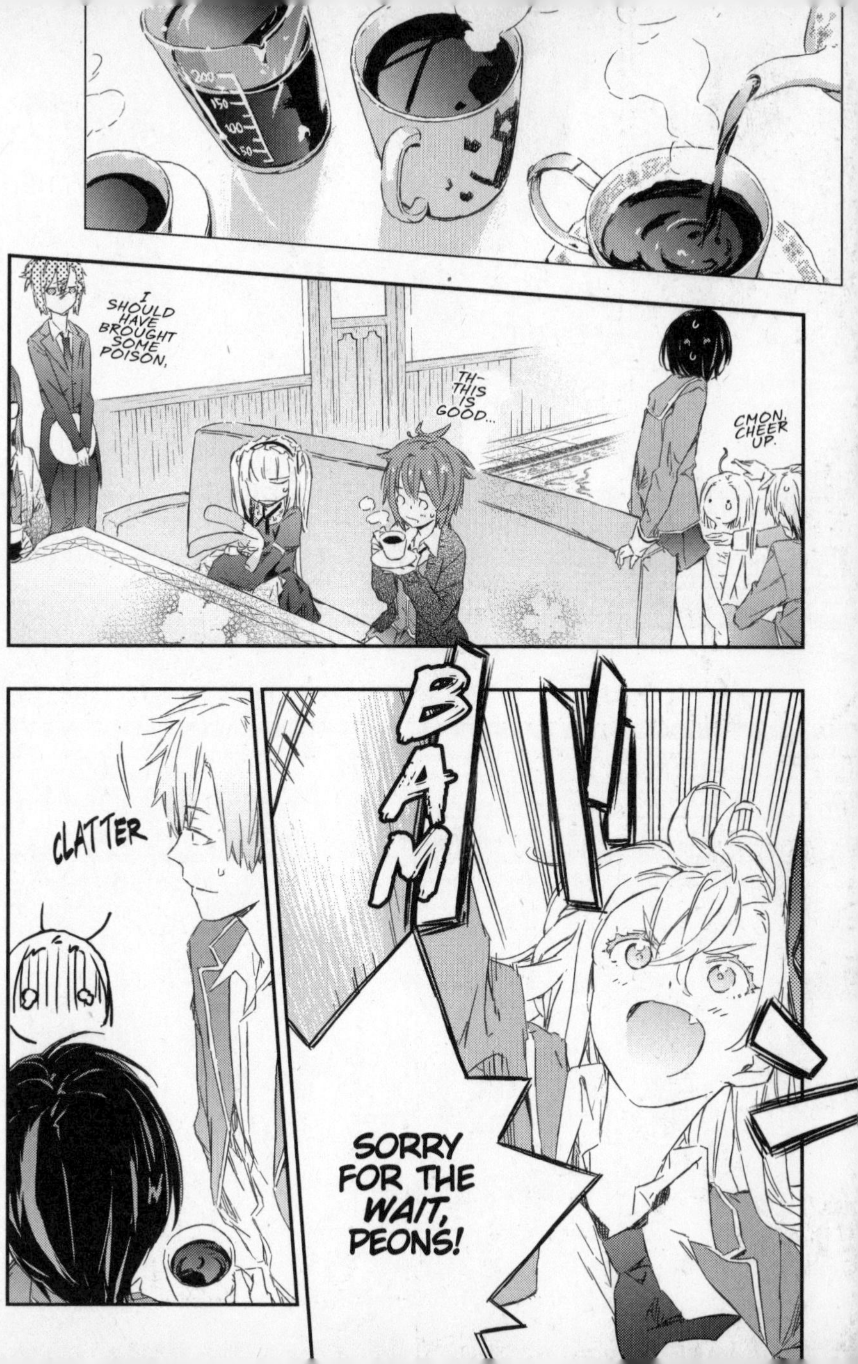
CMON, CHEER UP.
TH-THIS IS GOOD...
I SHOULD HAVE BROUGHT SOME POISON.
BAM
SORRY FOR THE WAIT, PEONS!
CLATTER

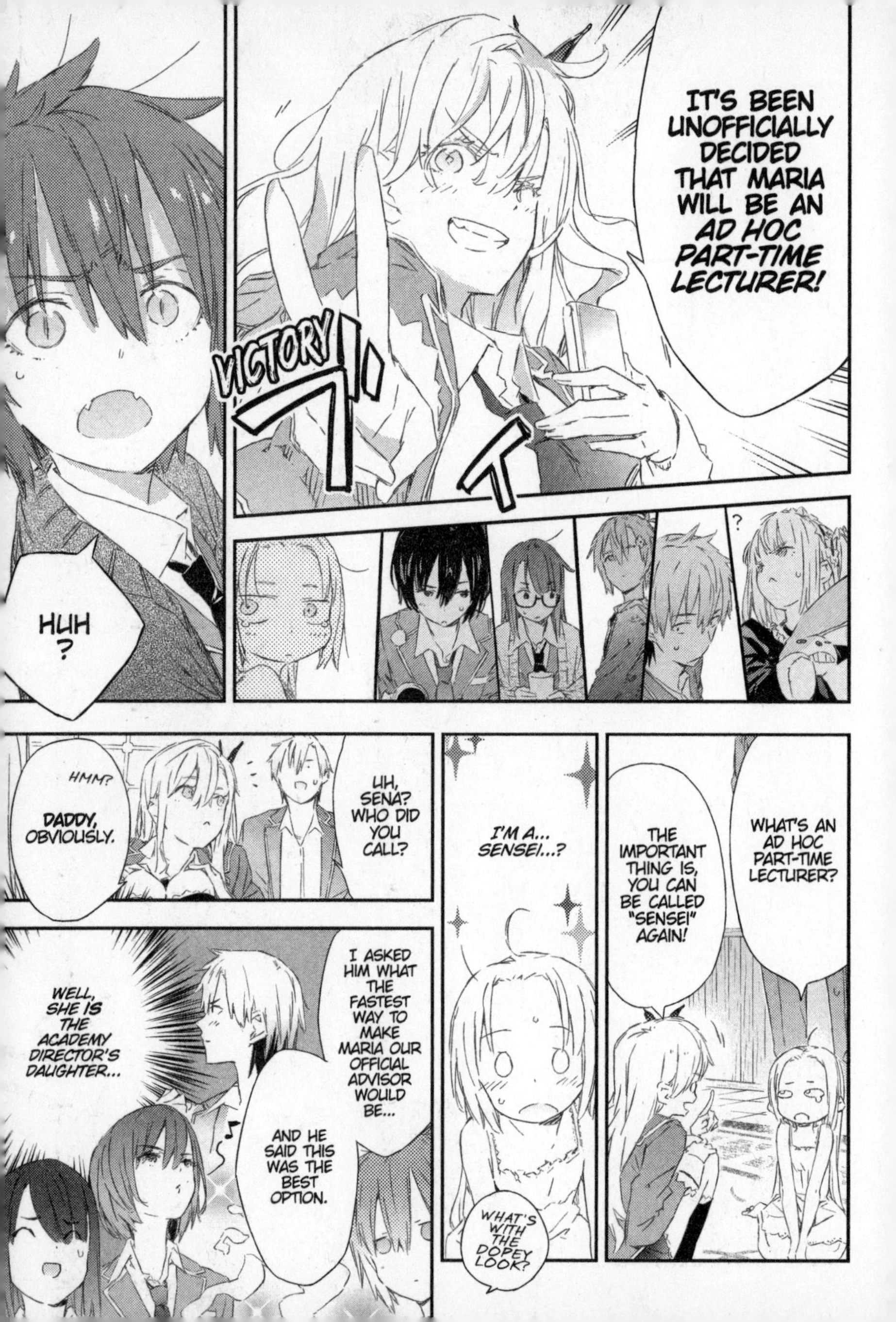
IT'S BEEN UNOFFICIALLY DECIDED THAT MARIA WILL BE AN *AD HOC PART-TIME LECTURER!*
VICTORY
HUH?
?
WHAT'S AN AD HOC PART-TIME LECTURER?
THE IMPORTANT THING IS, YOU CAN BE CALLED "SENSEI" AGAIN!
I'M A... SENSEI...?
WHAT'S WITH THE DOPEY LOOK?
UH, SENA? WHO DID YOU CALL?
HMM?
DADDY, OBVIOUSLY.
I ASKED HIM WHAT THE FASTEST WAY TO MAKE MARIA OUR OFFICIAL ADVISOR WOULD BE...
AND HE SAID THIS WAS THE BEST OPTION.
WELL, SHE IS THE ACADEMY DIRECTOR'S DAUGHTER...

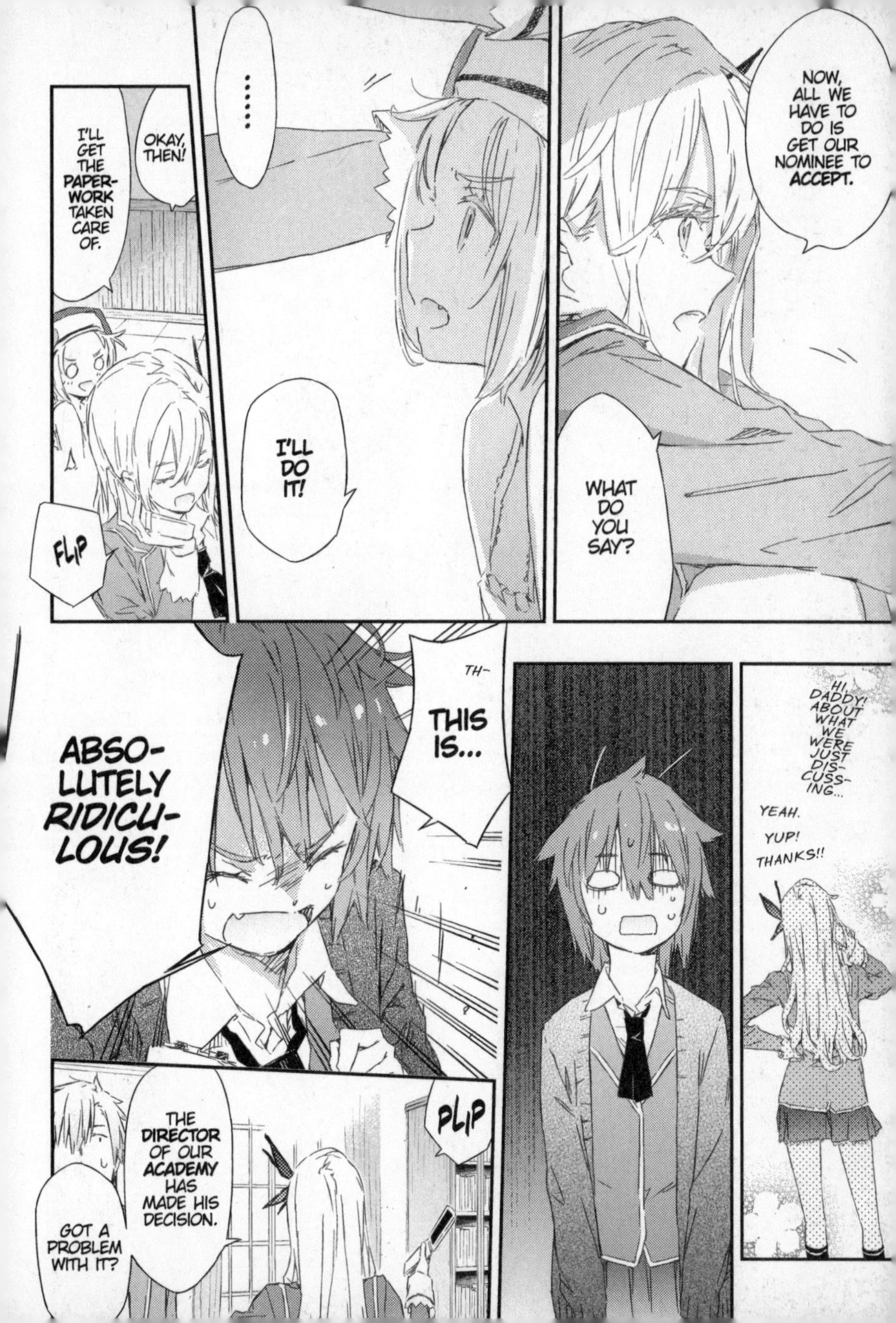
NOW, ALL WE HAVE TO DO IS GET OUR NOMINEE TO ACCEPT.
WHAT DO YOU SAY?
......
I'LL DO IT!
OKAY, THEN!
I'LL GET THE PAPER-WORK TAKEN CARE OF.
FLIP
HI, DADDY! ABOUT WHAT WE WERE JUST DIS-CUSS-ING...
YEAH.
YUP!
THANKS!!
TH-
THIS IS...
ABSO-LUTELY RIDICU-LOUS!
PLIP
THE DIRECTOR OF OUR ACADEMY HAS MADE HIS DECISION.
GOT A PROBLEM WITH IT?

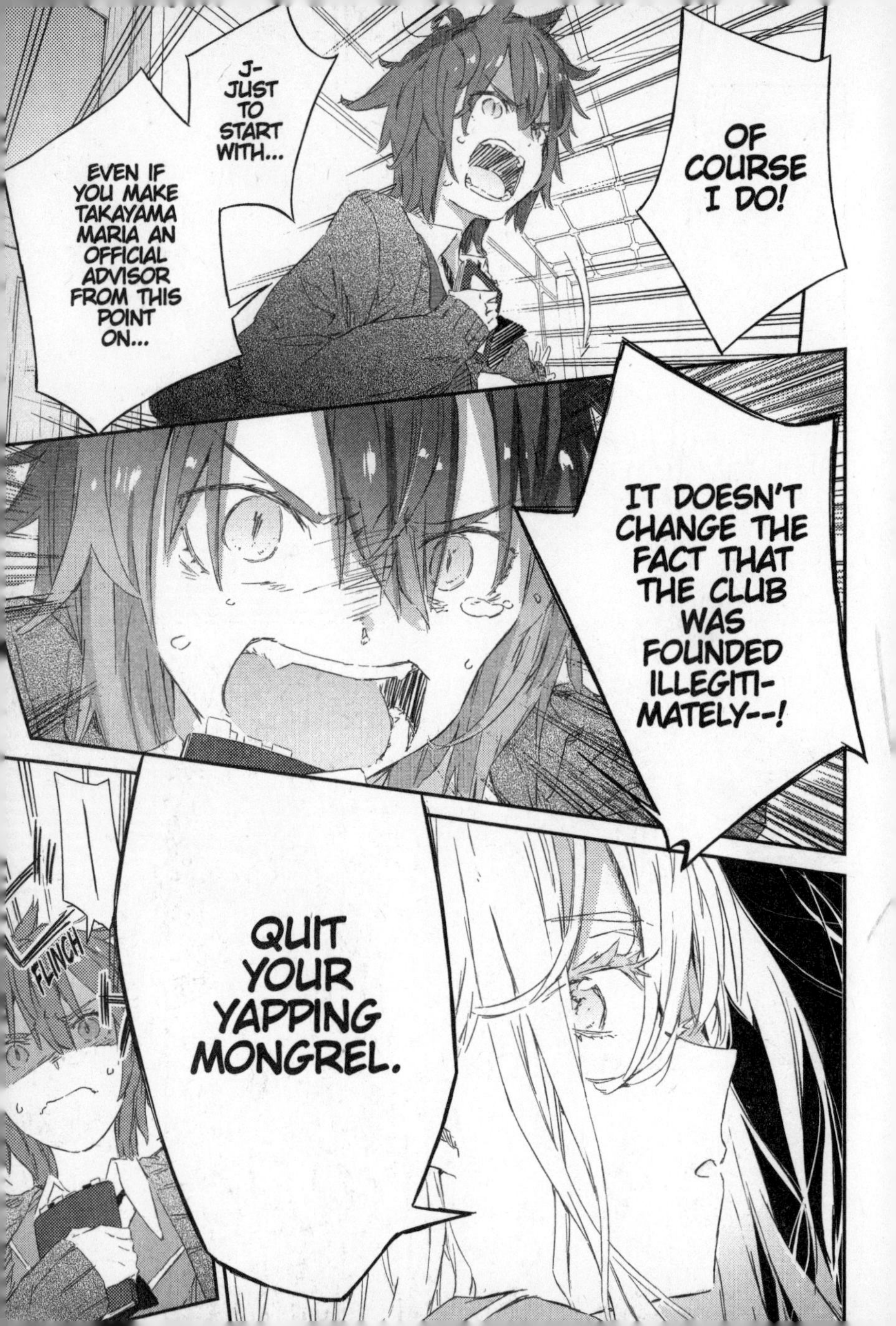
OF COURSE I DO!
J-JUST TO START WITH...
EVEN IF YOU MAKE TAKAYAMA MARIA AN OFFICIAL ADVISOR FROM THIS POINT ON...
IT DOESN'T CHANGE THE FACT THAT THE CLUB WAS FOUNDED ILLEGITI-MATELY--!
QUIT YOUR YAPPING MONGREL.
FLINCH

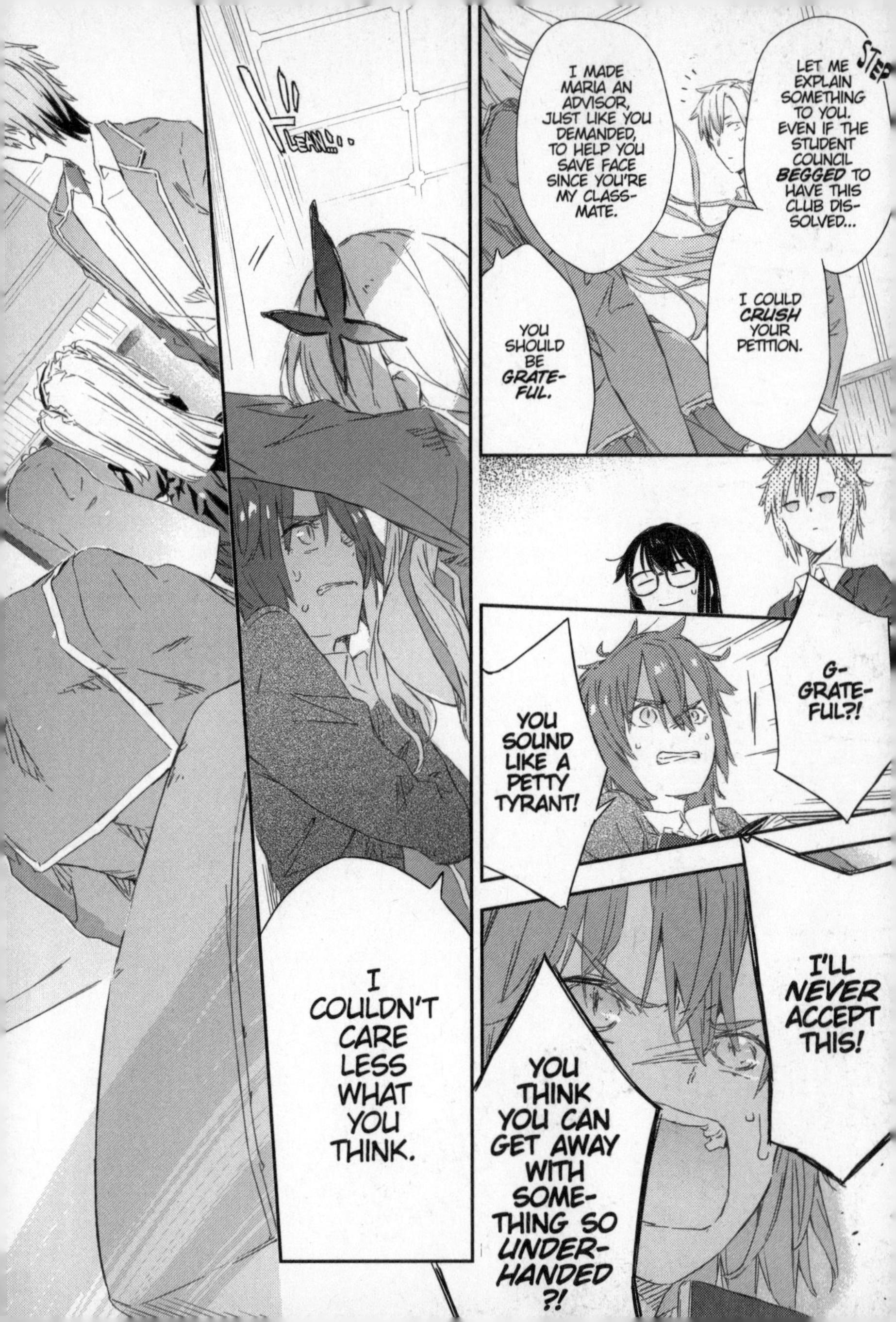
STEP
LET ME EXPLAIN SOMETHING TO YOU. EVEN IF THE STUDENT COUNCIL *BEGGED* TO HAVE THIS CLUB DISSOLVED...
I MADE MARIA AN ADVISOR, JUST LIKE YOU DEMANDED, TO HELP YOU SAVE FACE SINCE YOU'RE MY CLASSMATE.
I COULD *CRUSH* YOUR PETITION.
YOU SHOULD BE *GRATEFUL.*
G-GRATEFUL?!
YOU SOUND LIKE A PETTY TYRANT!
I'LL *NEVER* ACCEPT THIS!
YOU THINK YOU CAN GET AWAY WITH SOMETHING SO *UNDERHANDED* ?!
CLEAN...
I COULDN'T CARE LESS WHAT YOU THINK.

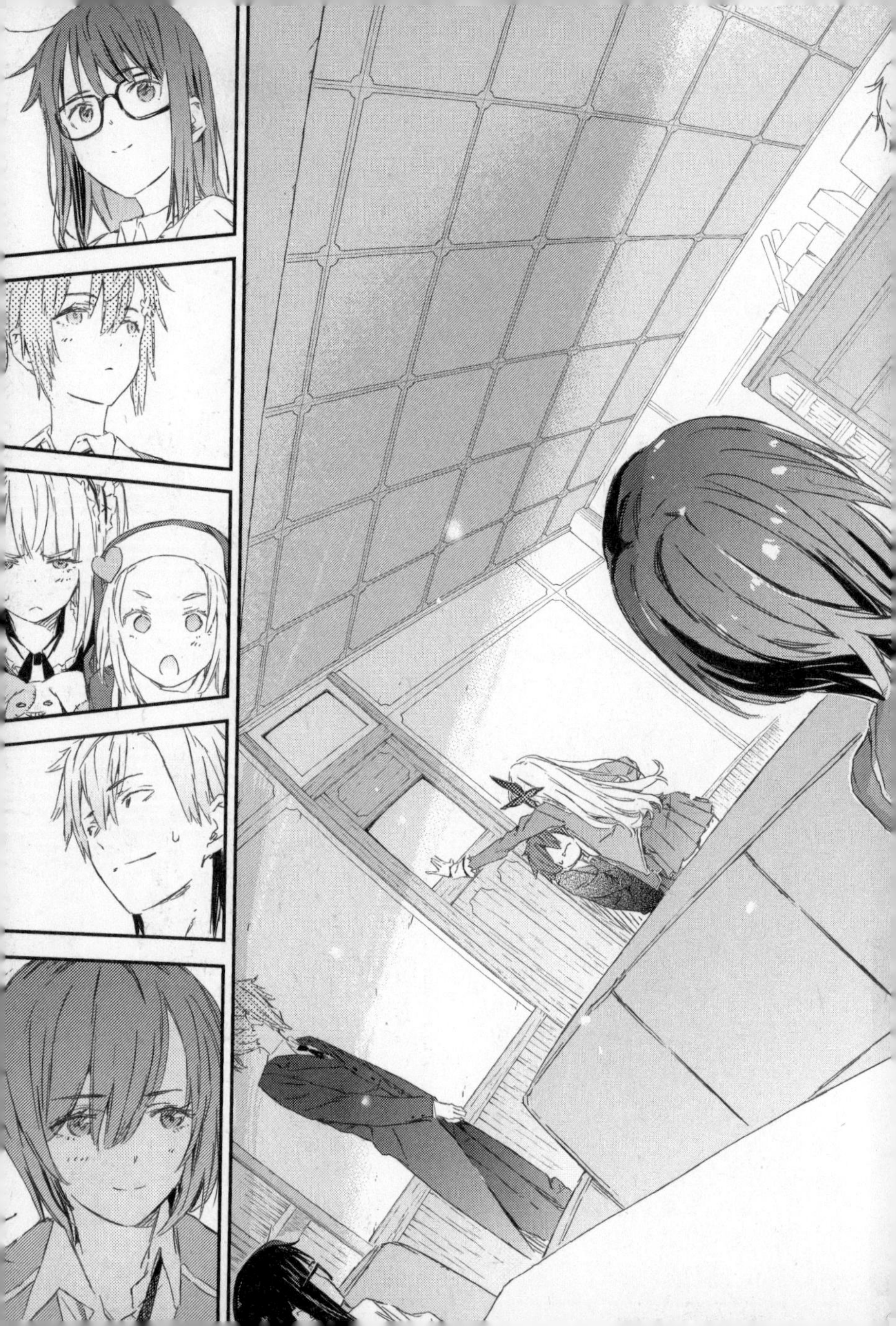

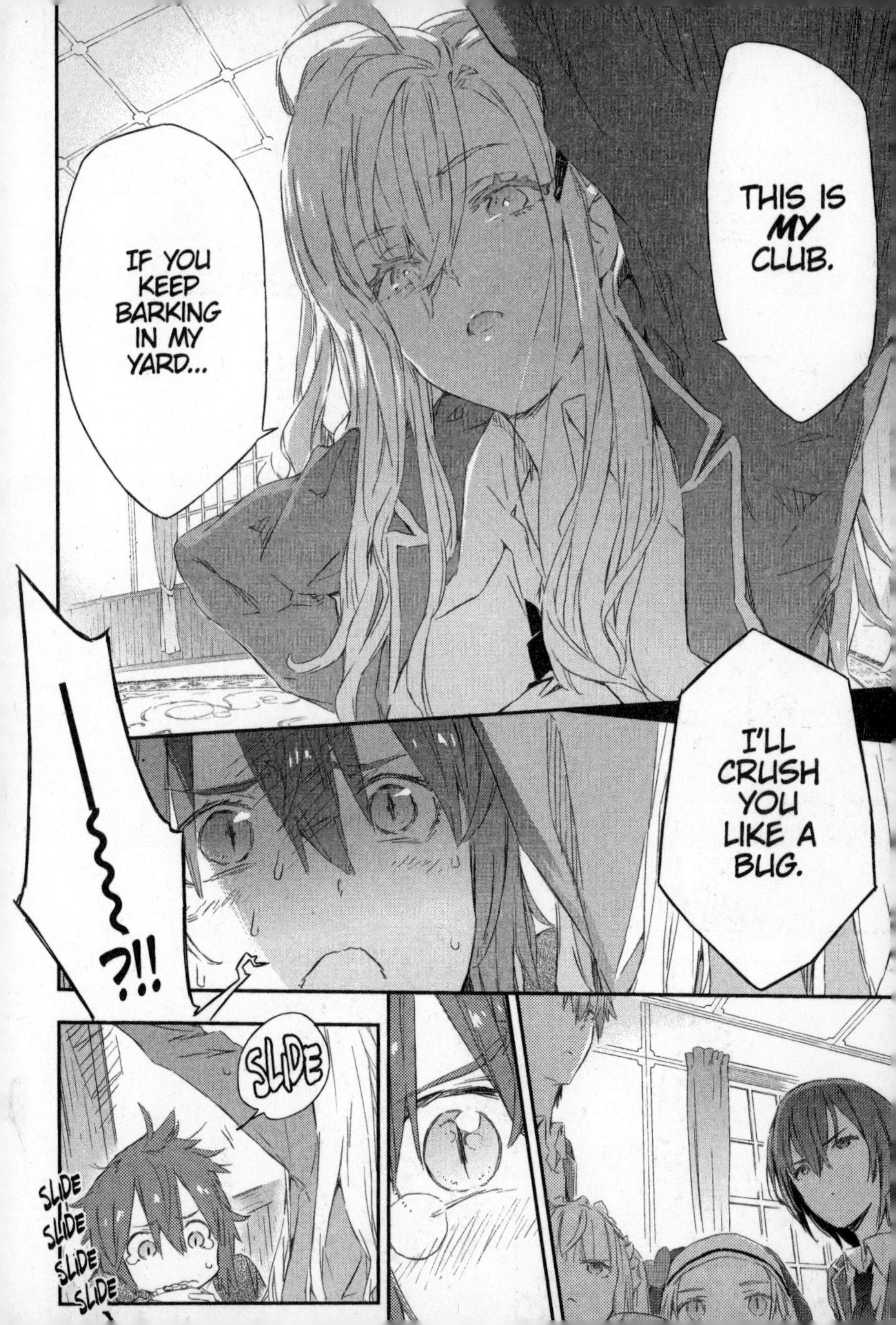
THIS IS MY CLUB.
IF YOU KEEP BARKING IN MY YARD...
I'LL CRUSH YOU LIKE A BUG.
—~~~~?!!
SLIDE
SLIDE SLIDE SLIDE SLIDE

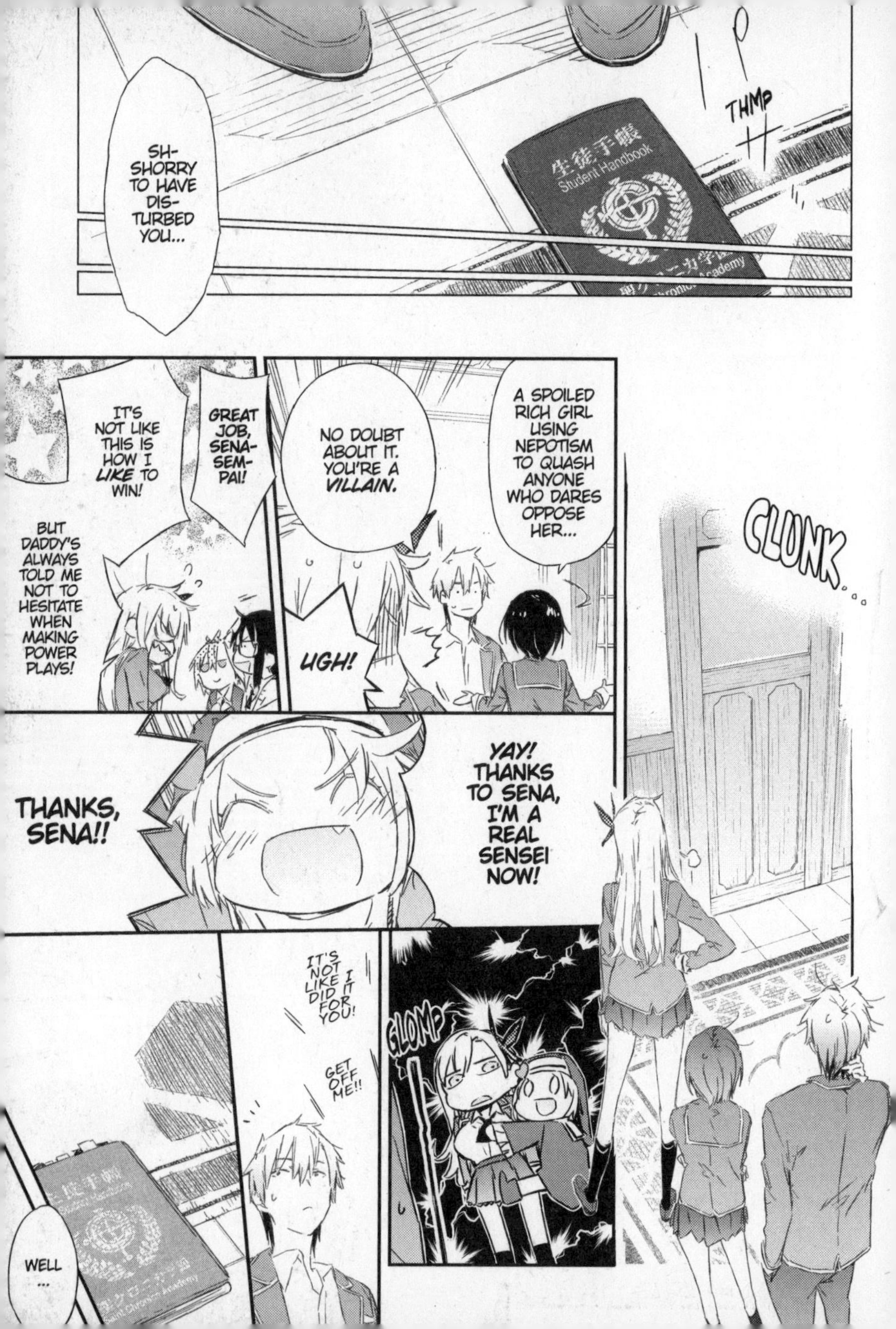
THMP
生徒手帳
Student Handbook
SH-SHORRY TO HAVE DIS-TURBED YOU...
CLUNK...
YAY! THANKS TO SENA, I'M A REAL SENSEI NOW!
A SPOILED RICH GIRL USING NEPOTISM TO QUASH ANYONE WHO DARES OPPOSE HER...
NO DOUBT ABOUT IT. YOU'RE A *VILLAIN.*
UGH!
GREAT JOB, SENA-SEMPAI!
IT'S NOT LIKE THIS IS HOW I *LIKE* TO WIN!
BUT DADDY'S ALWAYS TOLD ME NOT TO HESITATE WHEN MAKING POWER PLAYS!
THANKS, SENA!!
GLOMP
IT'S NOT LIKE I DID IT FOR YOU!
GET OFF ME!!
WELL ...

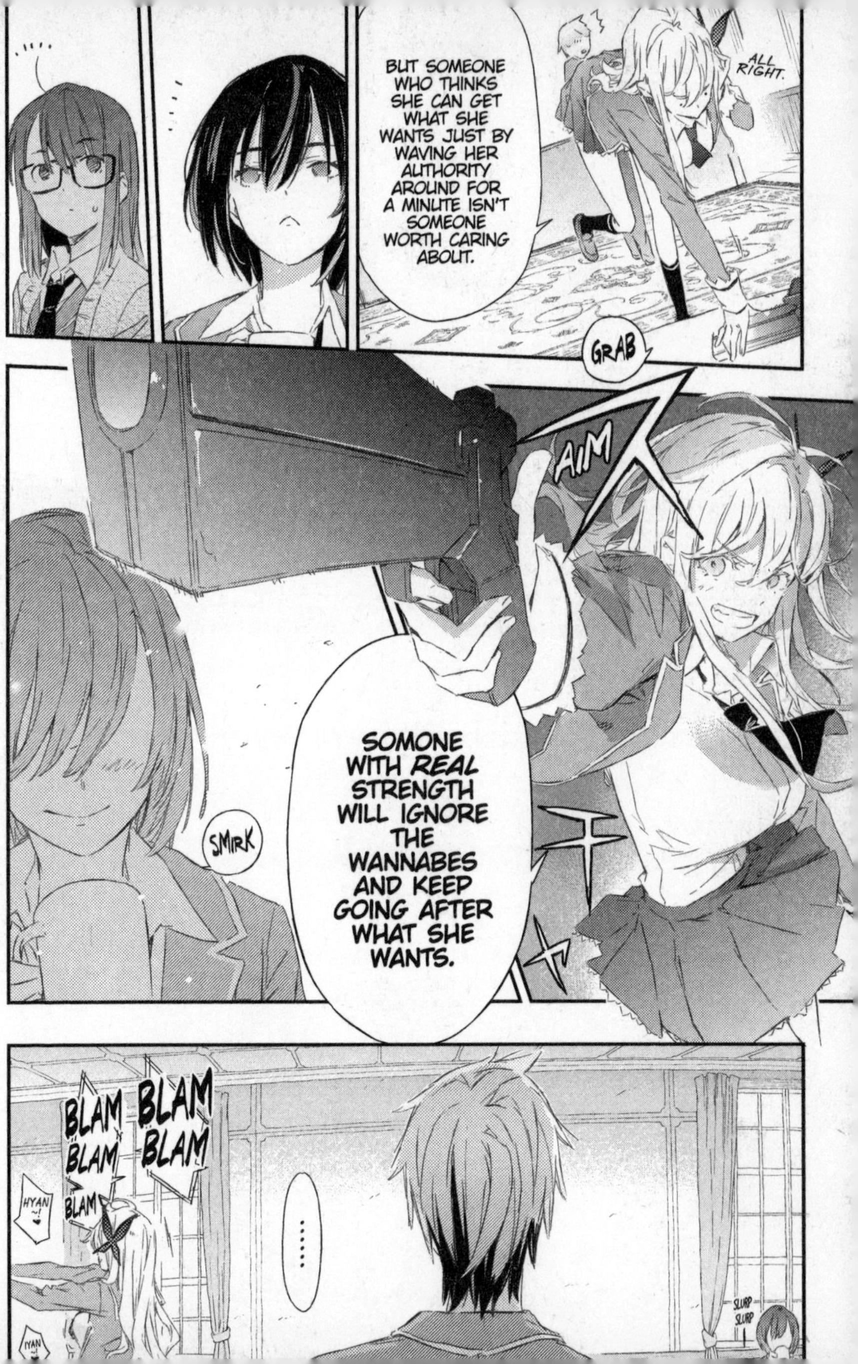
ALL RIGHT.
BUT SOMEONE WHO THINKS SHE CAN GET WHAT SHE WANTS JUST BY WAVING HER AUTHORITY AROUND FOR A MINUTE ISN'T SOMEONE WORTH CARING ABOUT.
...
...
GRAB
AIM
SOMONE WITH REAL STRENGTH WILL IGNORE THE WANNABES AND KEEP GOING AFTER WHAT SHE WANTS.
SMIRK
......
SLURP SLURP
BLAM BLAM
BLAM BLAM
BLAM
HYAN~!
IYAN~!

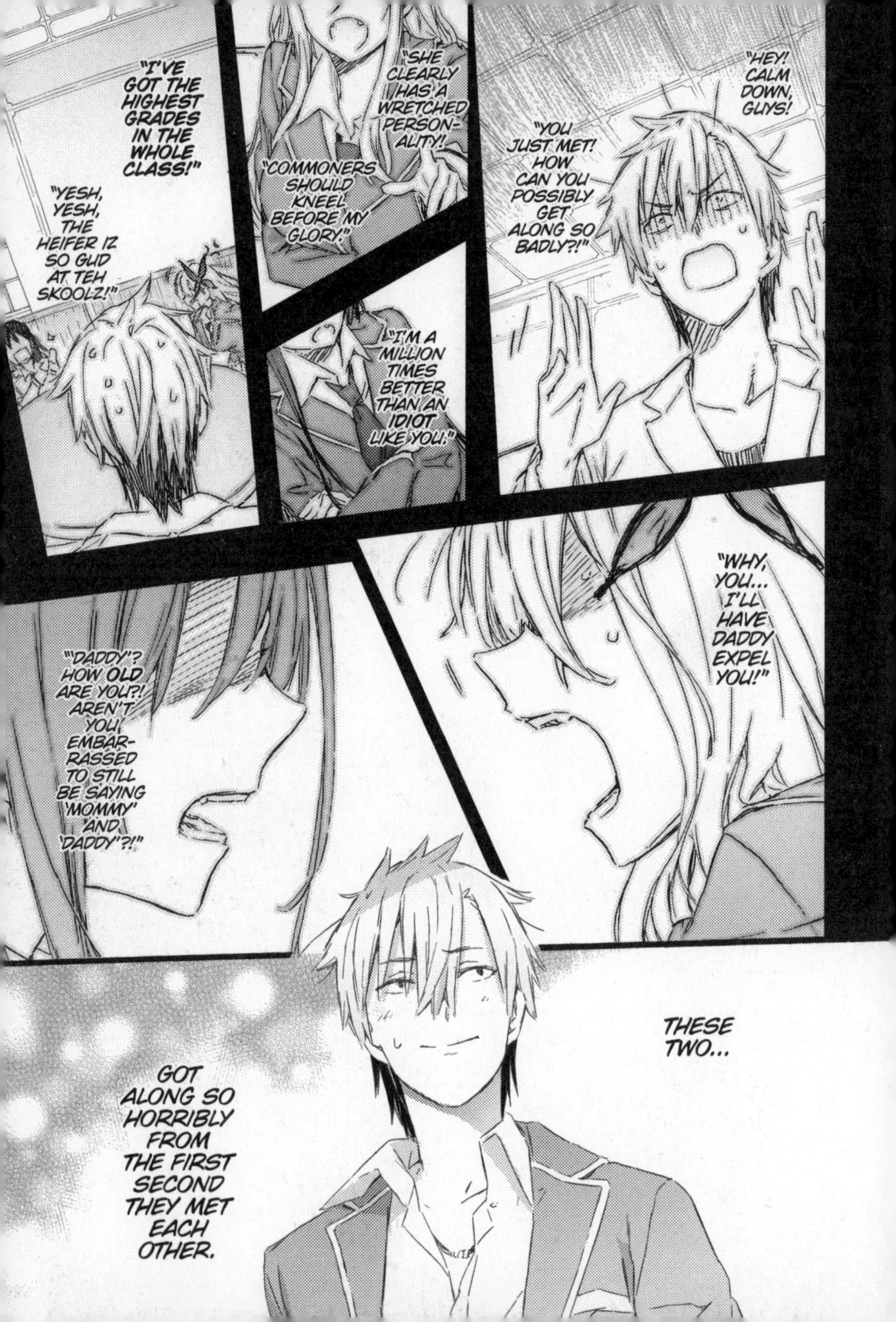
"HEY! CALM DOWN, GUYS!
"YOU JUST MET! HOW CAN YOU POSSIBLY GET ALONG SO BADLY?!"
"SHE CLEARLY HAS A WRETCHED PERSON-ALITY!
"COMMONERS SHOULD KNEEL BEFORE MY GLORY."
"I'M A MILLION TIMES BETTER THAN AN IDIOT LIKE YOU."
"I'VE GOT THE HIGHEST GRADES IN THE WHOLE CLASS!"
"YESH, YESH, THE HEIFER IZ SO GUD AT TEH SKOOLZ!"
"WHY, YOU... I'LL HAVE DADDY EXPEL YOU!"
"'DADDY'? HOW OLD ARE YOU?! AREN'T YOU EMBAR-RASSED TO STILL BE SAYING 'MOMMY' AND 'DADDY'?!"
THESE TWO...
GOT ALONG SO HORRIBLY FROM THE FIRST SECOND THEY MET EACH OTHER.

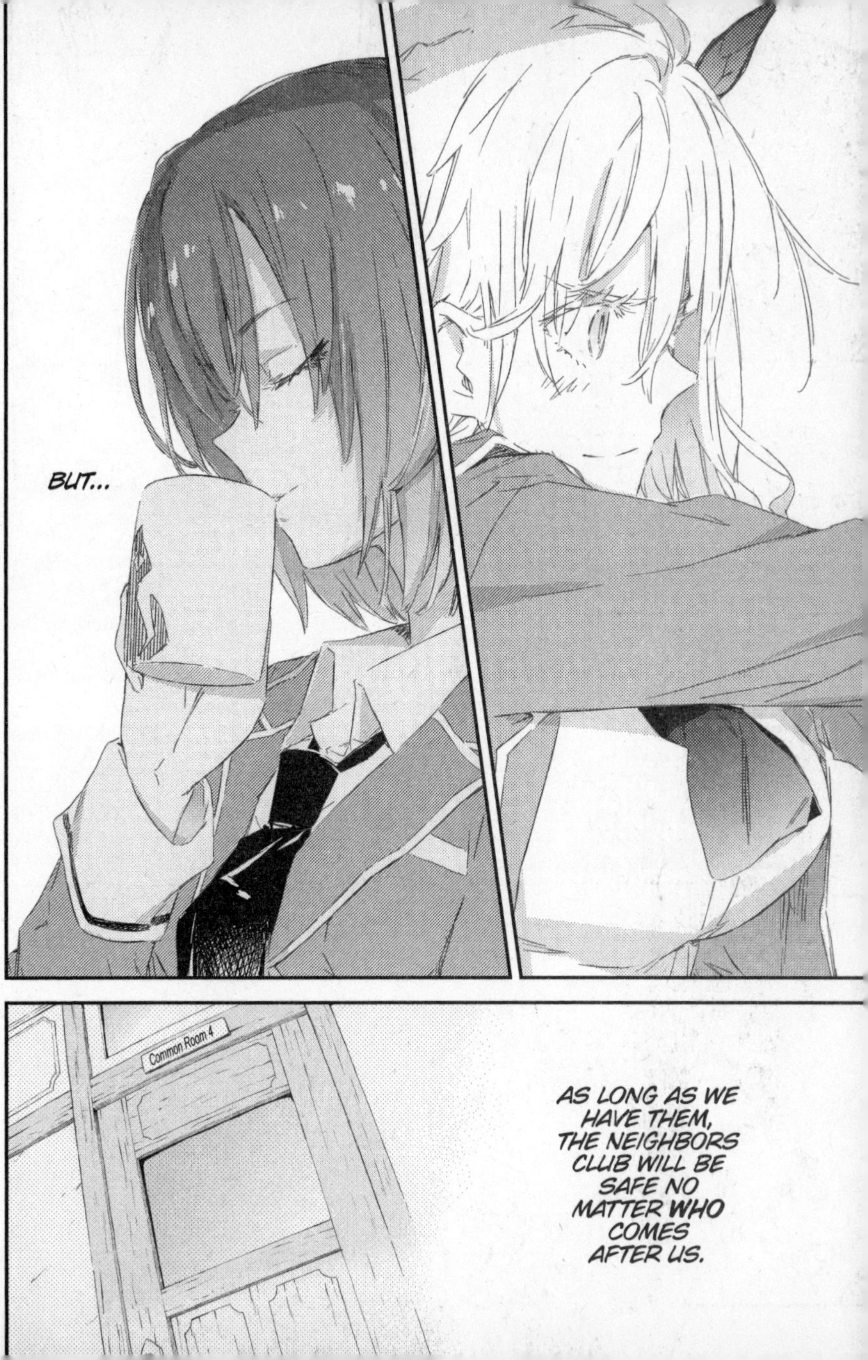
BUT...
Common Room 4
AS LONG AS WE HAVE THEM, THE NEIGHBORS CLUB WILL BE SAFE NO MATTER WHO COMES AFTER US.

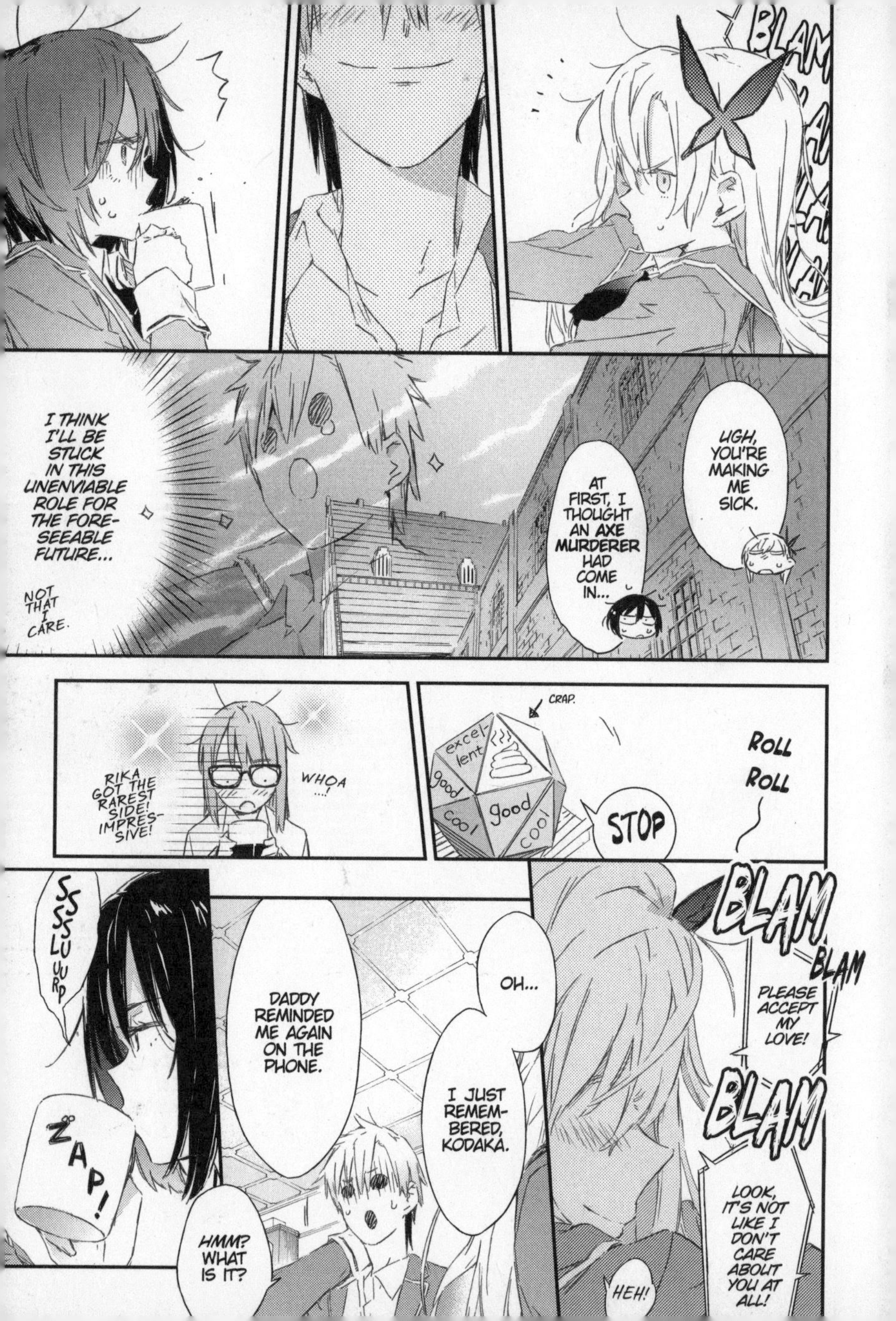
BLAM BLAM
UGH, YOU'RE MAKING ME SICK.
AT FIRST, I THOUGHT AN AXE MURDERER HAD COME IN...
I THINK I'LL BE STUCK IN THIS UNENVIABLE ROLE FOR THE FORESEEABLE FUTURE...
NOT THAT I CARE.
ROLL ROLL
STOP
CRAP.
excel-lent
good
cool
good
cool
WHOA...!
RIKA GOT THE RAREST SIDE! IMPRESSIVE!
BLAM
BLAM
PLEASE ACCEPT MY LOVE!
BLAM
LOOK, IT'S NOT LIKE I DON'T CARE ABOUT YOU AT ALL!
HEH!
OH...
I JUST REMEMBERED, KODAKA.
HMM? WHAT IS IT?
DADDY REMINDED ME AGAIN ON THE PHONE.
SSSLUUURP
ZAP!

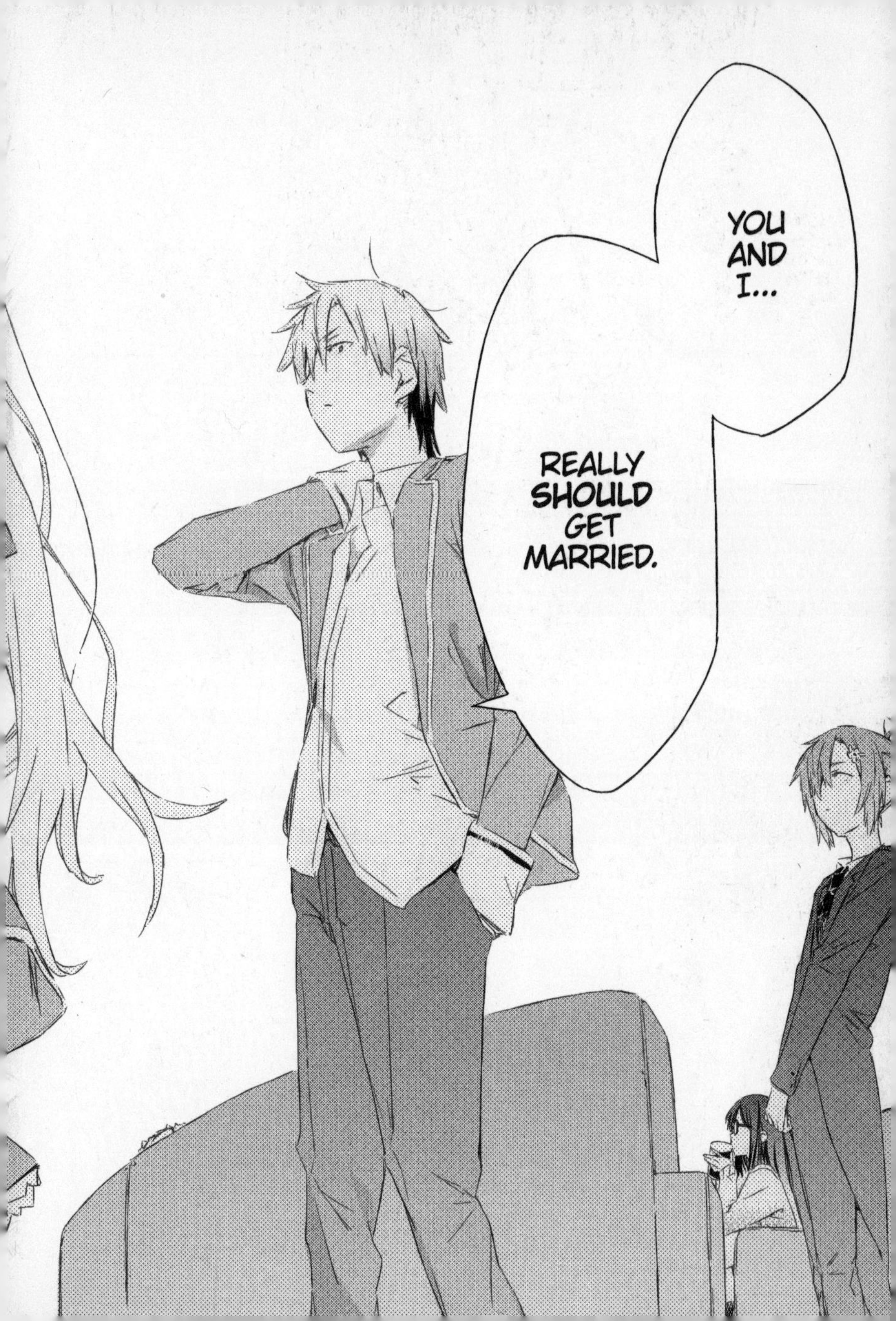
YOU AND I...
REALLY SHOULD GET MARRIED.

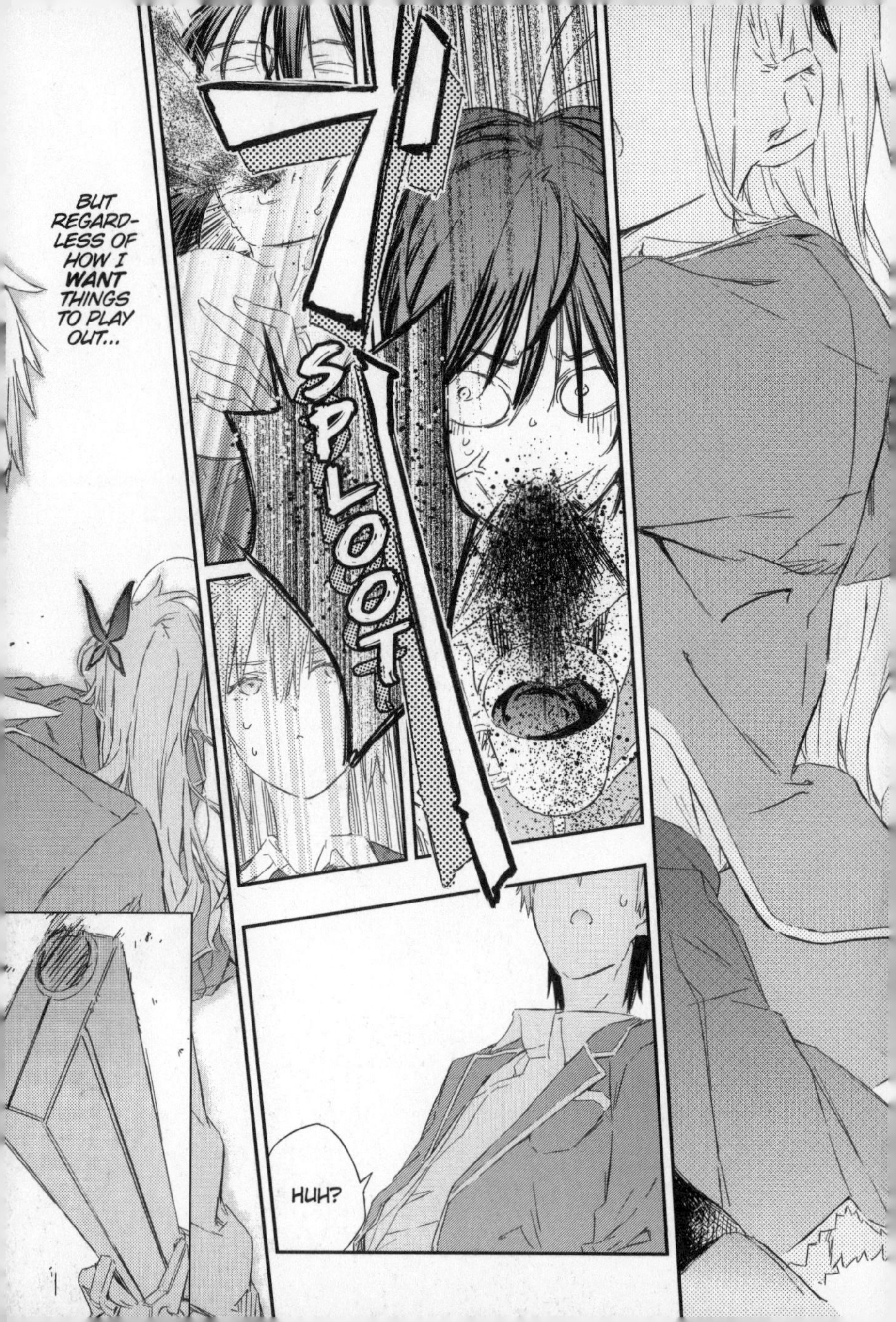
SPLOOT
BUT REGARDLESS OF HOW I WANT THINGS TO PLAY OUT...
HUH?

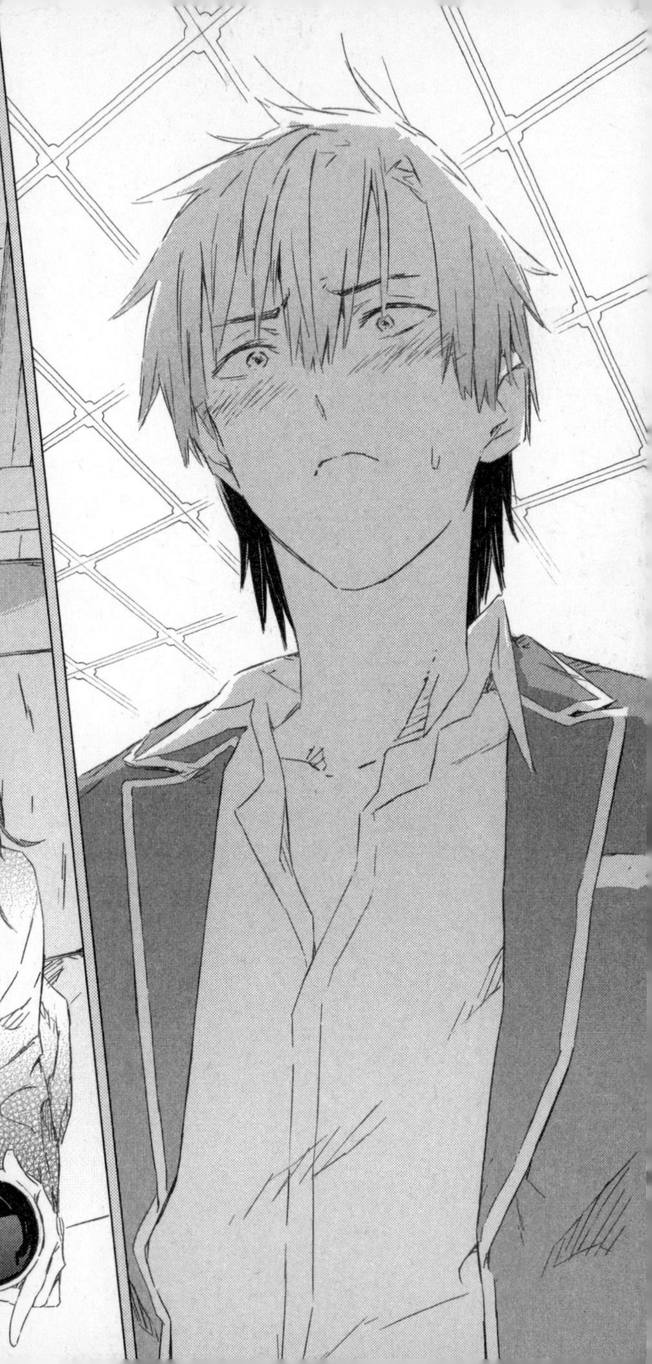
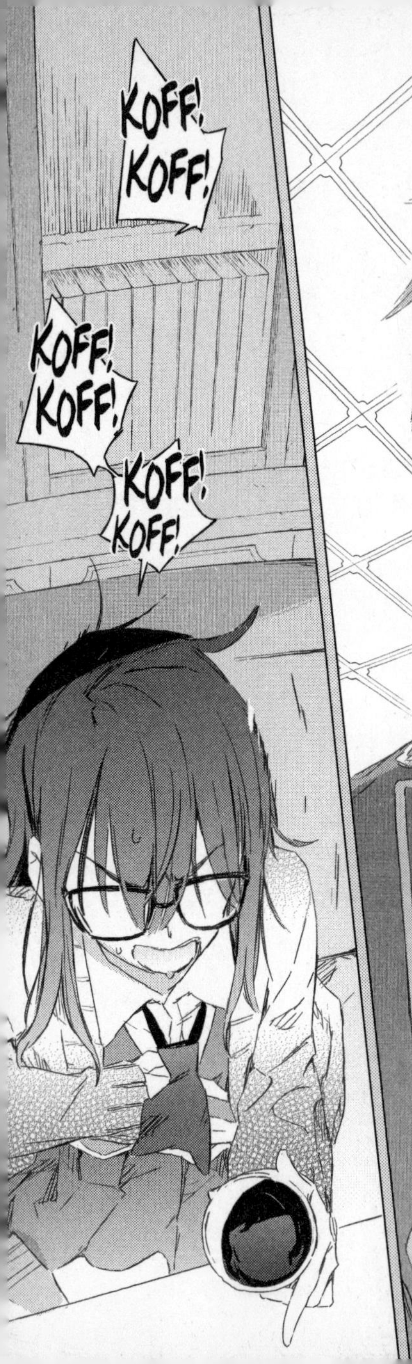
KOFF! KOFF!
KOFF! KOFF!
KOFF! KOFF!

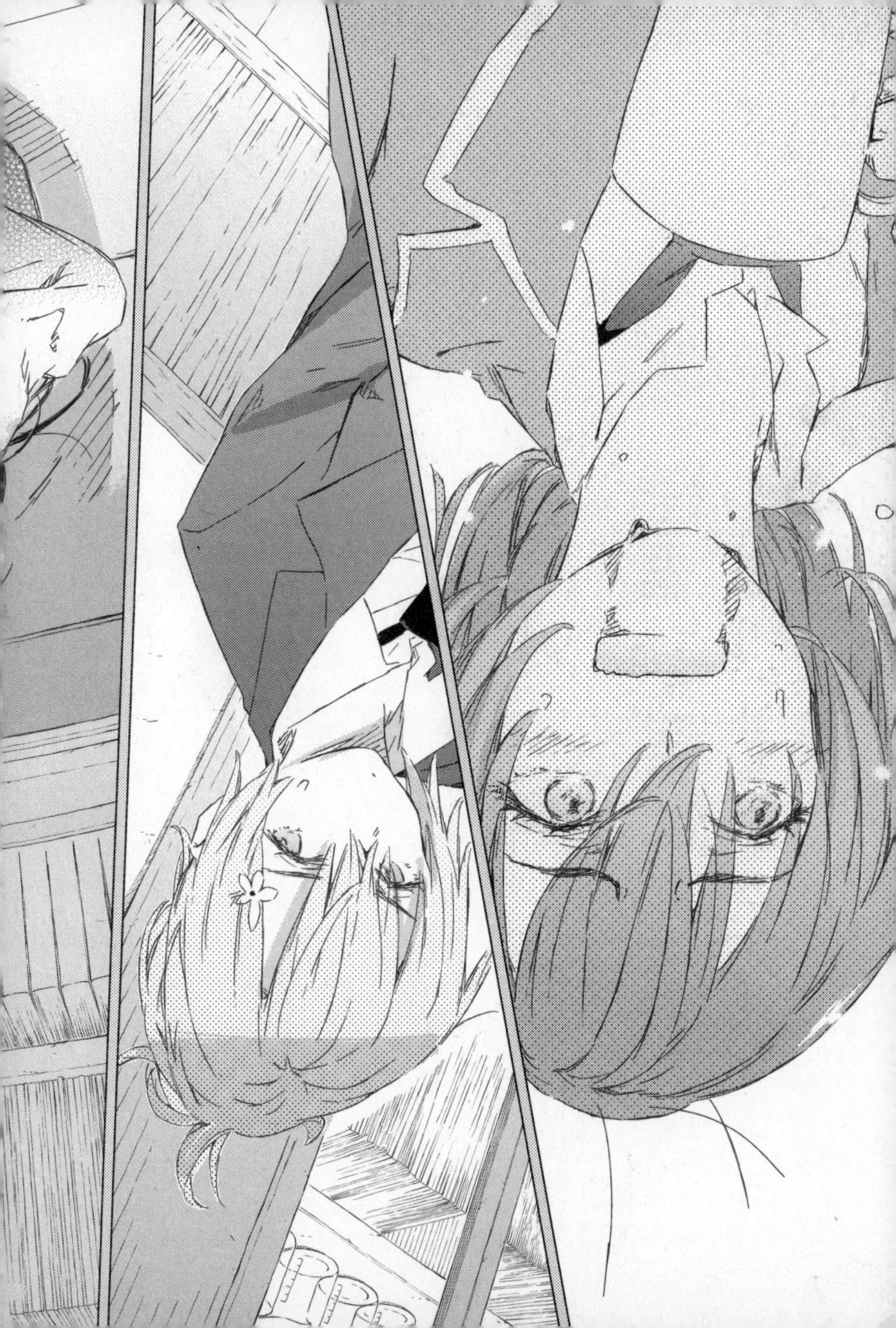

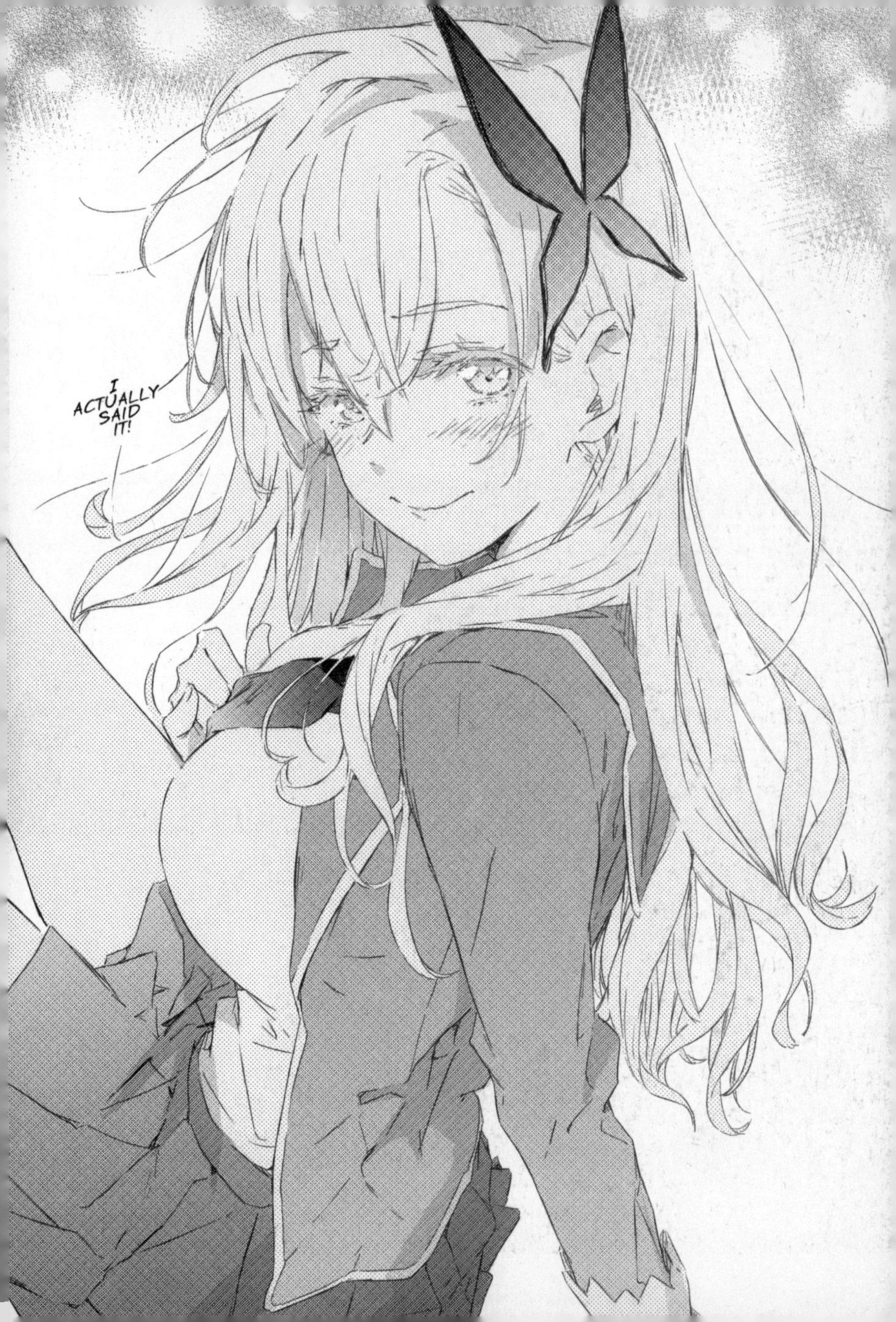
I ACTUALLY SAID IT!

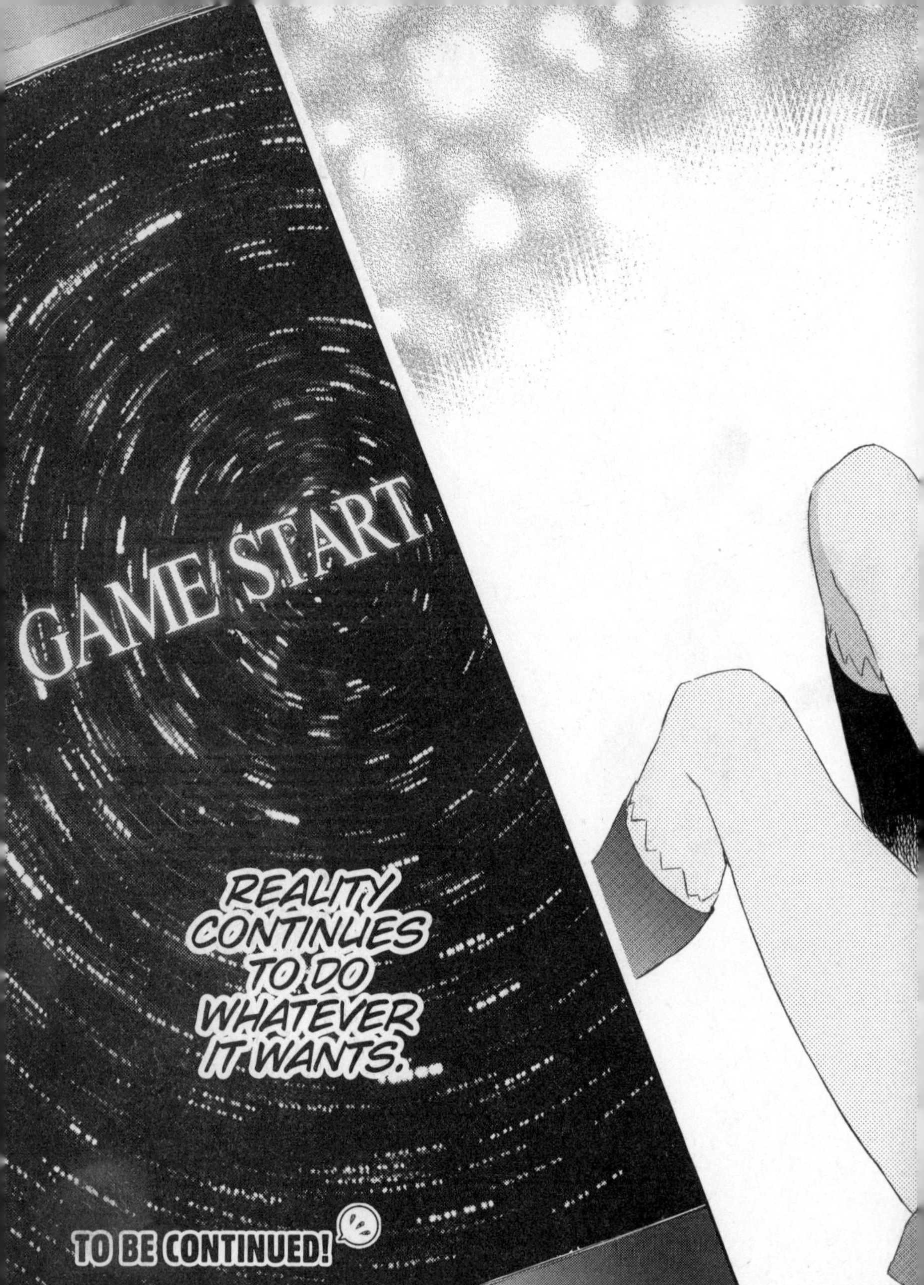
GAME START
REALITY CONTINUES TO DO WHATEVER IT WANTS...
TO BE CONTINUED!

SEE YOU NEXT VOLUME!

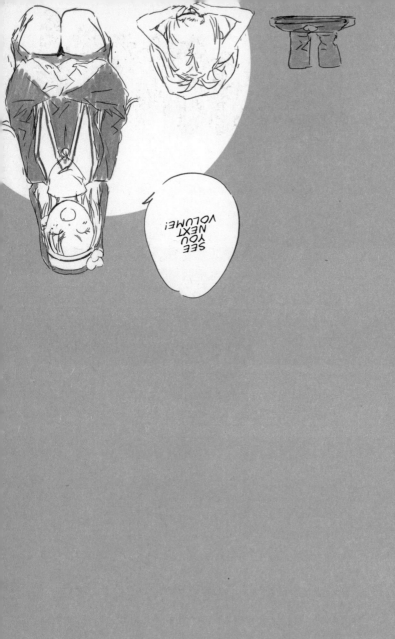

Haganai

I don't have many friends

あとがき
AFTERWORD

THANK YOU SO MUCH FOR PICKING UP VOLUME 13 OF HAGANAI: I DON'T HAVE MANY FRIENDS. I WENT THROUGH A LOT OF UPS AND DOWNS, IN TERMS OF BOTH PUBLIC AND PRIVATE THINGS. BUT BECAUSE YOU'VE ALL BEEN SO SUPPORTIVE, I'VE MADE IT THIS FAR!

THE LAST OF THE LIGHT NOVELS WAS PUBLISHED RECENTLY, BUT THIS MANGA VERSION WILL KEEP THROWING ITS HEART AND SOUL INTO CARRYING THE TORCH! PLEASE KEEP CHEERING ME ON!

ALL RIGHT. SEE YOU NEXT VOLUME!

IT'S SO SAD TO THINK THAT THE LIGHT NOVELS ARE OVER.

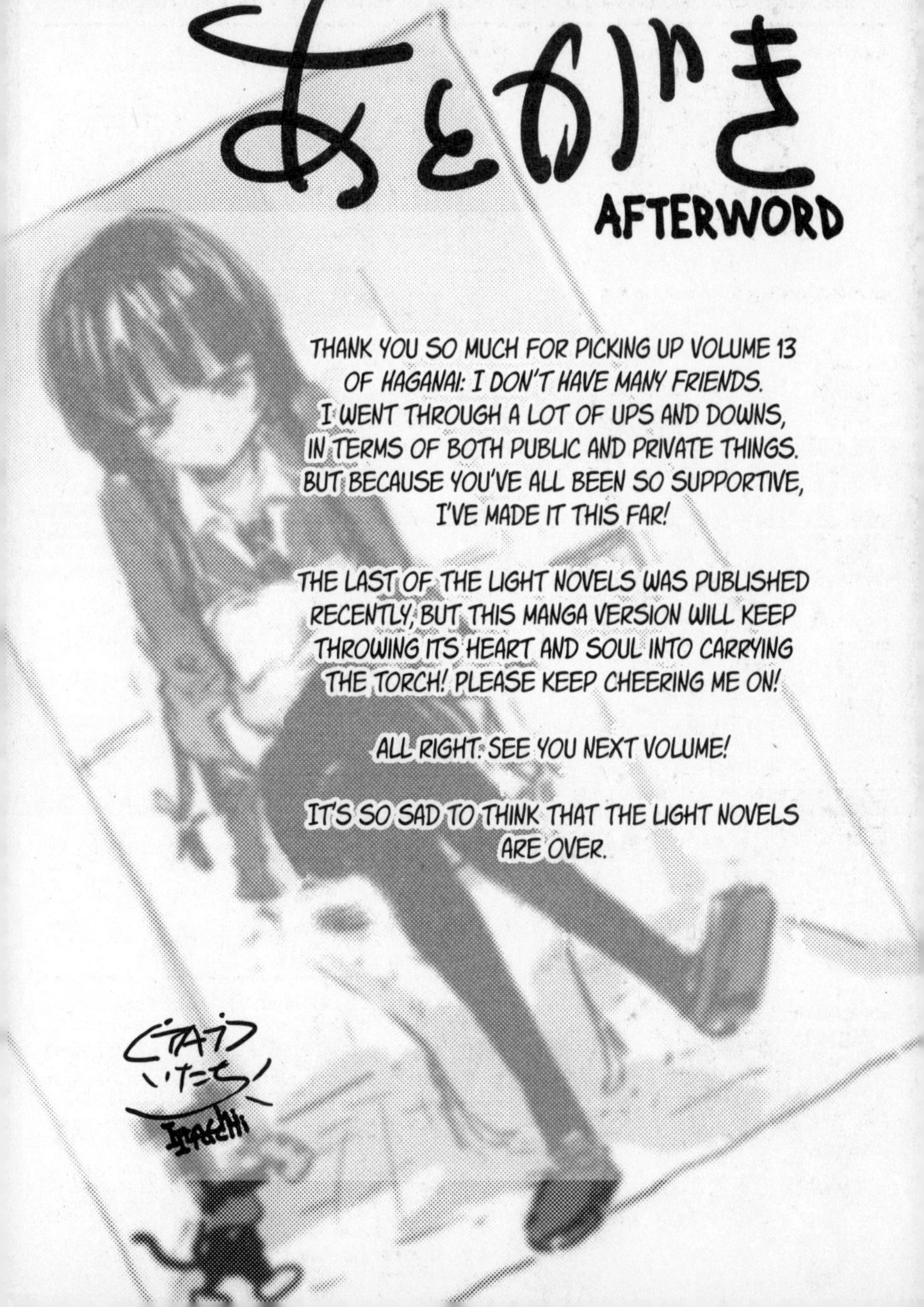
Itachi

In lieu of comments by Yomi Hirasaka, the original creator, the Neighbors Club is going to provide a bit of commentary for each chapter!

Club Activity Log 56: King Lear

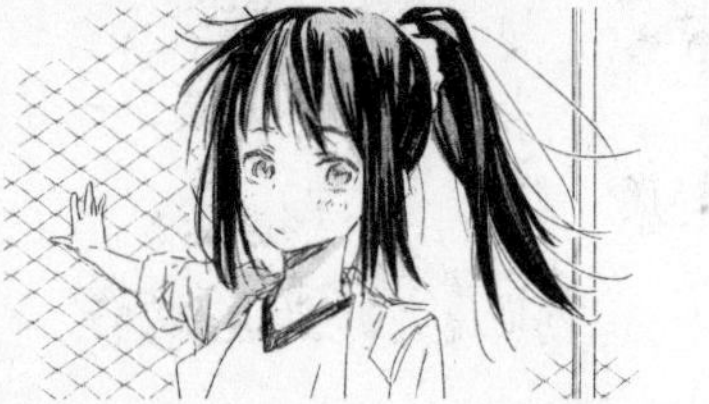

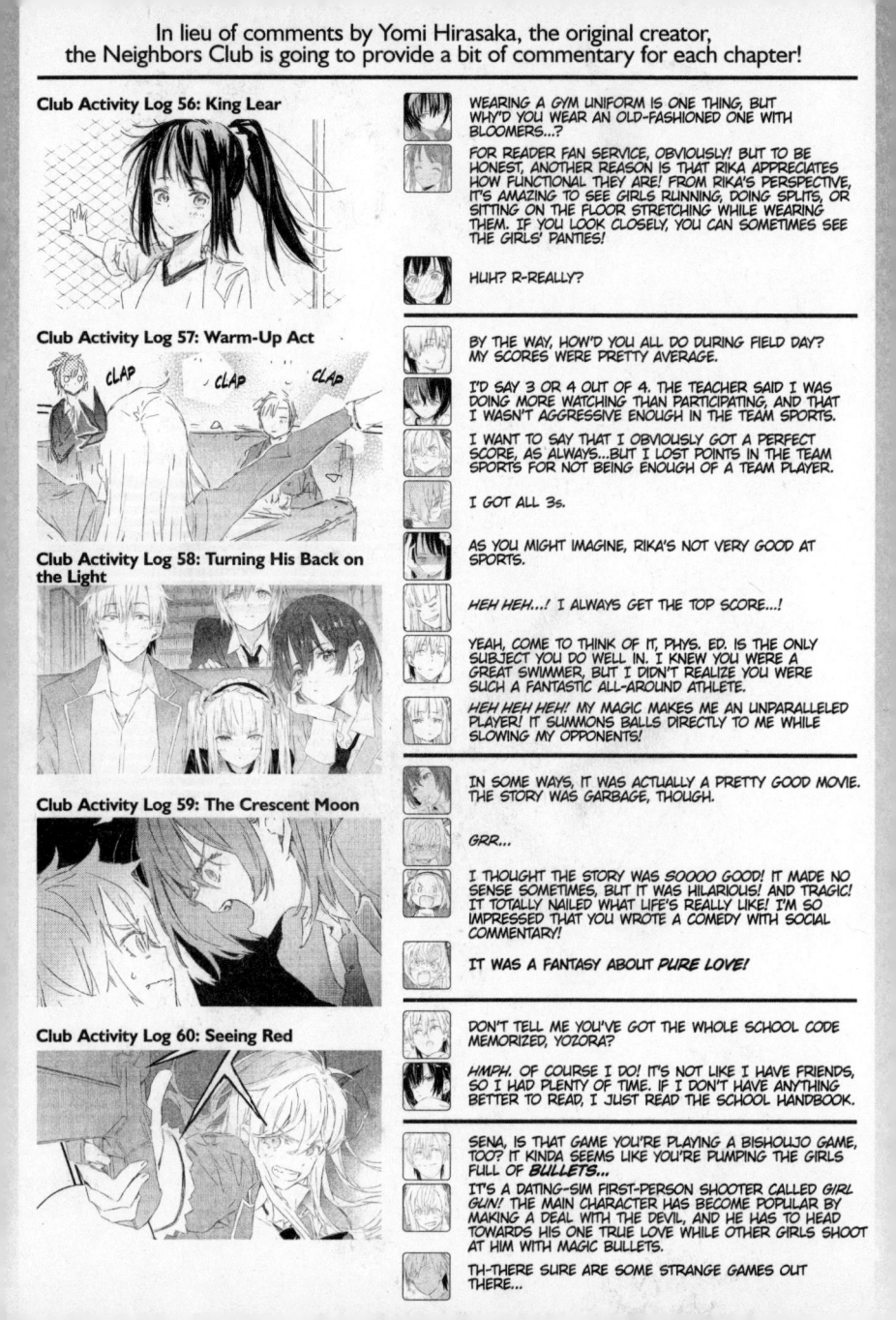

WEARING A GYM UNIFORM IS ONE THING, BUT WHY'D YOU WEAR AN OLD-FASHIONED ONE WITH BLOOMERS...?

FOR READER FAN SERVICE, OBVIOUSLY! BUT TO BE HONEST, ANOTHER REASON IS THAT RIKA APPRECIATES HOW FUNCTIONAL THEY ARE! FROM RIKA'S PERSPECTIVE, IT'S AMAZING TO SEE GIRLS RUNNING, DOING SPLITS, OR SITTING ON THE FLOOR STRETCHING WHILE WEARING THEM. IF YOU LOOK CLOSELY, YOU CAN SOMETIMES SEE THE GIRLS' PANTIES!

HUH? R-REALLY?

Club Activity Log 57: Warm-Up Act

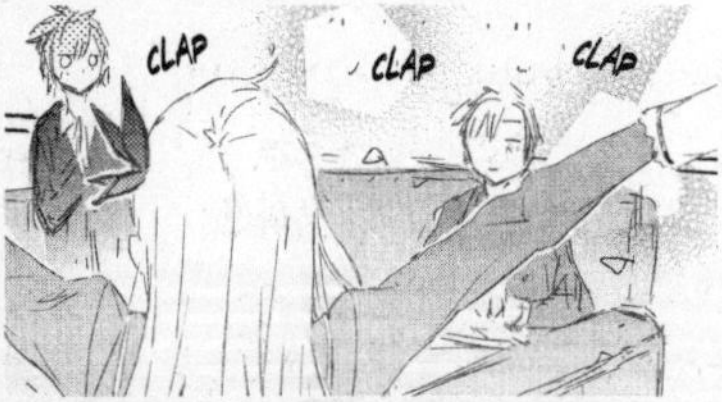
CLAP
CLAP
CLAP

BY THE WAY, HOW'D YOU ALL DO DURING FIELD DAY? MY SCORES WERE PRETTY AVERAGE.

I'D SAY 3 OR 4 OUT OF 4. THE TEACHER SAID I WAS DOING MORE WATCHING THAN PARTICIPATING, AND THAT I WASN'T AGGRESSIVE ENOUGH IN THE TEAM SPORTS.

I WANT TO SAY THAT I OBVIOUSLY GOT A PERFECT SCORE, AS ALWAYS...BUT I LOST POINTS IN THE TEAM SPORTS FOR NOT BEING ENOUGH OF A TEAM PLAYER.

I GOT ALL 3s.

AS YOU MIGHT IMAGINE, RIKA'S NOT VERY GOOD AT SPORTS.

HEH HEH...! I ALWAYS GET THE TOP SCORE...!

YEAH, COME TO THINK OF IT, PHYS. ED. IS THE ONLY SUBJECT YOU DO WELL IN. I KNEW YOU WERE A GREAT SWIMMER, BUT I DIDN'T REALIZE YOU WERE SUCH A FANTASTIC ALL-AROUND ATHLETE.

HEH HEH HEH! MY MAGIC MAKES ME AN UNPARALLELED PLAYER! IT SUMMONS BALLS DIRECTLY TO ME WHILE SLOWING MY OPPONENTS!

Club Activity Log 58: Turning His Back on the Light

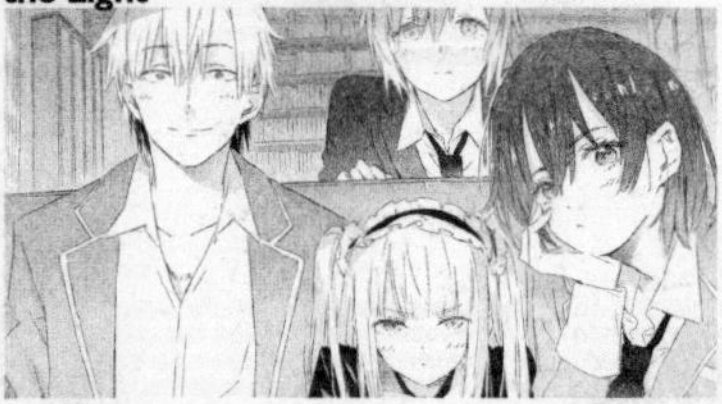

IN SOME WAYS, IT WAS ACTUALLY A PRETTY GOOD MOVIE. THE STORY WAS GARBAGE, THOUGH.

GRR...

I THOUGHT THE STORY WAS *SOOOO GOOD!* IT MADE NO SENSE SOMETIMES, BUT IT WAS HILARIOUS! AND TRAGIC! IT TOTALLY NAILED WHAT LIFE'S REALLY LIKE! I'M SO IMPRESSED THAT YOU WROTE A COMEDY WITH SOCIAL COMMENTARY!

IT WAS A FANTASY ABOUT *PURE LOVE!*

Club Activity Log 59: The Crescent Moon

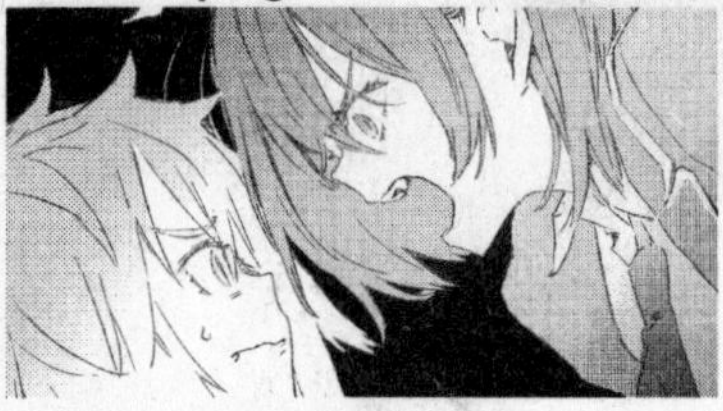

DON'T TELL ME YOU'VE GOT THE WHOLE SCHOOL CODE MEMORIZED, YOZORA?

HMPH. OF COURSE I DO! IT'S NOT LIKE I HAVE FRIENDS, SO I HAD PLENTY OF TIME. IF I DON'T HAVE ANYTHING BETTER TO READ, I JUST READ THE SCHOOL HANDBOOK.

Club Activity Log 60: Seeing Red

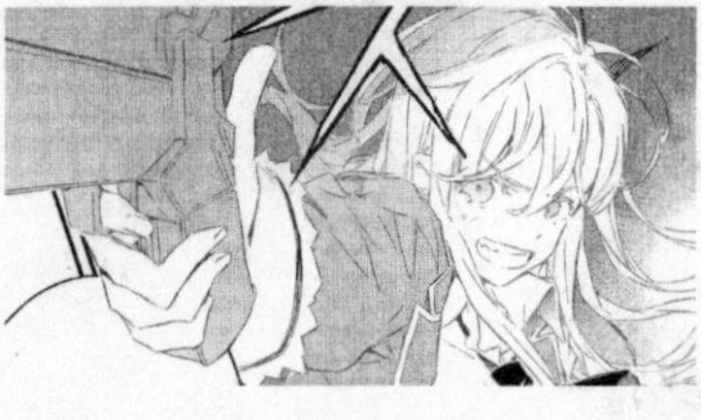

SENA, IS THAT GAME YOU'RE PLAYING A BISHOUJO GAME, TOO? IT KINDA SEEMS LIKE YOU'RE PUMPING THE GIRLS FULL OF ***BULLETS...***

IT'S A DATING-SIM FIRST-PERSON SHOOTER CALLED *GIRL GUN!* THE MAIN CHARACTER HAS BECOME POPULAR BY MAKING A DEAL WITH THE DEVIL, AND HE HAS TO HEAD TOWARDS HIS ONE TRUE LOVE WHILE OTHER GIRLS SHOOT AT HIM WITH MAGIC BULLETS.

TH-THERE SURE ARE SOME STRANGE GAMES OUT THERE...

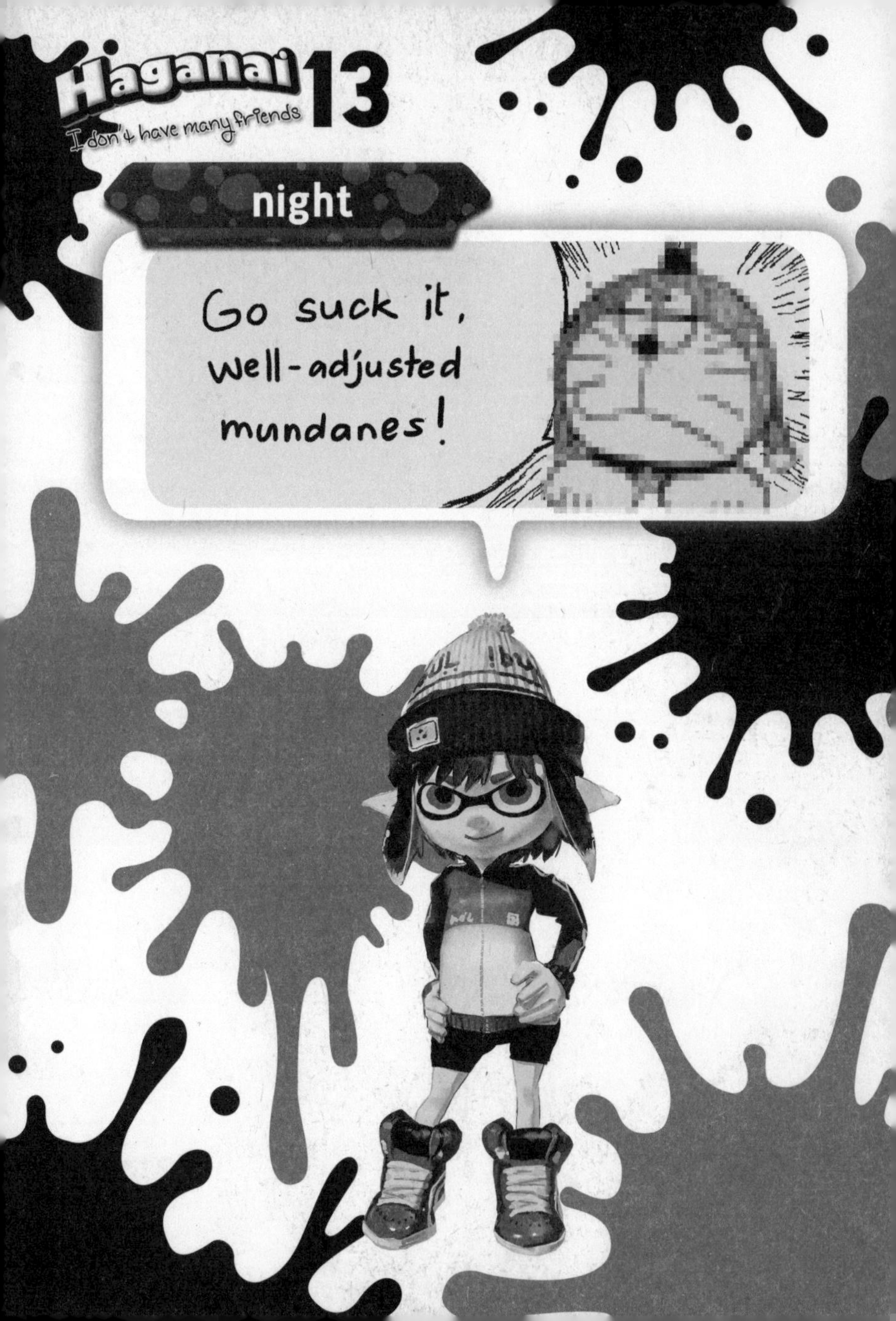
Haganai 13
I don't have many friends
night
Go suck it, well-adjusted mundanes!

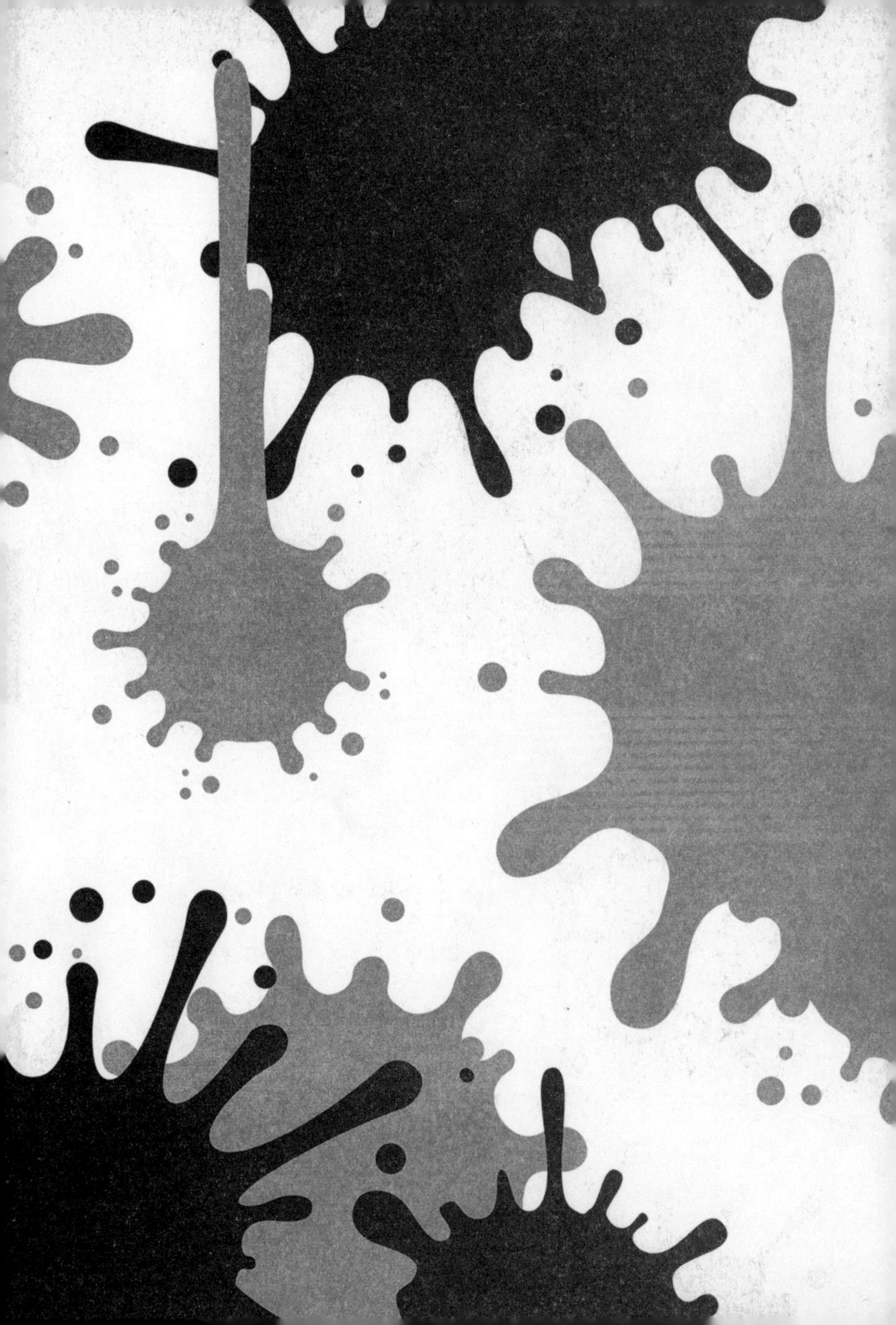

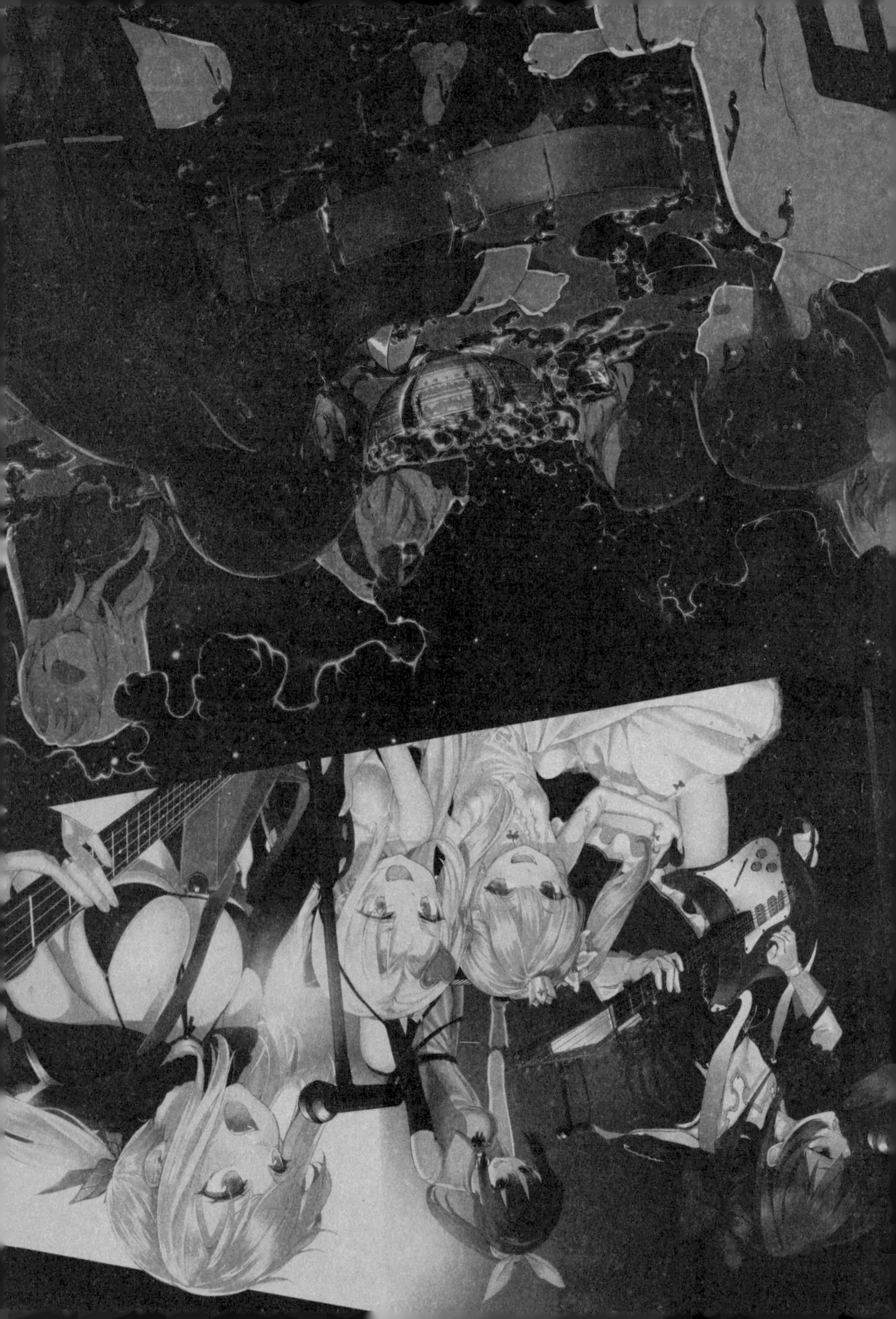

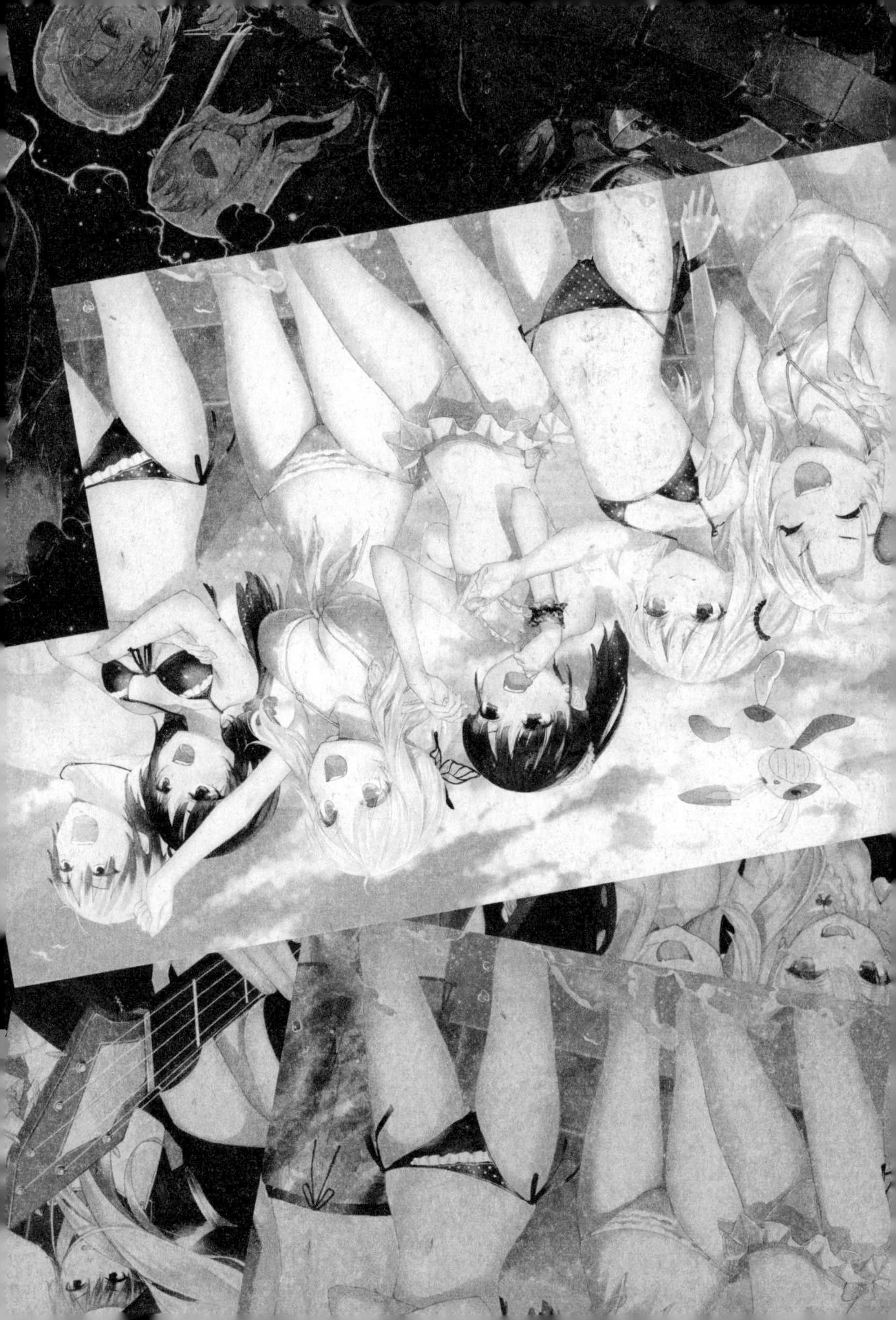

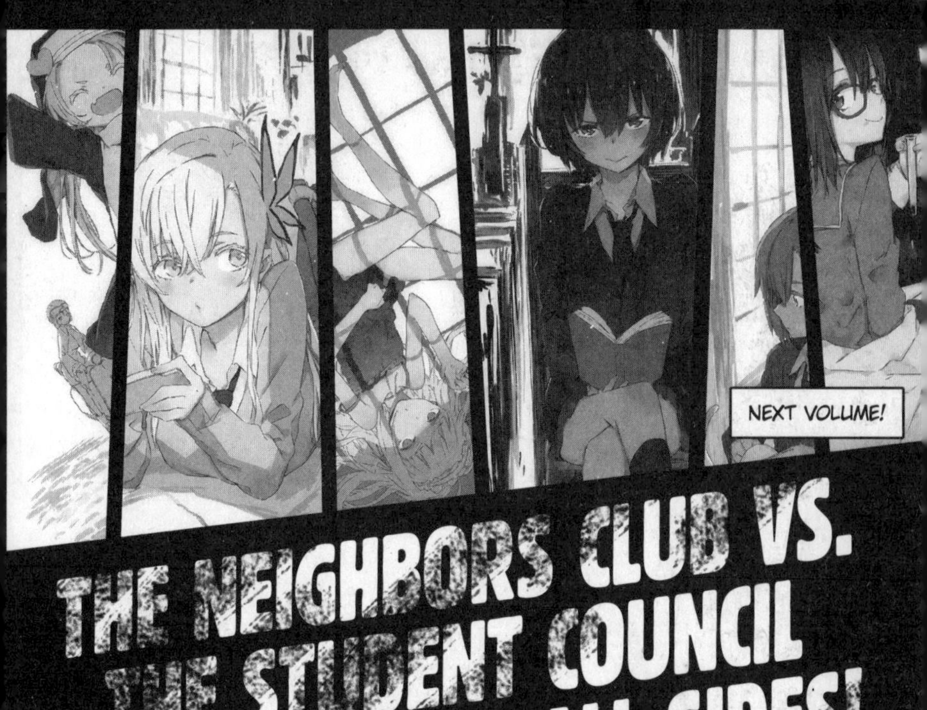
NEXT VOLUME!

THE NEIGHBORS CLUB VS. THE STUDENT COUNCIL ASSAULT FROM ALL SIDES!

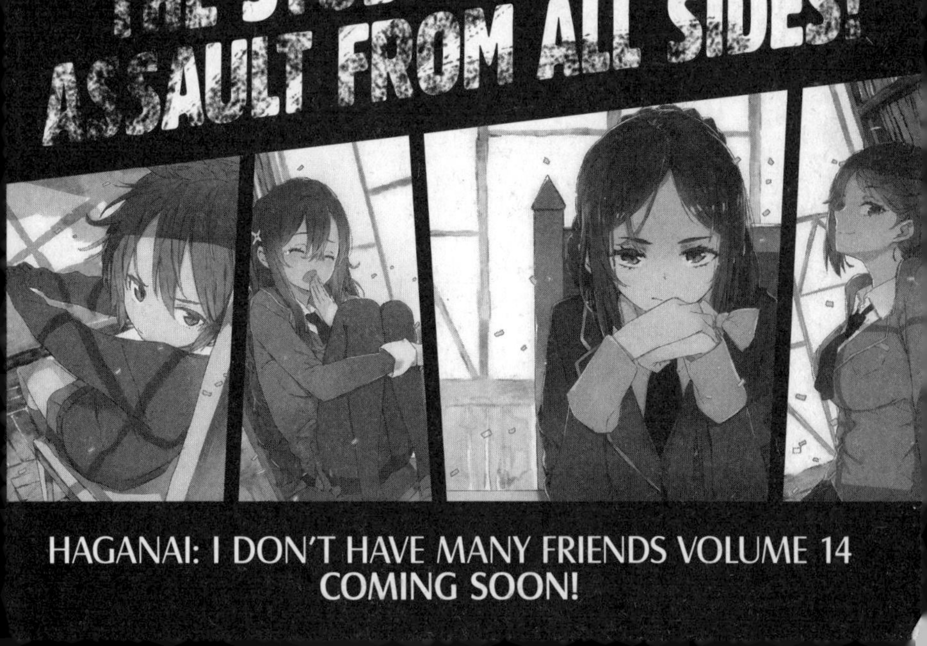

HAGANAI: I DON'T HAVE MANY FRIENDS VOLUME 14
COMING SOON!

Experience all that **SEVEN SEAS** has to offer!

Visit us online and follow us on Twitter!
WWW.GOMANGA.COM
WWW.TWITTER.COM/GOMANGA

SEVEN SEAS ENTERTAINMENT PRESENTS

Haganai²
I don't have many friends

VOLUME 13

art by **ITACHI** / story by **YOMI HIRASAKA** / character designs by **BURIKI**

TRANSLATION
Ryan Peterson

ADAPTATION
Ysabet Reinhardt MacFarlane

LETTERING
Roland Amago

LAYOUT
Bambi Eloriaga-Amago

COVER DESIGN
Nicky Lim

PROOFREADER
Shanti Whitesides

PRODUCTION MANAGER
Lissa Pattillo

EDITOR-IN-CHIEF
Adam Arnold

PUBLISHER
Jason DeAngelis

HAGANAI: I DON'T HAVE MANY FRIENDS VOL. 13
© Itachi 2015, Yomi Hirasaka 2015
Edited by MEDIA FACTORY.
First published in Japan in 2015 by KADOKAWA CORPORATION, Tokyo.
English translation rights reserved by Seven Seas Entertainment, LLC.
under the license from KADOKAWA CORPORATION, Tokyo.

No portion of this book may be reproduced or transmitted in any form without
written permission from the copyright holders. This is a work of fiction. Names,
characters, places, and incidents are the products of the author's imagination
or are used fictitiously. Any resemblance to actual events, locals, or persons,
living or dead, is entirely coincidental.

Seven Seas books may be purchased in bulk for educational, business, or
promotional use. For information on bulk purchases, please contact Macmillan
Corporate & Premium Sales Department at 1-800-221-7945 (ext 5442)
or write specialmarkets@macmillan.com.

Seven Seas and the Seven Seas logo are trademarks of
Seven Seas Entertainment, LLC. All rights reserved.

ISBN: 978-1-626922-22-8

Printed in Canada

First Printing: April 2016

10 9 8 7 6 5 4 3 2 1

FOLLOW US ONLINE: *www.gomanga.com*

READING DIRECTIONS

This book reads from *right to left*, Japanese style.
If this is your first time reading manga, you start
reading from the top right panel on each page and
take it from there. If you get lost, just follow the
numbered diagram here. It may seem backwards at
first, but you'll get the hang of it! Have fun!!

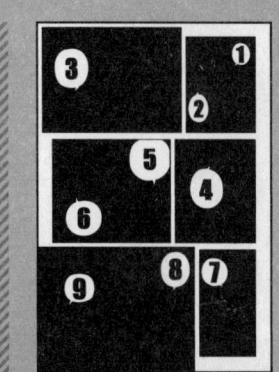